INTERNATIONAL MASS CLAIMS PROCESSES: LEGAL AND PRACTICAL PERSPECTIVES

International Mass Claims Processes:

Legal and Practical Perspectives

HOWARD M. HOLTZMANN
and
EDDA KRISTJÁNSDÓTTIR

Editors

Prepared under the Auspices of
the Permanent Court of Arbitration
Steering Committee on International Mass Claims

OXFORD
UNIVERSITY PRESS

OXFORD
UNIVERSITY PRESS

Great Clarendon Street, Oxford OX2 6DP

Oxford University Press is a department of the University of Oxford.
It furthers the University's objective of excellence in research, scholarship,
and education by publishing worldwide in

Oxford New York

Auckland Cape Town Dar es Salaam Hong Kong Karachi
Kuala Lumpur Madrid Melbourne Mexico City Nairobi
New Delhi Shanghai Taipei Toronto

With offices in

Argentina Austria Brazil Chile Czech Republic France Greece
Guatemala Hungary Italy Japan Poland Portugal Singapore
South Korea Switzerland Thailand Turkey Ukraine Vietnam

Oxford is a registered trade mark of Oxford University Press
in the UK and in certain other countries

Published in the United States
by Oxford University Press Inc., New York

British Library Cataloguing in Publication Data
Data available

Library of Congress Cataloging in Publication Data
Data available

Typeset by Newgen Imaging Systems (P) Ltd., Chennai, India
Printed in Great Britain
on acid-free paper by
Antony Rowe Ltd., Chippenham

ISBN 978-0-19-920744-2

1 3 5 7 9 10 8 6 4 2

Foreword

By Stephen M. Schwebel

The contemporary era of international arbitration is generally agreed to have begun with the arbitrations launched pursuant to provisions of the Jay Treaty of 1794 that concluded the Revolutionary War between the United States of America and Great Britain. The contemporary era of international arbitral institutions is generally agreed to have begun with the establishment in The Hague, a little more than a century later, in 1899, of the Permanent Court of Arbitration (PCA). Since the end of the eighteenth century, the body of international law has been invigorated by the production of international arbitral awards. That production was intermittent, but significant, in the nineteenth century. With the exception of the extraordinarily important award in 1872 in the *Alabama Claims* arbitration, and a few lesser exceptions such as the *Behring Sea* arbitration, arbitral awards were not of great political or economic importance. But they were of legal importance in the development of customary international law, particularly in the growth of the law of State responsibility. And naturally they were important for the parties.

With the institutionalization of the processes of international arbitration by the creation of the PCA at the outset of the twentieth century, and with the faith placed in and the impetus given to international arbitration by the peace movement of the era, the number and significance of international arbitral awards grew. Their importance was only somewhat displaced by the establishment and effectiveness of the Permanent Court of International Justice which functioned successfully in The Hague in the years 1922–1940 in the Peace Palace, built for the PCA, whose construction was financed by the munificence of Andrew Carnegie and the generosity of the Netherlands. In the current active days of the International Court of Justice, the successor to the Permanent Court of International Justice, international arbitration remains alive and well; in fact, with the direct access to international arbitration increasingly afforded to claimants in their own right, it has burgeoned.

Claims commissions and tribunals produced large numbers of international arbitral awards in the nineteenth century and in the course of the twentieth century. The table of contents of A.H. Feller's classic book, *The Mexican Claims Commissions* (1935) indicates that Mexican claims commissions were active as early as 1825 and recurrently sat in proceedings not only with the United States but France, Great Britain, Spain, Germany, Italy and Belgium; Mexican claims reached their zenith in the inter-War years of the twentieth century. The Venezuelan claims at the outset of the twentieth century were significant. The Mixed Arbitral Tribunals that were constituted by the Peace Treaties that ended World War I dealt with thousands of cases; the German-American Claims Commission set up after World War I alone dealt with many thousands of cases.

The innovative insight of that distinguished and ever energetic international arbitrator, Howard M. Holtzmann, and the readiness of the Permanent Court of Arbitration manifested since 1981 to undertake new initiatives, has resulted in the happy conjunction of this path-breaking book on *International Mass Claims Processes: Legal and Practical Perspectives.*

In response to a proposal of Judge Holtzmann made at its centenary conference, the PCA constituted a committee largely composed of persons who had experience in the work of two or more mass claims processes. Drawing on the expertise thus assembled, Judge Holtzmann and his long-time collaborator, Edda Kristjánsdóttir (an international lawyer who formerly was a member of the PCA's legal staff) have prepared a unique comparative survey and analysis of the issues that the establishment and functioning of international mass claims commissions engender. The procedures and processes of eleven mass claims commissions and tribunals are subjected to keen comparative analysis.

That analysis is at once detailed and pragmatic. A great body of uniformly organized information has been gathered and is set forth about each of the mass claims bodies considered; and the editors have provided a discerning commentary on each of the many topics that fall to be considered. The excellence of the volume's organization is suggested by its detailed Table of Contents; the utility of the volume is foreshadowed by its detailed Introduction.

This original volume may be one of the most unusual manuals ever produced. It will be of value to statesmen and scholars, to government officials, judges, arbitrators, special masters and accountants, to counsel and advocates, perhaps even to victims of misfortune and malice.

The editors, and the Permanent Court of Arbitration, are to be congratulated on the publication of *International Mass Claims Processes: Legal and Practical Perspectives.*

Stephen M. Schwebel
Washington, D.C.
February, 2006

Summary Table of Contents

Detailed Table of Contents

CHAPTER 1. ESTABLISHING THE CLAIMS PROCESS

1.01 Constituting Method

The types of constituting instrument(s) or procedures by which Claims Processes are created (e.g., treaty, agreement, judicial decision, or other), having regard to the major events and circumstances giving rise to the claims.

1.02 Constituting Instrument

Whether the contents of the constituting instrument are (i) a brief statement, or (ii) a detailed description of the Claims Process, with provisions, e.g., on who may

be claimants, deadlines, rules of procedure, etc. If rules of procedure are not included in the constituting instrument, who is authorized to establish rules and procedures.

1.03 Modifications and Amendments   46

Whether there is a body (e.g., consisting of the decision-makers) or a separate policy group that is empowered to modify or augment the procedural rules, administrative procedures, or structural aspects of the Claims Process in order to reflect emerging future needs.

The remedies available in the Claims Process. Whether the amounts of individual
compensation for various claimants, or categories of claimants, are included in the
constituting instruments or rules. Whether there is a maximum aggregate amount
to be paid pursuant to the Claims Process and, if there is such a maximum amount,
whether the expenses of the Claims Process are included when computing the
maximum amount, and the method of distribution of any funds remaining

after all individual claims are paid. (Note that the remedies may have an impact
on the mass claims methodologies used to process the claims.)

1.06 Location — 82

Where the Claims Process is physically located. Whether the location is a neutral
place. Legal and practical aspects.

CHAPTER 2. THE LEGAL NATURE OF THE CLAIMS PROCESS

2.01 Type of Process   97

Whether claims are resolved in a procedure akin to arbitration, or in an administrative proceeding, or by mediation/ conciliation, or in a combination thereof.

2.02 Exclusivity of Process   103

Whether the Claims Process is the sole recourse available to claimants or whether and when they may choose to sue in a national court.

CHAPTER 3. STARTING THE CLAIMS PROCESS

3.01 Outreach   141

How potential claimants are informed of the existence of the Claims Process, including the methods and extent of outreach.

CHAPTER 4. APPOINTING THOSE WHO WILL MAKE DECISIONS

4.01 Choice of Decision-Makers   179

**Who makes decisions on claims and by whom such decision-makers are
appointed. In that connection, whether any particular criteria, expertise,
or other qualifications are specified. To what extent policy-making,
executive, and adjudicative functions are differentiated and allocated
to the decision-makers or to different bodies.**

CHAPTER 5. PROCEDURES FOR CONDUCTING THE CLAIMS PROCESS

5.01 Procedural Rules   205

Whether an existing set of recognized procedural rules is incorporated by
reference (for example, the appropriate Permanent Court of Arbitration
Rules, which are based on the UNCITRAL Arbitration Rules), and where
there is such incorporation, what changes, if any, are made to reflect the
particular circumstances of the Claims Process. If an existing set of rules
is not incorporated by reference, whether a set of respected rules is used
as a guide.

5.06 Mass Claims Techniques   243

**The use of special mass claims processing methodologies such as grouping of
claims, statistical modeling and sampling, computerized matching, and
standardized valuation and verification methodologies.**

5.11 Awarding Interest   281

**Whether awards of compensation pursuant to the Claims Process include interest.
If so, how the interest rate is determined, for what period it is paid, and whether
simple or compound interest is awarded.**

CHAPTER 6. ADMINISTRATION, FACILITIES, AND COMPUTER SUPPORT

6.01 Management and Staffing 299

Legal, administrative, technical, and linguistic support required to implement the
Claims Process. The organizational and management structure created to execute
the identified functions. The type and level of expertise of the required personnel,
and the corresponding job descriptions.

6.02 Infrastructure 311

Whether the Claims Process creates its own staff, facilities, and administrative
organization, or uses an existing institution to provide all or part of such
infrastructure.

6.03 Secretariat Functions   317

The relationship between the Secretariat staff and the decision-makers. Defining their respective powers and functions. What role, if any, Secretariat staff has in conducting research, drafting orders and decisions, and whether the task of deciding certain claims is delegated to staff members.

6.04 Facilities 324

The facilities needed to implement the Claims Process (e.g., physical premises, copying and other office equipment and supplies, computers, telephone lines, etc.) What facilities need to be in place at the outset in order to handle claims as they are received.

6.05 Satellite Offices 331

If relevant in view of the geographic distribution of the claimant population, the various options and facilities available, including satellite offices, for reaching potential claimants, receiving and registering claims, and other functions.

7.02 Budget Process 353

The roles, if any, which Secretariat staff and decision-makers play in establishing periodic budgets.

CHAPTER 8. TRANSPARENCY

8.01 Informing the Public   369

Means for informing the public about the Claims Process, for example by publishing statistics on the caseload and/or texts of the awards.

Introduction

By the Editors

I. The Purpose and Scope of this Book

The Mass Claims Processes that are the subject of this book have been increasingly important phenomena in international dispute resolution. Each was established to consider claims that arose when a large number of parties—in one Process alone exceeding two and a half million—suffered damages resulting from the same historic event. These have come to be known as "Mass Claims," and the tribunals, commissions, and other mechanisms created to resolve them are called "Mass Claims Processes." They have been formed and function in a variety of ways, sometimes borrowing ideas from each other, but often inventing unique solutions. Thus, our task in considering them is akin to what Madame de Staël once described as "observing the similarities in things that are different and the differences in things that are similar."

Establishing a Mass Claims Process is a complex, multi-faceted task in which choices must be made with respect to a large number of elements and procedures ranging from legal theory to physical facilities. In order to assist systematic comparison of those numerous and divergent matters, it is necessary to view them from both their legal and practical perspectives. To do that, we have identified and listed forty-seven basic topics that experience shows typically arise when establishing an international Mass Claims Process. We then describe the approaches to those forty-seven topics taken by eleven of the most-used and highest-profile modern Mass Claims Processes. We use the term "modern" to characterize Mass Claims Processes beginning with the Iran–United States Claims Tribunal, established in 1981. Thus, the effort is to provide information about each of the eleven Claims Processes with respect to forty-seven separate topics—a total of at least 517 topics. Actually, there are more, because many of the topics listed include several sub-issues, resulting in the need to organize information concerning approximately 750 matters.

In view of the large number of topics, we have designed a format to facilitate recognizing and focusing on the specific issues and showing the ways they have been approached by each of the eleven Mass Claims Processes. To do this, each of the forty-seven principal topics is discussed in a separate Section that begins with a brief headnote—in contrasting type—directing attention to key matters related to the topic. Each Section then includes an Editors' Commentary and eleven separate subsections containing Annotations concerning how each of the eleven Claims Processes approached the particular matter.

It is important to recognize that this book does not presume to prescribe what practices are the best. Rather, our goal is to organize information systematically so that it is available to be used for a variety of purposes:

- First, we aim to provide an orderly framework for comparative study by those who seek to understand developments in a significant area of dispute resolution.
- In addition, on a practical level, the compilation of key issues may be a useful aid for those who have responsibilities for designing or revising Mass Claims Processes, and the Editors' Commentaries and Annotations may assist them in finding solutions and avoiding pitfalls.
- Another objective is to assist legal practitioners and scholars to evaluate the decisions of particular Mass Claims Processes by furnishing information concerning the procedures by which those decisions were made and the circumstances that may have molded them.
- Further, this book may aid in assessing the place of various Mass Claims Processes in the regime of international law, and in perceiving the differences among them in that regard.
- Finally, the information provided may lead to recognition that certain aspects of Mass Claims practice might have lessons for other forms of dispute resolution, both international and national.

In an effort to keep within manageable limits, we have focused on Mass Claims Processes that are primarily international, except for one interesting national case administered by the American Arbitration Association that used techniques not seen in the international systems covered. The eleven Claims Processes discussed in this book are an illustrative, not exhaustive, group. In choosing them the primary concern has been to present a wide variety of approaches and illustrate a spectrum of different techniques and procedures.

These eleven Mass Claims Processes should be viewed in their historical context. As a distinguished commentator has written,

"[m]ass claims mechanisms with large caseloads are not new. The 1794 Jay Treaty is best known for creating a commission that unanimously settled a crucial portion of the boundary between Canada and the United States, but it also established two other commissions to address large numbers of claims by British and US citizens. The first, created to address unlawful vessel seizures by the Royal Navy or by French privateers outfitted in US ports, was highly successful. It produced 565 awards, all but a few involving British seizures of US vessels. The other commission, dealing with colonial-era debts to British creditors, deadlocked and failed. Other commissions considering post-war claims by victorious parties or by injured neutrals, or claims growing out of civil unrest, were common throughout the nineteenth century. Writers identify about eighty nineteenth-century mixed claims commissions, and about thirty more between 1900 and 1918. Several mixed arbitral tribunals were established after World War I to address the victors' claims against each of the former Central Powers. Mexico, with a history of revolutionary upheaval, a large and assertive northern neighbor, and extensive European investments, was party to ten claims tribunals. However, only a handful of international commissions were created to address victors' claims or restitution issues related to World War II."[1]

The eleven modern Mass Claims Processes described in this book have made history of their own. The first of these was established by the 1981 Algiers Accords as a key element of the settlement of a crisis that arose when United States diplomats were held hostage in Tehran. The Accords included a provision for creation of the Iran–United States Claims Tribunal to decide thousands of claims resulting from the Islamic Revolution in Iran, including claims of business entities due to expropriations and alleged breaches of contract.

The 1990–1991 war resulting from Iraq's invasion and subsequent occupation of Kuwait led to the establishment of another Mass Claims Process, the United Nations Compensation Commission. Its purpose was to compensate large numbers of individuals from a variety of countries who had been working in Iraq or Kuwait and who incurred losses when they were forced to depart, or who suffered death or injury, as well as businesses whose property was damaged or whose commercial activities were disrupted. This Commission was also given the task of considering compensation for losses by affected governments, notably Kuwait itself.

War, and the disruptions of war, resulted in the creation of two claims commissions in the former Yugoslavia. The losses of persons who were displaced from their homes, largely for ethnic reasons, were specially addressed in the 1995 Dayton Peace Agreement by including a provision for creation of a

---

[1] John R. Crook, *Mass Claims Processes: Lessons Learned Over Twenty-Five Years*, in Redressing Injustices Through Mass Claims Processes: Innovative Responses To Unique Challenges, p. 41, at pp. 41–42 (Permanent Court of Arbitration ed., Oxford University Press 2006), citing, *inter alia*, David J. Bederman, *Historic Analogues of the UN Compensation Commission*, in The United Nations Compensation Commission: Thirteenth Sokol Colloquium p. 257 (R. Lillich ed., Transnational Publishers 1995), and *The United Nations Cmpensation Commission and the Tradition of International Claims Settlement*, 27 N.Y.U. J. Int'l L. & Pol. p. 1 (1994), (other citations omitted).

Commission for Real Property Claims for Displaced Persons and Refugees in Bosnia and Herzegovina. That was later followed by United Nations action in 1999 to establish a Housing and Property Claims Commission to settle claims concerning lost residential property in Kosovo. War, too, led to the Eritrea–Ethiopia Claims Commission, created by the 2000 Peace Agreement between those States to resolve claims of displaced persons, and for commercial losses, as well as for damages resulting from violations of humanitarian law.

In addition, a number of Claims Processes were instituted to deal with extensive losses of assets resulting from the Holocaust. The first of these was the Claims Resolution Tribunal for Dormant Accounts in Switzerland, established in 1997 to compensate holders of accounts in Swiss banks, and their heirs, who had been unable to recover those accounts since World War II. Later, when additional dormant accounts were uncovered as a result of further auditing, a second Claims Resolution Tribunal was established in 2000 to resolve claims related to those accounts by victims or targets of Nazi persecution. Similarly, three Mass Claims Processes were established beginning in 2000 to compensate persons who performed forced or slave labor, or who suffered loss of assets or unpaid insurance policies.

We also include discussion of the Mass Claims Process mentioned above, designed and administered by the American Arbitration Association for arbitrating tens of thousands of claims by policy-holders in the United States against a major American insurance company for damages arising from allegedly improper sales practices.

A brief history of each of the eleven Mass Claims Processes appears in the Annotations to Section 1.01 below. Also, information concerning each of those Processes can be found below in the "List of Mass Claims Processes Covered by This Book."

II. Background of the Project

The genesis of this book was a project suggested in a keynote address at the Centennial celebration of the Permanent Court of Arbitration (PCA) in The Hague, in May 1999. Speaking of the emergence of Mass Claims Processes, Howard M. Holtzmann noted:

"One thing is clear: there is no international arbitral institution where information concerning all of these mass claims processes is being collected, analyzed and compared by specialists in alternative dispute resolution. The PCA International Bureau is well-equipped to fill this gap.

As a first concrete step, the PCA might convene a meeting of individuals who have each been active in two or more of the mass claims processes that I have mentioned, either as arbitrators, administrators or counsel. ... Their experience is unique and their expertise is unparalleled. Working together, and with a few other experts, they might constitute a steering committee to recommend how the PCA could use its skills and facilities to assist in this complex field.

. . .

I suggest that if the PCA undertakes this new task it should do so promptly, while data can still be found in current files before being relegated to dusty archives, and while individuals who have first-hand knowledge are readily available."[2]

Following this suggestion, the Secretary-General of the PCA, Tjaco van den Hout, appointed a Steering Committee on Mass Claims Processes, consisting at first of nineteen Members, and later expanded to include several additional Members and Observers. Judge Holtzmann was designated Chairman. At least one Member of the Steering Committee was active in one, or more, of the eleven Claims Processes described in this book, either as someone who decided claims, as a staff member, as a government official who assisted in negotiation or administration, or as a lawyer of a party. Moreover, a broad, comparative perspective was assured by the fact that each Steering Committee Member had experience with at least two of the eleven Processes—indeed, one brought the experience of having participated at high levels in five of them—or on one of the eleven and also as a judge of a major international court. A list of Steering Committee Members and their experience appears in Annex A below, headed "Experience in Mass Claims Processes of Members of the Mass Claims Steering Committee of the Permanent Court of Arbitration."

III. Terminology and Nomenclature

A brief explanation of the terminology and nomenclature used in this book is necessary at the outset. It will be noted that some of the bodies that have been created to resolve international Mass Claims have the word "Tribunal" in their official name—such as the Iran–United States Claims Tribunal, and the Claims Resolution Tribunal for Dormant Accounts in Switzerland. In contrast, some others are officially named "Commission"—such as the Commission for Real Property Claims of Displaced Persons and Refugees, and the United Nations Compensation Commission. There is no uniform reason for this distinction and no legal significance derives from which term happens to be used.

---

[2] Reprinted in Howard M. Holtzmann, *Mass Claims Settlement Systems: Potentials and Pitfalls*, in INSTITUTIONAL AND PROCEDURAL ASPECTS OF MASS CLAIMS SETTLEMENT SYSTEMS, THE PERMANENT COURT OF ARBITRATION/PEACE PALACE PAPERS, p. 1, at pp. 6–7 (The International Bureau of the Permanent Court of Arbitration eds., Kluwer Law International 2000).

Therefore, the umbrella term "Mass Claims Process" is used for convenience in this book to cover a tribunal, a commission, or other dispute resolution body.

The persons who decide cases in those Mass Claims Processes are referred to in the respective constituting instruments and rules by such terms as "Judge," "Arbitrator," "Commissioner," and "Member." This book uses the generic term "decision-maker" to refer to those individuals.

As used herein, the term "Mass Claims Processes" includes proceedings known as "class actions" which exist under some, but not all, national laws.

IV. Identifying the Issues

Having determined that a list of basic issues would provide a convenient framework to aid comparing a large number of topics, the Steering Committee reviewed and polished a draft list of matters that had been prepared for it by its Chairman. In doing so, the Steering Committee recognized that all of the listed matters might not apply to all Claims Processes, and that the circumstances of particular Processes might require inclusion of additional matters. Thus, the list is a flexible guide, not a rigid mandate. It divides the issues into eight main categories, as follows:

1. *Establishing the Claims Process*—Whether the Claims Process is created by treaty, agreement, or other means; and the scope of the constituting instrument. (Chapter 1)
2. *The Legal Nature of the Claims Process*—Whether the Claims Process is akin to arbitration or to an administrative proceeding; whether the Claims Process is the exclusive recourse available to claimants; what law governs; and how awards are funded and enforced. (Chapter 2)
3. *Starting the Claims Process*—How potential claimants are informed of the existence of the Claims Process; procedures and deadlines for making claims; whether there is a means for initial screening to eliminate claims that *prima facie* do not fall within the jurisdiction of the Claims Process or clearly lack merit; and whether there are target schedules for conducting and completing the work. (Chapter 3)
4. *Appointing Those Who Will Make Decisions*—Who makes the appointments; whether any particular qualifications are specified; whether their duties are full-time or part-time; and how impartiality and independence are ensured. (Chapter 4)
5. *Procedures for Conducting the Claims Process*—How rules are adopted and amended; whether a set of recognized rules is incorporated by reference; what provisions are established concerning the equality of parties,

standards of proof, language, hearings, and document submission; how any interest is calculated; how costs are determined and paid; whether there is a means of appeal or review within the Claims Process itself; and the extent to which procedures are conducted by electronic means. (Chapter 5)

6. *Administration, Facilities, and Computer Support*—Levels and amounts of legal, technical and administrative support; whether there is reliance upon an existing organization; what are the respective roles of the Secretariat and the decision-makers; what facilities and equipment are needed. (Chapter 6)

7. *Funding the Claims Process*—The source of funds to pay for the Claims Process; estimated costs; the method for preparing periodic budgets; and the need for audits. (Chapter 7)

8. *Transparency*—The extent to which the activities of the Claims Process are made public. (Chapter 8)

V. Sources of Information

The information in the Annotations is based on a variety of sources. Some Mass Claims Processes have issued descriptive booklets and maintain websites, but these have been focused largely on providing information for potential claimants. Although they may include some background, they do not typically furnish information concerning many of the matters addressed in this book. Similarly, the constituting instruments, rules, and other documents referred to in the "List of Basic Documents" (Annex B), address some, but not all, of the issues.

In these circumstances, a major source of information has been the knowledge and experience of Members of the Steering Committee with respect to Claims Processes in which they personally participated, as shown in Annex A below that describes "Experience in Mass Claims Processes of the Members of the Mass Claims Steering Committee of the Permanent Court of Arbitration." Committee Members who were principal sources of information on particular Claims Processes are identified by asterisks in Annex A. In addition, some information has been supplied by persons, generally staff, who are not Committee Members. Thus, the Editors have necessarily relied on the extent of the information received from others. Further, a number of books, book chapters, monographs, and articles have been valuable sources of information or confirmation. (See Bibliographical Guide to Selected Sources of Information, in Annex C.) Materials received from all of these sources were organized and edited by the Editors and then submitted to the Steering Committee Members for comments and to check accuracy.

Many Mass Claims Processes make public the texts of their decisions, but some do not. Even when decisions are available, they generally are not directed toward many of the topics that we are addressing. Accordingly, we have not generally included analyses of decisions on claims made by various Mass Claims Processes, or by the few national courts that have considered matters related to each Process.

VI. Acknowledgments

In introducing this book the Editors acknowledge with deep thanks those who have assisted us in this effort. First, we must express our thanks to Judge Stephen M. Schwebel, former President of the International Court of Justice, for the honor he does us by contributing the Foreword. His experience as a jurist, scholar, leader of a great court, and arbitrator in major international cases is unmatched—indeed, unmatchable.

We thank, too, Tjaco van den Hout, Secretary-General of the Permanent Court of Arbitration, who has supported the project that resulted in this book from its inception and has placed the full facilities of the PCA International Bureau at our disposal.

As explained above, key sources of information in the Annotations that are a core element of this book were those members of the PCA Steering Committee on Mass Claims whose names are preceded by an asterisk in Annex A. We have chosen to use an asterisk to identify these individuals because the word "asterisk" is a synonym for "star," and they are stars in our firmament for whose light we are immensely grateful.

After drafts had been prepared, members and observers of the PCA Steering Committee were invited to make comments. In response, Arthur Rovine and Richard Mosk have graciously reviewed large portions of the manuscript and have made many valuable suggestions. Mr. Rovine has brought to the task insights gained from his wide experience as a government lawyer, as counsel in cases before Mass Claims Processes, and as an expert in arbitration of investment disputes. Justice Mosk, now a member of the California Court of Appeals, commented from the perspective of a lifetime in various aspects of litigation practice, including participation in Mass Claims Processes. Welcome comments on particular parts of the book have been made by Ronald Bettauer, Charles Brower, David Caron, John Crook, Veijo Heiskanen, Hans van Houtte, Andrew Jacovides, Clifton Johnson, Norbert Wühler, and Mark Appel.

Information concerning the work of the Conference on Jewish Material Claims Against Germany was provided by Alon Harnoy, its Director of Insurance Claims Programs, while working closely under the leadership of

Gideon Taylor, its Executive Vice President, and Gregory Schneider, its Chief Operating Officer. Also, updated information was furnished, (i) concerning the Iran–United States Claims Tribunal, by Maurizio Brunetti, its Deputy Secretary-General; (ii) concerning the United Nations Claims Commission, by Linda A. Taylor, Chief of Section of the UNCC's Legal Services Branch; (iii) concerning the Housing and Property Claims Commission in Kosovo, by Alan Dodson, Chairperson of the Commission, and Knut Rosandhaug, Executive Director; and (iv) concerning the Holocaust Victim Assets Programme at the International Organization for Migration, by Judith Cole, Deputy Director, Claims Programmes (GFLCP–HVAP), Cheryl Hill, Senior Legal Officer and Team Leader (HVAP), and Barbora Simerova, Special Projects Officer and Legal Successors Processing Coordinator (GFLCP–HVAP).

The team of the PCA that, under the leadership of Dr. van den Hout, significantly aided in the preparation of this book included Judith Freedberg, General Counsel; Bette Shifman, while Deputy Secretary-General and Principal Legal Counsel; Belinda Macmahon, Legal Counsel and Secretary of the Mass Claims Steering Committee in its later phases; and Anne Joyce, Deputy General Counsel.

Duco de Boer and the Stibbe law firm contributed much needed support, as did Ruth Bergman. Research assistance was provided by Cassandra Marshall, then a student at New York University School of Law.

We are grateful to the Delegates of the Oxford University Press for their confidence, and to John Louth, Senior Editor, Law, who, together with his colleagues, tactfully provided concrete assistance.

All books intrude into the lives of the families of those who write them. We thank our spouses, Carol Holtzmann and Duco de Boer, for the grace and understanding with which they have coped with our preoccupation. Finally, we express our hope that when Steinn and Thor de Boer come upon this book in the future they will understand why their mother spent so much time working on it during their earliest years.

Format and Use of this Book

By the Editors

The format of this book has been designed to permit easy access to a wide variety of separate topics and to facilitate comparative analysis of the ways different Mass Claims Processes have approached the basic matters that typically arise concerning their design and operation. To meet that need, this book is arranged in forty-seven Sections, each devoted to one basic topic. The Sections all follow the same format: each Section begins with a brief statement, printed in bold-face type, of key matters with respect to the topic covered in the Section. Following that is an "Editors' Commentary" and separate Annotations showing how each of eleven Mass Claims Processes has handled the matter. Each Annotation is headed by the name and identification of the Claims Process that is discussed. The Annotations in each Section appear in the chronological order of the dates of establishment of the Claims Process to which they relate, except that, to assist comparison, each Annotation concerning the second tribunal related to dormant accounts in Swiss banks (CRT-II) immediately follows discussion of the first such tribunal (CRT-I). The same system of headings and order of presentation is followed in each Section.

The book is arranged to facilitate reference by readers who have different interests. Those who have a general interest in the field may wish to read mainly the Editors' Commentaries, going deeper into the relevant Annotations if they seek further information on specific topics. Those interested in one, or a few, particular Claims Processes, may choose to concentrate on the Annotations relevant to those Claims Processes. Readers interested in a particular matter need refer only to the Sections where information can be found concerning the approaches to that matter by all eleven Claims Processes.

Recognizing that different readers may have different interests at different times, each Editors' Commentary and Annotation has been written with the aim that it can stand alone without having to read other parts of the book (except in the few instances where there is a cross-reference to material elsewhere).

A "Summary Table of Contents" shows the location of the main chapters and the other features. In addition, there is a detailed Table of Contents that is quite extensive in order to help readers quickly find what they are looking for.

As noted, the various Mass Claims Processes were established at different times, by different persons, and in different circumstances. It is therefore not surprising that no uniform practice was followed in naming them. Some have names that are reasonably descriptive of their function, e.g., "Iran–United States Claims Tribunal," "German Forced Labour Compensation Programme," and "Eritrea–Ethiopia Claims Commission." Others give some indication of the nature of the claims they handle, but are incomplete; for example, the title "Commission for Real Property Claims for Displaced Persons and Refugees" describes the nature of the claims but does not refer to Bosnia and Herzegovina, thereby giving no information as to where the claims arose. Some names, such as "United Nations Compensation Commission" give no hint of the type or source of the claims they were created to resolve. The lack of uniform approach is vividly illustrated by the names of the two tribunals created to handle claims relating to dormant accounts in Swiss banks—the first such tribunal has the useful title "Claims Resolution Tribunal for Dormant Accounts in Switzerland" but the second has only a mysterious name that reads in full "Claims Resolution Tribunal," with no indication of who, what, or where. Although most of the Claims Processes have abbreviated titles expressed in letters such as "GFLCP," "HVAP" and "ICHEIC," these acronyms are mere alphabetical mish-mash to most readers.

The Editors believe that readers should be able to identify the various Mass Claims Processes easily, without having to puzzle over incomplete or inscrutable titles, or to decipher and memorize unfamiliar sequences of letters. Therefore, to facilitate the task of our readers, we have adopted a uniform system of nomenclature for the headings of the Annotations. Each begins with the official title of the Claims Process because that may be needed for citation purposes, followed by the abbreviation in parenthesis, and augmented by a short phrase describing the claims to which the Claims Process relates, for example: "United Nations Compensation Commission (UNCC)—claims relating to the 1990–1991 Gulf War." This, of course, adds a few words, but faced with a choice between brevity and clarity, we have used the longer form in the hope that it will facilitate quick reference by those who work with these materials.

Throughout this book, we have generally used American spelling rather than British spelling, except where British spelling appears in official titles or quotations (e.g., "labor" and "program" rather than "labour" and "programme").

To assist those who wish to do further research, a "List of Basic Documents" governing the Mass Claims Processes covered by the book is included below in Annex B; a bibliographical guide to selected sources of information, prepared with the assistance of the staff of the Permanent Court of Arbitration, appears in Annex C; and "Tables of Sources Cited" are provided in Annex D.

Finally, a consolidated compilation of all the matters, headed "Checklist of Issues That Designers of Mass Claims Processes Might Wish to Consider," is provided in Annex E for the convenience of those to whom it might be useful for working purposes.

List of Mass Claims Processes Covered by this Book

(in chronological order of date of start of operations*)

Iran–United States Claims Tribunal (Iran–US CT), The Hague, the Netherlands

- Claims relating to the 1979 Islamic Revolution in Iran
- Period of operation: 1981–
- Website: www.iusct.org

United Nations Compensation Commission (UNCC), Geneva, Switzerland

- Claims relating to the 1990–1991 Gulf War resulting from Iraq's invasion and occupation of Kuwait
- Period of operation: 1991–
- Website: www.uncc.ch

Commission for Real Property Claims of Displaced Persons and Refugees (CRPC), Sarajevo, Bosnia and Herzegovina

- Claims relating to the 1992–1995 war in Bosnia and Herzegovina
- Period of operation: 1996 to 2003
- Website: [www.crpc.org.ba is no longer online; its contents are accessible via www.pca-cpa.org "Links to Completed Mass Claims Processes"]

Claims Resolution Tribunal for Dormant Accounts in Switzerland (CRT-I), Zurich, Switzerland

- First claims tribunal for assets deposited in Swiss banks
- Period of operation: 1998 to 2001
- Website: www.crt-ii.org/_crt-i

---

* Except that, to assist comparison, the second Claims Process relating to dormant accounts in Swiss banks (CRT-II) is listed immediately following the first such Claims Process (CRT-I). Note: where no date of conclusion of operations is shown, the Claims Process was still operating on 31 January 2006.

Claims Resolution Tribunal (CRT-II), Zurich, Switzerland

- Second claims tribunal for assets deposited in Swiss banks
- Period of operation: 2001–
- Website: www.crt-ii.org

Housing and Property Claims Commission (HPCC), Pristina, Kosovo

- Claims relating to the 1999 conflict in Kosovo
- Period of operation: 2000–
- Website: www.hpdkosovo.org

German Forced Labour Compensation Programme (GFLCP), International Organization for Migration, Geneva, Switzerland

- Claims against Germany and German industry for Nazi injustice
- Period of operation: 2000–
- Website: www.compensation-for-forced-labour.org

Holocaust Victim Assets Programme (HVAP), International Organization for Migration, Geneva, Switzerland

- Claims pursuant to 1999 Swiss banks class action settlement
- Period of operation: 2000–
- Website: www.swissbankclaims.iom.int

Eritrea–Ethiopia Claims Commission (EECC), The Hague, the Netherlands

- Claims relating to the 1998–2000 war between Eritrea and Ethiopia
- Period of operation: 2000–
- Website: www.pca-cpa.org

International Commission on Holocaust Era Insurance Claims (ICHEIC), The Conference on Jewish Material Claims Against Germany (JCC), New York, NY

- Humanitarian claims process
- Period of operation: 2003 to 2005
- Websites: www.icheic.org and www.claimscon.org

American Arbitration Association (AAA), New York, NY

- Claims relating to an insurance policy class action settlement
- Period of operation: 1997 to 2001
- Website: www.adr.org

List of Abbreviations

AAA	American Arbitration Association
ARF	Austrian Reconciliation Fund
BEG	Bundesentschädigungsgesetz (German Federal Indemnification Law)
BiH	Bosnia and Herzegovina
CQRT	Claimant Query Response Team (at CRPC)
CRPC	Commission for Real Property Claims of Displaced Persons and Refugees, Bosnia and Herzegovina
CRT-I	Claims Resolution Tribunal for Dormant Accounts in Switzerland
CRT-II	Claims Resolution Tribunal (second tribunal for dormant accounts in Switzerland)
E.D.N.Y.	Eastern District of New York
EECC	Eritrea–Ethiopia Claims Commission
F.R.	Federal Register (USA)
F.Supp.	Federal Supplement (USA)
GFLCP	German Forced Labour Compensation Programme (IOM)
GSF	General Settlement Fund for Victims of National Socialism in Austria
HABITAT	United Nations Centre for Human Settlements
HCPO	Holocaust Claims Processing Office (NY State Banking Department)
HPCC	Housing and Property Claims Commission, Kosovo
HPD	Housing and Property Directorate, Kosovo
HSP	Humanitarian and Social Programmes (IOM)
HVAP	Holocaust Victim Assets Programme (IOM)
ICEP	Independent Committee of Eminent Persons
ICHEIC	International Commission on Holocaust Era Insurance Claims
ICJ	International Court of Justice
ICRF	Independent Claims Resolution Foundation (Swiss banks)
I.L.M.	International Legal Materials
IOM	International Organization for Migration

IPCC	Iraq Property Claims Commission
ITS	International Tracing Service
JCC	Conference on Jewish Material Claims Against Germany—"Jewish Claims Conference"
Iran–US CT	Iran–United States Claims Tribunal
Iran–U.S. C.T.R.	Iran–United States Claims Tribunal Reports
MOU	Memorandum of Understanding
MOU Companies	Insurance companies participating in the ICHEIC Claims Process
NAIC	National Association of Insurance Commissioners (USA)
NATO	North Atlantic Treaty Organisation
OIOS	United Nations Office of Internal Oversight Services
PCA	Permanent Court of Arbitration
PCA Rules	Permanent Court of Arbitration Optional Rules for Arbitrating Disputes between Two States
SBA	Swiss Bankers Association
SFBC	Swiss Federal Banking Commission
UNCC	United Nations Compensation Commission
UNCITRAL	United Nations Commission on International Trade Law
UNDP	United Nations Development Program
UNHCR	United Nations High Commissioner for Refugees
UNMIK	United Nations Interim Administration Mission in Kosovo
UNOB	United Nations Office in Belgrade
UNOG	United Nations Office in Geneva
U.N.T.S.	United Nations Treaty Series
UNRWA	United Nations Relief and Works Agency for Palestine Refugees in the Middle East
U.S.C.	United States Code
USHMM	United States Holocaust Memorial Museum
VVSB	Verification and Valuation Support Branch (UNCC)
8A1	Referring to section 8A1 of the ICHEIC Memorandum of Understanding

Chapter 1

Establishing the Claims Process

1.01 Constituting Method

The types of constituting instrument(s) or procedures by which Claims Processes are created (e.g., treaty, agreement, judicial decision, or other), having regard to the major events and circumstances giving rise to the claims.

Editors' Commentary

The legal foundations of the Mass Claims Processes described in this book have been created by a number of different types of constituting instruments and procedures. Some adopt forms customarily used in public international law contexts; others resemble agreements to arbitrate, typically used to resolve commercial disputes; while still others have been formed by innovative means designed in the light of unique political circumstances. The methods for establishing these various Mass Claims Processes are described in this first section. Each description is accompanied by a brief history of the particular Claims Process so that the choice and effectiveness of the method used can be seen in context. Taken together, these descriptions demonstrate the wide variety of options available to designers of Mass Claims Processes to adopt or combine features of various approaches, or to invent new ones.

A frequently used public international law means for establishing Mass Claims Processes has been by agreements between States. Thus, for example, the Iran–United States Claims Tribunal (Iran–US CT) was established pursuant to a treaty between the two countries. Similarly, the Commission for Real Property Claims of Displaced Persons and Refugees (CRPC) in Bosnia and Herzegovina, and the Eritrea-Ethiopia Claims Commission (EECC), were each created by provisions included in a peace agreement. Other Claims Processes that have public international law roots include the United Nations Compensation Commission (UNCC) for claims resulting from the

1990–1991 Gulf War, and the Housing and Property Claims Commission (HPCC) in Kosovo, each created in accordance with action by the United Nations.

In contrast, the constituting instrument for the Claims Resolution Tribunal for Dormant Accounts in Switzerland (CRT-I) was established by an agreement to arbitrate, made between representatives of private banks and a non-governmental organization, to resolve claims to accounts in Swiss banks that had lain dormant since the end of World War II. That model, however, was not followed in forming a second such Claims Resolution Tribunal (CRT-II) that was created pursuant to a settlement agreement approved by a federal district court in the United States in an innovative class action on behalf of individual claimants. Although it is not uncommon in the United States for domestic mass claims to be resolved pursuant to processes established by national courts in class actions, such as some Claims Processes administered by the American Arbitration Association (AAA), it is an innovation to have a national court create and supervise a Claims Process to decide claims of large numbers of persons, most of whom have no connection with the United States and who seek compensation for wrongful acts that took place outside the United States.

Different approaches were used in constituting two Mass Claims Processes to compensate victims of Nazi persecution who were forced or slave laborers. One is the German Forced Labour Compensation Programme (GFLCP), which the International Organization for Migration (IOM) manages as one of seven partner organizations of the German Foundation "Remembrance, Responsibility and Future," established in 2000 to compensate certain victims of the Nazi regime. Establishing that Claims Process involved not only State negotiations (between the Governments of Germany and the United States, as well as Belarus, the Czech Republic, Israel, Poland, Russia, and Ukraine), but also national legislation, and commitments by private parties. Thus, German legislation implemented matters recorded in an agreement between the United States and Germany, by establishing a program, funded by the German Government and by German companies that agreed to participate, and to which parties in United States class action law suits and other private and State parties acceded. Somewhat similarly, a Claims Process to compensate for losses on unpaid insurance claims, known as the International Commission on Holocaust Era Insurance Claims (ICHEIC), was constituted by a Memorandum of Understanding and involved complex arrangements, including German legislation, as well as agreements by two States, a non-governmental organization, and a number of private insurance companies. That Claims Process included unique provisions for so-called "humanitarian awards" that are described below.

All of the Mass Claims Processes described in this book, with one exception, were designed to resolve claims having primarily an international character. The one exception is that this book includes information drawn from the experience of the American Arbitration Association (AAA) in administering the resolution of large numbers of domestic claims arising from settlements of class action law suits in either United States federal courts or in state courts. The Claims Processes administered by the AAA were developed in the light of their particular circumstances, and it is outside the scope of this book to describe them all. One illustrative case that involved more than 1.2 million claims has been included and described in this book, however, as it demonstrates techniques that may be useful in an international Mass Claims context.

Annotations

(a) Iran–United States Claims Tribunal (Iran–US CT)—claims relating to the 1979 Islamic Revolution

The Iran–US CT is an international arbitral tribunal created in 1981 by a legally binding agreement recognized as a treaty under international law.[1] As part of the efforts to resolve the crisis that arose when United States diplomats were held hostage in Tehran, the United States and Iran made a number of interdependent commitments, known as the Algiers Accords. These included a Claims Settlement Declaration by which the two States established a Tribunal for the purpose of deciding (i) claims and counterclaims by their nationals against the other State arising out of debts, contracts, expropriations, or other measures affecting property rights; (ii) official claims against each other arising out of contracts between them for the purchase or sale of goods and services; and (iii) disputes over the interpretation or performance of the Algiers Accords.[2] The Government of the Democratic Popular Republic of Algeria, which had served as an intermediary, declared on the basis of formal adherence received from each of the two Governments, that Iran and the United States had made these commitments.[3]

The hostage crisis between the United States and the Islamic Republic of Iran arose on 4 November 1979, when a group of Iranians seized the United

---

[1] Declaration of the Democratic and Popular Republic of Algeria concerning the Settlement of Claims by the Government of the United States of America and the Government of the Islamic Republic of Iran (19 January 1981), reprinted in 1 Iran-U.S. C.T.R. p. 9 [hereinafter Claims Settlement Declaration].   [2] Claims Settlement Declaration, Article II.
[3] Declaration of the Government of the Democratic and Popular Republic of Algeria (19 January 1981), reprinted in 1 Iran-U.S. C.T.R. p. 3 [hereinafter General Declaration], Introduction.

States Embassy compound in Tehran, detained fifty-two American nationals (who were subsequently held for 444 days), and demanded the return from the United States of the Iranian Shah and his assets. The United States subsequently froze all Iranian assets subject to its jurisdiction and imposed economic sanctions on Iran. Following that freeze order, many American individuals and companies that had suffered losses as a result of the Iranian Revolution instituted proceedings in United States courts to obtain judicial attachments of Iranian assets located in the United States, including bank accounts, cash, and securities. The United States attempted to, but did not, resolve the hostage crisis through diplomatic negotiation, an application to the International Court of Justice (ICJ), and then a military operation to free the hostages.

On 18 January 1981, following extensive indirect negotiations through the Government of Algeria as third-party intermediary, the Governments of Iran and the United States reached agreement: (i) Iran agreed to release the fifty-two American hostages; (ii) the United States agreed, subject to certain conditions, to return the frozen Iranian assets by transferring the largest part to special accounts to be used for payment of Iran's debts to banks and of awards against Iran by the new arbitral Tribunal established pursuant to the Claims Settlement Declaration, with the remaining amount to be paid directly to Iran; and (iii) the United States agreed to secure the dismissal in United States courts of litigation against Iran, which claims then could be submitted to the new arbitral Tribunal.

The architects of the Algiers Accords considered them to be an appropriate means to institute a Mass Claims Process in the complex situation negotiated in the midst of a tense diplomatic crisis.

According to a Communiqué issued by the Secretary-General of the Tribunal, the total number of cases finalized by Award, Decision, or Order of the Tribunal was, at the end of June 2005, 3,936.[4] This included 2,884 claims of less than US$250,000.[5] The Communiqué states the following with respect to amounts awarded:

"The total amount awarded to United States parties and notified to the Escrow Agent to date [is] US$2,166,998,515.43 and the US Dollar equivalent of £303,196.00, DM 297,051.00 and Rls. 97,132,598 (excluding any interest to be calculated by the Escrow Agent)...."

---

[4] Iran–US CT Communiqué No. 05/3, 26 July 2005, available at www.iusct.org.

[5] Out of the claims of less than US$250,000, 2,388 were terminated by Award on Agreed Terms, filed 22 June 1990, *The United States of America on behalf of and for the benefit of certain of its nationals* and *The Islamic Republic of Iran*, Award on Agreed Terms Nr 483—Claims of Less than US$250,000/86/B38/B76/B77-FT (22 June 1990), reprinted in 25 Iran-U.S. C.T.R. p. 327.

A total amount (excluding any interest to be calculated) of US$1,013,716,179.13 and the US Dollar equivalent of Rls. 7,977,343 was awarded to be paid to Iran and Iranian parties . . . ."[6]

(b) United Nations Compensation Commission (UNCC)—claims relating to the 1990–1991 Gulf War

Iraq invaded Kuwait on 2 August 1990 and thereafter occupied it until being expelled, on 2 March 1991, by an allied coalition operation under the authority of the United Nations. As the end of the military action drew nearer, the United Nations Security Council turned its focus to claims resolution. The Security Council had the previous fall already indicated that Iraq would be held liable for all damage resulting from its invasion and occupation of Kuwait.[7] It was further aware of the international community's grave concern over the environmental damage that Iraq had unleashed through actions such as setting fire to oil wells and releasing of oil into the Persian Gulf. Iraq had a very substantial debt prior to the invasion which might remain unpaid as a direct result thereof, and the Security Council knew that the number of claims would be in the millions and that the State of Kuwait alone would likely seek damages in the billions of dollars.[8]

Security Council Resolution 687 (1991) set forth the terms of the overall cease-fire and Iraq's liability in particular. It specifically included claims for environmental damage and expressly excluded claims for losses arising prior to the invasion and occupation of Kuwait.[9]

The UNCC was created in 1991 by a Resolution of the United Nations Security Council and is a subsidiary organ of the Security Council.[10] The

---

[6] Iran–US CT Communiqué No. 05/3, paragraph III, 26 July 2005, available at www.iusct.org.

[7] UN Security Council Resolution 674 (1990) of 29 October 1990, U.N. Doc. S/RES/674 (1990) (29 October 1990), paragraph 8, "[r]eminds Iraq that under international law it is liable for any loss, damage or injury arising in regard to Kuwait and third States, and their nationals and corporations, as a result of the invasion and illegal occupation of Kuwait by Iraq."

[8] The discussion of the UNCC in this book relates only to the period before commencement in 2003 of war between the United States and its coalition partners and Iraq. Later arrangements are outside the scope of the book.

[9] In UN Security Council Resolution 687 (1991) of 3 April 1991, U.N. Doc. S/RES/687 (1991) (8 April 1991), paragraph 16, the Security Council "reaffirms" that "Iraq, without prejudice to the debts and obligations of Iraq arising prior to 2 August 1990, which will be addressed through the normal mechanisms, is liable under international law for any direct loss, damage, including environmental damage and the depletion of natural resources, or injury to foreign Governments, nationals and corporations, as a result of Iraq's unlawful invasion and occupation of Kuwait."

[10] By its Resolution 687 (1991) of 3 April 1991, the UN Security Council decided to create a Compensation Fund and a Commission to administer it. U.N. Doc. S/RES/687 (1991) (8 April

Commission evaluates and decides claims for direct losses resulting from Iraq's 1990 invasion and subsequent occupation of Kuwait, and it pays compensation for such losses. The United Nations Secretary-General, in a Report in which he proposed the institutional structure of the Claims Process and outlined a system for funding its organization and paying awards, described the Commission as being "not a court or an arbitral tribunal . . . [but] a political organ that performs an essentially fact-finding function of examining claims, verifying their validity, evaluating losses, assessing payments and resolving disputed claims. It is only in this last respect that a quasi-judicial function may be involved."[11] It should be noted that this quoted passage appears in Part II of the Secretary-General's Report, which the United Nations Security Council only asked the UNCC Governing Council to "take into account" when implementing Resolution 687, and hence it is considered by the Governing Council, strictly speaking, not to be binding upon it.[12] In any event, the procedures that the Governing Council subsequently adopted were based on the reality of having to process 2.6 million claims in a limited amount of time, and the rules of procedure came to place great emphasis on administrative mechanisms, rather than on "quasi-judicial" action.[13]

The UNCC is the largest war reparations undertaking in history.[14] A total of 2.6 million claims were filed by the deadlines for filing claims, seeking a total of approximately US$368 billion in compensation. Approximately 6,700 claims were filed by corporations and other entities, close to 300 by governments and international organizations, and all remaining claims were filed by individuals.[15] As at 31 January 2006, one hundred percent of the total number

1991), paragraph 18. It also requested the UN Secretary-General to make recommendations, *inter alia*, with respect to the organization of the UNCC and its Claims Process (paragraph 19). The Secretary-General submitted his Report pursuant to paragraph 19 of Resolution 687, making recommendations regarding the institutional framework for the UNCC and the processing and payment of claims. *Report of the Secretary-General Pursuant to Paragraph 19 of Security Council Resolution 687 (1991)*, U.N. Doc. S/22559 (2 May 1991), [hereinafter Report of the Secretary-General of 2 May 1991, U.N. Doc. S/22559]. By Resolution 692 (1991) of 20 May 1991, the Security Council adopted Part I of the Secretary-General's Report and created the UNCC, U.N. Doc. S/RES/692 (1991) (20 May 1991), paragraph 3. In paragraph 5 of the same Resolution, the Security Council directed the UNCC's Governing Council to take "into account" the recommendations in Part II of the Secretary-General's Report when implementing Resolution 687.

[11] Report of the Secretary-General of 2 May 1991, U.N. Doc. S/22559, paragraph 20.

[12] UN Security Council Resolution 692 (1991) of 20 May 1991, U.N. Doc. S/RES/692 (1991) (20 May 1991), paragraph 5.

[13] See UNCC Governing Council Decision 10 of 26 June 1992, *Provisional Rules for Claims Procedure*, U.N. Doc. S/AC.26/1992/10 [hereinafter UNCC Provisional Rules].

[14] See, e.g., Veijo Heiskanen, *The United Nations Compensation Commission*, 296 Recueil des Cours p. 255, at p. 268 (2002).   [15] See www.uncc.ch.

of claims filed with the Commission had been resolved, and approximately US$19 billion had been paid out.

(c) Commission for Real Property Claims of Displaced Persons and Refugees (CRPC)—claims relating to the 1992–1995 war in Bosnia and Herzegovina

The CRPC was an international Commission established in 1996 under an international treaty, the Dayton Peace Agreement, to decide claims by Bosnians seeking to reestablish their rights to real property of which they had been dispossessed during the 1992–1995 conflict in Bosnia and Herzegovina.[16]

After the war in the region ended, the international community felt that the restoration of pre-conflict property rights was critical to the overall aims of the peace process and to the post-conflict rehabilitation in Bosnia and Herzegovina. Restoration of property rights to refugees and displaced persons was seen as a cornerstone of reversing the ethnic cleansing which had caused more than half of the country's pre-war inhabitants to flee their homes. An estimated one million persons were refugees outside Bosnia and Herzegovina when the Dayton Peace Agreement was signed, while another million persons were displaced internally. During the war, in an attempt to prevent the eventual return of minorities after the conflict, many of the cadastre records and property books had been destroyed or tampered with, making it very difficult for refugees and internally displaced persons to prove their ownership rights. The sensitivity of claims to homes in an ethnically divisive post-conflict situation called for the establishment of an international impartial body subject to international law. It was anticipated that the number of potential claims would be in the hundreds of thousands, but it was recognized that the war had so damaged the country's infrastructure that no viable institution existed in 1995 that could render formal decisions recognizing title to property.

The details of the Commission's mandate were contained in Annex 7 to the Dayton Peace Agreement, which provided that CRPC was to "receive and decide any claims for real property in Bosnia and Herzegovina, where the property has not voluntarily been sold or otherwise transferred since April 1, 1992, and where the claimant does not now enjoy possession of that property."[17]

The CRPC completed its work in 2003 and handed over its mandate to local authorities in Bosnia and Herzegovina. During its eight years of

---

[16] General Framework Agreement for Peace in Bosnia and Herzegovina, initialed in Dayton, 21 November 1995, signed in Paris, 14 December 1995 [hereinafter Dayton Peace Agreement], 35 I.L.M. p. 75, at p. 138.   [17] Dayton Peace Agreement, Annex 7, Article XI.

operation, the Commission rendered a total of 311,757 final and binding decisions concerning ownership, joint ownership, lawful possession and co-possession, occupancy rights and mixed rights to apartments and residential buildings, agricultural properties, business buildings and premises, land, and other real estate. Although Annex 7 had provided that claims could be made for "return of the property or for just compensation in lieu of return,"[18] the decisions of the Commission only established property "rights"; they did not award any amounts of money to be paid to claimants.[19] The decisions rendered by the CRPC are estimated to have benefitted close to one million people.[20]

(d) Claims Resolution Tribunal for Dormant Accounts in Switzerland (CRT-I)—first claims tribunal for assets deposited in Swiss banks

CRT-I was established in October 1997 as an independent international arbitral Tribunal under Swiss law to resolve claims to approximately 6,000 accounts in Swiss banks that had lain dormant, or inactive, since the end of World War II. An Independent Committee of Eminent Persons (ICEP)—also known as the Volcker Committee—had been formed in May 1996 by a Memorandum of Understanding between the Swiss Bankers Association (SBA), the World Jewish Restitution Organization, and the World Jewish Congress.[21] ICEP was chaired by Mr. Paul Volcker, former Chairman of the Board of Governors of the United States Federal Reserve System. Its mandate was to conduct an investigative audit of Swiss banks to determine whether there were any dormant accounts, financial instruments, or other assets that had been deposited in Swiss banks before, during, or immediately after World

---

[18] Dayton Peace Agreement, Annex 7, *The Agreement on Refugees and Displaced Persons*, Article XI. The parties to Annex 7 were the Republic of Bosnia and Herzegovina, the Federation of Bosnia and Herzegovina, and Republika Srpska. The parties to the Dayton Peace Agreement were the Republic of Bosnia and Herzegovina, the Republic of Croatia, and the Federal Republic of Yugoslavia, which undertook to promote fulfillment of the commitments of Annex 7. The Dayton Peace Agreement was signed by representatives of the following parties as witnesses: European Union Special Negotiator, French Republic, Federal Republic of Germany, Russian Federation, United Kingdom of Great Britain and Northern Ireland, and United States of America.

[19] See *Commission for Real Property Claims of Displaced Persons and Refugees (CRPC) End of Mandate Report (1996–2003)* [hereinafter CRPC End of Mandate Report], Annex B—*Annex 7 Compensation Fund Unrealised*, available at www.pca-cpa.org/MCP/index_MCP.htm "Links to Completed Mass Claims Processes."   [20] CRPC End of Mandate Report, Executive Summary.

[21] Memorandum of Understanding between The World Jewish Restitution Organization and The World Jewish Congress, representing also the Jewish Agency and Allied Organizations, and The Swiss Bankers Association, 2 May 1996 [hereinafter ICEP Memorandum of Understanding], Appendix A to Final ICEP Report (*Report on Dormant Accounts of Victims of Nazi Persecution in Swiss Banks*) (1999), available at www.crt-ii.org/icep_report.phtm.

War II, but that still remained in the possession of the banks. ICEP established the Independent Claims Resolution Foundation (ICRF), whose Board of Trustees in turn formed the Claims Resolution Tribunal.

In response to growing concerns that there were indeed unclaimed foreign assets that had been deposited with Swiss banks in the World War II era, and as part of the investigative audit, ICEP, SBA, and the Swiss Federal Banking Commission (SFBC) on 25 June 1997 agreed to establish a Claims Resolution Process to adjudicate claims to the dormant accounts that had been identified by Swiss banks or in the course of the ICEP audit.[22] On 23 July 1997, SBA published the names of 1,872 holders of accounts that had been opened by foreign nationals prior to the end of World War II and had lain dormant ever since. Additional names were published in October 1997 and, in total, the names of 5,570 owners of such accounts were published. Individuals who believed that they were the rightful owners of the published accounts were invited to file their claims within six months of the date of publication.

ICRF administered the Claims Resolution Process. On 15 October 1997, its Board of Trustees appointed a number of jurists and bankers, including a number of international arbitration specialists, to serve as arbitrators for the newly-established Tribunal, which eventually came to consist of seventeen Arbitrators, including a Chairman and a Vice Chairman. The Tribunal completed its work in October 2001. In total, CRT-I received 9,918 claims, from twenty-seven countries and in twenty different languages. It approved 3,121 claims, dismissed 6,797, and awarded, in Swiss Francs, approximately 65 million to claimants (including adjustment for interest and bank fees).[23]

(e) Claims Resolution Tribunal (CRT-II)—second claims tribunal for assets deposited in Swiss banks

CRT-II is a successor of the Claims Resolution Tribunal for Dormant Accounts in Switzerland (CRT-I). CRT-II was created in 2000 by a federal district court in the United States as part of the implementation of a Settlement Agreement reached in class action lawsuits brought in 1996 and 1997 against major Swiss banks in United States courts.[24] Those lawsuits were subsequently consolidated

---

[22] Joint Press Release of 25 June 1997 by the Chairmen of SFBC and ICEP, announcing agreement among SFBC and SBA on a comprehensive Claims Resolution Process, annexed to the Final ICEP Report (*Report on Dormant Accounts of Victims of Nazi Persecution in Swiss Banks*) (1999), available at www.crt-ii.org/icep_report.phtm (Appendices A–W, p. A-9).

[23] See www.crt-ii.org/_crt-i "Statistics."

[24] The U.S. District Court for the Eastern District of New York, per Korman, Chief Judge, approved the settlement on 26 July 2000, as corrected 2 August 2000. See *In re Holocaust Victim Assets Litig.*, 105 F.Supp. 2d 139 (E.D.N.Y. 2000). Text of the Settlement Agreement available at www.crt-ii.org.

in the United States District Court for the Eastern District of New York (Korman, Chief Judge, presiding), where they became known as the "Holocaust Victim Assets Litigation (Swiss Banks)."[25]

Plaintiffs in the lawsuits had alleged that the banks had failed to identify and return assets deposited in the banks by victims of Nazi persecution, and that the banks had accepted and laundered assets looted by the Nazis and profits generated by Nazi use of slave labor. The lawsuits were settled in January 1999, when the banks agreed to create a US$1.25 billion Settlement Fund. A world-wide notification program was implemented, under the supervision of the Court, to inform the potential beneficiaries of their eligibility to participate in the Settlement. Pursuant to a Plan of Allocation and Distribution that was proposed by a Special Master appointed by Judge Korman and approved by the Judge on 22 November 2000, CRT-II decides claims to assets deposited with Swiss banks by victims or targets of Nazi persecution in accounts that were open or opened during the period 1933 to 1945.[26]

The CRT-II Claims Process was launched in 2001 with the publication of a list of the names of owners of approximately 21,000 accounts that were believed to have belonged to victims of Nazi persecution. In January 2005, an additional list of approximately 2,700 names of account owners and 400 names of Power of Attorney holders was published. The 2005 list contains names that had been identified in the ICEP audit, described in section 1.01(d) on CRT-I above, as possibly belonging to Holocaust victims, but that had not been previously published.[27] In connection with the original list of 21,000 accounts, approximately 33,500 claims were filed with CRT-II.[28] In addition, approximately 40,000 completed "Initial Questionnaires" submitted to the Court in 1999 by potential class members are being processed as timely-filed

---

[25] Hereinafter referred to as the Holocaust Victim Assets Litigation.

[26] See Special Master's Proposed Plan of Allocation and Distribution of Settlement Proceeds [hereinafter Plan of Allocation and Distribution], approved by Judge Korman on 22 November 2000, *In re Holocaust Victim Assets Litig.*, Case No. CV 96-4849 (ERK)(MDG) 2000 WL 33241660 (E.D.N.Y. 22 November 2000), aff'd, *In re Holocaust Victim Assets Litig.*, 413 F.3d 183 (2d Cir. (N.Y.) 1 July 2005). The Special Master appointed by Judge Korman to assist in drawing up the Plan of Allocation and Distribution and in implementing the parts relating to claims other than deposited assets was Judah Gribetz. Two additional Special Masters, Paul Volcker and Michael Bradfield, were later appointed by the Court for purposes of administering the CRT-II Claims Process. On 13 April 2004, Judge Korman appointed Dr. Helen B. Junz as an additional CRT Special Master.

[27] See www.crt-ii.org.

[28] Over 32,500 claims were filed by the filing deadline of 31 August 2001, and close to 700 late filed claims were accepted by 31 December 2002. See Special Master's Report on the Claims Resolution Process, 30 June 2003, pp. 3–4, available at www.crt-ii.org.

claims.[29] As of January 2006, the Court had approved 1,962 awards certified to it, and US\$284.2 million had been awarded.[30]

All admissible claims in the CRT-II Claims Process are matched against approximately 36,000 accounts identified by audits conducted after the establishment of CRT-I as possibly or probably belonging to victims or targets of Nazi persecution.[31] These accounts are thus in addition to the approximately 6,000 accounts handled by CRT-I. Unlike CRT-I, CRT-II is not an arbitral tribunal with power to make final and binding awards. Its determinations regarding the rights of claimants to Swiss bank accounts have the legal effect of "recommendations" that must be certified by the Special Masters to the Court for payment and are subject to the Court's approval.[32]

(f) Housing and Property Claims Commission (HPCC)—claims relating to the 1999 conflict in Kosovo

The HPCC Claims Process was established in 1999 by a Regulation of the United Nations Interim Administration Mission in Kosovo (UNMIK), issued by a Special Representative of the Secretary-General of the United Nations, to create an independent tribunal to settle disputes concerning non-commercial residential property.[33] The Commission addresses claims arising out of discriminatory measures affecting property rights taken by the Government of Yugoslavia in Kosovo during the period 1989 to 1999, and events surrounding the air campaign in Kosovo in 1999 by the North Atlantic Treaty Organisation (NATO).

The constituting instrument, UNMIK Regulation 1999/23, also established a Housing and Property Directorate (HPD) in Kosovo. The purpose of HPD is to regularize housing and property rights in Kosovo and resolve disputes over residential property through the creation of an impartial and independent mechanism, using local and international legal expertise, mediation, and the HPCC.[34]

---

[29] Prior to the expiration of the 31 August 2001 filing deadline for claims, the Court decided that 560,000 Initial Questionnaires returned by potential claimants should be analyzed to identify those that could be processed as CRT-II claim forms. See First Report on the CRT-II Process, 31 July 2002, p. 4, available at www.crt-ii.org. Approximately 40,000 Initial Questionnaires qualified for claims processing.   [30] See www.crt-ii.org/ awards/index.phtm—updated as of 23 January 2006.

[31] See Plan of Allocation and Distribution, section III, A.4.

[32] See Rules Governing the Claims Resolution Process (As Amended), available at www.crt-ii.org. [Unless otherwise indicated, all references hereinafter to the CRT-II Governing Rules are to the Rules as amended.] See Introduction to the Rules.

[33] UNMIK Regulation No. 1999/23 of 15 November 1999, *On the Establishment of the Housing and Property Directorate and the Housing and Property Claims Commission*, U.N. Doc. UNMIK/REG/1999/23 (15 November 1999) [hereinafter UNMIK Regulation 1999/23].

[34] See UNMIK Regulation 1999/23, sections 1 and 3.

The subject-matter jurisdiction of the Commission has its roots in the 1989 revocation by the Yugoslav Government of Kosovo's autonomy, and the subsequent "special measures" taken by the Yugoslav Government which resulted in widespread protests and mass dismissals of ethnic Albanian employees in the region. Given the socialist economic system that prevailed in Yugoslavia at the time, loss of employment also led in certain cases to loss of socially-owned housing which was linked to employment. The Yugoslav Government subsequently took measures to restrict the sale of properties to stem the migration of the Serbian population from Kosovo. Those restrictions effectively prevented ethnic Albanians from purchasing real property from ethnic Serbs. To circumvent the restrictions, property transactions were thereafter concluded informally and were not properly registered. The property-related discrimination is believed to have played a central role in the conflict in Kosovo.[35]

The security situation continued to deteriorate throughout the 1990s, culminating in 1999 in widespread ethnic turmoil and violence and, eventually, in a NATO-led air campaign to end the conflict. During the air campaign, hundreds of thousands of people—ethnic Albanians as well as ethnic Serbs—fled Kosovo or were driven from their homes and internally displaced.[36] Thousands of homes were destroyed, and abandoned houses were illegally occupied.

Pursuant to United Nations Security Council Resolution 1244 (1999) of 10 June 1999, Kosovo was placed under United Nations administration pending a final political settlement concerning its future status.[37] One of the tasks of the United Nations administration was to restore order in the residential property market, by reversing the effects of the discriminatory measures taken in the

[35] See, e.g., HPCC Commissioners Veijo Heiskanen and Alan Dodson, *Housing and Property Restitution in Kosovo*, in RETURNING HOME: HOUSING AND PROPERTY RESTITUTION RIGHTS OF REFUGEES AND DISPLACED PERSONS, p. 225, at p. 227 (Scott Leckie ed., Transnational Publishers 2003).

[36] International law defines "internally displaced persons" as "persons or groups of persons who have been forced to flee or leave their homes or places of habitual residence as a result of armed conflicts, internal strife or systematic violations of human rights, and who have not crossed an internationally recognized State border." Declaration of International Law Principles on Internationally Displaced Persons, Article 1, Resolution No. 17/2000 adopted by the 69th Conference of the International Law Association, London, 25–29 July 2000.

[37] UN Security Council Resolution 1244 (1999) U.N. Doc. S/REG/1244 (10 June 1999). This Resolution called for "substantial autonomy and meaningful self-administration for Kosovo," and placed it under an interim UN administration, "under which the people of Kosovo can enjoy substantial autonomy within the Federal Republic of Yugoslavia, and which will provide transitional administration while establishing and overseeing the development of provisional democratic self-governing institutions to ensure conditions for a peaceful and normal life for all inhabitants in Kosovo." Preamble and paragraph 10.

preceding decade, and to ensure that refugees and internally displaced persons would be able to return to their homes.

As of 31 January 2006, the total number of claims filed with the HPCC Claims Process was 29,153, of which 27,175 were for repossession of property, 1,214 for restitution of property, and 764 for official registration of informal real estate transactions.[38] Over 29,000 claims (99.7% of filed claims), have been decided,[39] and over 22,000 decisions have been implemented.

(g) Mass Claims Processes administered by the International Organization for Migration (IOM)

The International Organization for Migration (IOM) administers two World War II-related Mass Claims Processes: the German Forced Labour Compensation Programme (GFLCP) and the Holocaust Victim Assets Programme (HVAP).[40] The purpose of both is to give financial reparations to the victims of certain injustices committed by the Nazi regime during World War II—mainly in the form of compensation for forced and slave labor, but also for certain property losses. The Claims Processes, each with its separate constituting instrument and procedures, were established pursuant to settlements, or private or governmental agreements, following numerous Holocaust-related lawsuits that had been brought in the United States against the German and Swiss Governments, banks, and corporations.

German Forced Labour Compensation Programme (GFLCP)—claims against Germany and German industry for Nazi injustice

In August 2000, IOM was designated as one of seven partner organizations of the German Foundation "Remembrance, Responsibility and Future" to resolve claims of former Nazi victims for slave and forced labor, personal injury, and lost property.[41] "Slave laborers," for purposes of this Claims Process, are

---

[38] See further section 1.04(f) below on different HPCC claims categories.

[39] See www.hpdkosovo.org/stat_cat.asp—updated as of 31 January 2006.

[40] Since 2003, IOM has also been involved in providing legal, technical and other assistance and advice to the Iraq Property Claims Commission (IPCC), the Iraqi authorities, and other partners involved in the Iraqi property claims program. See www.ipcciraq.org.

[41] Law on the Creation of a Foundation "Remembrance, Responsibility and Future" of 2 August 2000, entered into force 12 August 2000 (German Federal Law Gazette BGBl. 2000 I 1263), as amended 4 August 2001, entered into force 11 August 2001 (BGBl. 2001 I 2036) [hereinafter German Foundation Act], section 9, paragraph 2, number 6. Text of the Act available at www.compensation-for-forced-labour.org, and on the website of the German Foundation, www.stiftung-evz.de. The six other organizations designated by the German Foundation are the German-Czech Future Fund, the

persons who were detained in a concentration camp, ghetto, or similar place of confinement during World War II. "Forced laborers" are persons who were deported to the German Reich and forced to work.[42] The German federal law creating the Foundation, the "German Foundation Act," had been initiated by an association of leading German companies that had exploited forced labor during World War II, called the "Foundation Initiative." A special envoy of the German Chancellor had been sent to negotiate an overall solution with the United States and other governments, victims' organizations, and plaintiffs. After protracted negotiations, the parties agreed on an amount of DM 10 billion (5 billion to be paid by the German Government, and 5 billion by the companies, plus DM 100 million in interest) to be channeled into a Foundation, the basic tenets of a law establishing it, and a plan of allocation.

By an agreement between Germany and the United States of 17 July 2000,[43] the United States Government had agreed, in exchange for the creation of the Claims Process, to support dismissal of lawsuits against German companies for "all claims that have been or may be asserted against German companies arising from the National Socialist era and World War II," by intervening whenever legal action is initiated in United States courts for slave and forced labor and property loss.[44] The Governments of Israel and participating Eastern European States also undertook to implement appropriate measures in their national legal systems to bring about an "all-embracing and enduring legal peace," and any lawsuits pending in United States courts against German companies arising from the National Socialist era and World War II were dismissed by victims' lawyers.[45]

Under the German Foundation Act, the largest portion of the Settlement Fund, DM 8.1 billion, was designated for paying claims for slave and forced

German-Polish Reconciliation Foundation, the Belorussian Foundation "Understanding and Reconciliation," the Ukrainian National Foundation "Understanding and Reconciliation," the Russian Foundation "Understanding and Reconciliation," and the Conference on Jewish Material Claims Against Germany—also known as the "Jewish Claims Conference" (JCC).

[42] See section 1.04(g) below, on categories of eligible GFLCP claimants.

[43] Agreement between the Government of the United States of America and the Government of the Federal Republic of Germany concerning the Foundation "Remembrance, Responsibility and the Future," 17 July 2000 [hereinafter U.S.–German Agreement], available at www.compensation-for-forced-labour.org. See in particular Annex A.

[44] See U.S.–German Agreement, Article 2, referring to Article 1, paragraph 1, for the scope of the obligation. The obligation did not extend to suits against the German Government, which had the benefit of the United States Foreign Sovereign Immunities Act of 1976, 28 U.S.C. § 1330(a).

[45] See *Joint Statement on the occasion of the final plenary meeting concluding international talks on the preparation of the Foundation "Remembrance, Responsibility and the Future"* of 17 July 2000, Article 4, available at www.compensation-for-forced-labour.org.

labor.[46] Each of the seven partner organizations identified in the German Foundation Act—including IOM—process these claims and make payments out of the set maximum amount allotted to it (known as "*plafonds*") to eligible claimants residing within its jurisdiction. IOM was allotted DM 540 million to compensate non-Jewish, so-called "rest-of-the-world" victims. It was furthermore designated by the German Foundation Act as the sole partner organization to process claims for property losses suffered as a result of direct participation of German companies in Nazi takings of real property, for which DM 200 million were allocated under the Act.[47] In addition, DM 50 million were distributed among the seven partner organizations to compensate victims claiming in a category of "other personal injury" for having been subjected to medical experiments or for the death or injury of children lodged in certain homes for children of forced laborers during the war.[48]

At the end of the applicable deadlines for filing claims,[49] the GFLCP Claims Process had received over 330,000 claims for slave and forced labor. As of 31 January 2006, all claims had been resolved; approximately 92,000 were approved and paid a first instalment;[50] 235,000 were rejected; and the rest were withdrawn or transferred to other partner organizations. All compensable claims have been paid a first and second instalment. In the GFLCP personal injury claims category, all 42,000 claims received have been resolved, out of which 1,361 were approved and paid in full, and approximately 40,000 were rejected.[51] The IOM Property Claims Commission[52] received a total of 35,000 claims, all of which have been resolved: 10,500 property claims were approved, 24,500 were rejected. All requests for reconsideration of the

---

[46] German Foundation Act, section 9, paragraph 2. A remaining sum of DM 1 billion was designated for payments to persons who suffered property loss (section 9, paragraph 4); DM 50 million to persons who suffered "other personal injuries in connection with National Socialist injustice" (section 9, paragraph 3); DM 700 million for projects of the "Remembrance and Future" Fund (section 9, paragraph 7); and personnel and non-personnel costs are also to be paid from the Foundation's funds (section 9, paragraph 12).

[47] German Foundation Act, section 9, paragraph 4, sentence 2, numbers 1 and 2.

[48] See ibid., paragraph 3, and section 11, paragraph 1, sentence 3, number 5.

[49] See section 3.03(g) below on GFLCP and HVAP deadlines for submitting claims.

[50] The amounts paid out in the first instalment are Euro 5,752 for each slave labor claim, Euro 1,278 for each forced labor claim in industry, and Euro 511 for each forced labor claim in agriculture. The full amounts are Euro 7,670, Euro 2,556, and Euro 1,022 for those three categories of claims, respectively.

[51] The amount paid out initially to successful personal injury claimants was Euro 4,240. This was later increased by an additional payment of Euro 2,450. See further section 1.04(g) below on the different GFLCP claims categories.

[52] See further section 1.02(g) below, on the IOM Property Claims Commission.

decisions of the Property Claims Commission have been decided, and the actual amounts payable for lost property have been determined. Finally, at the end of 2005, IOM issued payments to over 11,600 legal successors and heirs of approximately 7,500 now deceased victims who would have been eligible for compensation.

Holocaust Victim Assets Programme (HVAP)—claims pursuant to 1999 class action Settlement

IOM was appointed in 2000 pursuant to the Settlement Agreement in the class action known as the Holocaust Victim Assets Litigation, described in section 1.01(e) above, as one of the organizations participating in the Settlement implementation according to the Plan of Allocation and Distribution proposed by Special Master Judah Gribetz and approved by Judge Korman of the United States District Court for the Eastern District of New York.[53] The constituting instruments of HVAP are thus the Settlement Agreement and the Plan of Allocation and Distribution in the Holocaust Victim Assets Litigation.[54] IOM processes claims of persons who, during the war, were forced to perform slave labor for entities under Nazi control because they were, or were believed to be, members of non-Jewish groups that were specifically targeted for Nazi persecution, namely Roma, Jehovah's Witnesses, homosexual, or physically or mentally handicapped (Slave Labor Class I), or who, in trying to flee from Nazi persecution, were either denied entry into Switzerland or were granted entry only to be detained and mistreated as refugees in Switzerland during the war (Refugee Class). IOM also awards compensation to any individuals, regardless of target group membership, who were forced to perform labor under the Nazi Regime for Swiss companies or their affiliates that were releasees under the Settlement Agreement (Slave Labor Class II). In addition, IOM administers a program of humanitarian support assistance (HSP) for the benefit of needy and elderly Roma, Jehovah's Witnesses, disabled, and homosexual victims of Nazi persecution.[55]

---

[53] See Plan of Allocation and Distribution, referred to in section 1.01(e) above on CRT-II, Exhibit 4. The two other organizations involved in the implementation of the Settlement Agreement are the Conference on Jewish Material Claims Against Germany, (referred to in some contexts as the "Jewish Claims Conference" (JCC) and by the Court as the "Claims Conference") responsible for slave labor and refugee claims submitted by Jewish claimants, and the Claims Resolution Tribunal (CRT-II), responsible for processing claims of owners of deposited bank assets.

[54] Text of the Settlement Agreement is contained in Exhibit 1 to the Plan of Allocation and Distribution, and is available at www.swissbankclaims.com.

[55] The Humanitarian and Social Programmes (HSP) arose from the Looted Assets Class in the litigation known as the Holocaust Victim Assets Litigation. Because looted assets were most often results

In the HVAP Claims Process, close to 60,000 claims were received. As of 31 January 2006, over 41,000 claims had been reviewed by IOM, and approximately 19,000 payments had been made.[56]

(h) Eritrea–Ethiopia Claims Commission (EECC)—claims relating to the 1998–2000 war between Eritrea and Ethiopia

The EECC is an arbitral body established by an agreement concluded between Eritrea and Ethiopia on 12 December 2000.[57] The Commission is administered under the auspices of the Permanent Court of Arbitration (PCA) in The Hague. The 12 December 2000 Agreement provides for a permanent end to the hostilities between the parties, and creates machinery to support the re-establishment of peaceful relations between them. Article 5 of the Agreement provides for the establishment of a neutral Claims Commission and gives it the mandate to decide claims by both parties for specified types of loss, damage, and injury related to the conflict, and resulting from violations of international humanitarian law or other violations of international law. The scope of this conflict is defined by reference to earlier instruments endorsed by the Organisation of African Unity.[58]

Between 1998 and 2000, Eritrea and Ethiopia engaged in a deadly war, with fighting on fronts all along their common border. The war took a heavy toll on civilians and the economies in both countries. Large areas were affected by

of Nazi persecution and generally applicable across the board to all persons targeted, "*cy pres*" remedies (meaning as close a remedy as possible) were fashioned to benefit (i) the entire class, and (ii) the neediest elderly victims. Thus, rather than create a claims resolution facility to determine individual claims on a case-by-case basis for all victims or to recommend a pro rata distribution where each "award" would total little more than a few dollars, the Settlement ultimately authorized, *inter alia*, humanitarian assistance projects for elderly survivors. See Plan of Allocation and Distribution, at pp. 110–142. Through HSP, these projects are managed to benefit IOM's target groups. Ibid., at pp. 138–142.

[56] Including direct and so-called "overlap" claims (relating to former slave or forced laborers who receive a payment from the German Fund and receive an additional payment from the "Swiss banks" Settlement Fund), HVAP received more than 40,000 claims in Slave Labor Class I alone. It received more than 16,000 claims in Slave Labor Class II, and approximately 1,200 in the Refugee Class. The amounts paid out are as follows: US$1,450 per claim in Slave Labor Class I; US$1,450 per claim in Slave Labor Class II; and varying amounts in the Refugee Class, dependent on the award category: US$3,625 (Expulsion); US$725 (Mistreatment); US$4,350 (Expulsion and Mistreatment). See further section 1.04(g) below, on the different types of HVAP claims.

[57] Agreement between the Government of the State of Eritrea and the Government of the Federal Democratic Republic of Ethiopia, 12 December 2000, Article 5 [hereinafter Eritrea–Ethiopia Agreement of 12 December 2000], available at www.pca-cpa.org.

[58] See Organisation of African Unity Framework Agreement and the Modalities for its implementation, endorsed by the 35th ordinary session of the Assembly of Heads of State and Government, held in Algiers, Algeria, 12–14 July 1999; Agreement on Cessation of Hostilities of 18 June 2000 between Eritrea and Ethiopia, U.N. Doc. S/2000/601 (18 June 2000); Eritrea–Ethiopia Agreement of 12 December 2000.

combat operations, by occupation by enemy forces, or by other consequences of the war. Hundreds of thousands of people were displaced.

The international community made substantial efforts in support of negotiations to end the conflict. In 2000, the two countries concluded an Agreement on the Cessation of Hostilities.[59] Subsequent negotiations then sought to bring a final end to the war. The details of those negotiations have not been published, but it is known that Eritrean and Ethiopian negotiators and their legal advisers met with legal experts familiar with the Permanent Court of Arbitration, the United Nations Compensation Commission (UNCC) in Geneva, and other contemporary Mass Claims Processes. The parties ultimately included in the 12 December 2000 Agreement several provisions indicating familiarity with these institutions and Claims Processes and authorizing use of mass claims techniques.

(i) Humanitarian insurance Claims Process administered by the Jewish Claims Conference (JCC) for the International Commission on Holocaust Era Insurance Claims (ICHEIC)

The International Commission on Holocaust Era Insurance Claims (ICHEIC) was established in 1998 by a Memorandum of Understanding (MOU) among the National Association of Insurance Commissioners (NAIC) in the United States, several European insurance companies, insurance regulators, representatives of several Jewish organizations, and the State of Israel.[60] ICHEIC is charged with establishing just processes for addressing and resolving, in an expeditious manner, claims for unpaid insurance policies that were issued to victims of the Holocaust.[61]

ICHEIC addresses the claims of Holocaust victims (or their heirs) who held life insurance with European insurers in Nazi-occupied territories during the Holocaust era. These claims can be grouped into several categories, the largest of which includes claims in which the claimant alleged that an insurance policy existed, but (i) the claimant no longer knew the name of the issuing insurance company (so-called "unnamed" claims), and (ii) the insurance companies in the ICHEIC Claims Process had been unable to find the insured's name in their

---

[59] Agreement on Cessation of Hostilities of 18 June 2000 between Eritrea and Ethiopia, U.N. Doc. S/2000/601 (18 June 2000).

[60] ICHEIC Memorandum of Understanding, signed on 25 August 1998, by several European insurance companies [hereinafter MOU Companies], available at www.icheic.org.

[61] Since its establishment, ICHEIC has been requested to create or assist with compensation structures for various other programs, such as the German Foundation Act, discussed above in section 1.01(g) on the German Forced Labour Compensation Programme, which in 2002 gave ICHEIC the mandate to process claims on unpaid Holocaust era insurance policies issued by German insurance companies. See German Foundation Act, section 9, paragraph 4, number 3.

records or a match with an existing policy (so-called "unmatched" claims). In ICHEIC's constituting instrument, the MOU, it was agreed that there should be a review of such unnamed and unmatched claims, referred to in section 8A of the MOU and hence known in the Claims Process as the "8A1 Claims."

The discussion of ICHEIC in this book focuses on the 8A1 humanitarian Claims Process because it employed unique procedures unlike those of any other Mass Claims Process. ICHEIC claims other than the 8A1 Claims are not covered by this book.[62]

The 8A1 humanitarian Claims Process was an administrative proceeding, conducted on a voluntary basis, in which ICHEIC offered a one-time humanitarian award of US$1,000 to claimants who demonstrated a likelihood that they were entitled to compensation for an unpaid Holocaust era life insurance claim, even though they could neither name the issuing insurance company nor be matched with existing insurance company records. The humanitarian awards were funded out of the ICHEIC Humanitarian Fund, established through ICHEIC's agreements with the companies participating in ICHEIC (the MOU Companies), as well as the German Foundation "Remembrance, Responsibility and Future" (described in section 1.01(g) above), and the German Insurance Association. The term "humanitarian" is used in this context to describe claims that insurance companies had no *legal* obligation to pay because of absence of evidence sufficient to prove that the policy ever existed. Thus, in recognition of the widespread destruction of documents during and after World War II, a special "Point Scoring System" was developed to award "points" to the unnamed and unmatched claims based on anecdotal information on the claim form about the alleged existence of a Holocaust era insurance policy.

The objective of the humanitarian payments was described by the Chairman of ICHEIC as follows:

"These payments are a symbolic acknowledgment of the fact that many insurance policy proceeds were never paid to victims of the Holocaust. The payments represent the long-delayed efforts to morally address the wrongs done to Holocaust victims who invested their hard-earned savings in insurance policies for their families. These payments are only a token, but they represent efforts to attain a small measure of justice."[63]

Thus, although the US$1,000 awards were small in monetary terms, they served another important purpose. As one Holocaust victim has been quoted as saying, "We need the recognition of compensation."[64]

---

[62] For further information about ICHEIC, see www.icheic.org.

[63] See ICHEIC Press Release of 30 March 2004, *$16 Million Paid to Holocaust-Era Insurance Claimants from ICHEIC Humanitarian Fund*, available at www.icheic.org.

[64] Joseph Berger, *After Scars of Holocaust, Fresh Pain Over Money*, N.Y. TIMES, 8 May 2005, Section 1, p. 33, col. 1, at p. 37.

Faced with the novel problems of the humanitarian Claims Process, which were far outside typical insurance claims practice, ICHEIC chose to contract the tasks of designing and administering it to an outside organization, rather than creating a new organization in-house or delegating the tasks to the staff of insurance companies whose experience related to solving quite different problems. For this purpose, ICHEIC chose the Conference on Jewish Material Claims Against Germany, also known as "the Jewish Claims Conference" (JCC), in New York City, in part because of its long and successful history of negotiating, designing, and conducting compensation programs worldwide.[65]

Processing of an initial batch of approximately 40,000 8A1 Claims began in October 2003, and was completed in March 2004, when payments in the amount of US$1,000 each, totaling approximately US$16 million, were sent to approximately 16,000 people, located in sixty countries. Based on the experience of this first phase, ICHEIC contracted with the JCC to process an additional group of approximately 38,000 claims, which in that second phase included unnamed and unmatched claims as well as some named claims where either the MOU Companies had been unable to find a match between their records and the information contained in the claim forms, or where the insurance companies referred to in the claim no longer existed. The second phase of claims processing began in December 2004 and ended in May 2005. In total, as of December 2005, payments of approximately US$26.68 million had been issued to approximately 26,680 people.

Whereas the overall constituting instrument of ICHEIC was the Memorandum of Understanding referred to above, the constituting instrument of the 8A1 humanitarian Claims Process was the Humanitarian Claims Processing Agreement between ICHEIC and the JCC, and amendments thereto.[66]

(j) American Arbitration Association (AAA)—an illustrative case

The Claims Process in the illustrative domestic case described in this book was created pursuant to a settlement in 1997 of a class action lawsuit in a United States federal district court, challenging various market practices in the sale of a very large number of insurance policies. The case involved a class of over

---

[65] The JCC has, e.g., since 1951 worked in partnership with the Israeli Government on negotiating and distributing payments from Germany, Austria, and other governments and industry, one result of which was the payment of lifetime pensions to nearly 300,000 survivors under the German Federal Indemnification Laws (*Bundesentschädigungsgesetz—BEG*), continuing to the present day. For further information about the JCC, see www.claimscon.org.

[66] Humanitarian Claims Processing Agreement between ICHEIC and the Jewish Claims Conference [hereinafter the JCC–ICHEIC Agreement], text of which is not officially available.

1.2 million plaintiffs. For the purpose of this case, the AAA established a mass claims administrative center to coordinate the scheduling of more than one thousand claims reviews per day, and it decided over 60,000 claims in sixteen months. This case has been chosen as an "illustrative case" because some of the innovative and interesting methods which it employed may be useful examples in designing and analyzing international Claims Processes.

The dispute in the illustrative case alleged fraudulent sales practices by an insurance company that sold insurance policies to customers throughout the United States. It was resolved in 1997 by a Settlement Agreement which was the constituting instrument of this Claims Process. The Settlement Agreement, which the parties agreed should be confidential, was drafted by plaintiffs' counsel and defendant's counsel and was approved by the United States federal district court Judge before whom the case was pending, as well as by chief legal officials of the fifty states in which the insurance policies had been sold. Initially, the claims were reviewed in-house by the defendant insurance company in an effort to resolve as many claims as possible by the company's own staff without having to resort to a much more costly arbitration process set out in the Settlement Agreement. Claimants who were not satisfied by the determinations made by the insurance company staff could appeal to have their case decided by an independent Arbitrator. Tens of thousands of claimants did appeal the initial determinations to arbitration, and it is those arbitrations that the AAA administered in the illustrative case.

1.02 Constituting Instrument

Whether the contents of the constituting instrument are (i) a brief statement, or (ii) a detailed description of the Claims Process, with provisions, e.g., on who may be claimants, deadlines, rules of procedure, etc. If rules of procedure are not included in the constituting instrument, who is authorized to establish rules and procedures.

Editors' Commentary

The constituting instruments of the various Mass Claims Processes described in this book differ as to the extent to which they include a detailed description of the procedures that are to govern the conduct of the Claims Process. The degree of specificity ranges from quite general statements concerning who may be claimants and the types of claims that may be brought, to the inclusion of a complete set of procedural rules. These differences derive not only from preferences as to style, but may also be due to the urgency or other circumstances surrounding the negotiation that made it difficult or not advisable for the parties to draft detailed provisions at the outset.

Mass Claims Processes typically have rules, either in the constituting instrument or adopted later, that govern the procedures to be followed in considering and resolving claims. The subjects covered by the rules include those customarily found in other dispute resolution rules, such as, for example, the UNCITRAL Arbitration Rules.[67] Typically, there are rules even if a Claims Process is more in the nature of an administrative proceeding rather than being an arbitration. Thus, the rules of the various Claims Processes described in this book often regulate such matters as (i) statements of claim by which the Claims Process is commenced; (ii) appointment of decision-makers, including provisions on challenges and replacement of decision-makers; (iii) conduct of the proceedings, including their location and language; (iv) conduct of hearings, if hearings are held; (v) time limits; (vi) the use of experts; and (vii) the form and effect of decisions and awards. These are all matters that designers of Mass Claims Processes and others who review the materials in this book may wish to consider, perhaps using as a checklist the Table of Contents of the UNCITRAL Arbitration Rules.

In addition to the matters generally found in dispute resolution rules, the rules of some Mass Claims Processes further include (i) detailed provisions concerning the jurisdiction of the Claims Process, i.e., what types of claims are admissible; (ii) provisions limiting what relief can be granted, i.e., establishing fixed or maximum amounts that can be awarded for certain categories of claims; (iii) provisions concerning the verification and valuation of claims, including evidentiary standards; (iv) formulas for calculation of interest; and (v) provisions for determining whether heirs of a victim qualify for an award and, if so, how to determine whether claimants are eligible heirs.

One approach for simplifying negotiation and drafting of constituting instruments followed in several Mass Claims Processes is to incorporate by reference, in some fashion, other systems of procedural rules, as is discussed further in section 5.01 below.

The subjects covered in the constituting instruments and rules of the various Mass Claims Processes are outlined in the Annotations to this section 1.02.

---

[67] United Nations Commission on International Trade Law (UNCITRAL) Arbitration Rules, 1976, United Nations Publication Sales No. E.93.V.6, also available at www.uncitral.org [hereinafter UNCITRAL Arbitration Rules].

(a) Iran–United States Claims Tribunal (Iran–US CT)—claims relating to the 1979 Islamic Revolution

The Claims Settlement Declaration, the constituting instrument of the Iran–US CT, contains provisions specifying who may be claimants, what claims can be brought, filing deadlines, method of appointment of Members of the Tribunal, composition of panels, applicable law, the seat of the Tribunal, and representation of the two Governments.[68] The Declaration does not include detailed descriptions of procedures, but it provides instead that the Tribunal shall conduct its business in accordance with the UNCITRAL Arbitration Rules, except to the extent modified by the Tribunal or the parties to ensure that the Claims Settlement Declaration can be carried out.[69] The actions to make modifications that were taken pursuant to that authority are described in section 5.01(a) below.

(b) United Nations Compensation Commission (UNCC)—claims relating to the 1990–1991 Gulf War

The structure of the UNCC is largely based on the recommendations made by the Secretary-General of the United Nations in a Report issued pursuant to United Nations Security Council Resolution 687 (1991). The Report contains, in Part I, provisions on (i) the structure and composition of the Claims Process and its three organs (the Governing Council, the Secretariat, and the panels of Commissioners); (ii) appointment of Commissioners; (iii) the rules under which the Secretariat of the Commission serves, including appointment of its Executive Secretary; and (iv) the seat of the Commission.[70] These recommendations of Part I of the Secretary-General's Report were adopted by the Security Council in Resolution 692 (1991) in May 1991 when it created the UNCC, and they are therefore binding on the Commission.[71] Part I of the Secretary-General's Report envisaged that the principal organ of the Commission, its Governing Council, would adopt "guidelines on all policy matters, in particular, those relating to . . . procedures to be applied to the processing of claims and to the settlement of disputed claims . . .".[72]

Security Council Resolution 692 (1991) directed the UNCC Governing Council expeditiously to implement section E of Resolution 687 (1991) that

---

[68] See Claims Settlement Declaration, Articles I–VI.   [69] Ibid., Article III, paragraph 2.

[70] Report of the Secretary-General of 2 May 1991, U.N. Doc. S/22559, Part I, paragraphs 3–12.

[71] UN Security Council Resolution 692 (1991) of 20 May 1991, U.N. Doc. S/RES/692 (1991) (20 May 1991), paragraph 3.

[72] Report of the Secretary-General of 2 May 1991, U.N. Doc. S/22559, Part I, paragraph 10.

established the Claims Process, "taking into account the recommendations in [Part] II of the Secretary-General's report."[73] Those recommendations related to claims procedures such as the filing of claims, who could be claimants, the categorization of claims, filing deadlines, priority treatment of certain categories of claims, the non-exclusive character of UNCC proceedings, payment of claims, funding of the Compensation Fund, and the expenses of the Commission. Also included were recommendations concerning the procedures to be used by the panels of Commissioners and the Secretariat for the assessment, verification, and evaluation of claims.[74] In Part II, the Secretary-General further proposed that, if disputes arose out of allegations by a claimant that a panel of Commissioners had made an error on a point of law and procedure or on a point of fact, such disputes would be resolved "by a board of commissioners who for this purpose should be guided by such guidelines as have been established by the Governing Council and the [UNCITRAL] Arbitration Rules."[75] In practice, this aspect of the Secretary-General's Report was not implemented and, consequently, the UNCC has no appeals process, only a procedure to correct technical errors, pursuant to Article 41 of the Provisional Rules.

Exercising its discretion in implementing section E of Resolution 687 (1991), the Governing Council in 1992 issued "Provisional Rules for Claims Procedure," which continue to be the procedural rules of the Claims Process.[76] The Provisional Rules provide that Commissioners, in making such additional procedural rules as may be necessary to complete work on particular cases, "may rely on the relevant UNCITRAL Rules for guidance," and request further procedural guidance at any time from the Governing Council.[77]

(c) Commission for Real Property Claims of Displaced Persons and Refugees (CRPC)—claims relating to the 1992–1995 war in Bosnia and Herzegovina

Annex 7 to the Dayton Peace Agreement, the constituting instrument of the CRPC Claims Process, contains provisions on the composition and appointment

---

[73] UN Security Council Resolution 692 (1991) of 20 May 1991, U.N. Doc. S/RES/692 (1991) (20 May 1991), paragraph 5, referring to section E of UN Security Council Resolution 687 (1991) of 3 April 1991, U.N. Doc. S/RES/687 (1991) (3 April 1991), paragraph 18, in which it " . . . *[d]ecides* to create a fund to pay compensation for claims . . . and to establish a Commission that will administer the fund."

[74] Report of the Secretary-General of 2 May 1991, U.N. Doc. S/22559, Part II, paragraphs 13–29.

[75] Ibid., paragraph 27.

[76] See UNCC Governing Council Decision 10 of 26 June 1992, *Provisional Rules for Claims Procedure*, U.N. Doc. S/AC.26/1992/10.   [77] UNCC Provisional Rules, Article 43.

of the Commission, establishing an Executive Secretariat and staff, and regulating who may be claimants, what claims can be brought, the conduct of proceedings, the types of remedies available, applicable law, financing of the Commission's operations, enforcement of its decisions, and diplomatic privileges and immunities.[78] Article XV of Annex 7 provides that "[t]he Commission shall promulgate such rules and regulations, consistent with this Agreement, as may be necessary to carry out its functions. In developing these rules and regulations, the Commission shall consider domestic laws on property rights."[79] Pursuant to this authority, the Commission adopted a "Book of Regulations" which covers legal, administrative and organizational issues, as well as procedural rules for the claims and decision process, including substantive and evidentiary standards.[80]

(d) Claims Resolution Tribunal for Dormant Accounts in Switzerland (CRT-I)—first claims tribunal for assets deposited in Swiss banks

The constituting instrument of CRT-I, a Memorandum of Understanding between the Swiss Bankers Association and two leading Jewish organizations, contained no rules of procedure, although it did contain quite detailed provisions on who could be claimants, what claims could be brought, with whom the claims should be filed, the filing deadline, etc.[81] More detailed "Rules of Procedure" were issued by the Independent Claims Resolution Foundation (ICRF), which later amended them from time to time.[82]

(e) Claims Resolution Tribunal (CRT-II)—second claims tribunal for assets deposited in Swiss banks

The Plan of Allocation and Distribution in the class action known as the Holocaust Victim Assets Litigation, which is a key constituting instrument of the CRT-II Claims Process, contains provisions on who may be claimants, what claims can be brought, maximum amounts of compensation per claim in

---

[78] Dayton Peace Agreement, Annex 7, Articles IX–XII.   [79] Ibid., Article XV.

[80] Book of Regulations on the Conditions and Decision Making Procedure for Claims for Return of Real Property of Displaced Persons and Refugees (Consolidated version, 8 October 2002) [hereinafter CRPC Book of Regulations on Procedure], available at www.pca-cpa.org/MCP/index_MCP.htm "Links to Completed Mass Claims Processes".

[81] See ICEP Memorandum of Understanding, Appendix A to Final ICEP Report (*Report on Dormant Accounts of Victims of Nazi Persecution in Swiss Banks*), p. 1 (1999), available at www.crt-ii/icep_report.phtm.

[82] Rules of Procedure for the Claims Resolution Process, adopted on 15 October 1997 by the Board of Trustees of the ICRF [hereinafter CRT-I Rules of Procedure], available at www.crt-ii, org/_crt-i.

different categories, filing deadlines, functions of the supervising federal district court, rules for the review of the claims, and the possibility for appeals. The Plan also contains a draft set of rules that were prepared by the CRT-II Secretariat, with the participation of the Chairman and Vice Chairman of the CRT-II.[83] The Rules were proposed to the United States District Court for the Eastern District of New York by the two Court-appointed Special Masters,[84] and were approved as the "Governing Rules" by the Court.[85] The Governing Rules constitute a complete procedural framework for CRT-II that deals with all relevant aspects of the Claims Process. The Rules have since been amended by the Special Masters, with the Court's approval.[86]

(f) Housing and Property Claims Commission (HPCC)—claims relating to the 1999 conflict in Kosovo

UNMIK Regulation 1999/23, the constituting instrument of the HPCC Claims Process, contains provisions on who may be claimants, what claims can be brought, composition of the Commission and appointment of Commissioners, the exclusivity of the Commission's jurisdiction, applicable law, and the possibility for appeals.

A detailed description of the Claims Process is not contained in the constituting Regulation, but rather in a subsequent UNMIK Regulation 2000/60 containing the procedural rules that the Commission is to follow.[87] Regulation 2000/60 was promulgated by the Special Representative of the United Nations Secretary-General upon recommendation of the Commission. It contains substantive legal principles covering the types of claims that can be made and the remedies available to claimants. Chapter II of Regulation 2000/60 contains the rules of the Housing and Property Directorate (HPD),[88] including matters such as the registration of claims, content of claims, and the

---

[83] Plan of Allocation and Distribution, Exhibit 5.

[84] The Special Masters were appointed by order of the Court, on 8 December 2000, "to establish, organize and supervise" the Claims Resolution Process, using the CRT. See *In re Holocaust Victim Assets Litig.*, Memorandum and Order, 2000 WL 33281701 (E.D.N.Y. 8 December 2000).

[85] Order of 5 February 2001 adopting CRT Governing Rules, *In re Holocaust Victim Assets Litig.*, Memorandum and Order, CV 96-4849 (ERK)(MDG) (E.D.N.Y. 5 February 2001), available at www.crt-ii.org. The Governing Rules were amended on 22 March 2003.

[86] CRT-II Governing Rules, Article 43, sets out the procedure for amendments.

[87] UNMIK Regulation 2000/60 of 31 October 2000, *On Residential Property Claims and the Rules of Procedure and Evidence of the Housing and Property Directorate and the Housing and Property Claims Commission*, UNMIK Official Gazette, p. 10, U.N. Doc. UNMIK/REG/2000/60 (31 October 2000) [hereinafter UNMIK Regulation 2000/60], available at www.hpdkosovo.org and www.unmikonline.org.

[88] UNMIK Regulation 2000/60, Chapter II, *Rules of the Housing and Property Directorate*.

rights of parties to the claim, the resolution of claims, uncontested claims, execution of decisions and eviction orders, reconsideration requests, and cooperation and delegation. Chapter III sets forth the rules of procedure of the HPCC, relating to matters such as the organization of the Commission, its plenary sessions, proceedings, panels, evidence, decisions, summary procedure, provisional measures, and reconsideration of decisions.[89]

(g) Mass Claims Processes administered by the International Organization for Migration (IOM)

German Forced Labour Compensation Programme (GFLCP)—claims against Germany and German industry for Nazi injustice

The German Foundation Act, the constituting document of the GFLCP Claims Process, contains provisions on who may be claimants, what claims may be brought, maximum amounts of compensation per claim in different categories, allocation of funds for each of the claims categories, filing deadlines, organization and functions of the supervisory organs of the German Foundation, composition and appointment of a Property Claims Commission, the evidentiary standard for the review of the claims, appeals, priority of payment to certain groups of claimants, and relations to other related Claims Processes.[90]

For slave and forced labor and personal injury claims under GFLCP, rules of procedure are not contained in one single document, but rather in a number of instruments, including various provisions of the German Foundation Act, the contract between the German Foundation and IOM, decisions of the Foundation Board of Trustees, and in legal circulars issued by the Board of Directors—a separate body appointed by and reporting to the Board of Trustees. These provisions set out general principles, and where they include details, they deal mostly with the relationship between the Foundation and IOM, and with the collection and payment of claims; they leave the elaboration of the details of the processing, review, and determination of the claims to IOM.

In contrast, as to property claims, the IOM Property Claims Commission, acting pursuant to an authorization under the German Foundation Act,[91]

---

[89] UNMIK Regulation 2000/60, Chapter III, *Rules of Procedure of the Housing and Property Claims Commission.*

[90] These matters are also regulated by Annex A of the U.S.–German Agreement discussed in section 1.01(g) above, but the German Foundation Act is the governing instrument of the Claims Process.

[91] German Foundation Act, section 9, paragraph 6.

established Supplemental Rules concerning the content and procedure of its determinations. These Supplemental Rules cover matters such as the submission, registration and initial review of claims, causation, substantive determinations and evidentiary standard, decision-making, and appeals.[92]

Holocaust Victim Assets Programme (HVAP)—claims pursuant to 1999 class action Settlement

The Plan of Allocation and Distribution in the class action known as the Holocaust Victim Assets Litigation is the constituting document of the HVAP Claims Process. The Plan contains provisions on who may be claimants, what claims can be brought, maximum amounts of compensation per claim in the different categories, filing deadlines, functions of the supervising United States federal district court, rules for the review of the claims, appeals, and priority of payment to certain groups of claimants. For those categories of claims for which IOM is responsible,[93] the Plan of Allocation and Distribution sets out proposed rules of procedure which are to be elaborated by IOM in consultation with the Court.[94] These proposed rules deal with the filing and acceptance of claims, the form and content of their determination, and the review of decisions, and IOM is authorized to amend them subject to the Court's approval.[95]

(h) Eritrea–Ethiopia Claims Commission (EECC)—claims relating to the 1998–2000 war between Eritrea and Ethiopia

The 12 December 2000 Agreement constituting the EECC Claims Process establishes the Commission's basic framework. It defines the Commission's jurisdiction, authorizes the filing of claims in respect of Governments, nationals and certain non-nationals, sets the deadline for filing claims, and specifies the Commission's composition and appointment, the applicable law, and the

---

[92] IOM Property Claims Commission Supplemental Principles and Rules of Procedure [hereinafter IOM Property Commission Supplemental Rules], available at www.compensation-for-forced-labour.org.   [93] See section 1.04(g) below, on types of eligible claims.
[94] Plan of Allocation and Distribution, pp. 164–167 (proposed rules for Slave Labor Class II) and pp. 176–179 (proposed rules for Refugee Class). In addition to so-called "direct" (HVAP) claims submitted to IOM generally from countries outside IOM's GFLCP jurisdiction areas, Slave Labor Class I "overlap" claims relate to former slave or forced laborers who receive a payment from the German Fund and receive an additional payment from the "Swiss banks" Settlement Fund. These claims are handled by the distribution mechanisms of the IOM and Jewish Claims Conference (JCC) used for German slave labor claims.   [95] Plan of Allocation and Distribution, pp. 167 and 179.

seat of the Claims Process. The Agreement also authorizes the Commission to use mass claims processing methods such as expedited procedures and sampling techniques to complete its work expeditiously.[96]

The 12 December 2000 Agreement, however, leaves the specific procedures for handling claims to be spelled out through separate rules of procedure to be adopted by the Commission "based upon" the Permanent Court of Arbitration Optional Rules for Arbitrating Disputes Between Two States.[97] The Commission's Rules were thus not definitively established by the constituting document, but were instead a task assigned to the Commission.

Taking account of comments from the parties on a draft circulated to them, the Commission adopted its Rules of Procedure in October 2001, in the first year of its work.

(i) Humanitarian insurance Claims Process administered by the Jewish Claims Conference (JCC) for the International Commission on Holocaust Era Insurance Claims (ICHEIC)

The contents of the constituting instruments of the 8A1 humanitarian Claims Process gradually developed from the general to the more specific as the various constituting instruments listed in section 1.01(i) above were drafted and approved. The initial instruments avoided specificity, and thus permitted degrees of flexibility through amendments and supplements as might become necessary or appropriate once experience was gained from processing the actual claims. Although the JCC-ICHEIC Agreement did specify certain procedural requirements, extending from the database design phase through to issuance of humanitarian payments, this was but a frame-work for the claims processing plan.

The JCC–ICHEIC Agreement provided that the 8A1 Claims should be processed in accordance with a methodology and a "Point Scoring System" approved by the Senior Counselor of the 8A1 humanitarian Claims Process, who was appointed by the Chairman of ICHEIC to approve evaluation criteria and supervise the payment process. The Agreement stated that processing of the 8A1 Claims should be set out with greater specificity in the Point Scoring System.

---

[96] Eritrea–Ethiopia Agreement of 12 December 2000, Article 5, paragraphs 1, 3, 5 and 8. The various mass claims techniques are described in more detail in section 5.06(h) below.

[97] Ibid., Article 5, paragraph 7. See also Permanent Court of Arbitration, Optional Rules for Arbitrating Disputes between Two States, in PERMANENT COURT OF ARBITRATION BASIC DOCUMENTS, p. 41 (1998), also available at www.pca-cpa.org [hereinafter PCA Rules].

The procedures of this Claims Process were thus developed in a collaborative effort between the claims processing unit (JCC), the Senior Counselor, and the ICHEIC administration, the latter having final authority to set policy.

(j) American Arbitration Association (AAA)—an illustrative case

In the illustrative case, the constituting instrument, the Court-approved Settlement Agreement between the defendant insurance company and the class of claimants, was a detailed document, consisting of hundreds of pages. It set forth the rules of procedure for the initial in-house review of claims, which the insurance company handled, such as the requirements for filing a claim and the criteria for evaluating the claim. The Settlement Agreement also contained the rules of procedure to be used in the arbitrations that the AAA administered if the claimant was not satisfied with the initial decision.

1.03 Modifications and Amendments

Whether there is a body (e.g., consisting of the decision-makers) or a separate policy group that is empowered to modify or augment the procedural rules, administrative procedures, or structural aspects of the Claims Process in order to reflect emerging future needs.

Editors' Commentary

It is a practical fact that even the best drafted procedural rules may require future modifications during the course of the Claims Process in light of changing circumstances or "gaps" which are perceived only after the procedures have been set in place. To reflect and deal with changes, it is advisable to keep the original procedures flexible enough to allow them to adapt to future needs.

It is generally easier and quicker for an authorized body to modify existing rules than it is for the parties to re-negotiate the constituting instruments, particularly when the parties include governments or large non-governmental organizations. As time passes it may become necessary to change the overall structure of the Claims Process, and it is useful for the modalities for making such changes to be anticipated in the constituting documents themselves. Therefore, the advisability of designating an authorized body to modify the rules ought to be considered. The constituting instrument of each of the Mass Claims Processes described in this book provides authority for a body—often the Tribunal or Commission itself, or sometimes a supervisory or governing body—to modify or add to the procedural rules in order to carry out functions effectively or to improve efficiency based on emerging experience.

(a) Iran–United States Claims Tribunal (Iran–US CT)—claims relating to the 1979 Islamic Revolution

The constituting instrument of the Iran–US CT, the Claims Settlement Declaration, gave the Tribunal power to modify the UNCITRAL Arbitration Rules to ensure that the Declaration could be carried out.[98] Exercising that authority, the Full Tribunal of nine Members initially modified the UNCITRAL Arbitration Rules in several respects, and later made further amendments, to create its own Tribunal Rules.[99] Thus, while any structural changes to the Claims Process itself can be made only by the two Government parties, the Tribunal itself, or the two Governments, may at any time modify the Tribunal Rules.[100] The Full Tribunal also adopted Internal Guidelines,[101] Staff Rules, and Financial Regulations.[102]

(b) United Nations Compensation Commission (UNCC)—claims relating to the 1990–1991 Gulf War

The Governing Council of the UNCC, whose membership is the same as that of the United Nations Security Council, is the policy-making organ of the Commission. As such, it established the criteria for the eligibility for compensation of claims, the rules and procedures for processing the claims, the guidelines for the administration and financing of the Compensation Fund, and the procedures for the payment of compensation to claimants.[103] The Governing

---

[98] Claims Settlement Declaration, Article III, paragraph 2.

[99] Iran–US CT Final Tribunal Rules of Procedure of 3 May 1983, 2 Iran–U.S. C.T.R. p. 405, also available at www.iusct.org [hereinafter Iran–US CT Tribunal Rules].

[100] Iran–US CT Tribunal Rules, Article 1, paragraph 1.

[101] Iran–US CT Internal Guidelines of the Tribunal, 1 Iran–U.S. C.T.R. p. 98.

[102] The Iran–US CT Staff Rules and Financial Regulations are not public documents.

[103] See, e.g., UNCC Governing Council Decision 1 of 2 August 1991, *Criteria for Expedited Processing of Urgent Claims*, U.N. Doc. S/AC.26/1991/1 (2 August 1991); Decision 2 of 2 August 1991, *Arrangements for ensuring payment to the Compensation Fund*, U.N. Doc. S/AC.26/1991/2 (2 August 1991); Decision 6 of 18 October 1991, *Arrangements for ensuring payment to the Compensation Fund*, U.N. Doc. S/AC.26/1991/6 (23 October 1991); Decision 7 of 28 November 1991, as revised on 16 March 1992, *Criteria for additional Categories of Claims*, U.N. Doc. S/AC.26/1991/7/Rev.1 (17 March 1992); Decision 10 of 26 June 1992, *Approving the Provisional Rules for Claims Procedure*,

Council is empowered to adopt, modify, and augment the Commission's Provisional Rules, as well as the administrative procedures and structural aspects of the Claims Process when circumstances warrant.[104] For example, in December 2000, the Governing Council amended the Claims Process relating to the larger and more complex claims, by instructing panels of Commissioners to hold oral hearings and prepare separate reports for any claims having an asserted value of US$1 billion or more.[105]

The procedures set out in the Provisional Rules for the processing of the larger individual, corporate, and governmental claims filed with the UNCC were further elaborated in a five-year work program, prepared by the Commission's Executive Secretary in 1997 and adopted by the Governing Council in 1998, and in subsequent updates of the work program.[106] Under the Provisional Rules, the Secretariat is authorized to hire external expert consultants to assist panels of Commissioners with the verification and valuation of claims.[107] The UNCC's extensive use of expert consultants—a novel approach among international Mass Claims Processes and the need for which may not have been fully realized at the time this Claims Process was constituted—became a defining feature of its procedures. It is but one example of a Claims Process adapting its procedures to meet its mandate once its actual scope has become fully known.

The panels of Commissioners were also authorized, subject to the provisions of the Provisional Rules, to make such additional procedural rulings as might be necessary to expedite work on particular cases or categories of cases. In so doing, they could rely on the relevant UNCITRAL Arbitration Rules for guidance, although in practice that was not done.[108] They were also authorized to request the Governing Council to provide further guidance with respect to the Provisional Rules at any time.[109] The UNCC Secretariat also developed standard operating procedures covering the various stages of the Claims Process, as well as the relationships between (i) the Secretariat and the panels of Commissioners; (ii) the Commission and the claimants and Iraq; and (iii) the Commission and external experts.

U.N. Doc. S/AC.26/1992/10 (26 June 1992); Decision 17 of 23 March 1994, *Priority of Payment and Payment Mechanisms*, U.N. Doc. S/AC.26/Dec.17 (1994) (24 March 1994); and Decision 18 of 23 March 1994, *Distribution of Payments and Transparency*, U.N. Doc. S/AC.26/Dec.18 (1994) (24 March 1994).

[104] UNCC Provisional Rules, Article 43.

[105] UNCC Governing Council Decision 114 of 7 December 2000, *Decision concerning the review of current UNCC procedures*, U.N. Doc. S/AC.26/Dec.114 (2000) (7 December 2000), paragraph 12.

[106] UNCC Work Programme, U.N. Doc. S/AC.26/1997/WP.1 (1998). The Work Programme is not a public document.　　　　[107] UNCC Provisional Rules, Article 36, paragraph b.

[108] Ibid., Article 43. See further section 5.01(b) below, on procedural rules.　　　[109] Ibid.

(c) Commission for Real Property Claims of Displaced Persons and Refugees (CRPC)—claims relating to the 1992–1995 war in Bosnia and Herzegovina

The constituting instrument of the CRPC Claims Process, Annex 7 to the Dayton Peace Agreement, provides that the Commission shall promulgate such rules and regulations, consistent with the Peace Agreement, as may be needed to carry out its functions.[110] Accordingly, the Commission adopted Books of Regulations concerning the right to give authentic interpretation of the provisions of those Regulations. Any procedural matters not regulated by the Regulations were to be governed by the provisions of the Law on Civil Procedure of Bosnia and Herzegovina, as defined in the Dayton Peace Agreement.[111]

In practice, each time a question arose which was not yet covered by the Books of Regulations, the Commission reviewed the criteria that needed to be addressed and, if it deemed it appropriate, introduced a new rule in the applicable Book of Regulations. The Books of Regulations were thus continuously updated throughout the life of this Claims Process, and their most up-to-date versions were always posted on the CRPC website.

(d) Claims Resolution Tribunal for Dormant Accounts in Switzerland (CRT-I)—first claims tribunal for assets deposited in Swiss banks

The Board of Trustees of the Independent Claims Resolution Foundation (ICRF) created the initial CRT-I Rules of Procedure and had the power to amend them. While the Members of the Tribunal thus had no role in drafting the Rules nor power to amend them, they did have the limited authority "to enact such guidelines and procedures, consistent with [the] Rules, as are required to fill gaps in [the] Rules and to deal with unforeseen circumstances."[112] The Members several times exercised this authority to supplement and interpret the Rules, but such interpretations and supplements were considered to be internal guidelines and the Chairman elected not to make them public. The Tribunal later adopted Internal Rules regulating the proceedings and internal organization of the Tribunal in order to secure the uniform handling of claims submitted to it.[113]

---

[110] Dayton Peace Agreement, Annex 7, Article XV.

[111] CRPC Book of Regulations on Procedure, Article 91.

[112] CRT-I Rules of Procedure, Article 42.

[113] Ibid., Article 26, provided that the Tribunal could, "if necessary, promulgate rules of its practice and internal rules consistent with these Rules . . . ." The Internal Rules were not made public.

(e) Claims Resolution Tribunal (CRT-II)—second claims tribunal for assets deposited in Swiss banks

The Rules Governing the Claims Resolution Process of CRT-II were prepared by its Secretariat, proposed by the Special Masters to the United States federal district court supervising the class action known as the Holocaust Victim Assets Litigation, and approved by the Court. Significant amendments to the Rules have been made following the same procedure.[114] The Special Masters may further promulgate guidelines and procedures that are deemed necessary for the fair and expeditious functioning of the Claims Process and that are consistent with the Rules.[115]

(f) Housing and Property Claims Commission (HPCC)—claims relating to the 1999 conflict in Kosovo

Both the Housing and Property Directorate (HPD) and the HPCC may adopt additional rules for carrying out their respective functions, provided they are consistent with the constituting Regulation.[116] In practice, both bodies have adopted such additional rules.

(g) Mass Claims Processes administered by the International Organization for Migration (IOM)

German Forced Labour Compensation Programme (GFLCP)—claims against Germany and German industry for Nazi injustice

The principal policy organ of GFLCP is the Board of Trustees of the German Foundation. The Board of Trustees has the right to decide all fundamental matters having to do with the tasks of the Foundation and to establish guidelines for the use of resources insofar as their use is not already specified in the German Foundation Act.[117] The Board of Trustees may change the guidelines it establishes by a majority vote of its members.[118] A Board of Directors, appointed by and reporting to the Board of Trustees, oversees the partner organizations' adherence to the German Foundation Act and to the guidelines established by the Board of Trustees.[119] In this capacity, the Board of Directors

---

[114] CRT-II Governing Rules, Article 43, authorizes amendments by the Special Masters with the approval of the Court.   [115] Ibid., Article 10, paragraph 2.

[116] UNMIK Regulation 2000/60, sections 16 (HPD) and 26 (HPCC).

[117] German Foundation Act, section 5, paragraphs 5 and 7.

[118] Statutes of the German Foundation, *Satzung*, available on the Foundation's website, www.stiftung-evz.de, section 6, paragraph 1.

[119] German Foundation Act, section 6, paragraph 3. See also Statutes of the German Foundation, *Satzung*, available on the Foundation's website, www.stiftung-evz.de, section 8, paragraph 2.

issues further guidelines and interpretations of the German Foundation Act which IOM and the other partner organizations must follow.

The German Foundation has entered into a contract with IOM (as it has with each of its other partner organizations that carry out other portions of the Claims Process under the German Foundation Act) in which the respective rights and obligations of the Foundation and IOM are elaborated. This includes further guidelines as to the review of and the decisions on the claims. IOM consults with the Foundation and the other partner organizations on an on-going basis to harmonize the work, receive guidance, and share emerging experiences.

Holocaust Victim Assets Programme (HVAP)—claims pursuant to 1999 class action Settlement

In administering HVAP and distributing payments thereunder, IOM makes all necessary arrangements in consultation with the United States federal district court supervising the class action known as the Holocaust Victim Asset Litigation, which is assisted in this by recommendations of the Special Masters. Subject to the Court's approval, IOM receives, processes, and reviews the claims. Any additional provisions or modifications to the Claims Process require the authorization of the Court.[120]

(h) Eritrea–Ethiopia Claims Commission (EECC)—claims relating to the 1998–2000 war between Eritrea and Ethiopia

The 12 December 2000 Agreement, which establishes the EECC, contains considerable detail regarding its makeup and jurisdiction. However, it leaves the specific procedures for handling claims to Rules of Procedure to be adopted by the Commission.[121] The Rules as adopted may be modified by the Commission after consultation with the parties.[122]

The Commission may also clarify or supplement its procedures through "Decisions" establishing procedural principles of general application not related to the merits of particular claims.[123] The Commission's first Decision addressed questions regarding its mandate and the temporal scope of its

---

[120] See, e.g., Plan of Allocation and Distribution, at pp. 164 and 176, recognizing the Court's supervisory authority and IOM's intention to work closely with the Court and consult with it on all significant decisions affecting all stages of the claims review.

[121] Eritrea–Ethiopia Agreement of 12 December 2000, Article 5, paragraph 7.

[122] Eritrea–Ethiopia Claims Commission Rules of Procedure [hereinafter EECC Rules of Procedure], available at www.pca-cpa.org. See Article 1, paragraph 2.

[123] EECC Rules of Procedure, Article 18, paragraph 1.

jurisdiction. Other early Decisions addressed remedies, evidence, and questions related to the possible use of mass claims processing techniques such as grouping claims into categories, claim forms that could be scanned by computer, and issues related to multiple claims by the same claimant. (Largely because of the shortness of time, the parties elected to file their claims as Government-to-Government claims, and thus to avoid filing large numbers of individual claims.)

The Commission's original mandate was to endeavor to complete its work by December 2004, three years after the deadline for filing claims. Faced with an unexpectedly large volume of cases and issues, the parties and the Commission agreed to extend the time-frame for the Commission's work. The Commission completed hearings on the merits of all of the parties' claims in April 2005. Final awards on liability were issued on 19 December 2005.[124] The mechanisms described above have provided sufficient flexibility to respond to emerging needs within the Commission's mandate—including extending the time-frame after consultation with the parties, and consulting with the parties about how to conduct a damages phase after the completion of the liability phase.

(i) Humanitarian insurance Claims Process administered by the Jewish Claims Conference (JCC) for the International Commission on Holocaust Era Insurance Claims (ICHEIC)

ICHEIC set forth general guidelines for claims review, based upon which the JCC reviewed the claims and made recommendations in accordance with the Point Scoring System described in section 1.02(i) above. ICHEIC had appointed a Senior Counselor to approve the evaluation criteria and supervise the payment process. Thus, the Point Scoring System was approved by the Senior Counselor and authorized by ICHEIC. Clarifications were obtained from ICHEIC where appropriate. ICHEIC responded to such requests by means of policy memoranda with guidance on the matter in question. To the extent that such memoranda established or clarified a common rule, they became part of the official record in the 8A1 Point Scoring System Guidelines and constituted a practical approach to meeting unforeseen needs.

(j) American Arbitration Association (AAA)—an illustrative case

Despite the specificity of the Settlement Agreement in the illustrative case as to the rules of the Claims Process, when the actual review of the claims began,

---

[124] Completed awards of the EECC are publicly available at www.pca-cpa.org.

numerous unforeseen circumstances arose which needed to be addressed before the claims could be decided. Modifications could only be made by unanimous agreement of an *ad hoc* committee of three, consisting of representatives of, respectively, plaintiffs' counsel, defendant's counsel, and the insurance regulators of the states. Thus, the parties and the Arbitrators could not themselves modify the Settlement Agreement.

1.04 Jurisdiction

The jurisdiction of the Claims Process, including the types of claims that can be made. Eligible claimants, including any issues of nationality and dual nationality. Whether heirs of victims are eligible to be claimants. (Note that the types of claims may have an impact on the mass claims methodologies used to process the claims.)

Editors' Commentary

Some Mass Claims Processes take the form of arbitral tribunals that decide legal issues of liability of the party against which the claims are made, before determining individual claimants' eligibility for payment and the value of the claims. An example of this is the Eritrea–Ethiopia Claims Commission (EECC). Other Claims Processes, such as the United Nations Compensation Commission (UNCC), are given a mandate to perform the verification and valuation function after another organ—judicial or political—has determined the liability.

The architects of the constituting instruments or procedural rules for each of the Mass Claims Processes described in this book attempted to be quite precise in defining the types of claims that could be made in the particular Claims Process, and in identifying who are eligible claimants. Most also defined the time limits as to when a claim had to have arisen in order to qualify for compensation. Generally, these efforts have been successful, although they have not in all cases eliminated disagreements as to interpretation and application.

The designers of a number of the Claims Processes did not expressly deal with the eligibility of heirs to make claims, presumably because it was considered that if the initial person who had a right to make a claim had died, that right would pass to his or her heirs in accordance with applicable laws of inheritance. Others opted to avoid implicit or explicit reference to applicable laws of inheritance for fear that doing so might slow down the Claims Process by lengthy and complex disputes over conflicts of law and the need to determine and apply numerous domestic laws. Some established a defined hierarchy of heirs that were determined to be eligible for the purposes of the particular Claims Process without regard to otherwise applicable inheritance law.

Although eligibility to claim is often conditioned upon the nationality of the claimant, the wording of the documents governing some of the Claims Processes described in this book has led to differing interpretations and subsequent disputes concerning the rights of dual nationals. This has resulted in uncertainty and delay in some Claims Processes, and where, for example, the eligibility of a dual national is based on his or her "dominant and effective nationality"—the test the Arbitrators of the Iran–United States Claims Tribunal (Iran–US CT) decided to apply—the determination of which nationality is "dominant" has presented vexing factual issues in some individual cases. Accordingly, in a world of transient populations, designers of future Mass Claims Processes may wish to consider including explicit and detailed provisions relating to persons of dual or multiple nationality.

The descriptions that follow include some extensive quotations of the jurisdiction provisions of various Claims Processes. This is done, rather than paraphrasing or describing those provisions, because the exact wording used may be the most helpful way of understanding and comparing them.

(a) Iran–United States Claims Tribunal (Iran–US CT)—claims relating to the 1979 Islamic Revolution

Types of claims

The jurisdiction of the Iran–US CT and the types of claims that can be made are determined in the Claims Settlement Declaration, which provides that the Tribunal is to decide

" . . . claims of nationals of the United States against Iran and claims of nationals of Iran against the United States, and any counterclaim which arises out of the same contract, transaction or occurrence that constitutes the subject matter of that national's claim, if such claims and counterclaims are outstanding on the date of [the Claims Settlement Declaration], whether or not filed with any court, and arise out of debts, contracts (including transactions which are the subject of letters of credit or bank guarantees), expropriations or other measures affecting property rights, excluding claims [of the U.S. hostages and claims arising out of U.S. counter measures], and excluding claims arising under a binding contract between the parties specifically providing [for a forum selection clause in favor of Iranian courts]."[125]

The Claims Settlement Declaration further provides that the Tribunal has jurisdiction over "official claims of the United States and Iran against each other arising out of contractual arrangements between them for the purchase and sale of goods and services,"[126] and "over any dispute as to the interpretation or performance of any provision of [the General Declaration]."[127]

Eligible claimants

The application of the above-quoted provision requires a determination of who are "nationals." Accordingly, the Claims Settlement Declaration contains the following definitions of "nationals," "claims of nationals," and "Iran" and the "United States":

"1. A 'national' of Iran or of the United States, as the case may be, means (a) a natural person who is a citizen of Iran or the United States; and (b) a corporation or other legal entity which is organized under the laws of Iran or the United States or any of its states or territories, the District of Columbia or the Commonwealth of Puerto Rico, if, collectively, natural persons who are citizens of such country hold, directly or indirectly, an interest in such corporation or entity equivalent to fifty per cent or more of its capital stock.

2. 'Claims of nationals' of Iran or the United States, as the case may be, means claims owned continuously, from the date on which the claim arose to the date on which this Agreement enters into force, by nationals of that state, including claims that are owned indirectly by such nationals through ownership of capital stock or other proprietary interests in juridical persons, provided that the ownership interests of such nationals, collectively, were sufficient at the time the claim arose to control the corporation or other entity, and provided, further, that the corporation or other entity is not itself entitled to bring a claim under the terms of this Agreement. Claims referred to the arbitration Tribunal shall, as of the date of filing of such claims with the Tribunal, be considered excluded from the jurisdiction of the courts of Iran, or of the United States, or of any other court.

3. 'Iran' means the Government of Iran, any political subdivision of Iran, and any agency, instrumentality, or entity controlled by the Government of Iran or any political subdivision thereof.

4. The 'United States' means the Government of the United States, any political subdivision of the United States, and any agency, instrumentality or entity controlled by the Government of the United States or any political subdivision thereof."[128]

---

[125] Claims Settlement Declaration, Article II, paragraph 1.
[126] Ibid., Article II, paragraph 2.   [127] Ibid., Article II, paragraph 3.
[128] Ibid., Article VIII.

Interpreting the provisions of the Claims Settlement Declaration, the Tribunal determined that, for purposes of jurisdiction, the nationality of a person having dual nationality shall be his or her "real and effective nationality,"[129] a standard based on a precedent established in 1955 by the International Court of Justice (ICJ) in the *Nottebohm* case.[130]

(b) United Nations Compensation Commission (UNCC)—claims relating to the 1990–1991 Gulf War

Types of claims

The basic provision governing the types of claims that could be made before the UNCC, as well as who were eligible as claimants, was contained in its constituting instrument, United Nations Security Council Resolution 687 (1991). That Resolution confirmed the Council's determination that Iraq, without prejudice to pre-existing debts or obligations, was "liable under international law for any direct loss, damage, including environmental damage and the depletion of natural resources, or injury to foreign Governments, nationals and corporations, as a result of Iraq's unlawful invasion and occupation of Kuwait."[131] The jurisdiction of the UNCC was thus limited to providing compensation for damages stemming from Iraq's 1990 invasion and occupation of Kuwait, but Iraq's pre-invasion debts and obligations were excluded from the Commission's jurisdiction. Iraq's liability having thus already been determined in Resolution 687 (1991), the UNCC did not need to render a decision on liability. Rather, one of the initial tasks of the UNCC Governing Council was to develop criteria for interpreting and applying the requirements in Resolution 687 (1991) that compensable losses had to have been a "direct" result of Iraq's invasion and occupation of Kuwait, as the Resolution did not contain a test for determining which losses were direct or indirect.

With respect to the types of claims that could be filed with the Commission, the Governing Council created six categories, labeled "A" through "F"; four for individual claimants, one for corporations, and one for Governments and international organizations. The Governing Council decided, for humanitarian and other policy reasons, and as the United Nations Secretary-General

---

[129] *Iran and United States*, Case No. A/18 *Concerning the Jurisdiction of the Tribunal over Claims Presented by Dual Iranian–United States Nationals Against the Government of Iran*, Decision No. 32-A18-FT (6 April 1984), 5 Iran–U.S. C.T.R. p. 251. A number of subsequent decisions determined which nationality was the "dominant" one in the circumstances of the particular case.

[130] *Nottebohm Case (Liechtenstein v. Guatemala)*, Second Phases, (1955) ICJ Reports p.4, at p.22.

[131] UN Security Council Resolution 687 (1991), U.N. Doc. S/RES/687 (1991), paragraph 16.

recommended in a Report of 2 May 1991, to give priority to processing smaller individual claims over the large individual, corporate, and government claims.[132]

Classified as the three most urgent categories were claims for fixed amounts by individuals who, as a result of Iraq's invasion and occupation of Kuwait, left or fled Iraq or Kuwait during the relevant period[133] (category "A"); or suffered serious personal injury, or the loss of a spouse, child or parent (category "B"); and claims by individuals for up to US$100,000 for departure costs, personal injury or death, loss of income or support, housing, personal property, bank accounts, securities, or individual business loss (category "C").[134]

Deadlines were set for filing claims in the various categories, but some extensions were granted,[135] the latest of which was to 15 January 2002 for category "F4" claims for environmental damage.

The less urgent categories included claims of individuals for more than US$100,000 (category "D") for losses similar to those brought below the US$100,000 limit in category "C"; claims of corporations and public sector enterprises, including oil sector losses (category "E"); and claims by governments and international organizations for loss or damage to government property and costs incurred in evacuating foreign nationals from Iraq and Kuwait and providing relief, for damage to diplomatic premises and government property, and for direct environmental damage and natural resources depletion as a result of Iraq's invasion and occupation of Kuwait (category "F").[136] Losses suffered

---

[132] UNCC Governing Council Decision 1 of 2 August 1991, *Criteria for Expedited Processing of Urgent Claims*, U.N. Doc. S/AC.26/1991/1 (2 August 1991); UNCC Governing Council Decision 7 of 28 November 1991, as revised on 16 March 1992, *Criteria for Additional Categories of Claims*, U.N. Doc. S/AC.26/1991/7/Rev.1 (17 March 1992); Report of the Secretary-General of 2 May 1991, U.N. Doc. S/25599, paragraph 24.

[133] The UNCC Governing Council defined the relevant period as 2 August 1990 to 2 March 1991. See its Decision 1 of 2 August 1991, *Criteria for Expedited Processing of Urgent Claims*, U.N. Doc. S/AC.26/1991/1 (2 August 1991), paragraph 10.

[134] UNCC Governing Council Decision 1 of 2 August 1991, *Criteria for Expedited Processing of Urgent Claims*, U.N. Doc. S/AC.26/1991/1 (2 August 1991). The claim forms that the UNCC distributed contained further details on the types of claims, and a subsequent decision elaborated on the criteria for personal injury claims. See UNCC Governing Council Decision 3 of 18 October 1991, *Personal Injury and Mental Pain and Anguish*, U.N. Doc. S/AC.26/1991/3 (23 October 1991).

[135] See UNCC Governing Council Decision 12 of 24 September 1992, *Claims for which Established Deadlines are Extended*, U.N. Doc. S/AC.26/12 (25 September 1992).

[136] UNCC Governing Council Decision 7 of 28 November 1991, as revised on 16 March 1992, *Criteria for Additional Categories of Claims*, U.N. Doc. S/AC.26/1991/7/Rev.1 (17 March 1991). The Council clarified in a subsequent decision what types of business losses were eligible for compensation. UNCC Governing Council Decision 9 of 6 March 1992, *Propositions and Conclusions on Compensation for Business Losses: Types of Damages and Their Valuation*, U.N. Doc. S/AC.26/1992/9

exclusively as a result of the trade embargo imposed on Iraq were excluded from the Commission's jurisdiction.[137]

Eligible claimants

Provisions on who may submit a claim are contained in the Commission's Provisional Rules.[138] Iraqi nationals or companies were not allowed to file claims with the Commission, except for dual nationals with a bona fide nationality of a State other than Iraq.[139] The panel of Commissioners deciding claims of individuals who departed from Kuwait or Iraq (category "A") applied the standard of "dominant and effective" nationality to claims by dual nationals, construing "bona fide" non-Iraqi nationality to mean nationality acquired prior to 2 August 1991, the date of Governing Council Decision 1 which set forth the eligibility criteria for individual claimants. These procedures obviated the need for determining whether a claimant's non-Iraqi nationality was "dominant and effective" at the time the claim arose.[140]

Claims on behalf of all claimants—individuals as well as legal entities—were to be gathered and submitted by governments and international organizations; private parties and bodies did not in principle have a right to initiate a claims procedure. In the interest of treating all potential claimants equally and to simplify claims collection, governments were given discretion beyond what are otherwise traditional rules of international claims and diplomatic protection, in that they could submit claims not only on behalf of their own citizens but also on behalf of nationals of other countries residing within their territories.[141] Thus, claimants' eligibility was not limited by their displacement outside their country of citizenship. International organizations were generally allowed to submit claims only on their own behalf, except that the UNCC Executive Secretary appointed several international organizations to submit claims on behalf of refugees or stateless persons who were not in a position to

---

(6 March 1991). In particular, this decision deals with losses in connection with contracts or past business practice, losses relating to tangible assets, and losses relating to income-producing properties.

[137] UNCC Governing Council Decision 15 of 18 December 1992, *Compensation for Business Losses Resulting from Iraq's Unlawful Invasion and Occupation of Kuwait Where the Trade Embargo and Related Measures Were also a Cause*, U.N. Doc. S/AC.26/1992/ 15 (4 January 1993), paragraph 3.

[138] UNCC Provisional Rules, Article 5.

[139] See UNCC Governing Council Decision 1 of 2 August 1991, *Criteria for Expedited Processing of Urgent Claims*, U.N. Doc. S/AC.26/1991/1 (2 August 1991), paragraph 17; Decision 7 of 28 November 1991, as revised on 16 March 1992, *Criteria for Additional Categories of Claims*, U.N. Doc. S/AC.26/1991/7/Rev.1 (17 March 1991), paragraph 11.

[140] See *Nottebohm Case (Liechtenstein v. Guatemala)*, Second Phase, (1955) ICJ Reports, at pp. 22–23; Case A18 (6 April 1984), 5 Iran–U.S. C.T.R. p. 251 (1984).

[141] UNCC Provisional Rules, Article 5, paragraph 1(a).

have their claims submitted by a government.[142] This was mostly relevant for Palestinian claimants. Another exception to the rule against private parties filing claims was that corporations were allowed to file claims directly on their own behalf if the State of incorporation failed to bring the claim. This was done in order to protect companies controlled by foreign interests.[143]

With respect to eligibility of heirs to make claims, it is to be noted that "claimant" is defined in the UNCC's Provisional Rules to mean "any individual . . . that files a claim with the Commission."[144] There is no reference in the UNCC's constituting documents to the question of heirs; that question was left to be addressed by the panels of Commissioners reviewing claims in the individual claims categories ("A", "B", "C" and "D").

In the situation where an individual filed a claim with the UNCC and subsequently died, the claim would continue to be processed and any award of compensation would be made in the name of the deceased claimant, to be distributed by the claimant government or other submitting entity in accordance with relevant domestic law. In the situation where an otherwise eligible individual died before filing a claim with the UNCC, the authorized representative(s) of the heirs or the executor or administrator of the deceased's estate was permitted to file the claim. In such cases, any award of compensation was still made in the name of the deceased "claimant" (again, to be distributed by the claimant government or other submitting entity in accordance with domestic law). Non-pecuniary losses personal to the deceased did not survive the death of the individual and could not be claimed by the authorized representative(s) of the heirs or the executor or administrator of the estate.[145]

---

[142] UNCC Governing Council Decision 5 of 18 October 1991, *Guidelines Relating to Paragraph 19 of the Criteria for Expedited Processing of Urgent Claims*, U.N. Doc. S/AC26/1991/5 (23 October 1991); UNCC Governing Council Decision 1 of 2 August 1991, *Criteria for Expedited Processing of Urgent Claims*, U.N. Doc. S/AC.26/1991/1 (2 August 1991), paragraph 19. This special procedure authorized a number of international organizations with offices in the Middle East, such as the United Nations Development Program (UNDP), the Office of the United Nations High Commissioner for Refugees (UNHCR), and the United Nations Relief and Works Agency for Palestine Refugees in the Middle East (UNRWA), to file claims on behalf of stateless persons and refugees.

[143] See UNCC Governing Council Decision 4 of 18 October 1991, *Business Losses of Individuals Eligible for Consideration under the Expedited Procedures*, U.N. Doc. S/AC.26/1991/4 (23 October 1991). Claims of corporations and other legal entities (category "E") were to be submitted by the State in which, and under whose law, the entity was, on the date the claim arose, incorporated or organized. UNCC Provisional Rules, Article 5, paragraph 1(b). If the State failed to submit a timely claim, the corporation or entity itself was allowed to file its claim directly. UNCC Provisional Rules, Article 5, paragraph 3.   [144] UNCC Provisional Rules, Article 1, paragraph 12.

[145] See, e.g., *Recommendations Made by the Panel of Commissioners Concerning Individual Claims for Serious Personal Injury or Death (Category "B" Claims)*, U.N. Doc. S/AC.26/1994/1 (26 May 1994), at pp. 19–20.

The Governing Council decided that members of the Allied Coalition armed forces in the Gulf War were not eligible for compensation for loss or injury arising as a consequence of their involvement in military operations against Iraq, unless: " . . . they were prisoners of war as a consequence of their involvement in Coalition military operations against Iraq in response to its unlawful invasion and occupation of Kuwait; and . . . the loss or injury resulted from mistreatment in violation of international humanitarian law (including the Geneva Conventions of 1949)."[146]

(c) Commission for Real Property Claims of Displaced Persons and Refugees (CRPC)—claims relating to the 1992–1995 war in Bosnia and Herzegovina

Types of claims

The CRPC had jurisdiction to resolve claims for real property lost during the war in Bosnia and Herzegovina.[147] The constituting instrument, Annex 7 to the Dayton Agreement, provided that the claimants could choose between three options: (i) they could seek to return into the possession of the claimed property; (ii) they could seek compensation for property that could not be restored to them; or (iii) they could keep both options open if they were un-decided as to what they wanted to do with the property. Claimants could also ask the Commission to set aside a wartime sale or transfer that had been concluded under duress.[148] In practice, CRPC decisions only confirmed the pre-war property rights of the claimants, authorizing them to return into possession of the property or to engage in lawful real estate transactions on the private property market. With approximately half of the property records destroyed during the war, and many of the surviving records outdated, the certificates issued by the CRPC implementing its decisions provided conclusive evidence of the claimants' entitlement to the claimed properties.

Eligible claimants

Persons who could file claims with the Commission were primarily internally displaced persons and refugees, but other "natural persons with a legal interest in the claimed real property" were also entitled to submit a claim.[149] Such other

---

[146] UNCC Governing Council Decision 11 of 26 June 1992, *Eligibility for Compensation of Members of the Allied Coalition Armed Forces*, U.N. Doc. S/AC.26/1992/11 (26 June 1992), paragraphs (b) and (c).   [147] Dayton Peace Agreement, Annex 7, Article I, paragraph 1.

[148] Ibid., Article XII, paragraph 3.

[149] CRPC Book of Regulations on Procedure, Article 10.

persons could include heirs of owners who died after 1 April 1992. Decisions sought by heirs, however, would only indicate that the deceased had had property rights as of 1 April 1992; they did not decide the heirs' title to such rights. The Commission's decision certificates indicated merely who was the "historic" owner or possessor of the property in question as of 1 April 1992—whether alive or deceased—which avoided inheritance disputes from having to be resolved in the Claims Process. The CRPC Book of Regulations on Procedure provided that, if a claimant to real property died before the Commission issued a decision, the claimant's heirs could either pursue or withdraw the claim.[150]

(d) Claims Resolution Tribunal for Dormant Accounts in Switzerland (CRT-I)—first claims tribunal for assets deposited in Swiss banks

Types of claims

The Rules of Procedure of CRT-I stated that it was established to resolve claims:

> "i. to accounts opened by non-Swiss nationals or residents that are dormant since May 9, 1945 and were made public by the Swiss Bankers Association on July 23, 1997 or at a later date; and
> ii. to accounts opened by Swiss nationals that are dormant ever since May 9, 1945 and will be made public by the Swiss Bankers Association in October 1997 or at a later date, *if and to the extent* a Sole Arbitrator determines, after consultation with [ICEP], that such accounts may have been held by a Swiss intermediary for a victim of Nazi persecution."[151]

The Rules included the useful definition that:

"For the purposes of these Rules of Procedure, the term 'account' shall include all kinds of accounts, including, without limitation, current, savings and securities accounts, passbooks, safety deposit boxes, and any other form of dormant bank liability, including, without limitation, bank cheques, bonds and bank-issued medium-term notes (Kassenobligationen)."[152]

Eligible claimants

As the above-quoted provision shows, CRT-I had jurisdiction over claims of all holders of dormant accounts, including victims of Nazi persecution as well as persons who were not such victims.

---

[150] CRPC Book of Regulations on Procedure, Article 32.
[151] CRT-I Rules of Procedure, Article 1 (emphasis in original).
[152] CRT-I Rules of Procedure, Article 1.

With respect to heirs, the Rules provided that the Arbitrators were to apply "the law with which the matter in dispute has the closest connection in deciding matters concerning the relationship between the published account holder or holder of power of attorney and the claimant (e.g., to inheritance matters or fiduciary agreements)." If all parties involved, other than the Swiss banks, so wished, the Tribunal could resolve inheritance matters in accordance with Talmudic law.[153]

(e) Claims Resolution Tribunal (CRT-II)—second claims tribunal for assets deposited in Swiss banks

Types of claims

In contrast to CRT-I, which dealt with claims to accounts that had lain dormant since World War II and which had been published by the Swiss Bankers Association in 1997, CRT-II has jurisdiction over assets deposited in accounts that were identified during the audit described in section 1.01(e) above as having been open or opened during the period from 1933 to 1945 in Swiss banks, regardless of the present disposition of those accounts.[154]

Claims can be made for any type of bank accounts (including securities accounts, safety deposit boxes, and precious metals) that were "open and dormant, suspended, closed to bank profits or because fees or charges exhausted the Accounts, or were paid to Nazi authorities"; to accounts that were "Closed Unknown by Whom"; or to accounts that "had unique, almost unique or confirming factors matches [*sic*.] between Victims and Account Owners."[155]

Eligible claimants

CRT-II was established to provide victims or targets of Nazi persecution—or their heirs—with an opportunity to make claims for deposited assets. The CRT-II Governing Rules define "Victim" as "any person or entity persecuted or targeted for persecution by the Nazi regime because they were or were believed to be Jewish, Romani, Jehovah's Witness, homosexual, or physically or mentally disabled or handicapped."[156] The Claims Process can make an award of the value of an account to a claimant who has: identified a person with the same or similar name as the account owner; provided satisfactory information consistent with unpublished information in bank records; provided plausible evidence that the account owner was a Victim; and that the

---

[153] CRT-I Rules of Procedure, Article 16.   [154] CRT-II Governing Rules, Article 14.
[155] Ibid., Article 1.   [156] Ibid., Article 46, paragraph 26.

relationship between claimant and the account owner justifies making an award.[157]

With respect to heirs, the Governing Rules set out detailed criteria regulating the distribution of awards in the absence of a will or other inheritance documents, as well as of awards in cases where there is a will.[158] These Governing Rules apply uniformly to all claimants, instead of the respective national laws of inheritance that would otherwise govern a particular claimant, as was the more conventional system used in CRT-I. The Rules also establish which presumptions will be applied to questions of joint accounts, unrelated claimants, and accounts of legal and other entities.[159]

(f) Housing and Property Claims Commission (HPCC)—claims relating to the 1999 conflict in Kosovo

Types of claims

The HPCC's mandate is to resolve disputes over residential property in Kosovo. UNMIK Regulation 1999/23, establishing the Claims Process, identifies three categories of property claims that can be made and provides as follows:

"As an exception to the jurisdiction of the local courts, the [Housing and Property] Directorate shall receive and register the following categories of claims concerning residential property including associated property:

   a. Claims by natural persons whose ownership, possession or occupancy rights to residential real property have been revoked subsequent to 23 March 1989 on the basis of legislation which is discriminatory in its application or intent;
   b. Claims by natural persons who entered into informal transactions of residential real property on the basis of the free will of the parties subsequent to 23 March 1989;[160]
   c. Claims by natural persons who were the owners, possessors or occupancy right holders of residential property prior to 24 March 1999 and who do not enjoy possession of the property, and where the property has not voluntarily been transferred.

The Directorate shall refer these claims to the Housing and Property Claims Commission for resolution or, if appropriate, seek to mediate such disputes and, if

---

[157] CRT-II Governing Rules, Article 22.   [158] Ibid., Article 23.

[159] See ibid., Articles 23–27.

[160] Category "B" claims thus could arise between 23 March 1989 and 13 October 1999, the date of promulgation of UNMIK Regulation 1999/10 *On the Repeal of Discriminatory Legislation Affecting Housing and Rights in Property*, U.N. Doc. UNMIK/REG/1999/10 (13 October 1999).

not successful, refer them to the Housing and Property Claims Commission for resolution."[161]

Excluded from the Commission's jurisdiction are claims for compensation for damage to or destruction of property.[162]

Eligible claimants

As the above-quoted Regulation makes clear, eligibility in this Claims Process is limited to claims by *natural* persons; claims by legal persons, such as corporations or government entities, are excluded. If the person who suffered the property loss cannot make a claim, a member of the family household of that person may pursue the claim.[163] In addition to the claimant, any current occupant of the claimed property and any other natural person with a legal interest in the property shall also be parties to the claim. UNMIK Regulation 2000/60 further provides:

"A person with a legal interest in the claim, who did not receive [timely] notification of a claim, may be admitted as a party at any point in the proceedings, provided the claim has not been finally adjudicated. The current or former allocation right holder to a claimed apartment may make submissions or present evidence in connection with the claim."[164]

(g) Mass Claims Processes administered by the International Organization for Migration (IOM)

German Forced Labour Compensation Programme (GFLCP)—claims against Germany and German industry for Nazi injustice

Types of claims

The German Foundation Act clearly sets out the three types of claims that may be filed in the GFLCP Claims Process: (i) claims by former slave laborers who were held in concentration camps, ghettos or other places of confinement, and claims by former forced laborers who were deported to Germany or German-occupied areas and were held in prisons or similar extremely harsh living conditions, and were forced to work; (ii) personal injury claims, in particular by victims of medical experiments and by children who were held in homes for children of forced laborers; and (iii) claims for certain property losses as a consequence of persecution because of race, political or religious

---

[161] UNMIK Regulation 1999/23, section 1.2.
[162] UNMIK Regulation 2000/60, section 2.6.   [163] Ibid., section 7.2.
[164] Ibid., section 9.2 and 9.3.

conviction or faith, with both direct and harm-causing participation of German companies.[165]

Eligible claimants

IOM's mandate under GFLCP is to process and resolve claims of non-Jewish, so-called "rest-of-the-world" forced and slave labor claimants, namely, claimants who do not fall under the jurisdiction of one of the other partner organizations or of the Austrian Reconciliation Fund.[166] Western European claimants (i.e., from Belgium, France, Italy, Luxembourg, and the Netherlands) are in general ineligible for compensation under the German Foundation Act unless they can show that they were held in a concentration camp or ghetto, were deported and put in prison for racial, political or similar reasons, or were detained in a labor reform or penal camp.[167] The reason for this is that most of the non-Jewish, non-Roma forced laborers of Western European origin were not specific targets of discriminatory official decrees or regulations of the Nazi regime. Former prisoners of war and Italian "Military Internees" are also excluded from eligibility under the German Foundation Act unless they can show that they were detained in a concentration camp.[168]

The German Foundation Act and the Agreement between the Governments of the United States and Germany[169] define which heirs are eligible for compensation, rather than leaving that determination to domestic laws.[170] Heirs or legal successors of victims who died after 16 February 1999 are eligible to be claimants. Priority is given, however, to the processing of claims by actual victims rather than those by heirs, as the victims are often elderly and in urgent need of assistance. Further, as among the various classes of eligible heirs, the German Foundation Act establishes a strict priority for inheritance, giving the highest priority to surviving spouses and children of a claimant.[171] Juridical

---

[165] German Foundation Act, section 11, paragraph 1. See also IOM Property Commission Supplemental Rules, section 18, defining who is an eligible claimant for property.

[166] The Austrian Reconciliation Fund (ARF) is a compensation program under Austrian domestic law, distributing voluntary payments by the Republic of Austria to former slave and forced laborers of the Nazi regime in the territory of present-day Austria. ARF is wholly separate from GFLCP, but it maintains ongoing dialog and cooperation with the German Foundation because of "overlap claims" for forced labor. ARF does accept claims by Western Europeans. For information about ARF, see www.reconciliationfund.at.

[167] See section 5.02(g) below, on evidence to establish detention.

[168] German Foundation Act, section 11, paragraph 3.

[169] U.S.–German Agreement, described in section 1.01(g) above.

[170] See German Foundation Act, section 13, paragraph 1; U.S.–German Agreement, paragraph 8. See also Annex B to the U.S.–German Agreement, paragraphs 7 and 8.

[171] German Foundation Act, section 13, paragraph 1.

persons, such as corporations, are not eligible, except religious communities or organizations that may claim for property losses under the Rules of the Property Claims Commission.[172]

Holocaust Victim Assets Programme (HVAP)—claims pursuant to 1999 class action Settlement

Types of claims

Under the Settlement Agreement approved by the United States District Court for the Eastern District of New York in the class action known as the Holocaust Victim Assets Litigation, five categories of claims were created: Deposited Assets Class, Slave Labor Class I, Slave Labor Class II, Refugee Class, and a Looted Assets Class.[173] IOM processes claims in the two Slave Labor Classes and in the Refugee Class.

Eligible claimants

Under HVAP, three groups of claimants can claim, corresponding to the three classes for which IOM is responsible under the Settlement Agreement:

(i) Slave Labor Class I comprises victims or targets of Nazi persecution, as defined in the Settlement Agreement,[174] who performed slave labor for private entities, entities owned or controlled by Germany or by the Nazi authorities, or by concentration camp or ghetto authorities. IOM is in charge of claims by non-Jewish members of this class.

(ii) Slave Labor Class II comprises *any* individuals (regardless of whether they were targets of Nazi persecution) who performed slave labor for a Swiss entity, which is defined as any facility or work site, wherever located, actually or allegedly owned, controlled, or operated by any corporation or other business concern headquartered, organized, or based in Switzerland, or any affiliate thereof. A list of those Swiss companies and their affiliates that have identified themselves as having actually or potentially used slave labor has been published.[175] To qualify for compensation under HVAP, a Slave Labor Class II

---

[172] German Foundation Act, section 13, paragraph 2. See IOM Property Commission Supplemental Rules.

[173] The definitions of these five classes are summarized in the Plan of Allocation and Distribution, p. 8.

[174] The term "target of Nazi persecution" is defined in the Settlement Agreement, section 1, as "any individual, corporation, partnership, sole proprietorship, unincorporated association, community, congregation, group, organization, or other entity persecuted or targeted for persecution by the Nazi Regime because they were or were believed to be Jewish, Romani, Jehovah's Witness, homosexual, or physically or mentally disabled or handicapped."   [175] See www.swissbankclaims.iom.int.

claimant must have worked in one of the Swiss companies or its subsidiaries on that list.

(iii) The Refugee Class comprises victims or targets of Nazi persecution who sought entry into Switzerland to avoid Nazi persecution and who were denied entry into or expelled from Switzerland, or who were admitted into Switzerland as refugees and were detained or mistreated there.[176] IOM is in charge of claims by non-Jewish members of this class.

Because there are millions of potentially eligible heirs in this Claims Process, but a finite Settlement Fund of US$1.25 billion (of which US$800 million was allocated to paying claims to Swiss bank accounts), it was recognized that there might not be enough money in the Fund to pay all heirs in the Slave Labor and Refugee classes.[177] As of 31 January 2006, HVAP had only made direct payments to Holocaust survivors. Eligible legal successors or heirs of a former slave laborer or refugee who died on or after 16 February 1999, began to receive payments in 2006, in the same order of priority as is described in the preceding section on the German Forced Labour Compensation Programme (GFLCP).

(h) Eritrea–Ethiopia Claims Commission (EECC)—claims relating to the 1998–2000 war between Eritrea and Ethiopia

Types of claims

Under the constituting instrument of the EECC Claims Process, the 12 December 2000 Agreement,

"[t]he mandate of the Commission is to decide through binding arbitration all claims for loss, damage or injury by one Government against the other, and by nationals (including both natural and juridical persons) of one party against the Government of the other party or entities owned or controlled by the other party that are (a) related to the conflict that was the subject of the Framework Agreement, the Modalities for its

---

[176] A list of refugees expelled from or denied entry into Switzerland has been published. See www.swissbankclaims.iom.int. A list of refugees admitted into Switzerland that the Swiss Federal Archives provided to the United States Court has been made available to IOM, but it has not been published. Apart from Jehovah's Witnesses, however, almost none of IOM's target group members can be found in those lists, largely due to the victims' lifestyles and social attitudes at the time. The Court has therefore accepted plausible personal histories where sufficient detail can be provided.

[177] According to the Plan of Allocation and Distribution, paragraph III.C.2, depending upon the amount of the Settlement Fund remaining (if any) after all claims have been evaluated, the Court may be able to make additional distributions to survivors, certain heirs, and organizations which have sought recovery under the lawsuit as permitted by the terms of the Settlement Agreement. In practice, however, it is not expected that legal successors of victims who died before 16 February 1999 will receive payment.

Implementation and the Cessation of Hostilities Agreement, and (b) result from violations of international humanitarian law, including the 1949 Geneva Conventions, or other violations of international law. The Commission shall not hear claims arising from the cost of military operations, preparing for military operations, or the use of force, except to the extent that such claims involve violations of international humanitarian law."[178]

The two Government parties thus are authorized to file traditional State-to-State claims under the principles of the law of State responsibility for injury they suffered, including for injury to the State occurring by reason of injuries to its nationals in violation of international law. (This was the course both parties followed in their claims filings in December 2001.) In addition, the 12 December 2000 Agreement authorizes the Government parties to file claims both of individual nationals and of certain non-nationals.

The EECC Rules of Procedure introduced a further distinction giving the Government parties the option of electing one of two basic types of claims procedures. They could file claims to be individually arbitrated ("individual claims"); these could be either claims of the Governments or of individual nationals or eligible non-nationals. Alternatively, the parties could file claims for large numbers of individuals or household groups, each of whom would be eligible to receive a fixed amount of compensation (in a "mass claims procedure"). The parties could file both types of claims so long as there would be no double recovery. The Rules of Procedure were divided into three chapters to reflect this structure. Chapter One applies to all proceedings. Chapter Two applies to individual claims, defined as "all claims by the government of one party on its own behalf against the government of the other party, all claims for compensation in excess of US$100,000 on behalf of persons, and any other claims for which individual treatment is required by Chapter Three."[179] Chapter Three establishes procedures for mass claims. As to these, the Commission authorized a system of fixed-sum remedies for claimants electing to utilize the mass claims procedure.[180] It initially authorized such claims by persons (as opposed to the claims of the Governments) in five different categories:

"(a) Category 1—Claims of natural persons for unlawful expulsion from the country of their residence;

(b) Category 2—Claims of natural persons for unlawful displacement from their residence;

---

[178] Eritrea–Ethiopia Agreement of 12 December 2000, Article 5, paragraph 1.

[179] EECC Rules of Procedure, Article 23.

[180] EECC Decision Number 2: Claims Categories, Forms and Procedures (24 July 2001), available at www.pca-cpa.org.

(c) Category 3—Claims of prisoners of war for injuries suffered from unlawful treatment;

(d) Category 4—Claims of civilians for unlawful detention and for injuries suffered from unlawful treatment during detention; and

(e) Category 5—Claims of persons for loss, damage or injury other than those covered by the other categories."[181]

The Commission's Decision Number 5 authorized the cumulative filing of claims on behalf of one claimant in more than one of Categories 1 to 5 in the mass claims procedure.[182]

Under the 12 December 2000 Agreement, all claims had to be filed by 31 December 2001. The Rules of Procedure then required each Government party to group its mass claims into sub-categories, grouping together all those alleged to arise from a particular violation of international law.[183] The Commission anticipated holding proceedings to decide the core issues posed in each such sub-category. The resulting awards were expected to establish precedents that could be applied to all claims in the same sub-category, utilizing mass claims techniques such as random sampling.[184]

In its Decision Number 2, the Commission added a sixth category, namely "Claims of Governments for loss, damage or injury."[185] Any claims in Category 6, and those claims in Categories 1 to 5 seeking to prove *actual damages* or otherwise requiring individual consideration, had to be filed as individual claims requiring individualized review under Chapter Two of the Rules of Procedure.[186]

Eligible claimants

Under the 12 December 2000 Agreement, all claims must be submitted by one of the Governments party to the Agreement, either on its own behalf or on behalf of its nationals, including both natural and juridical persons.[187] The Agreement also authorizes each Government to file claims on behalf of persons of Eritrean or Ethiopian origin who may not be its nationals. The Commission

---

[181] EECC Rules of Procedure, Article 30, paragraph 1; see also EECC Decision Number 2: Claims Categories, Forms and Procedures (July 24, 2001), available at www.pca-cpa.org, adding a 6th Category for "Claims of Governments for loss, damage or injury."

[182] EECC Decision Number 5: Multiple Claims in the Mass Claims Process, Fixed-Sum Compensation at the $500 and $1500 Levels, Multiplier for Household Claims (29 August 2001), available at www.pca-cpa.org.   [183] EECC Rules of Procedure, Article 31.

[184] See further section 5.06(h) below on mass claims techniques.

[185] EECC Decision Number 2: Claims Categories, Forms and Procedures (24 July 2001), available at www.pca-cpa.org.

[186] Ibid. See also EECC Rules of Procedure, Article 30, paragraph 2.

[187] Eritrea–Ethiopia Agreement of 12 December 2000, Article 5, paragraph 8.

is to consider these on the same basis as claims submitted on behalf of the party's nationals.[188] This provision was added to provide for a significant number of persons of Eritrean origin initially resident in Ethiopia who left that State under circumstances alleged to have been in violation of international law, but who were not nationals of Eritrea or whose nationality was in dispute. Statements of Claim are required to specify whether a particular claimant is "the government of a Party or an agency of such government, whether the claim is solely of that government or agency or whether it includes the claims of persons, and, if the latter, the identification of such persons, including their names, places of residence and nationalities."[189]

The Commission and the two Government parties devoted considerable attention to possible procedures for mass claims involving families or other groups of related persons. All agreed that it would be desirable to have procedures creating an option for collection of such claims, although in practice neither party ultimately had time to utilize those procedures. The Commission concluded that "household" was a more appropriate and workable concept than "family" for these purposes. It established a framework for collecting mass claims for wrongful expulsion or wrongful displacement (Categories 1 and 2) based on households, as these events often appeared to have affected members of a household collectively. Mass claims for other types of injury or loss suffered by individuals would be collected on an individual basis.

Drawing on the parties' advice regarding social realities in each of the countries, the Commission adopted the following working definition of "household": a mother and/or father, their children under the age of eighteen and other individuals under the age of eighteen who reside with them and are considered their dependants.[190] Under this definition, a household could be as few as two persons, but it could include many more. The Commission also sought a reasonable balance between over-complicating the Claims Process and preventing abuses in the collection of household claims. It anticipated requiring proof of actual size of the household to be verified by the claims-collector, who would also verify that no person included in the household would file a claim individually or be included in any other household claim.

The Commission made several other preliminary decisions regarding procedures for household claims. It decided that the amount of lump sum compensation for household claims for wrongful expulsion and for wrongful displacement should be three times the amount authorized for an individual.

---

[188] Eritrea–Ethiopia Agreement of 12 December 2000, Article 5, paragraph 9.
[189] EECC Rules of Procedure, Article 24, paragraph 3(b).
[190] EECC non-published internal guidelines.

It also decided to allow household claims for expulsion even if some members of the household were not expelled; not to allow both a household expulsion claim and an individual expulsion claim for a member of that household; and that a person's age at the time of expulsion controls, so that a person under eighteen years of age at the time of expulsion would fall within the household even if he or she was over eighteen at the time of filing the claims.[191]

The 12 December 2000 Agreement and the Rules of Procedure and the Decisions issued to date do not refer specifically to heirs of claimants. As the parties filed their claims as Government-to-Government claims, the position of heirs has not been addressed by the Commission. The issue of heirs may have to be resolved at the damages phase of the Claims Process. Experience in other Claims Processes suggests that the availability of sufficient funds to pay all claims may be considered in this regard.

(i) Humanitarian insurance Claims Process administered by the Jewish Claims Conference (JCC) for the International Commission on Holocaust Era Insurance Claims (ICHEIC)

Types of claims

Eligible claims in the ICHEIC Claims Process were those for unpaid Holocaust era life insurance. Any claims submitted after the deadline for filing claims, 31 March 2004, were ineligible for compensation. Claims received by ICHEIC that did not name a specific insurance company or included information that could be matched with either ICHEIC's internal research database or the records of any MOU Company (unnamed and unmatched claims) were forwarded to the 8A1 humanitarian Claims Process. JCC evaluated the claims and any supporting documentation, and if such materials demonstrated, in accordance with ICHEIC standards, that an uncompensated policy may have existed, the claim was eligible for a US$1,000 award.

Claims which asserted that policies were held in certain parts of the Former Soviet Union were deemed ineligible for review by ICHEIC for historical reasons, as citizens of such States were, in the period before the Nazi seizures, unable to acquire private insurance policies or maintain preexisting policies. Policies which were held in Former Soviet Union States where such policies could have been acquired were, however, submitted for review by the JCC.

---

[191] EECC Decision Number 5: Multiple Claims Process, Fixed-Sum Compensation at the $500 and $1,500 Levels, Multiplier for Household Claims (29 August 2001), paragraph C. Available at www.pca-cpa.org.

Eligible claimants

Eligible claimants in the 8A1 humanitarian Claims Process included, but were not limited to, beneficiaries of life insurance policies that existed during the Holocaust era. Heirs and even distant relatives of beneficiaries could also be eligible.

Only one award was granted per successful *claimant* in the 8A1 humanitarian Claims Process, regardless of the number of claims submitted or the number of policies alleged to have existed.

(j) American Arbitration Association (AAA)—an illustrative case

Eligible claimants in the illustrative case had all purchased a particular type of insurance from one insurance company (the defendant in the class action), during a specific time period. All of the policies that were the subject of the class action lawsuit had been sold to United States nationals. Heirs of persons who purchased the policies were also eligible to be claimants.

1.05 Remedies

The remedies available in the Claims Process. Whether the amounts of individual compensation for various claimants, or categories of claimants, are included in the constituting instruments or rules. Whether there is a maximum aggregate amount to be paid pursuant to the Claims Process and, if there is such a maximum amount, whether the expenses of the Claims Process are included when computing the maximum amount, and the method of distribution of any funds remaining after all individual claims are paid. (Note that the remedies may have an impact on the mass claims methodologies used to process the claims.)

Editors' Commentary

The remedies provided by the Mass Claims Processes described in this book fall into two main categories: (i) monetary compensation, for breach of contract and expropriation (e.g., the Iran–United States Claims Tribunal (Iran–US CT)), and to compensate former slave or forced laborers from the Holocaust era (e.g., the German Forced Labour Compensation Programme (GFLCP) and the Holocaust Victim Assets Programme (HVAP) administered by the International Organization for Migration); or (ii) restitution, for example, of assets in dormant bank accounts (e.g., by the Claims Resolution Tribunal for Dormant Accounts in Switzerland (CRT-I)), or of real property losses (by the Commission for Real Property Claims of Displaced Persons and Refugees (CRPC) in Bosnia and Herzegovina, and the Housing and Property Claims Commission (HPCC) in Kosovo).[192] Some Claims Processes also provide for a range of remedies, as the Eritrea–Ethiopia Claims Commission (EECC), which indicates in principle that the remedy to be awarded in its cases will be monetary compensation but does not foreclose the possibility of providing other types of remedies in appropriate cases. The Iran–US CT, in addition to monetary damages, has ordered specific performance in a few cases where it considered that remedy appropriate.

Some Claims Processes for humanitarian reasons provide fixed sums of money to deserving claimants who cannot demonstrate a legal entitlement to compensation, such as, for example, the 8A1 humanitarian Claims Process under the International Commission on Holocaust Era Insurance Claims (ICHEIC), and certain humanitarian programs funded by the German Foundation "Remembrance, Responsibility and Future."[193]

Generally, the Claims Processes described in this book provide for no maximum aggregate amount that may be awarded for successful claims. Exceptions are the second Claims Resolution Tribunal (CRT-II) in Switzerland, as to which a maximum aggregate amount of US$800 million is available for payment of awards, interest, and costs of conducting the Claims Process, and the two Claims Processes implemented by IOM, respectively, under the German Foundation Act, and the Settlement Agreement in the class action known as the Holocaust Victim Assets Litigation.[194]

---

[192] The IOM Property Claims Commission, however, awards monetary compensation for persecution-related property losses suffered during the National Socialist era. See sub-section 1.05(g) below on the German Forced Labour Compensation Programme.

[193] A special remedy is available to certain groups of beneficiaries in the two Holocaust-related Claims Processes implemented by IOM: it would consist of a lump sum allocation, e.g., to community organizations for humanitarian payments or in-kind assistance, because determining the amount of compensation for individuals would involve such high costs that it would not be feasible. Such humanitarian payments were determined through application of the "*cy pres*" doctrine (meaning as close a remedy as possible) by the U.S. federal district court supervising the class action known as the Holocaust Victim Assets Litigation, and through the allocation of a certain amount under the German Foundation Act for the German Forced Labour Compensation Programme.

[194] For a discussion of costs and the sources of funds to pay the costs of the various Claims Processes, see sections 5.03 (costs incurred by parties) and 7.03 (source of funds to pay for the Claims Process) below. For a discussion of awards of interest, see section 5.11 below.

(a) Iran–United States Claims Tribunal (Iran–US CT)—claims relating to the 1979 Islamic Revolution

The Iran–US CT generally awards monetary compensation, but it may order other forms of relief, including injunctions and specific performance, if it determines that it is justified. Amounts of awards are decided on a case-by-case basis. There is no maximum aggregate amount that can be paid pursuant to this Claims Process.

(b) United Nations Compensation Commission (UNCC)—claims relating to the 1990–1991 Gulf War

As its name would indicate, the remedy under the UNCC Claims Process is monetary compensation. The panels of Commissioners who reviewed the claims recommended the amounts of compensation to the Commission's Governing Council. The Council reviewed the amounts and, where it determined that the circumstances so required, could increase or reduce them.[195] The Governing Council set fixed and maximum amounts that could be awarded for certain categories of claims,[196] but there was no maximum aggregate amount that could be paid pursuant to the Claims Process.

Thus, in category "A", persons who departed from Iraq or Kuwait between 2 August 1990 and 2 March 1991 received a fixed sum of US$2,500, with a cap of US$5,000 per family. In category "B" for serious personal injury or loss of a spouse, child, or parent, a fixed sum of US$2,500 was awarded to successful claimants. Cumulative awards under categories "A" and "B" claims were allowed up to a cap of US$10,000 for personal injury affecting one family. For claims in category "C", covering various types of individual losses such as departure costs, real property losses, loss of income or support, or business losses, there were no fixed amounts, nor were fixed sums awarded in categories "D", "E" or "F" (individual claims in excess of US$100,000; corporate claims, and government claims, respectively). There was, however, a cap for non-pecuniary damages for mental pain and anguish for the category "C" and "D" claims, and a cap of

---

[195] UNCC Provisional Rules, Article 40, paragraph 1.

[196] UNCC Governing Council Decision 1 of 2 August 1991, *Criteria for Expedited Processing of Urgent Claims*, U.N. Doc. S/AC.26/1991/1 (2 August 1991), paragraphs 10–13, establishing fixed amounts for certain claimants. See also Governing Council Decision 225 of 2 July 2004, *Filing of "late" claims of the "bedoun"*, U.N. Doc. S/AC.26/Dec.225 (2004) (2 July 2004), establishing the fixed sum of US$2,500 for those "*bedoun*" who met the eligibility criteria established by the Council.

US$100,000 for awards in category "C".[197] The panels of Commissioners made a case-by-case determination as to the value of these losses.

(c) Commission for Real Property Claims of Displaced Persons and Refugees (CRPC)—claims relating to the 1992–1995 war in Bosnia and Herzegovina

The CRPC Claims Process was a real property restitution program. When the constituting instrument, the Dayton Peace Agreement, was negotiated, two basic remedies were envisioned: (i) the return of the claimed real property into possession of the claimant, or the setting aside of a wartime sale or transfer concluded under duress, with restitution of that which had been exchanged;[198] and (ii) monetary compensation in lieu of return of the lost property, or a compensation bond issued for the future purchase of real estate.[199]

During the course of the Claims Process, however, it became clear that no funds were available for compensation payments and that no monetary awards would be made to claimants. As a result, successful claimants could either return into possession of the property or engage in lawful transactions on the private property market. It also soon became clear that the planned compensation fund could not be replenished at sufficient levels through income-producing activities of the CRPC, as had been envisaged in Annex 7 of the Dayton Agreement.[200] Such activities would have required a certain level of market activity and capital from buyers, which was non-existent in the devastated economy of Bosnia and Herzegovina. Furthermore, the CRPC never found it feasible to issue the compensation bonds contemplated in Annex 7.[201] These factors, combined with the limited funds available to set up and run the CRPC's decision-making work, resulted in the compensation fund never coming into existence; the property was not evaluated and no compensation

---

[197] See UNCC Governing Council Decision 3 of 18 October 1991, *Personal Injury and Mental Pain and Anguish*, U.N. Doc. S/AC.26/1991/3 (23 October 1991), and Decision 8 of 24 January 1992, *Determination of Ceilings for Compensation for Mental Pain and Anguish*, U.N. Doc. S/AC.26/1992/8 (27 January 1992).

[198] Dayton Peace Agreement, Annex 7, Article XII, paragraphs 2 and 3.

[199] Ibid., Article XI and Article XII, paragraphs 2 and 5.

[200] Ibid., Article XIV ("The Fund shall be replenished through the purchase, sale, lease and mortgage of real property which is the subject of claims before the Commission. It may also be replenished by direct payments from the Parties, or from contributions by States or international or nongovernmental organizations").

[201] Ibid., Article XII, paragraph 6. See also CRPC End of Mandate Report, Annex B—*Annex 7 Compensation Fund Unrealised.*

was paid.[202] Hence, there was no issue of a maximum aggregate amount to be paid out. The CRPC's decisions, however, serve the useful purpose of providing formal recognition of property title.

(d) Claims Resolution Tribunal for Dormant Accounts in Switzerland (CRT-I)—first claims tribunal for assets deposited in Swiss banks

The only remedy available under the CRT-I Claims Process was restitution of the amount of the dormant accounts to their rightful owners or their heirs. Such amounts were adjusted to add interest and to compensate for bank fees that had been charged to the account, both computed in accordance with the Rules of Procedure, which also took account of inflation. There was no maximum remedy for any category of claims and no maximum aggregate amount payable pursuant to the Claims Process.

(e) Claims Resolution Tribunal (CRT-II)—second claims tribunal for assets deposited in Swiss banks

Restitution of assets is the remedy available under the CRT-II Claims Process. In cases where the amount of the assets in the dormant account owned by a victim of Nazi persecution is known, claimants are awarded the amount of the deposit, adjusted for unpaid interest, inflation, and bank fees charged since 1945. In cases where the amount of the assets in the account is not known, the CRT-II Governing Rules include a schedule of presumed amounts, based on the amount that was typical of similar accounts held in Swiss banks during the relevant period. In contrast to CRT-I, where neither the constituting instrument nor Rules of Procedure provided for an aggregate maximum amount that could be paid pursuant to the Claims Process, for CRT-II, the Settlement Agreement in the class action known as the Holocaust Victim Assets Litigation limits aggregate payments for Swiss bank accounts to a total of US$800 million, including both the awards and the expenses of running the Claims Process.

According to the Plan of Allocation and Distribution proposed by the Special Master and approved by the Court overseeing the class action settlement, in the event that any residual funds remain unclaimed from the US$800 million allocated to the Deposited Assets Class, a portion of the remaining funds can be allocated to cultural, memorial or educational projects that have been proposed to the Special Master.[203] The Court, in November 2003,

---

[202] See CRPC End of Mandate Report, Annex B—*Annex 7 Compensation Fund Unrealised*.
[203] Plan of Allocation and Distribution, pp. 19–20.

requested proposals on suggested uses for such potential residual funds.[204] Numerous proposals were received, but the Court later observed that there was insufficient data to estimate how much, if any, of the US$800 million would be paid out by CRT-II, partly because of restricted access to information concerning approximately 4.1 million Holocaust era accounts that had not yet been published.[205] In order to ensure that the claimants in the Deposited Assets Class—whose claims, according to the Court, had the greatest legal merit among the settlement classes in the class action—the Court decided to postpone any decision on the use of residual funds until such time as CRT-II has had the opportunity to decide all claims to Holocaust era bank accounts, published or as yet unpublished.[206]

(f) Housing and Property Claims Commission (HPCC)—claims relating to the 1999 conflict in Kosovo

The HPCC Claims Process is essentially a property restitution program. Monetary compensation is only available in category "A" (claims of natural persons whose property rights were revoked by discriminatory legislation) in instances where the claimed property cannot be restored to the rightful owner because it has been sold in the interim period to a third party.[207] The remedies available otherwise are: restitution (category "A"); an order for registration of ownership in the appropriate public record (category "B"); or an order for

---

[204] See Special Master's Interim Report on Distribution and Recommendations for Allocation of Unclaimed Residual Funds, 2 October 2003, available at www.swissbankclaims.com, and Order of the Court adopting the Special Master's 2 October 2003 recommendations, *In re Holocaust Victim Assets Litig.*, No. CV 9604849, slip. op. at 2 (E.D.N.Y. Nov. 17, 2003).

[205] See *In re Holocaust Victim Assets Litig.*, 302 F.Supp.2d 59 (E.D.N.Y. February 19, 2004), opinion amended and superseded by *In re Holocaust Victim Assets Litig.*, 319 F.Supp.2d 301 (E.D.N.Y. June 1, 2004)(concerning Swiss banks and access to information).

[206] See Special Master's Recommendations for Allocation of Possible Unclaimed Residual Funds, April 16, 2004, available at www.swissbankclaims.com; and *In re Holocaust Victim Assets Litig.*, 302 F.Supp.2d 89 (E.D.N.Y. March 9, 2004)(opinion addressing legal strength of Deposited Assets Class claims and examining relative needs among survivor groups), *aff'd* 424 F.3d 132 (C.A.2 (N.Y.) September 9, 2005).

[207] See UNMIK Regulation 2000/60, sections 3.3 and 4.4–4.5. But see section 4.2, regarding category "A" claims and related category "C" claims for repossession, where a claim affects a so-called "First Owner"—i.e., a current owner of a socially owned apartment purchased from the allocation right holder under the Law on Housing. In such cases, the claimant is to pay a fair purchase price (as determined in section 4.2(a)) into a trust fund maintained by HPD, out of which a First Owner losing the ownership of the apartment can be compensated by the Directorate for "the amount s/he paid for the purchase of the apartment, a percentage of the current market value of the apartment, as determined by the Directorate, as well as for the cost of any improvements s/he made to the apartment" (section 4.2(c)).

repossession (category "C"),[208] with respect to which UNMIK Regulation 2000/60 states that "[a]ny refugee or displaced person with a right to property has a right to return to the property, or to dispose of it in accordance with the law . . . ."[209]

No remedies other than those provided for in the governing UNMIK Regulation may be awarded,[210] and the Commission is allowed to "limit its decision to rights of possession of the claimed property where that would provide an effective remedy for the claim."[211] The Claims Process has no maximum aggregate amount of payments that can be made.

(g) Mass Claims Processes administered by the International Organization for Migration (IOM)

German Forced Labour Compensation Programme (GFLCP)—claims against Germany and German industry for Nazi injustice

The remedy available for slave and forced labor claims in the GFLCP Claims Process is monetary compensation.[212] Out of the DM 10 billion Settlement Fund described in section 1.01(g) above, an overall aggregate amount of DM 8.1 billion has been allocated for the payment of claims, with specific base amounts (so-called "*plafonds*") allotted to each of the seven partner organizations implementing the German Foundation Act. Each partner organization has to cover its expenses for running the Process from its *plafonds*.[213]

Except for property claims lodged with the Property Claims Commission, a maximum amount of individual compensation for each category of claims is specified in the German Foundation Act.[214] Each of the partner organizations may, for certain types of claims, create sub-categories of claims based on the severity of the fate of the claimant, for which different (lower) amounts of compensation may be paid. This requires the approval by the Foundation's Board of Trustees.[215] The partner organizations may also use the so-called "opening clause" in the Foundation Act to award compensation, with the Foundation's approval, to other victims of Nazi crimes than are defined in the Act.[216] Payments under the opening clause must, however, come from the funds allocated in the German Foundation Act to each partner organization

---

[208] UNMIK Regulation 2000/60, sections 2–4. Section 2.2 provides that "[r]estitution may take the form of restoration of the property right (. . . 'restitution in kind') or compensation."

[209] Ibid., section 2.5.   [210] Ibid., section 22.3.   [211] Ibid., section 22.5.

[212] However, from the German Foundation Fund, an amount of DM 300 million has been allocated for social programs for the benefit of Holocaust survivors. This humanitarian assistance may be provided in cash or in kind. See German Foundation Act, section 9, paragraph 4, number 4.

[213] Ibid., section 9, paragraph 1.   [214] Ibid., section 9, paragraph 1.

[215] Ibid., section 9, paragraph 8.

[216] The opening clause is section 11, paragraph 1, sentences 2–3, of the German Foundation Act.

(its *plafonds*), and they must not reduce the payments for the highest category of slave labor claimants.[217] In practice, due to the high number of claimants falling within its jurisdiction, the IOM has not resorted to the opening clause but rather awarded the maximum amount of available compensation to each successful claimant. The one exception to this is that IOM used the opening clause for forced labor in agriculture in order to treat those claimants consistently with what a number of other partner organizations had done.

Despite provisions in the constituting instrument and the Agreement between the Governments of the United States and Germany that contemplated the reallocation of any excess funds among the partner organizations with the aim of providing equal levels of payments for slave and forced laborers,[218] it was clear from the outset that the *plafonds* allocated to IOM would not be sufficient to pay all its claimants the full amount of compensation. This has now been confirmed: even after the allocation of a portion of the interest accrued in the Compensation Fund, there is a shortfall in IOM's funding, and, as result, IOM has had to reduce the compensation payments to heirs. Where victims died after receiving the first instalment payment, heirs will receive no further payment.

Compensation payments under GFLCP are exempt from inheritance, income, or gift tax and are not supposed to lead to a reduction of income which claimants may receive from social security or health care systems in the countries where they reside.[219]

The IOM Property Claims Commission awarded compensation for persecution-related property losses out of the DM 200 million allocated to such losses under the German Foundation Act.[220]

Holocaust Victim Assets Programme (HVAP)—claims pursuant to 1999 class action Settlement

The only remedy available under the HVAP Claims Process is monetary compensation.[221]

A maximum amount of individual compensation for each category of claims is specified in the Plan of Allocation and Distribution approved by the United States federal district court in the class action known as the Holocaust Victim

---

[217] German Foundation Act, section 11, paragraph 1, sentences 2 and 3.

[218] See U.S.–German Agreement, Annex A, paragraph 4, and German Foundation Act, section 9, paragraph 9.

[219] Ibid., section 11, paragraph 4, and section 15, paragraph 1.

[220] See ibid., section 9, paragraph 4, sentences 1 and 2, and IOM Property Commission Supplemental Rules, sections 17.1 and 18.2.

[221] From the Swiss Banks Settlement Fund, an amount of US$100 million has been allocated for two "*cy pres*" (meaning as close a remedy as possible) payments to compensate members of the Looted

Assets Litigation.[222] While the overall amount of the Settlement Fund in the class action is an established figure,[223] no maximum aggregate amount has been set for the various claims categories.

The expenses of the HVAP Claims Process are paid out of the Settlement Fund.[224]

The Plan of Allocation and Distribution originally provided for allocation and distribution of payments in two stages. "Stage 1" payments were to include compensation to surviving Nazi victims (and certain heirs of victims who died on or after 16 February 1999) as well as expenses of the Claims Process. In the event that any portion of the Settlement Fund remained after "Stage 1" payments, it was envisioned that additional "Stage 2" payments would be made to surviving Nazi victims and potentially to needy spouses and children of deceased Nazi victims.[225] In practice, the idea of a two-stage payment process was abandoned early in the Claims Process in favor of a one-time payment of higher fixed amounts to eligible claimants. As of 31 January 2006, payments had only been made to actual survivors. Eligible legal successors of victims who died on or after 16 February 1999 began to receive payments in 2006.

(h) Eritrea–Ethiopia Claims Commission (EECC)—claims relating to the 1998–2000 war between Eritrea and Ethiopia

There is no ceiling on either the amount of individual claims or on the total amounts that may potentially be awarded by the EECC Claims Process.

In its early stages, the Commission and the Government parties considered whether the Commission could indicate interim measures or provide other types of relief in addition to awards of compensation. In Decision Number 3, the Commission decided that:

" . . . in principle, the appropriate remedy for valid claims submitted to it should be monetary compensation. However, the Commission does not foreclose the possibility of providing other types of remedies in appropriate cases, if the particular remedy can be

Assets Class; one to benefit the neediest survivors of Nazi persecution, and a second to benefit all members of the Looted Assets Class and all the other classes. See Plan of Allocation and Distribution, p. 23. US$10 million of this amount are distributed by IOM to Roma, Jehovah's Witnesses, homosexuals, and handicapped; the rest by the Jewish Claims Conference to Jewish survivors. This humanitarian assistance to the neediest survivors of Nazi persecution may be provided in cash or in kind. See Plan of Allocation and Distribution, pp. 25 and 118.

[222] Ibid., p. 30 (Slave Labor Class I), p. 34 (Slave Labor Class II), p. 37 (Refugee Class).

[223] See section 1.01(g) above, on the background of the Settlement.

[224] Plan of Allocation and Distribution, p. 19; Settlement Agreement, section 7.5.

[225] Plan of Allocation and Distribution, p. 19. It was recommended that a portion of the remaining funds also be allocated to some of the cultural, memorial, or educational projects for which proposals have been submitted to the Special Master.

shown to be in accordance with international practice, and if the Tribunal determines that a particular remedy would be reasonable and appropriate in the circumstances."[226]

Prior to this Decision, some Commissioners expressed concern that large cash awards to individuals might not be the appropriate or optimum response to aspects of the social and economic disruption caused by the conflict between the two States. They asked whether other types of remedies more closely aimed at re-establishing the social and economic infrastructure and resources of affected areas would not be of greater value in addressing the negative socio-economic impact of the crisis on the civilian population.

Neither the 12 December 2000 Agreement establishing the Commission nor its Rules of Procedure specify any amounts for individual compensation. However, the Commission made several Decisions during its early months that were intended to permit a system of simplified mass claims collection and processing, should either Government party desire to utilize such procedures. The Commission's Decision Number 2 authorized two possible tiers of fixed amount compensation linked to the type of evidence available to individual claimants in a mass claims procedure.[227] Decision Number 5 then established that the level of fixed-sum compensation would be US$500 per individual in the first tier, and US$1,500 per individual in the second tier. The US$500 amount was authorized for persons (including juridical persons) for whom there is simple evidence showing that they belong to a category entitled to receive compensation under the Commission's rulings. The larger amount was authorized for persons able to produce additional evidence sufficient in the circumstances to show damages or injury of a higher amount. In setting these sums, the Commission took into account that the parties could file multiple claims on behalf of an individual in the mass claims procedure.[228] The Commission also was concerned that the levels must not be unreasonably high and that they must be capable of implementation in light of the circumstances of the parties.

(i) Humanitarian insurance Claims Process administered by the Jewish Claims Conference (JCC) for the International Commission on Holocaust Era Insurance Claims (ICHEIC)

While the 8A1 humanitarian Claims Process was designed to issue a humanitarian award in acknowledgment of the likelihood that a claimant may have had an insurance policy, the fixed humanitarian award payment of US$1,000 was

---

[226] EECC Decision Number 3: Remedies (24 July 2001), available at www.pca-cpa.org.

[227] EECC Decision Number 2: Claims Categories, Forms and Procedures (24 July 2001), Part B. Available at www.pca-cpa.org.

[228] EECC Decision Number 5: Multiple Claims Process, Fixed-Sum Compensation at the $500 and $1500 Levels, Multiplier for Household Claims (29 August 2001), Part B. Available at www.pca-cpa.org.

not set by ICHEIC until shortly after the 8A1 training phase for claims analysts began. Once it became clear what amount of funds ICHEIC would have available from the various settlements reached with insurance companies participating in the overall ICHEIC Claims Process, and that those funds would be sufficient to make humanitarian payments, the US$1,000 amount was fixed by ICHEIC and it is not subject to any possible subsequent change or adjustment.

(j) American Arbitration Association (AAA)—an illustrative case

Awards in the illustrative case were monetary compensation prescribed by a formula, but remedies involving individuals' insurance policies ranged from opportunities to purchase more insurance, to payment in full of the individuals' policy. Claims were processed in two stages, or "levels." At the first level, based on minimal documentation, a grid established the awards that were available based on the amount lost. A second level offered the claimants a simplified alternative dispute resolution process, handled by representatives of the defendant insurance company.

At the appeals level, which was the portion of the Claims Process handled by AAA Arbitrators, monetary ranges were prescribed for the amount of awards. There was no "cap" on the amount for which the defendant was responsible. Only the law firm representing claimants was given a cap, which meant that it had to provide representation for all claimants within the budget to which it had originally agreed. The defendant paid AAA's fees, the fees of the Arbitrators, and all expenses of the Claims Process, in addition to the awards.

1.06 Location

Where the Claims Process is physically located. Whether the location is a neutral place. Legal and practical aspects.

Editors' Commentary

A widely-accepted principle in international dispute resolution is that it is strongly preferable for a commission or arbitral tribunal to be located in a "neutral" place, i.e., a locale where none of the parties has its principal residence or business headquarters or is a national. This principle has been followed in the Mass Claims Processes described in this book, with the exceptions noted below, whether they resolve claims through arbitration or in an administrative procedure.

The Claims Processes described in this book that have not followed the principle of neutral location are (i) the two Claims Resolution Tribunals for dormant accounts in Swiss banks (CRT-I and CRT-II), which faced national laws prohibiting bank records from being removed outside of Switzerland, and (ii) the two Claims Processes for real property claims in the former Yugoslavia (CRPC and HPCC), which were located in Bosnia and Herzegovina and Kosovo, respectively, for strong practical reasons: the claimants, the properties that were the subjects of the claims, and the relevant public land records were all located there. In the light of those circumstances, it was thought to be highly impractical to conduct those Claims Processes elsewhere.

(a) Iran–United States Claims Tribunal (Iran–US CT)—claims relating to the 1979 Islamic Revolution

The seat of the Iran–US CT, as mandated by the Claims Settlement Declaration,[229] is The Hague, the Netherlands, a neutral locale where the United States and Iran each maintains an Embassy.

(b) United Nations Compensation Commission (UNCC)—claims relating to the 1990–1991 Gulf War

Pursuant to United Nations Security Council Resolution 692 (1991), adopting the recommendations of the United Nations Secretary-General, the UNCC is located at the United Nations Office in Geneva, Switzerland. Geneva is considered to be a neutral locale, and most of the governments and international organizations submitting claims maintain permanent missions and offices there.[230]

(c) Commission for Real Property Claims of Displaced Persons and Refugees (CRPC)—claims relating to the 1992–1995 war in Bosnia and Herzegovina

The Executive Secretariat of the CRPC was located in Sarajevo, but because of the limited freedom of movement in post-war Bosnia and Herzegovina, the Commission immediately established regional offices in the Bosnian-, Croat-, and

---

[229] Claims Settlement Declaration, Article VI, paragraph 1, provides that the Tribunal may also be located at "any other place agreed by Iran or the United States."

[230] UN Security Council Resolution 692 (1991), U.N. Doc. S/RES/692 (1991) (20 May 1991), paragraph 3, deciding "that the Governing Council will be located at the United Nations Office at Geneva and that the Governing Council may decide whether some of the activities of the Commission should be carried out elsewhere."

Serb-dominated parts of the country. It subsequently opened offices in Croatia, Serbia and Montenegro, and various other locations in Europe in order to serve the refugee population located in those countries.[231] Being a Claims Process charged with deciding claims for real property, it was essential that the Commission's staff have easy access to local property registers, all the affected parties, and the actual property sites for on-site inspections. Setting up the Claims Process in a distant locale would thus not have been a practical option.

(d) Claims Resolution Tribunal for Dormant Accounts in Switzerland (CRT-I)—first claims tribunal for assets deposited in Swiss banks

CRT-I was located in Zurich, Switzerland. All of the dormant accounts were in Swiss banks. The Claims Process was constituted by an arbitration agreement between the Swiss banks and a non-governmental organization, the Independent Committee of Eminent Persons (ICEP), located in Switzerland. As such, the Tribunal could only be formed with the agreement of the Swiss banks, who, it is understood, insisted on locating the Claims Process in Switzerland where the bank records and personnel were located. Further, Swiss law requires that certain bank records be kept in Switzerland, and that might have created serious practical problems had the Tribunal been located elsewhere.

(e) Claims Resolution Tribunal (CRT-II)—second claims tribunal for assets deposited in Swiss banks

The CRT-II Claims Process is located in Zurich, Switzerland, and all of the listed accounts are in Swiss banks. CRT-II is the successor of CRT-I and it inherited the institutional structure, personnel, and know-how from CRT-I, including, at its inception, the CRT-I Arbitrators who were to serve as Senior Claims Judges for CRT-II. However, in the summer of 2002, CRT-II announced a number of procedural and organizational changes influenced by new information which suggested that there had been significantly more Swiss bank transfers of Nazi victim accounts to Nazi authorities than was earlier thought.[232] The Governing Rules of CRT-II were modified so that CRT-II staff attorneys would make recommendations in Zurich regarding claimants' rights to Swiss bank accounts, to be sent to the United States District Court for

---

[231] CRPC had offices in Croatia, Denmark, Germany, the Netherlands, Norway, Serbia and Montenegro, and Sweden.

[232] See CRT-II Press Release of 15 July 2002, *New Actions to Expedite Claims Processing*, available at www.crt-ii.org.

the Eastern District of New York for payment by the Special Masters, subject to the approval by the Court. Compensation to claimants is paid out of the Settlement Fund in New York.[233]

In 2004, an additional CRT-II office was opened in New York at the premises of the Conference on Jewish Material Claims Against Germany (the "Jewish Claims Conference" (JCC)), where JCC attorneys and claims analysts review and make recommendations to the Court on certain CRT-II claims.

(f) Housing and Property Claims Commission (HPCC)—claims relating to the 1999 conflict in Kosovo

The headquarters of the Housing and Property Directorate (HPD) and the seat of the Commission are located in Pristina, Kosovo, with regional and field offices elsewhere. Just as the Commission for Real Property Claims of Displaced Persons and Refugees (CRPC) in Bosnia and Herzegovina, discussed in section 1.06(c) above, HPCC is a real property Claims Process and as such needs access to local property registers, affected parties, and the actual property sites for on-site inspections.[234]

(g) Mass Claims Processes administered by the International Organization for Migration (IOM)

German Forced Labour Compensation Programme (GFLCP)—claims against Germany and German industry for Nazi injustice

Although the seat of the German Foundation, under whose authority IOM implements this Claims Process, is Berlin, Germany, five national partner organizations have their seat in their respective countries (Belarus, the Czech Republic, Poland, Russia, and Ukraine); and the Conference on Jewish Material Claims against Germany (JCC) has its seat in the United States. IOM runs the GFLCP Claims Process out of its own headquarters in Geneva, Switzerland, and it has also used its field offices in almost sixty countries during various phases of activities.

Holocaust Victim Assets Programme (HVAP)—claims pursuant to 1999 class action Settlement

The Court supervising the implementation of HVAP is the United States District Court for the Eastern District of New York, located in New York City. The Claims Process is managed from IOM's offices in Geneva, and IOM has

---

[233] See CRT-II Governing Rules, Introduction.
[234] See also section 6.05(f) below, on establishing satellite offices for HPCC.

also used many of its field offices to assist with outreach and claims intake as part of the Claims Process.[235]

(h) Eritrea–Ethiopia Claims Commission (EECC)—claims relating to the 1998–2000 war between Eritrea and Ethiopia

The two Government parties agreed in the 12 December 2000 Agreement that the EECC Claims Process be located in a neutral place, The Hague, the Netherlands, and the Commission's Rules of Procedure require that all of its awards be made there.[236] However, the Agreement also authorizes the Commission to hold hearings and conduct investigations in the territory of either party, or at other locations it deems expedient.[237] The Rules add that any persons appointed by the Commission may enter the territory of either Eritrea or Ethiopia to obtain information related to the Commission's work. The parties are to be given adequate notice so that representatives of both can be present at such visits or inspections, including measures required to permit participation by representatives of the other party.[238]

(i) Humanitarian insurance Claims Process administered by the Jewish Claims Conference (JCC) for the International Commission on Holocaust Era Insurance Claims (ICHEIC)

Prior to the launch of the 8A1 humanitarian Claims Process, most of the ICHEIC claims processing was conducted in Europe, and all insurance claim documents were also handled by the participating insurance companies (the MOU Companies) in Europe.

The claims evaluated in the 8A1 Claims Process were processed in New York City, taking advantage of the JCC's existing claims processing and administrative facilities and equipment. All relevant documentation was scanned into digital media and was reviewed and evaluated in electronic form, which obviated the need for physically removing paper records from the places where claims were collected and where insurance records were stored. This allowed the location of the Claims Process to be based on practical factors such as the

---

[235] Two other organizations participate in the implementation of the Settlement Agreement: claims of Jewish applicants in Slave Labor Class I and the Refugee Class are processed by the Jewish Claims Conference (JCC) in New York, and claims for deposited assets are processed by CRT-II in Zurich, Switzerland.   [236] EECC Rules of Procedure, Article 11, paragraph 1.
[237] Eritrea–Ethiopia Agreement of 12 December 2000, Article 5, paragraph 5.
[238] EECC Rules of Procedure, Article 11, paragraph 1.

availability of staff, equipment, and facilities, and access to the claimant population through the network and resources of the JCC.

(j) American Arbitration Association (AAA)—an illustrative case

The AAA headquarters are located in New York City, but the location was not really relevant in the illustrative case because, in the initial round of claims settlements, awards were made based on documents only. At the appeals level, which was the part of the Claims Process handled by the AAA, there was a mandatory telephonic mediation that preceded a separate telephonic arbitration. Both the mediations and the arbitrations were presided over by the same Arbitrator, and that Arbitrator could conduct the telephone conference from any location.

1.07 Privileges and Immunities

Whether privileges and immunities are provided for decision-makers and staff in the Claims Process.

Editors' Commentary

Each of the international Mass Claims Processes described in this book recognizes that it is highly desirable to protect those engaged in the Claims Process from interference by the State in which the Process is located, or from personal liability for acts done in performance of their duties. Accordingly, each Claims Process provides in its constituting instrument or procedural rules that decision-makers and staff engaged in the Claims Process will enjoy the benefit of diplomatic immunity and/or will be protected from personal liability for acts or omissions other than the consequences of conscious and deliberate wrongdoing. None of the Claims Processes described in this book include an express waiver of sovereign immunity.

(a) Iran–United States Claims Tribunal (Iran–US CT)—claims relating to the 1979 Islamic Revolution

The Members of the Tribunal and its Secretary-General enjoy the same privileges and immunities as the heads of diplomatic missions in the Netherlands. Immunities and privileges are accorded to staff members by the Government of the Netherlands in the interest of the Tribunal. These privileges and immunities furnish no excuse for non-performance of private obligations or failure to observe laws and police regulations.[239] Details are laid down in several exchanges of letters between the Tribunal and the Government of the Netherlands.

(b) United Nations Compensation Commission (UNCC)—claims relating to the 1990–1991 Gulf War

Pursuant to the UNCC Provisional Rules, Commissioners, when performing their functions for the Commission, had the status of "experts on mission" within the meaning of Article VI of the Convention on the Privileges and Immunities of the United Nations of 13 February 1946.[240] Staff members of the Commission's Secretariat are subject to the United Nations Staff Rules and Regulations. Higher officials of the Claims Process enjoy privileges and immunities equivalent to those of members of diplomatic missions in Geneva.

(c) Commission for Real Property Claims of Displaced Persons and Refugees (CRPC)—claims relating to the 1992–1995 war in Bosnia and Herzegovina

The international Commissioners and international staff of the CRPC were accorded the same privileges and immunities, respectively, as diplomatic agents and members of the staff of a diplomatic mission under the 1961 Vienna Convention on Diplomatic Relations.[241] This protection also extended to the families of the Commissioners and CRPC staff.[242] National Commissioners and staff enjoyed the immunities provided under the Vienna Convention to the extent necessary for them to fulfill their duties; they were not to be held criminally or civilly liable for any acts carried out in furtherance of their responsibilities.[243]

(d) Claims Resolution Tribunal for Dormant Accounts in Switzerland (CRT-I)—first claims tribunal for assets deposited in Swiss banks

The CRT-I Arbitrators were not liable to any party for any act or omission in connection with any Claims Resolution Process conducted under the CRT-I

---

[239] Iran–US CT Staff Rules, Article 1, paragraph 5.

[240] UNCC Provisional Rules, Article 26. See Convention on the Privileges and Immunities of the United Nations, 1 U.N.T.S. 15 (13 February 1946), Article VI.

[241] Vienna Convention on Diplomatic Relations of 18 April 1961, U.N.T.S. Nos 7310–7312.

[242] Dayton Peace Agreement, Annex 7, Article X, paragraph 3; CRPC Headquarters Agreement, Article 1, paragraph 3 (text not officially available).

[243] CRPC Headquarters Agreement, Article 2, paragraph 2 (text not officially available).

Rules of Procedure, except that they could be liable to a party for the consequences of conscious and deliberate wrongdoing. The liability of the Arbitrators was governed by Swiss law.[244] As this was a private Claims Process created by private parties, diplomatic immunity did not apply.

(e) Claims Resolution Tribunal (CRT-II)—second claims tribunal for assets deposited in Swiss banks

The CRT-II Governing Rules provide that, by filing a claim with CRT-II, a claimant agrees that the Special Masters, the members of CRT-II, including staff attorneys, members of the Secretariat, and persons acting under the direction of the Special Masters, the audit firms under the mandate of the Independent Committee of Eminent Persons (ICEP), and the participating banks, are not liable for acts or omissions in connection with any matter they conduct under the Rules; and that any issue as to any liability of such entities and persons is governed by United States federal law.[245] The Governing Rules also state that the above-mentioned provision "shall not prejudice the immunities granted to the ICEP entities under the terms of the Settlement Agreement of the Holocaust Victim Assets Litigation."[246] As this is a private Claims Process created by private parties, diplomatic immunity does not apply.

(f) Housing and Property Claims Commission (HPCC)—claims relating to the 1999 conflict in Kosovo

The HPCC Commissioners and the staff members of the Commission and the Housing and Property Directorate (HPD) are immune from criminal or civil proceedings for any acts carried out within the scope of their official duties.[247]

(g) Mass Claims Processes administered by the International Organization for Migration (IOM): *German Forced Labour Compensation Programme (GFLCP) for claims against Germany and German industry for Nazi injustice, and Holocaust Victim Assets Programme (HVAP) for claims pursuant to 1999 class action Settlement*

IOM enjoys the normal privileges and immunities of an international organization in the implementation of both the GFLCP and HVAP Claims

---

[244] CRT-I Rules of Procedure, Article 41.
[245] CRT-II Governing Rules, Article 44, paragraph 1.   [246] Ibid., Article 44, paragraph 2.
[247] UNMIK Regulation 2000/60, section 17.6.

Processes. IOM staff members working in the two Claims Processes are subject to the IOM Staff Rules and Regulations. According to IOM officials, higher officials of the Claims Process enjoy privileges and immunities equivalent to those of members of diplomatic missions in Geneva.

(h) Eritrea–Ethiopia Claims Commission (EECC)—claims relating to the 1998–2000 war between Eritrea and Ethiopia

The constituting instrument of EECC, the 12 December 2000 Agreement, requires both Government parties to accord to the Commissioners and the Commission's employees the privileges and immunities accorded to diplomatic agents under the 1961 Vienna Convention on Diplomatic Relations.[248] No waiver of sovereign immunity is provided in the Agreement or the Rules of Procedure.

The EECC operates with the support of the Permanent Court of Arbitration (PCA) in The Hague. The PCA's Headquarters Agreement with the Government of the Netherlands provides for immunities for arbitrators in proceedings administered by the PCA, or under its auspices, corresponding to those accorded to diplomatic agents. The EECC has held informal discussions with representatives of the Government of the Netherlands regarding its juridical position and the status of its Commissioners in the Netherlands, but no separate agreements or understandings have been concluded between the Commission and the Netherlands.

(i) Humanitarian insurance Claims Process administered by the Jewish Claims Conference (JCC) for the International Commission on Holocaust Era Insurance Claims (ICHEIC)

The JCC–ICHEIC Agreement included extensive provisions indemnifying the JCC against ICHEIC for any liability that it might incur, except in cases of gross negligence or willful misconduct. It was understood that the claims evaluation performed by JCC staff constituted merely a recommendation; authorization for payments resided with the Senior Counselor appointed by ICHEIC, *inter alia*, to oversee the payment procedures, although actual payments, for the sake of convenience, were executed by JCC Payment Operations staff.

---

[248] Eritrea–Ethiopia Agreement of 12 December 2000, Article 5, paragraph 18. See Vienna Convention on Diplomatic Relations of 18 April 1961, U.N.T.S. Nos 7310–7312.

(j) American Arbitration Association (AAA)—an illustrative case

The illustrative case involved United States claimants and a private United States insurance company and was thus an exclusively domestic process. Hence, domestic United States law determining liability applied, and the issue of diplomatic privileges and immunities did not arise.

1.08 Participation of Claimants in Planning

Whether representatives of the claimants take part in planning the Claims Process.

Editors' Commentary

The designers of the Mass Claims Processes described in this book generally did not conduct formal consultations with prospective parties concerning the planning of the organization and procedures of the respective Claims Processes, although, as noted below, in some cases the views and recommendations of claimants were expressed informally. An exception was where a State that was a potential party engaged in the negotiations for constituting the Claims Process. Another exception involved the two Claims Resolution Tribunals dealing with Swiss bank accounts (CRT-I and CRT-II). There, the Swiss banks on the one hand, and Jewish organizations on the other, participated in negotiating the agreements that established the Claims Processes. Moreover, in the case of CRT-II, the constituting instrument, the Settlement Agreement in the class action known as the Holocaust Victim Assets Litigation, had to be approved by the United States federal district court overseeing the class action, as to which United States law required that public notice be given so that interested parties might have the opportunity to express their views. Although victims covered by the German Forced Labour Compensation Programme (GFLCP) did not participate in establishing that Claims Process, a number of claimant representatives participated in setting up the German Foundation that created the Claims Process. Finally, in the American Arbitration Association (AAA) illustrative case, counsel for the plaintiffs and counsel for the defendant insurance company were actively and equally involved in all phases of the Claims Process, including the design of administrative procedures.

(a) Iran–United States Claims Tribunal (Iran–US CT)—claims relating to the 1979 Islamic Revolution

The two Government parties took part in the initial planning for the Iran–US CT Claims Process. Representatives of the private claimants did not participate directly as such, although some in the United States made their views and recommendations known to the United States Government. After the Tribunal was formed, the Agents appointed to the Tribunal by the two Government parties made proposals at various stages with respect to the planning and organization of the Tribunal and the drafting of the Tribunal Rules, taking into account any views that may have been expressed by claimants.

(b) United Nations Compensation Commission (UNCC)—claims relating to the 1990–1991 Gulf War

Representatives of the participating governments—other than Iraq—took part in the planning of the UNCC, but private claimants did not.

(c) Commission for Real Property Claims of Displaced Persons and Refugees (CRPC)—claims relating to the 1992–1995 war in Bosnia and Herzegovina

Representatives of the claimants did not take part in the planning of the CRPC. The Commission planned its own procedures without the involvement of the signatories of the Dayton Peace Agreement.

(d) Claims Resolution Tribunal for Dormant Accounts in Switzerland (CRT-I)—first claims tribunal for assets deposited in Swiss banks

Representatives of the largest group of potential claimants took part in the planning and implementation of CRT-I. Thus, the Memorandum of Understanding between the World Jewish Restitution Organization, the World Jewish Congress, and the Swiss Bankers Association resulted in the formation of an Independent Committee of Eminent Persons (ICEP) that included officials of those organizations. ICEP then established the Independent Claims Resolution Foundation (ICRF), with the Secretary-General of the World Jewish Congress as one of the three members of the Board of Trustees. The Board of Trustees then created CRT-I, planned and adopted its Rules of Procedure, appointed the Arbitrators, and employed Secretariat staff. Inasmuch as the same procedures governed all claimants equally, the participation in the planning process of a representative of the largest group of potential claimants effectively provided a voice for other claimants as well.

(e) Claims Resolution Tribunal (CRT-II)—second claims tribunal for assets deposited in Swiss banks

CRT-II arose out of the Settlement Agreement in the class action known as the Holocaust Victim Assets Litigation in the United States District Court for the Eastern District of New York, and from the subsequent Plan of Allocation and Distribution proposed by a Special Master and approved by the Court.[249] To the extent that the Settlement Agreement contributed to the planning of CRT-II, the representatives of the claimants took part therein. A number of them submitted comments and formal proposals to the Special Masters regarding the Plan of Allocation and Distribution, which contained proposals for the framework of CRT-II. The Special Masters met with claimant representatives to hear their views. There was also a hearing conducted by the Special Masters on the proposed Governing Rules.

Under the Governing Rules, the Special Masters may establish an Advisory Committee that may include persons drawn from among victims, the plaintiffs in the class action, Jewish organizations with experience in claim matters, organizations providing assistance to potential claimants, governmental entities, or other persons who can contribute to the administration of the Claims Process.[250]

(f) Housing and Property Claims Commission (HPCC)—claims relating to the 1999 conflict in Kosovo

The wording of UNMIK Regulation 2000/60—the document which governs the work of the HPCC Claims Process—was the result of lengthy consultations between the Special Representative of the Secretary-General of the United Nations and interim bodies established for the purpose of representing the interests of the local Kosovar population. It can therefore be said that representatives of the claimants—albeit not personal representatives—were involved in planning the Claims Process.

(g) Mass Claims Processes administered by the International Organization for Migration (IOM)

German Forced Labour Compensation Programme (GFLCP)—claims against Germany and German industry for Nazi injustice

Although Holocaust victims did not participate in establishing the GFLCP, there was wide representation of claimant groups in creating the German

---

[249] See section 1.01(d) above, on background of CRT-I.
[250] CRT-II Governing Rules, Article 47.

Foundation, which in turn created, and supervises the administration of, the Claims Process. Among such representatives were: lawyers representing claimants in United States class action litigations who, after the lawsuits were dropped, became claimants under the German Foundation Act; victims associations; the entities (other than IOM) that subsequently became the partner organizations under the Act; the German Government, and the United States Government. Representatives of the same groups or entities are members of the Board of Trustees of the German Foundation, and as such participate in the policy-making of the Foundation.

Holocaust Victim Assets Programme (HVAP)—claims pursuant to 1999 class action Settlement

The HVAP Claims Process arose out of the Settlement Agreement in the class action known as the Holocaust Victim Assets Litigation in the United States District Court for the Eastern District of New York, and from the Plan of Allocation and Distribution approved by the Court. The representatives of the claimants had a voice in the establishment of the Settlement Agreement, and thus, to the extent that the Settlement Agreement influenced the planning of HVAP, the representatives had an influence on that planning. In addition, when establishing the Plan of Allocation and Distribution, the Court-appointed Special Master considered suggestions directly from members of the classes of claimants.[251]

(h) Eritrea–Ethiopia Claims Commission (EECC)—claims relating to the 1998–2000 war between Eritrea and Ethiopia

The two Governments party to the EECC Claims Process in their 12 December 2000 Agreement planned and established the key elements of the structure and organization of the Commission and the Claims Process.[252] No other representatives of the ultimate claimants took part in the planning. After the Commission was constituted, it carried on substantial consultations with representatives of the two Government parties regarding the Commission's Rules of Procedure and other aspects of the Claims Process.

---

[251] A representative sample of proposals submitted from around the world as part of this process was placed on the notice website which received approximately 316,000 visits. See Plan of Allocation and Distribution, p. 6 and Annex A (Summaries of Proposals Received by the Special Master).

[252] See generally Eritrea–Ethiopia Agreement of 12 December 2000, Article 5.

(i) Humanitarian insurance Claims Process administered by the Jewish Claims Conference (JCC) for the International Commission on Holocaust Era Insurance Claims (ICHEIC)

As was set forth in the constituting Memorandum of Understanding, ICHEIC's members include United States insurance regulatory authorities, companies participating in ICHEIC (MOU Companies), and global Jewish and survivor organizations.[253]

(j) American Arbitration Association (AAA)—an illustrative case

Representatives of the plaintiffs in the class action which resulted in the Settlement Agreement in the illustrative case were equal participants in the planning of the Claims Process. They were also involved in the training of the Mediators and Arbitrators, and in monitoring the effectiveness of the appeals process which the AAA administered.

---

[253] ICHEIC Memorandum of Understanding, paragraph 1.

Chapter 2

The Legal Nature of the Claims Process

2.01 Type of Process

Whether claims are resolved in a procedure akin to arbitration, or in an administrative proceeding, or by mediation/conciliation, or in a combination thereof.

Editors' Commentary

Some of the Mass Claims Processes described in this book are designed as arbitrations—notably the Iran–United States Claims Tribunal (Iran–US CT), the Claims Resolution Tribunal for Dormant Accounts in Switzerland (CRT-I), and the Eritrea–Ethiopia Claims Commission (EECC)—while others resolve claims by administrative procedures. Several factors may influence the choice.

Those who choose arbitration are electing to use a well-known process with established procedures that have stood the tests of time. However, arbitration procedures were largely developed in order to regulate single cases and may not be considered appropriate when there is a need to resolve as quickly as possible thousands, or hundreds of thousands, of claims by individuals who have urgent personal needs. In such situations, administrative solutions may be preferable because they allow for the use of efficient and innovative dispute resolution methods that might be problematic in the context of traditional arbitration.

Although conciliation and mediation—the two terms are interchangeable—are increasingly used to resolve many types of disputes arising in international trade and relations, these techniques have not been utilized in most of the Mass Claims Processes described in this book. One exception is that the Regulations governing the Housing and Property Claims Commission (HPCC) in Kosovo permit the administrators of that Claims Process to mediate disputes, but the use of mediation has been limited. An interesting use of mediation which is worthy of study, in part because of how speedily it was carried out, is that of the American Arbitration Association (AAA) in its insurance policy Claims Process described in sub-section (j) below.

Annotations

(a) Iran–United States Claims Tribunal (Iran–US CT)—claims relating to the 1979 Islamic Revolution

The Iran–US CT is an "international arbitral tribunal"[1] that decides claims through "binding third-party arbitration"[2] in accordance with the UNCITRAL Arbitration Rules as modified by the parties or the Tribunal.[3] As in typical international arbitration practice, proceedings before the Tribunal include the exchange of written pleadings (statement of claim, statement of defense, reply, rejoinder), sometimes a pre-hearing conference with the parties, and usually an oral hearing, followed by deliberations and an award. The Tribunal Rules and its Internal Guidelines[4] contain a number of typical arbitration provisions for dealing with various aspects of the proceedings.

(b) United Nations Compensation Commission (UNCC)—claims relating to the 1990–1991 Gulf War

The decisions by the UNCC's panels of Commissioners were made in an administrative proceeding rather than by arbitration. Although some large cases before it have been adversarial and argued,[5] the Commission is more of an inquisitorial, fact-finding model of claims resolution than an adversarial one. Parties have tended to play a secondary role to that of the UNCC Secretariat in investigating claims and gathering evidence for consideration by the panels of Commissioners.[6]

The administrative methods employed to evaluate and decide the more than 2.6 million claims submitted to the UNCC include mass claims techniques such as computerized matching of claims information against outside data,

---

[1] Claims Settlement Declaration, Article II, paragraph 1.   [2] Ibid., Article I.
[3] Ibid., Article III, paragraph 2.
[4] Iran–US CT Internal Guidelines of the Tribunal, 1 Iran–U.S. C.T.R. p. 98.
[5] See UNCC Provisional Rules, Articles 36(a) and 38(d), authorizing the use of oral proceedings in unusually large or complex cases. See also UNCC Governing Council Decision 114 of 7 December 2000, *Review of current UNCC procedures*, U.N. Doc. S/AC.26/Dec.114 (2000) (7 December 2000). Oral proceedings have been held in respect of one category "D" claim and in respect of a number of claims in each of categories "E" and "F".   [6] See UNCC Provisional Rules, Article 36.

statistical modeling and sampling, and the grouping of similar claims into categories to be decided *en masse*.[7] The initial screening and review of the claims were delegated to the UNCC Secretariat, and much of the valuation work was outsourced to accounting and loss adjustment firms.[8]

(c) Commission for Real Property Claims of Displaced Persons and Refugees (CRPC)—claims relating to the 1992–1995 war in Bosnia and Herzegovina

The CRPC was an independent international body that decided property rights in administrative proceedings. Considering the large number of claims, their similarity, and the limited resources of the Claims Process, the Commission only took up groups of claims for decision after they had been examined and their evidence verified by the CRPC Secretariat. The procedure was basically a document-based process that relied heavily on computer support, including software programs for matching claims against data in public property records.

(d) Claims Resolution Tribunal for Dormant Accounts in Switzerland (CRT-I)—first claims tribunal for assets deposited in Swiss banks

CRT-I was an arbitral Claims Process in which claims were decided in accordance with Swiss law on arbitration.[9] Claimants who wished to have their claims resolved by the Tribunal were required to sign an arbitration agreement—the "Claims Resolution Agreement"—the filing of which initiated the claims procedure.[10] Swiss banks could enter into a master arbitration agreement with the Independent Claims Resolution Foundation (ICRF), submitting to the jurisdiction of the Tribunal all claims to their dormant accounts with respect to which claimants had signed Claims Resolution Agreements.[11]

(e) Claims Resolution Tribunal (CRT-II)—second claims tribunal for assets deposited in Swiss banks

Unlike its predecessor CRT-I, CRT-II is not an arbitral tribunal. Rather than having arbitrators acting pursuant to arbitration law, with the power to issue

---

[7] See further section 5.06(b) below, on mass claims techniques used at the UNCC.

[8] See further section 6.03(b) below, on the relationship between the UNCC Secretariat staff and the decision-makers.   [9] CRT-I Rules of Procedure, Article 16, paragraph 2.

[10] Ibid., Article 2, paragraph 1.   [11] Ibid., paragraph 2.

final and binding awards as in CRT-I, CRT-II staff attorneys prepare draft decisions that have the legal character of recommendations and are submitted by Special Masters to the United States District Court for the Eastern District of New York in the class action known as the Holocaust Victim Assets Litigation, for approval by the Court.[12]

(f) Housing and Property Claims Commission (HPCC)—claims relating to the 1999 conflict in Kosovo

Under the applicable UNMIK Regulations, where appropriate, the Housing and Property Directorate (HPD) may seek to mediate disputes and promote the amicable settlement of disputes through an agreement of the parties.[13] To this end, the Directorate is authorized to develop standardized settlement agreements for use by the parties and may certify such settlement agreements.[14] In practice, however, recourse has not been had to the mediation mechanism. Having "fought" for their rights for a long time, the parties did not opt for an intervention of HPD that they perceived might lead to a compromise outcome.

The Commission generally decides claims in administrative proceedings on the basis of written submissions only.[15] Exceptionally, however, oral hearings may be held in particular cases if the Commission so decides.[16] To facilitate this administrative Claims Process, the Commission is authorized to employ mass claims techniques, such as grouping of claims that share common legal and factual issues; delegation to the Registrar and the Directorate of review functions with respect to claims and evidence; use of computer databases, programs, and other electronic tools; and other appropriate means.[17] A summary procedure is available for uncontested claims for the repossession of property.[18]

---

[12] CRT-II Governing Rules, Article 16 provides: "The CRT shall certify draft claims decisions, prepared by Staff Attorneys, for approval by the Court. These decisions shall be in writing and shall contain the relevant facts and the reasons for the decision."

[13] UNMIK Regulation 1999/23, section 1.2, and UNMIK Regulation 2000/60, section 10.

[14] UNMIK Regulation 2000/60, section 10.1.

[15] Ibid., section 19.1 and 19.8, providing that, for purposes of Kosovo criminal law concerning false testimony, the proceedings before both the Directorate and the Commission, including the completion and submission of claim and reply to claim forms, are legally deemed to be administrative proceedings.   [16] Ibid., section 19.2.

[17] Ibid., section 19.5.

[18] Ibid., section 23 "Summary Procedure." See also section 5.06(f) below, on mass claims techniques used at HPCC.

(g) Mass Claims Processes administered by the International Organization for Migration (IOM)

German Forced Labour Compensation Programme (GFLCP)—claims against Germany and German industry for Nazi injustice

The decisions on the vast majority of claims under GFLCP are made in an administrative setting rather than in a procedure akin to arbitration. The more than one million slave and forced labor claims which were filed in the overall Claims Process, using standardized claim forms, were reviewed by the Secretariat staff of the partner organization in whose jurisdiction the claimants reside. In processing the claims that fell under its jurisdiction, IOM has employed methods such as computerized matching of claims information against central archives and other databases, list searches in other public archives, checks against previous Holocaust compensation programs, and statistical modeling and sampling.[19]

Claims submitted to the Property Claims Commission—which is administered by IOM on behalf of all the partner organizations implementing the German Foundation Act—were divided into two categories: simple cases and complex cases.[20] For the many similarly situated simple cases, the Commission only performed quality checks of standardized draft decisions prepared by the IOM Secretariat, whereas it reviewed in more detail the much smaller number of complex claims, using a procedure closer to arbitration.

Holocaust Victim Assets Programme (HVAP)—claims pursuant to 1999 class action Settlement

HVAP decisions are made in an administrative proceeding. The individual claims review conducted by IOM staff includes searches against lists from companies and from Swiss Government entities, searches in public archives, and checks against previous Holocaust compensation programs, in addition to research assistance and advice from experts in Holocaust history, primarily based at the United States Holocaust Memorial Museum (USHMM). Based on these analyses, and on methods set forth in the Plan of Allocation and Distribution in the class action known as the Holocaust Victim Assets Litigation, IOM staff makes recommendations to the United States federal

---

[19] See further section 5.06(g) below, on mass claims techniques used at GFLCP.
[20] See IOM Property Commission Supplemental Rules.

district court that oversees the class action as to whether a claim qualifies for compensation or not. If the Court approves the recommendation, compensation is awarded.[21]

(h) Eritrea–Ethiopia Claims Commission (EECC)—claims relating to the 1998–2000 war between Eritrea and Ethiopia

The EECC's mandate is to decide the claims submitted to it "through binding arbitration,"[22] and its Rules of Procedure are based upon the Permanent Court of Arbitration Optional Rules for Arbitrating Disputes between Two States (PCA Rules), which in turn are based on the UNCITRAL Arbitration Rules.[23] However, the Government parties also authorized the Commission to deviate from conventional bilaterally-focused arbitration as necessary in order to deal expeditiously with very large numbers of claims. The 12 December 2000 Agreement authorizes it to adopt "such methods of efficient case management and mass claims processing as it deems appropriate, such as expedited procedures for processing claims and checking claims on a sample basis for further verification . . . ."[24]

The Commission may conduct the arbitration in such manner as it considers appropriate and shall itself decide whether to hold hearings or decide claims on the basis of documents only.[25] It may appoint consultants to advise it and experts to report on particular matters,[26] and it may appoint such persons to enter the territory of either party in order to obtain information related to the Commission's work.[27] The Rules of Procedure provide for a Registrar who acts as a channel of communication between the parties and the Commission.[28]

(i) Humanitarian insurance Claims Process administered by the Jewish Claims Conference (JCC) for the International Commission on Holocaust Era Insurance Claims (ICHEIC)

Claims in the 8A1 humanitarian Claims Process were decided in an administrative procedure.[29]

---

[21] The same decision-making mechanism is also followed by the two other organizations implementing the Settlement Agreement, the Jewish Claims Conference (JCC) processing Slave Labor Class I and Refugee Class claims by Jewish claimants, and the CRT-II, processing claims for deposited assets.   [22] Eritrea–Ethiopia Agreement of 12 December 2000, Article 5, paragraph 1.

[23] Ibid., Article 5, paragraph 7.   [24] Ibid., Article 5, paragraph 10.

[25] EECC Rules of Procedure, Article 10.   [26] Ibid., Article 16.

[27] Ibid., Article 11, paragraph 2.   [28] Ibid., Article 9.

[29] See further sections 1.01(i) and 5.05(i) for descriptions of the design and decision-making procedures of the 8A1 humanitarian Claims Process.

(j) American Arbitration Association (AAA)—an illustrative case

In the initial claims review conducted by the defendant insurance company itself, claimants in the illustrative case could have their claims resolved on the basis of documentary evidence alone. If they rejected the amount proposed, the claim was sent to mediation. Each matter involved a single neutral third party, acting first as Mediator and then, failing settlement, as Sole Arbitrator. In the first phase, mediation was conducted over the telephone, with the Arbitrator acting as Mediator, and was restricted to a ten-minute presentation by each side. The total time for these mediation hearings was forty-five to sixty minutes. Almost half of the cases were resolved in this type of mediation, during which the claimant was represented by counsel paid for by the defendant insurance company. The insurance company had a representative on the telephone as well, representing the company's position. The Mediator had the authority to mediate the claim, within certain restrictions, according to the Settlement Agreement. If the mediation was unsuccessful, a telephonic arbitration hearing was scheduled. At the arbitration hearing, an attorney representing the claimant and a representative for the insurance company participated, as well as the claimant himself or herself, on the line with the Arbitrator. The decision-making procedure which the Arbitrator was mandated to follow was regulated by the Settlement Agreement.

2.02 Exclusivity of Process

Whether the Claims Process is the sole recourse available to claimants or whether and when they may choose to sue in a national court.

Editors' Commentary

Each of the Mass Claims Processes described in this book seeks to prevent duplicate payments for the same claim that might result from action in a national court or other body. The mechanisms to achieve that legal result vary.

In some Claims Processes, such as the Claims Resolution Tribunal for Dormant Accounts in Switzerland (CRT-I), claimants must agree to arbitration as a condition for having their claim considered. That effectively bars recourse to litigation in most national courts. In other Claims Processes, successful claimants must sign a release before they can receive payment. The release clauses in the Holocaust-related Claims Processes administered by the International Organization for Migration (IOM) and the International Commission on Holocaust Era Insurance Claims (ICHEIC) are illustrations of detailed and comprehensive release provisions.

Where a Mass Claims Process involves a choice for individual claimants either to participate or to pursue a claim elsewhere, designers may give thought to whether the Claims Process will be an attractive choice in terms of procedures, remedies, and speed.

(a) Iran–United States Claims Tribunal (Iran–US CT)—claims relating to the 1979 Islamic Revolution

The Iran–US CT Claims Process is the sole recourse available to United States claimants for the claims within the Tribunal's jurisdiction. The United States agreed in the Algiers Accords that legal proceedings should not be pursued in United States courts involving claims of United States persons and institutions against Iran and its State enterprises.[30] The Claims Settlement Declaration excludes from the Tribunal's jurisdiction claims arising under a binding contract between the parties, specifically providing that any disputes thereunder shall be within the sole jurisdiction of the competent Iranian courts.[31] The Declaration also excludes claims not outstanding on 19 January 1981, the date of the Algiers Accords.[32]

(b) United Nations Compensation Commission (UNCC)—claims relating to the 1990–1991 Gulf War

The UNCC is not an exclusive forum for the claims within its jurisdiction. Nothing prevents a claimant from bringing a claim before another competent forum. Therefore, to avoid multiple recovery of compensation by claimants for the same losses in another proceeding—national or international—the UNCC Governing Council, in response to the 2 May 1991 Report of the United Nations Secretary-General, introduced several measures.[33] It requested

---

[30] General Declaration, General Principles B.

[31] Claims Settlement Declaration, Article II, paragraph 1.   [32] Ibid.

[33] UNCC Governing Council Decision 1, *Criteria for Expedited Processing of Urgent Claims*, U.N. Doc. S/AC.26/1991/1 (2 August 1991), paragraph 16; Decision 7 of 28 November 1991, as revised on 16 March 1992, *Criteria for additional Categories of Claims*, U.N. Doc. S/AC.26/1991/7/Rev.1 (17 March 1992), paragraphs 10, 25 and 39 (deductions to be made from awards of compensation from other sources); followed by UNCC Governing Council Decision 13 of 25 September 1992, *Further Measures to Avoid Multiple Recovery of Compensation by Claimants*, U.N. Doc. S/AC.26/1992/13 (25 September 1992)(calling on Iraq to inform the Commission of any claims against it in national

Iraq to provide the Commission with information about claims against Iraq in national courts and other fora for losses that would also be eligible for compensation by the Commission, and information about any compensation awarded for such losses. Iraq had a strong incentive to provide that information in order to protect itself against double payments. The Governing Council also invited governments to seek to obtain and to provide the Commission with information regarding lawsuits within their jurisdiction, or any compensation granted for losses resulting from Iraq's invasion and occupation of Kuwait.

The UNCC also has deducted from the compensation to be paid from the Compensation Fund, compensation that a claimant has received elsewhere for the same loss, upon learning, from the claimant or through other means, of such earlier payments. Claimants were instructed to disclose on the claim form any compensation received from other sources. Finally, the UNCC put claimants at the end of the processing queue in their category of claims when it learned through sources other than the claimant that a lawsuit had been brought by the claimant for the same losses as were also claimed before the Commission.

(c) Commission for Real Property Claims of Displaced Persons and Refugees (CRPC)—claims relating to the 1992–1995 war in Bosnia and Herzegovina

The CRPC, although it was an independent Commission entrusted with a specific mandate, formed part of a cluster of international bodies created by the Dayton Peace Agreement.[34] In particular, there was a relationship between CRPC and the Commission on Human Rights and the Human Rights Chamber—both created under Annex 6 to the Dayton Peace Agreement.[35] The property rights that were to be determined by the CRPC were at the same time a protected human right, and thus fell also under the jurisdiction of the Annex 6 institutions.[36]

Claimants could submit a claim regarding the same property issue before both the CRPC and the Human Rights Chamber.[37] However, the CRPC only determined who was the holder of the property right as of 1 April 1992, while the Human Rights Chamber decided on allegations of infringement of

---

courts or other fora). See also Report of the UN Secretary-General of 2 May 1991, U.N. Doc. S/25599, paragraph 22.

[34] Dayton Peace Agreement, Annex 7, Article X, paragraph 5, "The Commission shall cooperate with other entities established under the General Framework Agreement, agreed by the Parties, or authorized by the United Nations Security Council."   [35] Ibid., Annex 6, Articles II and VII, respectively.

[36] Ibid., Annex 6, Article I, Fundamental Right No. 11 is "the right to property."

[37] Ibid., Annex 6, Article VIII.

property rights. That Chamber was not to address any claim which was substantially the same as a matter already submitted to another procedure for international settlements. A permanent exchange of information regarding pending cases was therefore necessary between these two bodies.[38] There was no other mechanism for limiting duplicate claims in local courts or elsewhere.

(d) Claims Resolution Tribunal for Dormant Accounts in Switzerland (CRT-I)—first claims tribunal for assets deposited in Swiss banks

In order for a claim to come before CRT-I, the parties first had to sign a Claims Settlement Agreement that expressly agreed to arbitration under Swiss law. That law barred the claimant from recourse to courts in Switzerland or in other States party to the Convention on the Recognition and Enforcement of Foreign Arbitral Awards (New York, 1958),[39] as well as in a number of other States.

(e) Claims Resolution Tribunal (CRT-II)—second claims tribunal for assets deposited in Swiss banks

The Governing Rules of CRT-II require that each person receiving an award under the Claims Process shall submit to the Tribunal an acknowledgment that releases all claims as defined in the Settlement Agreement in the class action known as the Holocaust Victim Assets Litigation in the United States District Court for the Eastern District of New York.[40]

(f) Housing and Property Claims Commission (HPCC)—claims relating to the 1999 conflict in Kosovo

The HPCC has exclusive jurisdiction to settle the three categories of claims under its mandate, as defined in the constituting instrument, UNMIK Regulation 1999/23,[41] until such time as the Special Representative of the Secretary-General of the United Nations determines that local courts in

---

[38] It had been suggested that proceedings before the CRPC should precede those before the Human Rights Commission, since it was for the former to determine property rights and to grant a remedy, and for the latter to intervene when the remedy needed implementation by the authorities and when they failed to implement it. It had also been suggested that the Human Rights Chamber could request the CRPC to issue opinions or "preliminary rulings" regarding property issues, to be used in proceedings before the Chamber. However, no specific mechanism was set up. Finally, a right of appeal against CRPC decisions for alleged violation of human rights before the Human Rights Chamber, which some also suggested, seemed to be contrary to the principle that the decisions of the CRPC were final.

[39] Convention on the Recognition and Enforcement of Foreign Arbitral Awards, New York, 10 June 1958, 330 U.N.T.S. 38 (New York Convention).

[40] CRT-II Governing Rules, Article 31, paragraph 4.

[41] UNMIK Regulation 1999/23, section 1.2.

Kosovo are able to carry out the functions entrusted to the Commission.[42] Once the Commission has rendered a decision, local courts retain jurisdiction to adjudicate any legal issue not decided by the Commission.[43] In practice, there are thus two ways in which local courts come into play. First, the Commission may refer a specific aspect of a claim to the competent local court, such as, for example, a request for revision of the purchase price of a property sold subsequently by the claimant to the current occupant.[44] Secondly, in particular with respect to category "C" claims for repossession, the Commission ordinarily issues an eviction order entitling the claimant to repossession, stating specifically in its decision that such order only resolves the issue of *possession*, and not issues of ownership, inheritance, etc., that may be subject to further dispute in local courts.[45]

Local courts in Kosovo have jurisdiction to resolve claims of illegal occupation of property that are not linked to the events of 1999. Thus, illegal occupation stemming, for example, from riots in 2004, are outside the HPCC jurisdiction and fall under the jurisdiction of the local courts.

(g) Mass Claims Processes administered by the International Organization for Migration (IOM)

German Forced Labour Compensation Programme (GFLCP)—claims against Germany and German industry for Nazi injustice

GFLCP is the sole and exclusive recourse of claimants who filed a claim under the Claims Process against the German Government and German companies for the types of exploitation and crimes described in section 1.04(g) above. All claim forms used by each of the partner organizations implementing the German Foundation Act—including IOM—contain a waiver which the claimant must sign, and pursuant to which the claimant, upon receipt of a payment, is precluded from bringing any further claims for forced labor and property damage or claims in connection with Nazi injustice against German and Austrian Government entities or against German and Austrian enterprises.[46]

Holocaust Victim Assets Programme (HVAP)—claims pursuant to 1999 class action Settlement

Eligible claimants under the Settlement Agreement in the class action known as the Holocaust Victim Assets Litigation who filed claims with the HVAP

---

[42] Ibid., section 2.1.   [43] UNMIK Regulation 2000/60, section 22.6.
[44] Ibid., section 22.1.   [45] See ibid., section 22.6.
[46] See German Foundation Act, section 16, paragraphs 1 and 2.

Claims Process have no other recourse available.[47] They were required to sign a waiver on the claim form with respect to Swiss entities similar to that which the claimants under GFLCP had to sign with respect to Germany and German entities, as described in the immediately preceding section. Individuals were free to opt out of the underlying class action against Swiss banks in the United States federal district court overseeing the class action, and those who did were free to seek recourse elsewhere, but they could then not participate in the HVAP Claims Process.

(h) Eritrea–Ethiopia Claims Commission (EECC)—claims relating to the 1998–2000 war between Eritrea and Ethiopia

The EECC is the sole recourse for claims within its jurisdiction. Except for claims submitted to another mutually-agreed settlement mechanism, or filed in another forum prior to the signing of the 12 December 2000 Agreement, the Commission is the sole forum for adjudicating the claims described in that Agreement. Any such claims which could have been but were not submitted by the 12 December 2001 deadline for filing claims are extinguished in accordance with international law.[48] If, however, before the Commission issues an award in a claim or group of claims, the parties agree on a settlement of that claim or claims, the Commission will either terminate the relevant arbitral proceedings or record the settlement as an arbitral award on agreed terms.[49]

(i) Humanitarian insurance Claims Process administered by the Jewish Claims Conference (JCC) for the International Commission on Holocaust Era Insurance Claims (ICHEIC)

Claimants who accepted an award for a *matched* claim[50] from an MOU Company through ICHEIC were required to sign a waiver relinquishing

---

[47] See Settlement Agreement, section 12 ("Releases and Covenant not to Sue"), and Final Order approving the Settlement, *In re Holocaust Victim Assets Litig.*, 105 F.Supp.2d 139, at pp. 142–143 (E.D.N.Y. 2000) ("In exchange for the settlement amount paid by the settling defendants, settling plaintiffs and settlement class members have agreed irrevocably and unconditionally to release, acquit and forever discharge certain releasees from any and all claims relating to the Holocaust, World War II and its prelude and aftermath, victims or targets of Nazi persecution, transactions with or actions of or in connection with the Nazi regime, treatment by the Swiss Confederation or other releasees of refugees fleeing persecution, or any related cause or thing whatever.").

[48] Eritrea–Ethiopia Agreement of 12 December 2000, Article 5, paragraph 8.

[49] EECC Rules of Procedure, Article 20, paragraph 1.

[50] "Matched claims" are claims that name an insurance policy which matches with the MOU Company's records or with ICHEIC's research database.

further claims and recognizing the Claims Process as their sole remedy. In the case of 8A1 Claims, however, the Claims Process was not a sole remedy; awards were granted on a voluntary basis for humanitarian, not legal, reasons and it did not constitute admission of liability on the part of MOU Companies. Recipients of 8A1 humanitarian awards were therefore not required to sign a release form or waiver, nor were they barred from pursuing their claims elsewhere.

(j) American Arbitration Association (AAA)—an illustrative case

Because the illustrative case was a class action certified by a United States federal district court Judge, potential claimants had a period of time within which they could choose to opt out of the Claims Process and litigate their claims elsewhere. The vast majority of claimants agreed to use the Claims Process and accordingly were bound by the terms of the Settlement Agreement.

2.03 Applicable Law

What substantive law, if any, is applied and whether procedural law at the place where the Claims Process is located applies.

Editors' Commentary

Express provisions on the choice of applicable substantive law are included in the constituting instruments and rules of the Iran–United States Claims Tribunal (Iran–US CT), the two Claims Processes that deal with real property claims in the Former Yugoslavia (CRPC in Bosnia and Herzegovina, and HPCC in Kosovo), and the Eritrea–Ethiopia Claims Commission (EECC). The other Mass Claims Processes described in this book contain no such provisions.

None of the constituting instruments or rules includes express mention of procedural law. However, in the case of the Claims Resolution Tribunal for Dormant Accounts in Switzerland (CRT-I), because the parties agreed to arbitration under Swiss law, the Swiss procedural law of arbitration applied. The Claims Processes which are administrative and not arbitral may be considered to be outside the scope of local procedural laws of arbitration. It may be useful for designers of future Mass Claims Processes to anticipate that questions may arise as to whether or not the particular Claims Process is intended to create an international body that is not subject to local procedural law, and to draft the governing instruments in a way that would resolve any such questions.

(a) Iran–United States Claims Tribunal (Iran–US CT)—claims relating to the 1979 Islamic Revolution

The constituting instrument of the Iran–US CT, the Claims Settlement Declaration, states that "[t]he Tribunal shall decide all cases on the basis of respect for law, applying such choice of law rules and principles of commercial and international law as the Tribunal determines to be applicable, taking into account relevant usages of the trade, contract provisions and changed circumstances."[51] The Tribunal is allowed to decide *ex aequo et bono* "only if the arbitrating parties have expressly and in writing authorized it to do so."[52] Although the Tribunal takes the position that it is an international body and, as such, the procedural law of the Netherlands—the seat of the Claims Process— does not apply, it has followed the Dutch practice of filing its awards in a Dutch court as a matter of precaution in the event issues may arise with respect to enforcement.[53]

(b) United Nations Compensation Commission (UNCC)—claims relating to the 1990–1991 Gulf War

According to the UNCC Provisional Rules,

"[i]n considering the claims, Commissioners will apply [United Nations] Security Council resolution 687 (1991) and other relevant Security Council resolutions, the criteria established by the [Commission's] Governing Council for particular categories of claims, and any pertinent decisions of the Governing Council. In addition, where necessary, the Commissioners will apply other relevant rules of international law."[54]

Resolution 687 (1991) reaffirmed that Iraq, without prejudice to its debts and obligations arising prior to its invasion of Kuwait (which are addressed

---

[51] Claims Settlement Declaration, Article V.

[52] Iran–US CT Tribunal Rules, Article 33, paragraph 2.

[53] See ibid., Article 32, paragraph 7, "If the arbitration law of the country where the award is made requires that the award be filed or registered by the arbitral tribunal, the tribunal shall comply with this requirement within the period of time required by law."

[54] UNCC Provisional Rules, Article 31.

through traditional mechanisms), is liable under international law for any direct loss, damage, including environmental damage and the depletion of natural resources, or injury to foreign governments, nationals, and corporations, as a result of Iraq's unlawful invasion and occupation of Kuwait in 1990 and 1991.[55]

The more detailed legal criteria, and guidance established by the Commission's Governing Council as to how to interpret and apply such criteria, are contained in Governing Council decisions.[56] It is worth recalling in this context that the UNCC Governing Council is essentially an alter ego of the United Nations Security Council, and that its quasi-legislative function is properly understood as an extension of Security Council Resolution 692 (1991) constituting the Claims Process.

(c) Commission for Real Property Claims of Displaced Persons and Refugees (CRPC)—claims relating to the 1992–1995 war in Bosnia and Herzegovina

The constituting instrument of CRPC, Annex 7 to the Dayton Peace Agreement, required that, in developing the rules and regulations necessary to carry out its functions, the CRPC was to consider domestic laws on property rights in Bosnia and Herzegovina.[57] In practice, the CRPC, to the extent possible, took account of domestic substantive law. However, it had to ignore acts that, if considered, would lead to an unfair result, as instructed by the

---

[55] UN Security Council Resolution 687 (1991), U.N. Doc. S/RES/687 (1991) (8 April 1991), paragraph 16.

[56] See, e.g., UNCC Governing Council Decision 1 of 2 August 1991, *Criteria for Expedited Processing of Urgent Claims*, U.N. Doc. S/AC.26/1991/1 (2 August 1991); Decision 3 of 18 October 1991, *Personal Injury and Mental Pain and Anguish*, U.N. Doc. S/AC.26/1991/3 (23 October 1991); Decision 4 of 18 October 1991, *Business Losses of Individuals Eligible for Consideration under the Expedited Procedures*, U.N. Doc. S/AC.26/1991/4 (23 October 1991); Decision 7 of 28 November 1991, as revised on 16 March 1992, *Criteria for Additional Categories of Claims*, U.N. Doc. S/AC.26/1991/7/Rev.1 (17 March 1992); Decision 8 of 24 January 1992, *Determination of Ceilings for Compensation for Mental Pain and Anguish*, U.N. Doc. S/AC.26/1992/8 (27 January 1992); Decision 9 of 6 March 1992, *Propositions and Conclusions on Compensation for Business Losses: Types of Damages and Their Valuation*, U.N. Doc. S/AC.26/1992/9 (6 March 1992); Decision 11 of 26 June 1992, *Eligibility for Compensation of Members of the Allied Coalition Armed Forces*, U.N. Doc. S/AC.26/1992/11 (26 June 1992); Decision 15 of 18 December 1992, *Compensation for Business Losses Resulting from Iraq's Unlawful Invasion and Occupation of Kuwait where the Trade Embargo and Related Measures Were also a Cause*, U.N. Doc. S/AC.26/1992/15 (4 January 1993); Decision 16 of 18 December 1992, *Awards of Interest*, U.N. Doc. S/AC.26/1992/16 (4 January 1993); Decision 19 of 24 March 1994, *Military Costs*, U.N. Doc. S/AC.26/Dec.19 (1994) (24 March 1994); and Decision 23 of 20 October 1994, *Notification of the Governing Council's Intention Not to Accept Further Individual Claims After 1 January 1995*, U.N. Doc. S/AC.26/Dec. 23 (1994) (21 October 1999).

[57] Dayton Peace Agreement, Annex 7, Article XV.

Dayton Peace Agreement, which provided that, "[i]n determining the lawful owner of any property, the Commission shall not recognize as valid any illegal property transaction, including any transfer that was made under duress, in exchange for exit permission or documents, or that was otherwise in connection with ethnic cleansing."[58]

The legal criterion for compensation was that it be "just." For this purpose, the constituting instrument provided that the Commission establish fixed rates that could be applied to determine the value of all real property in Bosnia and Herzegovina that was the subject of claims before it. The rates were to be based on an assessment or survey of properties in the territory of Bosnia and Herzegovina undertaken prior to 1 April 1992, or on other reasonable criteria as determined by the Commission.[59]

(d) Claims Resolution Tribunal for Dormant Accounts in Switzerland (CRT-I)—first claims tribunal for assets deposited in Swiss banks

The Rules of Procedure of CRT-I stated that the Arbitrators should "apply the law with which the matter in dispute has the closest connection in deciding matters concerning the relationship between the published account holder or holder of power of attorney and the claimant (e.g., to inheritance matters or fiduciary agreements)."[60] At the request of all parties involved, other than the Swiss banks, inheritance matters could be resolved according to Talmudic law.

The Rules of Procedure also provided that "[t]he relationship between the claimant and the Swiss bank shall be governed by Swiss law, except as provided by these Rules of Procedure. In deciding matters relating to interest, fees and charges, the [arbitrators] shall apply the Interest Guidelines [adopted by the Board of Trustees of the ICRF]."[61] As Interest Guidelines were so adopted, they applied rather than Swiss law.

(e) Claims Resolution Tribunal (CRT-II)—second claims tribunal for assets deposited in Swiss banks

The Governing Rules of CRT-II leave it to the Tribunal to determine the law to be applied to the relationship between an account owner and a bank.[62] As to

---

[58] Dayton Peace Agreement, Annex 7, Article XII, paragraph 3.

[59] Ibid., Article XII, paragraph 4.   [60] CRT-I Rules of Procedure, Article 16, paragraph 1.

[61] Ibid., Article 16, paragraph 2. See also Board of Trustees, ICRF, Rules on Interest, Charges, and Fees for Arbitral Decisions of the Claims Resolution Tribunal [hereinafter CRT-I Interest Guidelines], available at www.crt-ii.org/_crt-i.   [62] CRT-II Governing Rules, Article 27, paragraph 2.

matters relating to inheritance, the Tribunal is required to apply certain rules of distribution that govern the determination of who are heirs, as set out in the Governing Rules, notwithstanding any contrary provisions of national law that would otherwise apply.[63] In applying the rules of distribution, the Tribunal shall "seek to achieve the result that is most fair and equitable under the circumstances."[64]

The inheritance regime set forth in the Governing Rules, approved by the United States federal district court overseeing the class action known as the Holocaust Victim Assets Litigation, is generally recognized as fair, and establishing such a regime was designed to expedite the decision of some claims by eliminating the need for ascertaining and applying the particular national laws applicable to the claimants. Nevertheless, questions may arise as to whether it is appropriate for a court in the United States to adopt rules that supersede national laws that would otherwise govern inheritance of individuals, particularly where the claimants have not lived in the United States and the distribution of their estates would be governed by national laws having different provisions.

(f) Housing and Property Claims Commission (HPCC)—claims relating to the 1999 conflict in Kosovo

United Nations Security Council Resolution 1244 (1999) established the United Nations Interim Administration Mission in Kosovo (UNMIK).[65] UNMIK Regulation 1999/1 provided that the administration of the judiciary in Kosovo, as well as legislative and executive authority, was vested in UNMIK.[66] A subsequent UNMIK Regulation held that housing and property rights would be governed by the law applicable and in force in Kosovo on 22 March 1989—immediately prior to the revocation by Serbia of Kosovo's autonomy.[67]

Chapter I of that Regulation is entitled "Substantive Provisions" and it establishes several substantive legal provisions in addition to rules of procedures. For example, "any property right which was validly acquired . . . at

---

[63] See CRT-II Governing Rules, Article 23, setting forth the general rule on distribution (i) where there is no will or other inheritance document, and (ii) where there is a will or other inheritance document. [64] Ibid., Article 27, paragraph 1. See also Article 23, paragraphs 1(g) and 2(c).

[65] UN Security Council Resolution 1244 (1999) of 10 June 1999, U.N. Doc. S/RES/1244 (1999) (10 June 1999).

[66] UNMIK Regulation 1999/1 of 25 July 1999, *On the Authority of the Interim Administration in Kosovo*, U.N. Doc. UNMIK/REG/1999/1 (25 July 1999), section 1.

[67] UNMIK Regulation 1999/24 of 12 December 1999, *On the Law Applicable in Kosovo*, U.N. Doc. UNMIK/REG/1999/24 (12 December 1999), section 1.1.

the time of its acquisition remains valid notwithstanding the change in the applicable law in Kosovo, except where [Regulation 2000/60] provides otherwise."[68] This is the law that the HPCC applies.

Regulation 2000/60 further states that the Commission may be guided, but is not bound, by the rules of evidence applied in local courts in Kosovo.[69]

(g) Mass Claims Processes administered by the International Organization for Migration (IOM)

German Forced Labour Compensation Programme (GFLCP)—claims against Germany and German industry for Nazi injustice

The German Foundation has created a special regime[70] in which no international or national law applies other than the provisions of the German Foundation Act and decisions of the Foundation Board of Trustees, which govern both the substance and procedures of the GFLCP Claims Process.[71]

With respect to claims for real property, the Supplemental Principles and Rules of Procedure developed by the Property Claims Commission require that Commission to make its determinations pursuant to the terms of the German Foundation Act, the Supplemental Rules, and "on the basis of respect for established principles of international law and practice regarding causation and directness of loss. In applying these principles, the Commission shall take into account the [relaxed evidentiary standard specified in the German Foundation Act]."[72]

Holocaust Victim Assets Programme (HVAP)—claims pursuant to 1999 class action Settlement

The Settlement Agreement and the Plan of Allocation and Distribution in the class action known as the Holocaust Victim Assets Litigation, establish a

---

[68] UNMIK Regulation 2000/60, section 2.1.   [69] Ibid., section 21.1.

[70] This Claims Process has sometimes been called a "self-contained system." See, however, International Law Commission Special Rapporteur Martti Koskenniemi, *Study on the Function and Scope of the Lex Specialis Rule and the Question of "Self-Contained Regimes"*, U.N. Doc. ILC (LVI)/SG/FIL/CRD.1/Add.1 (2002), suggesting that the term "special regime" be used instead, as "there is no support for the view that anywhere general law would be fully excluded" paragraph 134.

[71] The U.S.–German Agreement and the *Joint Statement on the occasion of the final plenary meeting concluding international talks on the preparation of the Foundation "Remembrance, Responsibility and the Future"* of 17 July 2000 (available at www.compensation-for-forced-labour.org) can be said to provide the international law context or backdrop of the German Foundation Act, but the Act remains the only law applicable to the Claims Process.

[72] IOM Property Commission Supplemental Rules, section 17.2.

special regime—albeit one which is ultimately controlled by the United States federal district court overseeing the class action—for the substance and the procedures of the HVAP Claims Process.[73]

(h) Eritrea–Ethiopia Claims Commission (EECC)—claims relating to the 1998–2000 war between Eritrea and Ethiopia

The 12 December 2000 Agreement provides that, in considering claims, the EECC "shall apply relevant rules of international law," and it states expressly that the Commission does not have the power to make decisions *ex aequo et bono*.[74] Drawing on the familiar provisions of Article 38 of the Statute of the International Court of Justice (ICJ), the Commission's Rules of Procedure elaborate on the elements of international law to be applied, stating that the Commission must look to:

> "a. International conventions, whether general or particular, establishing rules expressly recognized by the parties;
> b. International custom, as evidence of a general practice accepted as law;
> c. The general principles of law recognized by civilized nations;
> d. Judicial and arbitral decisions and the teachings of the most highly qualified publicists of the various nations, as subsidiary means for the determination of rules of law."[75]

The 12 December 2000 Agreement and the Rules of Procedure are silent as to whether the procedural law of the location of the Claims Process (the Netherlands) will apply. However, should relevant issues arise, the Commission is authorized to "refer to national laws in appropriate circumstances."[76]

(i) Humanitarian insurance Claims Process administered by the Jewish Claims Conference (JCC) for the International Commission on Holocaust Era Insurance Claims (ICHEIC)

In the case of the 8A1 humanitarian Claims Process, there was no applicable substantive law or procedural law. Awards in this Claims Process were granted on a voluntary basis and in the absence of any definitive connection to an insurance policy; there was no contractual or other legal basis of liability or obligation on the part of the MOU Companies. Given the range of countries in which the participating insurance companies are located, where the policies

---

[73] See note on special regime in the preceding section on GFLCP.
[74] Eritrea–Ethiopia Agreement of 12 December 2000, Article 5, paragraph 13.
[75] EECC Rules of Procedure, Article 19, paragraph 2.   [76] Ibid., Article 19, paragraph 3.

were originally sold, and where the claimants reside presently, the designers of the Claims Process considered that there was no single legal system whose laws could rationally be applied.

(j) American Arbitration Association (AAA)—an illustrative case

In the illustrative case, provisions on the applicable substantive and procedural law were agreed upon and set forth in the Settlement Agreement. The Settlement Agreement had been approved by the presiding United States federal district court Judge in the class action, and it was in final form before the AAA became involved. The provisions differ from existing Rules that the AAA has developed in the light of its extensive experience and which may be a preferred model in other cases.[77]

2.04 Effect of Decisions

Whether decisions made in the Claims Process are final and binding. Whether the principle of *stare decisis* applies within the Claims Process itself.

Editors' Commentary

The constituting instruments or procedural rules of the Mass Claims Processes described in this book all have as their goal that awards will be final and binding. As to those Claims Processes that conduct arbitration, the awards are subject only to such recourse as may be available in vacating arbitral awards under national law. Claims Processes which resolve claims by administrative procedures rather than by arbitration often provide for systems of appeal or reconsideration within the Claims Process itself.

Mass Claims Processes are created to decide large volumes of claims—reaching as high as 2.6 million claims at the United Nations Compensation Commission (UNCC)—with one of the primary goals being the equal treatment of all the claimants. Claims Processes therefore face the task of designing practices for achieving consistent decisions, especially when there are

---

[77] See AAA Supplementary Rules for Class Arbitrations, effective October 2003, available at www.adr.org, under Rules/Procedures.

many decision-makers working separately. Applying the legal rule of *stare decisis* is one way that some national court systems seek to promote consistency. In the absence of formal rules of binding precedent and *stare decisis* in arbitration generally, formal application of such rules may not be practical in Claims Processes that must decide large numbers of cases more or less simultaneously. In that circumstance, the Mass Claims Processes described in this book have devised a variety of methods to achieve the consistency needed for equal treatment of the parties. The innovative systems utilized by the UNCC, those adopted by the Jewish Claims Conference (JCC) in administering the humanitarian program of the International Commission for Holocaust Era Insurance Claims (ICHEIC), as well as other procedures described below, are useful illustrations of techniques that can be used. Further procedures for harmonizing claims processing are described in section 5.07 below, and provisions for review or reconsideration of awards and appeals within a Claims Process are discussed in section 5.13.

(a) Iran–United States Claims Tribunal (Iran–US CT)—claims relating to the 1979 Islamic Revolution

Awards made by the Iran–US CT are final and binding on the Government parties and they undertake to carry them out without delay.[78] The constituting instrument, the Claims Settlement Declaration, provides that any award rendered by the Tribunal against either Government party "shall be enforceable against such government in the courts of any nation in accordance with its laws."[79]

There is no formal rule of *stare decisis* in the practice of the Full Tribunal of nine Members or its three Chambers of three Members each. However, the Tribunal has taken a number of measures to promote, to the extent possible, the consistent resolution of similar issues and claims. An example of a situation in which the Tribunal acted to promote consistent results in a number of cases is found in the so-called "forum selection case," described in section 5.07(a) below. There, the Tribunal purposely created precedents that would guide the decision of similar questions later.[80]

---

[78] Iran–US CT Tribunal Rules, Article 32, paragraph 2.

[79] Claims Settlement Declaration, Article IV, paragraph 3.

[80] See *Gibbs and Hill, Inc.* and *Iran Power Generation and Transmission Co. (TAVANIR) of the Ministry of Energy of the Government of Iran, et al.*, Award No. ITL 1-6-FT (5 November 1982), 1 Iran–U.S. C.T.R. p. 236; *Halliburton Company, et al.* and *Doreen/IMCO, et al.*, Award No. ITL 2-51-FT (5 November 1982), 1 Iran–U.S. C.T.R. p. 242; *Howard, Needles, Tammen and Bergendoff (HNTB)* and *The Government of The Islamic Republic of Iran, et al.*, Award No. ITL 3-68-FT

A further measure is that the Tribunal Rules provide that awards and decisions shall be published.[81] The parties and Members of the Tribunal can refer to past cases in the interest of fostering uniformity, and submissions by parties and awards typically include references to earlier decisions which, while not binding, are often influential. Thus, publication has tended towards a certain harmonization of the Tribunal's jurisprudence. All awards of the Claims Process are, moreover, circulated among all the Members as soon as they are filed, so that, even before publication, the Members of the Tribunal know about past decisions and can act consistently, although no formal *stare decisis* rules apply.

Where a Chamber of three Members has formally requested the Full Tribunal of nine Members to decide an important issue or an issue that might result in inconsistent decisions or awards by the Tribunal, that Chamber is bound by the Full Tribunal's decision on that issue.[82] On occasion, issues that confronted the Chambers on a regular basis have been determined by the Full Tribunal. In practice, all Full Tribunal rulings have been observed as precedent by the individual Chambers, and decisions by individual Chambers have generally, but not always, been followed by other Chambers.[83]

(b) United Nations Compensation Commission (UNCC)—claims relating to the 1990–1991 Gulf War

Decisions of the UNCC's Governing Council with respect to compensation awards of the panels of Commissioners are final and not subject to appeal or

(5 November 1982), 1 Iran–U.S. C.T.R. p. 248; *George W. Drucker, Jr.* and *Foreign Transaction Co., et al.*, Award No. ITL 4-121-FT (5 November 1982), 1 Iran–U.S. C.T.R. p. 252; *T.C.S.B., Inc.* and *Iran*, Award No. ITL 5-140-FT (5 November 1982), 1 Iran–U.S. C.T.R. p. 261; *Ford Aerospace and Communications Corp., et al.* and *The Air Force of the Islamic Republic of Iran, et al.*, Award No. ITL 6-159-FT (5 November 1982), 1 Iran–U.S. C.T.R. p. 268; *Zokor International, Inc.* and *The Government of the Islamic Republic of Iran, et al.*, Award No. ITL 7-254-FT (5 November 1982), 1 Iran–U.S. C.T.R. p. 271; *Stone and Webster Overseas Group, Inc.* and *National Petrochemical Co., et al.*, Award No. ITL 8-293-FT (5 November 1982), 1 Iran–U.S. C.T.R. p. 274; *Dresser Industries, Inc.* and *The Government of the Islamic Republic of Iran, et al.*, Award No. ITL 9-466-FT (5 November 1982), 1 Iran–U.S. C.T.R. p. 280.

[81] Iran–US CT Tribunal Rules, Article 32, paragraph 5. The Tribunal's awards and decisions have been published in 34 volumes, to date, of the Iran–United States Claims Tribunal Reports, published by Cambridge University Press, and they are also available in electronic legal databases such as Westlaw. See also section 8.01(a) below, on transparency.

[82] Iran–US CT Presidential Order No. 1 of 19 October 1981, 1 Iran–U.S. C.T.R. p. 95, paragraph 6.

[83] See, e.g., *Reza Said Malek* and *The Government of the Islamic Republic of Iran*, Interlocutory Award No. ITL 68-193-3 (23 June 1988), 19 Iran–U.S. C.T.R. p. 48 (Chamber 3 applying the "dominant and effective nationality" test established by the Full Tribunal in Case No. A18, Decision No. DEC 32-A18-FT, 5 Iran–U.S. C.T.R. p. 251).

review on procedural, substantive, or other grounds.[84] The reports and recommendations of the panels became final only after they were approved by the Governing Council, and that is when they became part of the body of UNCC precedent that the panels could subsequently apply in practice.

There is no formal rule of *stare decisis* in the practice of the UNCC and its panels of Commissioners. However, a number of provisions in the Provisional Rules, as well as measures that the Commission has taken, were designed to promote, to the extent possible, that similar issues and claims would be decided in a consistent manner and that inconsistencies would be avoided. As was set forth in the Rules, in order to facilitate the work of the panels of Commissioners and to ensure uniformity in the treatment of similar claims, the Secretariat consistently categorized claims according to their type or size and the similarity of legal and factual issues they raised.[85] The Governing Council, already in Decision 1, created six main categories for what turned out to be more than 2.6 million claims.[86] After further sub-categorization by the Secretariat, sub-categories of claims were assigned to the (as many as nineteen) panels of Commissioners in such a way that, so far as possible, claims with significant common legal and factual issues could be processed together.[87] In practice, it was one of the chief tasks of the senior legal staff in the Secretariat to coordinate and ensure the consistency of legal advice presented to the panels of Commissioners.

Quarterly reports concerning the claims received by the Commission (issued by the Executive Secretary to the Governing Council, the Government of Iraq, as well as governments that submitted claims) indicated significant legal and factual issues raised by the claims.[88] Information and views submitted by the recipients pursuant to these reports were then made available to all panels of Commissioners, who took them into account in their consideration of the claims, thereby fostering uniformity.[89]

For the larger individual, corporate, and government claims (categories "D", "E" and "F"), the panels of Commissioners adopted "special procedures appropriate to the character, amount and subject-matter of the particular types of claims under consideration."[90] While the Provisional Rules required that each of these claims be reviewed individually, the similarity of types of loss and of issues across significant numbers of claims enabled the UNCC to employ precedent-setting procedures which ensured equal treatment in the

---

[84] UNCC Provisional Rules, Article 40, paragraph 4.   [85] Ibid., Article 17.

[86] UNCC Governing Council Decision 1 of 2 August 1991, *Criteria for Expedited Processing of Urgent Claims*, U.N. Doc. S/AC.16/1991/1 (2 August 1991).

[87] UNCC Provisional Rules, Article 38(a).   [88] Ibid., Article 16.

[89] Ibid., Article 32, paragraph 1 and Article 34, paragraph 2.   [90] Ibid., Article 38(b).

processing of similar claims. The panels attempted to resolve common issues and develop standard valuation methods during their review of the first group of similarly situated claims, and they then applied the legal, factual, and valuation precedents in the review of subsequent groups of claims assigned to them.

Finally, the chairpersons of the panels of Commissioners were instructed to organize the work of their respective panels so as to achieve the consistent application of the relevant legal criteria and the Provisional Rules.[91] To that end, different panels of Commissioners met with each other, as the need arose, to consider legal, factual, and valuation issues common to the claims before their respective panels. The chairpersons of all panels have also met once a year with senior Secretariat staff for the same purpose.

(c) Commission for Real Property Claims of Displaced Persons and Refugees (CRPC)—claims relating to the 1992–1995 war in Bosnia and Herzegovina

The constituting instrument of CRPC, Annex 7 of the Dayton Peace Agreement, stated that the Commission's decisions should be final, and that "any title, deed, mortgage or other legal instrument created or awarded by the Commission shall be recognized as lawful throughout Bosnia and Herzegovina."[92]

Although the constituting instrument allowed for division into separate panels of Commissioners, the Commission in practice preferred to render its decisions in plenary sessions. This served to promote consistency in the decision-making, since the body making the decisions was always composed of the same Commissioners. Thus, although no formal *stare decisis* rule applied in the Claims Process, the decisions of the Commission were consistent.

(d) Claims Resolution Tribunal for Dormant Accounts in Switzerland (CRT-I)—first claims tribunal for assets deposited in Swiss banks

The CRT-I awards were final and binding in accordance with Swiss law, subject to the right of claimants under that law to challenge an award on certain limited grounds within thirty days after its issuance. Decisions by Sole Arbitrators or claims panels were not considered binding on other Sole Arbitrators or claims panels; they each exercised their functions and rendered

---

[91] UNCC Provisional Rules, Article 29.
[92] Dayton Peace Agreement, Annex 7, Article XII, paragraph 7.

their decisions independently. However, in order to avoid inconsistent decisions and to enhance the consistency of the Tribunal's overall jurisprudence, policy committees were set up, headed by the Chairman of the Tribunal. There was a General Policy Committee, as well as special committees for specific tasks, such as Interest and Fees, and for Victim and Non-Victim Accounts. These committees issued non-binding instructions in the form of "recommendations."

(e) Claims Resolution Tribunal (CRT-II)—second claims tribunal for assets deposited in Swiss banks

Awards issued by CRT-II become final and binding only upon approval by the United States federal district court overseeing the class action known as the Holocaust Victim Assets Litigation. Once CRT-II has certified an award to the Court and the Court has approved it, the Special Masters appointed by the Court are required to pay such award in full.[93]

The Court's decisions and orders are typically observed as *stare decisis* within the Claims Process in its continuing work. The extent to which the Court's actions are subject to appeal to higher Courts is governed by the applicable United States law relating to appeals from federal district courts.

(f) Housing and Property Claims Commission (HPCC)—claims relating to the 1999 conflict in Kosovo

The HPCC's final decisions are binding and enforceable and not subject to review by any other judicial or administrative body.[94]

UNMIK Regulation 2000/60 provides that a panel of Commissioners "shall be bound by the principles established in: (a) Its own decisions and the decisions of another Panel, unless compelling reasons exist for deviating from those principles; and (b) The decisions of the plenary Commission."[95] In practice, one panel has been sufficient for handling all of the Commission's decisions. Thus, although the need for maintaining consistency between different panels has not arisen, the principle of *stare decisis* has bound Panel 1 to follow its own precedent, save where the Panel sits in an appellate capacity in deciding requests for reconsideration. In such capacity, the Commission has

---

[93] CRT-II Governing Rules, Article 31, paragraph 3.

[94] UNMIK Regulation 1999/23, section 2.7. The Commission may refer specific aspects of claims to local courts or administrative organs if the adjudication of such parts does not raise issues that fall within the Commission's jurisdiction. See section 2.02(f) above, on recourse to other bodies.

[95] UNMIK Regulation 2000/60, section 22.2.

considered itself entitled to revisit precedents established when deciding claims in the first instance.

(g) Mass Claims Processes administered by the International Organization for Migration (IOM)

German Forced Labour Compensation Programme (GFLCP)—claims against Germany and German industry for Nazi injustice

Decisions rendered under the German Foundation Act are final and binding. While the principle of *stare decisis* is not formally applicable to GFLCP, the administrative nature of the Claims Process and the mass claims methods applied to all received claims are designed to promote, and have the effect of promoting, consistency in the treatment of the many similarly situated claims.

Neither the Property Claims Commission nor the IOM Appeals Body for Forced Labour Claims have any formal *stare decisis* rules, but both have in practice developed criteria and standards to be applied consistently to similarly situated claims.

Holocaust Victim Assets Programme (HVAP)—claims pursuant to 1999 class action Settlement

Decisions rendered under the HVAP Claims Process are final and binding upon approval by the United States federal district court overseeing the class action known as the Holocaust Victim Assets Litigation. *Stare decisis* does not formally apply to the Claims Process, but the administrative nature of the Claims Process—i.e., applying the Special Master's Plan of Allocation and Distribution, and certifying all decisions to the Court for approval—and the mass claims methods applied to all received claims serve to promote consistency in the decision-making.

(h) Eritrea–Ethiopia Claims Commission (EECC)—claims relating to the 1998–2000 war between Eritrea and Ethiopia

The 12 December 2000 Agreement provides that decisions and awards of the EECC shall be final and binding. The parties agree to honor all decisions and to pay any monetary awards rendered against them promptly.[96] As there is only

---

[96] Eritrea–Ethiopia Agreement of 12 December 2000, Article 5, paragraph 17. "Decisions" are significant actions the Commission takes regarding jurisdiction, procedure or other matters not related to the merits of particular claims. EECC Rules of Procedure, Article 18, paragraph 1. As at 31 January 2006, the Commission has issued six such Decisions, available at www.pca-cpa.org.

one panel of Arbitrators, the issue of *stare decisis* as between different panels does not arise, but the Commission, in practice, follows its own precedent.

(i) Humanitarian insurance Claims Process administered by the Jewish Claims Conference (JCC) for the International Commission on Holocaust Era Insurance Claims (ICHEIC)

The 8A1 humanitarian Claims Process was purely voluntary and the US$1,000 awards represented a symbolic gesture. ICHEIC therefore decided not to allow any appeals of such awards; all 8A1 decisions were final and binding.

No *stare decisis* applied formally to this Claims Process, but in evaluating the claims, all the JCC claims analysts followed the same Point Scoring System Guidelines, that were designed and tested to yield consistent results no matter which analyst used them to score a claim. The analysts also underwent a training phase for the same purpose.

(j) American Arbitration Association (AAA)—an illustrative case

Awards in the illustrative case were final and binding, and they were based upon standards set forth in the constituting instrument, the Settlement Agreement in the underlying class action. Although there was formally no rule of *stare decisis*, the awards of different appeals reviewers were available to representatives both of the plaintiffs and the defendant insurance company so that they could review them for consistency. In practice, inconsistency of awards was one of the bases for not assigning further cases to an Arbitrator.

2.05 Approval of Decisions

Whether decisions rendered in the Claims Process require approval of another body before becoming effective.

Editors' Commentary

A major goal of Mass Claims Processes is to dispose of claims as quickly as possible. Recognizing this objective, the designers of the Claims Processes described in this book have, with few exceptions, minimized the number of procedural steps needed in order to provide that decisions rendered in the Claims Process will become effective without further approval. Exceptions are the United Nations Compensation Commission (UNCC), where recommendations by panels of Commissioners require the approval of the Governing Council, which has the power to modify them as to the amount of compensation or return them for further proceedings; the German Forced Labour Compensation Programme (GFLCP), where decisions by the partner organizations require approval of the German Foundation before funds can be allocated to pay compensation; and the Holocaust Victim Assets Programme (HVAP) and the Claims Resolution Tribunal (CRT-II), where decisions do not become effective until approved by the United States federal district court that supervises the class action known as the Holocaust Victim Assets Litigation.

Designers of future Mass Claims Processes and others who might review the materials in this book may wish to consider whether the extra step of having decisions of decision-makers subject to further approval provides benefits that outweigh the advantages of a single-step procedure in which such decisions become effective without further approval. In doing so, they will wish to balance, on the one hand, the advantages of having cases finally decided in a speedy manner by those who are closest to them, against the value, on the other hand, that review by a central body can have in promoting consistency in the jurisprudence of Claims Processes where decision-making is delegated to a number of different panels or claims reviewers. Review by a central body can also be useful in Claims Processes where it is necessary to control the flow of limited funds.

(a) Iran–United States Claims Tribunal (Iran–US CT)—claims relating to the 1979 Islamic Revolution

Awards made by the Iran–US CT are final and binding on the parties, and approval of no other body is required.[97] Pursuant to the pertinent provision of the Tribunal Rules, awards granting monetary compensation are filed with the competent Dutch court at the seat of the Tribunal at The Hague, but only for recording purposes, not review.[98] See section 2.03(a) above.

[97] Claims Settlement Declaration, Article IV, paragraph 1; Iran–US CT Tribunal Rules, Article 32, paragraph 2.

[98] Iran–US CT Tribunal Rules, Article 32, paragraph 7, provides: "If the arbitration law of the country where the award is made requires that the award be filed or registered by the arbitral tribunal, the tribunal shall comply with this requirement within the period of time required by law."

(b) United Nations Compensation Commission (UNCC)—claims relating to the 1990–1991 Gulf War

The UNCC panels of Commissioners made reports on the claims they reviewed and the amounts of compensation they recommended. These reports were submitted through the UNCC's Executive Secretary to the Governing Council,[99] and they generally applied to all the claims submitted to the panel as part of a group of claims. The amounts recommended by the panels of Commissioners were subject to approval by the Governing Council, which could review those amounts and, where it determined circumstances required, increase or reduce them.[100] The Governing Council, in its discretion, could return a particular claim or group of claims to Commissioners for further review.[101] In practice, the Governing Council has approved all panel recommendations. The Council's decisions follow a standard format that does not include giving reasons for its decisions.

Although the Governing Council is a subsidiary organ of the United Nations Security Council, it does not refer questions to it, except that a dissenting Member State of the Governing Council could have referred to the Security Council questions concerning the methods for ensuring that payments are made to the Compensation Fund, but this never happened in practice.

(c) Commission for Real Property Claims of Displaced Persons and Refugees (CRPC)—claims relating to the 1992–1995 war in Bosnia and Herzegovina

Decisions of the CRPC were final.[102] While the Commission required the cooperation of various local authorities under the supervision of the international bodies mandated by the Dayton Peace Agreement for the implementation of its decisions, approval of no other body was needed before those decisions became effective.

The Commission's decisions had to be implemented by the local authorities on the basis of the Law on Implementation of CRPC Decisions that was enacted in the Federation of Bosnia and Herzegovina, as well as in Republika Srpska.[103] Further, the local law on property books recognizes CRPC decisions

---

[99] UNCC Provisional Rules, Article 37(e).   [100] Ibid., Article 40, paragraph 1.

[101] Ibid., Article 40, paragraph 2.

[102] Dayton Peace Agreement, Annex 7, Article XII, paragraph 7.

[103] Law on Implementation of CRPC Decisions, Official Gazette of the Federation of Bosnia and Herzegovina, Nos 43/99, 51/00, 56/01, and 24/03; Official Gazette of the Republika Srpska, Nos 31/99, 39/00, 65/01, and 39/03.

as having the force of legal evidence that may be used in administrative, judicial, or other legal proceedings, most importantly, the proceedings to register ownership.

(d) Claims Resolution Tribunal for Dormant Accounts in Switzerland (CRT-I)—first claims tribunal for assets deposited in Swiss banks

CRT-I claims were decided in certain cases by a Sole Arbitrator and, in others, by a three-Member claims panel. In neither case was approval of another body required before awards became effective.

(e) Claims Resolution Tribunal (CRT-II)—second claims tribunal for assets deposited in Swiss banks

Awards issued by CRT-II have the legal character of recommendations. They are certified by Special Masters to the United States federal district court overseeing the class action known as the Holocaust Victim Assets Litigation, for payment out of the Settlement Fund established in that class action. The awards do not become binding unless and until they are approved by the Court.[104]

(f) Housing and Property Claims Commission (HPCC)—claims relating to the 1999 conflict in Kosovo

The Commission's final decisions are binding.[105] Approval of no other body is required before they become effective.

(g) Mass Claims Processes administered by the International Organization for Migration (IOM)

German Forced Labour Compensation Programme (GFLCP)—claims against Germany and German industry for Nazi injustice

Decisions on slave and forced labor and personal injury claims under GFLCP require the approval of the Board of Directors of the German Foundation in order to become final. Each time approval is requested for a group—or *tranche*—of claims, these are "spot checked" on-site by an audit team from the Foundation before they can be approved. The Board of Directors has established this audit practice pursuant to its mandate to monitor the partner

---

[104] CRT-II Governing Rules, Article 31, paragraphs 2 and 3.
[105] UNMIK Regulation 1999/23, section 2.7.

organizations' adherence to the provisions of the German Foundation Act and the guidelines established by the Board of Trustees.[106]

By contrast, the Property Claims Commission and the IOM Appeals Body for Forced Labour Claims are independent bodies, and the German Foundation has no formal oversight function over their work. However, the Foundation can bring its views to the attention of the Commissioners on the basis of sample reviews of their decisions.

Holocaust Victim Assets Programme (HVAP)—claims pursuant to 1999 class action Settlement

As in the case of CRT-II, described in section 2.05(e) above, awards issued by HVAP have the legal character of recommendations. They are certified by Special Masters to the United States federal district court overseeing the class action known as the Holocaust Victim Assets Litigation, for payment out of the Settlement Fund established in the settlement of that class action. The awards do not become binding unless and until they are approved by the Court.[107]

(h) Eritrea–Ethiopia Claims Commission (EECC)—claims relating to the 1998–2000 war between Eritrea and Ethiopia

The constituting instrument, the 12 December 2000 Agreement, provides that decisions and awards of the EECC shall be final and binding on the parties.[108] Approval by no other body is required before they become effective. The Commission has responded to requests from the Secretary-General of the United Nations for information on the progress of its work, but it is not subject to direction by the Secretary-General.

(i) Humanitarian insurance Claims Process administered by the Jewish Claims Conference (JCC) for the International Commission on Holocaust Era Insurance Claims (ICHEIC)

The scoring of claims carried out by JCC staff in the 8A1 humanitarian Claims Process constituted recommendations; authorization for payments resided with the Senior Counselor appointed by ICHEIC. Thus, awards in this Claims Process needed to be approved by ICHEIC before they became effective.

---

[106] German Foundation Act, section 6, paragraph 3.
[107] Plan of Allocation and Distribution, pp. 156, 166 and 178.
[108] Eritrea–Ethiopia Agreement of 12 December 2000, Article 5, paragraph 17.

(j) American Arbitration Association (AAA)—an illustrative case

The awards issued in the illustrative case did not require the consent or approval of another body before becoming effective.

2.06 Mandates from Other Bodies

Whether there are any aspects of claims as to which decision-makers are mandated to follow and apply decisions by another body.

Editors' Commentary

Typically, those who decide claims in a Mass Claims Process, whether in an arbitral or administrative setting, have wide discretion in determining facts and applying the governing law. Consistent with that general approach, those responsible for deciding cases in the Claims Processes described in this book generally are not, or were not, mandated to follow and apply decisions by any other body. Exceptions include: (i) the United Nations Compensation Commission (UNCC), where the panels of Commissioners had to apply decisions of the Commission's Governing Council as to criteria for the eligibility of claims and their verification and valuation; (ii) the German Forced Labour Compensation Programme (GFLCP), where the partner organizations—including the International Organization for Migration (IOM)—must apply decisions by the Board of Directors of the German Foundation as to criteria for the eligibility of claims and their verification; (iii) the Claims Resolution Tribunal for Dormant Accounts in Switzerland (CRT-I), where the Arbitrators were required to follow guidelines on interest and bank fees determined by the Board of Directors of the Foundation that established the Claims Process; and (iv) the second Claims Resolution Tribunal (CRT-II), whose Governing Rules, approved by a United States federal district court, require the Tribunal to apply certain presumptions of fact, to follow specific formulas in determining the amounts of awards, and to decide who are heirs in cases in which there is no will, by applying rules of distribution set out in the Governing Rules, notwithstanding that the otherwise applicable national law might establish a different inheritance scheme.

Choosing between establishing a Claims Process in which decision-makers have wide discretion, or one in which they are mandated to follow fixed rules on certain issues, requires a balancing of the advantages and disadvantages of each system. The strong case for limiting the areas of discretion of the decision-makers is that doing so accelerates the processing of claims by narrowing the task. It may also be the only feasible alternative where a number of different decision-makers have to resolve very large numbers of claims in a consistent manner. On the other hand, establishing in advance rules that limit discretion imposes a rigidity upon the Claims Process that may make it difficult to handle unexpected circumstances and unintended consequences. Although fixed rules and presumptions can be changed if they prove to be unworkable, incomplete, or inappropriate, it may be difficult to apply changes retroactively once the Claims Process is underway, and repeated amendments may undermine confidence in its stability.

(a) Iran–United States Claims Tribunal (Iran–US CT)—claims relating to the 1979 Islamic Revolution

There are no decisions by another body that Members of the Iran–US CT are mandated to follow and apply.

(b) United Nations Compensation Commission (UNCC)—claims relating to the 1990–1991 Gulf War

The panels of Commissioners of the UNCC were mandated to follow and apply relevant Resolutions of the United Nations Security Council and pertinent decisions of the Commission's Governing Council.[109]

(c) Commission for Real Property Claims of Displaced Persons and Refugees (CRPC)—claims relating to the 1992–1995 war in Bosnia and Herzegovina

There were no decisions by another body that the CRPC Commissioners were mandated to follow and apply.

(d) Claims Resolution Tribunal for Dormant Accounts in Switzerland (CRT-I)—first claims tribunal for assets deposited in Swiss banks

When awarding interest and compensation for fees that may have been deducted from accounts by banks, the CRT-I Arbitrators were obligated to

---

[109] UNCC Provisional Rules, Article 31.

follow "Guidelines" on interest and fees recommended by an international panel and adopted by the Board of Trustees of the Independent Claims Resolution Foundation (ICRF).[110] There were no other decisions by another body that the Arbitrators were mandated to follow and apply. In making determinations on the entitlement of claimants, the Arbitrators were permitted to obtain the advice of the Independent Committee of Eminent Persons (ICEP),[111] but they were not required to seek such advice or to follow any advice given.

(e) Claims Resolution Tribunal (CRT-II)—second claims tribunal for assets deposited in Swiss banks

The CRT-II Governing Rules, which were proposed by the Special Masters and adopted by the United States federal district court overseeing the class action known as the Holocaust Victim Assets Litigation, provide that CRT-II staff attorneys prepare draft decisions, containing the relevant facts and the reasons for the recommended decision, that are certified to the Court for approval.[112]

The Rules mandate the application of various presumptions, recommended by the Plan of Allocation and Distribution as approved by the Court, in order to overcome factual gaps in the records and in recognition of certain war-time realities.[113] Thus, the Governing Rules establish presumptions to be applied in deciding whether account holders had already received the proceeds of accounts for which they claimed,[114] and for determining the value of accounts whose amounts were unavailable from bank records.[115] Further, the Rules require that awards be adjusted by designated amounts on account of interest and bank fees, and they provide that such adjustments shall be "in accordance with a formula established by the Special Masters with Court approval."[116] Finally, in contrast to CRT-I, where Arbitrators decided inheritance questions by the application of what they determined to be the applicable national law, at CRT-II, questions of who are heirs in cases where there is no will are to be decided by applying a "General Rule on Distribution" set out in the Governing Rules.[117]

---

[110] CRT-I Rules of Procedure, Article 12.   [111] Ibid., Article 15, paragraph 3.

[112] CRT-II Governing Rules, Article 16.

[113] See ibid., Introduction, Part III. See also Article 28 "Presumptions Relating to Claims to Certain Closed Accounts," and Article 29 "Value Presumptions for Accounts with Unknown or Low Values."   [114] Ibid., Article 28.

[115] Ibid., Article 29.   [116] Ibid., Article 31, paragraph 1.   [117] Ibid., Article 23.

(f) **Housing and Property Claims Commission (HPCC)—claims relating to the 1999 conflict in Kosovo**

The HPCC Commissioners are not mandated to follow and apply the decisions of any other body.

(g) **Mass Claims Processes administered by the International Organization for Migration (IOM)** *German Forced Labour Compensation Programme (GFLCP) for claims against Germany and German industry for Nazi injustice; and Holocaust Victim Assets Programme (HVAP) for claims pursuant to 1999 class action Settlement*

In deciding claims under the GFLCP and HVAP Claims Processes, IOM is mandated to follow and apply the decisions of the respective overseeing bodies, namely, the German Foundation on "Remembrance, Responsibility and Future" for GFLCP, and the United States District Court for the Eastern District of New York for HVAP. IOM is not required to follow and apply the decisions of any other bodies.

(h) **Eritrea–Ethiopia Claims Commission (EECC)—claims relating to the 1998–2000 war between Eritrea and Ethiopia**

EECC Commissioners are not mandated to follow and apply the decisions of any other body. The Commission has responded to requests from the Secretary-General of the United Nations for information on the progress of its work, but it is not subject to direction by the Secretary-General.

(i) **Humanitarian insurance Claims Process administered by the Jewish Claims Conference (JCC) for the International Commission on Holocaust Era Insurance Claims (ICHEIC)**

ICHEIC membership is comprised of groups involved on a voluntary basis through private agreements. ICHEIC is not mandated to apply the decisions of any other body.

(j) **American Arbitration Association (AAA)—an illustrative case**

In the illustrative case, the claims reviewers who first considered the claims in-house at the defendant insurance company, as well as the AAA Arbitrators who decided appeals, were required to follow the mandates of the Settlement

Agreement approved by the United States federal district court in the underlying class action. Several appeals reviewers wished to change certain provisions, for example, by allowing more discovery, lengthening the hearing time, and so forth. No changes were allowed, as the Settlement Agreement had been vigorously negotiated and approved by the Court with no option for amendment.

2.07 Enforcement

How decisions in the Claims Process are enforced. If they are not enforceable as arbitral awards, what legal force do they have, and what is the source of their legal authority. The mechanism for paying out awards of compensation, and whether there is a special fund to secure the payment of awards.

Editors' Commentary

A Mass Claims Process may be an exercise in futility if the award is not enforceable and payments do not reach the claimants. The designers of the Claims Processes described in this book, in cases where States are parties, have relied, in the first instance at least, on international law holding States responsible to fulfill their promises. Where only private entities are involved, the Claims Processes tend to rely on methods of enforcement generally available for international arbitration awards.

As to funding, it has been possible in several Claims Processes to provide security by establishing special funds from which awards are paid. Examples of various modalities for doing that include: (i) a fixed sum deposited in advance, combined with an obligation to replenish it if additional funds become necessary to maintain the fund at an agreed level, as is done at the Iran–United States Claims Tribunal (Iran–US CT); (ii) a fixed negotiated sum deposited in advance that is not required to be replenished and is, therefore, the limit of the debtor's liability, as was the case for the compensation fund from which the German Forced Labour Compensation Programme (GFLCP) was funded, and for the second Claims Resolution Tribunal for bank assets in Switzerland (CRT-II); (iii) a fund that receives periodically a percentage of certain future income of the debtor until all awards have been paid, as at the United Nations Compensation Commission for claims arising out of the 1990–1991 Gulf War (UNCC); and (iv) other payment systems devised in the light of particular circumstances, such as for example at the Housing and Property Claims Commission (HPCC) in Kosovo. In other Claims Processes, the constituting instrument or procedural rules include no mechanisms for securing payment of awards, and thus rely on the commitment of the party found responsible to honor its obligations, as for example the first Claims Resolution Tribunal for Dormant Accounts in Switzerland (CRT-I) and the Eritrea–Ethiopia Claims Commission (EECC).[118]

However, even if there is a question as to whether funds are available, there can be value in having a Claims Process that can put an objective price-tag on awards. Much time may pass before political or other circumstances evolve in ways that make payment possible. Hence, United States claims practice (and other national practice as well) has not infrequently been to have Claims Processes adjudicate claims to provide a considered basis for future diplomatic settlement, even if it takes years before the eventual settlement occurs. In practice, this has often been very useful, even if frustrating to individual claimants.

If it is anticipated, as was the case initially, for example, at the UNCC, that the value of successful claims will exceed the funds available to the Mass Claims Process, designers of a Claims Process and others might consider the recommendation of the United Nations Secretary-General when establishing the UNCC, namely, to adopt rules on the priority of payment to the most urgent categories of needy claimants. A first phase of payments can then be made to the neediest claimants, even perhaps consisting of only a percentage of the full award. This was done at the German Forced Labour Compensation Programme, whose claimants were often elderly and needy. Once all claims have been resolved, the balance—or what funds remain—can then be paid out as a second phase payment pro rata.

Establishing a special fund from which awards are to be paid involves resolving complex issues. First, a financial institution must be found and agreed upon—often a national central bank, and sometimes in a third country—and it must be willing to undertake the responsibility. Then, detailed technical agreements that will be acceptable to the opposing parties must be negotiated and drafted.

---

[118] For further discussion of funding the Claims Process, see section 7.03 below.

(a) Iran–United States Claims Tribunal (Iran–US CT)—claims relating to the 1979 Islamic Revolution

Decisions of the Iran–US CT are enforceable as international arbitration awards.[119] To assure enforcement, a security account at the Central Bank of the Netherlands was established in agreement with the Algerian Central Bank for the purpose of securing the payment of, and paying, awards made by the Tribunal against Iran in accordance with the Claims Settlement Declaration. This account was initially funded with US$1 billion, and Iran is obliged by treaty to make deposits sufficient always to maintain a minimum balance of US$500 million until all awards against it have been satisfied (at which point any amount remaining in the account shall be transferred back to Iran).[120] The funds are kept in the Settlement Bank of the Netherlands, a bank established and managed by the Dutch Central Bank pursuant to a series of technical agreements between the Algerian Central Bank, Bank Markazi Iran, the Federal Reserve Bank of New York, and the Dutch Central Bank.[121] There is no provision for securing payment of awards made by the Tribunal against the United States.

The payment necessary for the execution of an award rendered by the Tribunal in favor of a United States claimant is made by the Dutch depositary bank to the Federal Reserve Bank of New York, pursuant to instructions that the Algerian Central Bank, as escrow agent, issues after it receives a notification from the President of the Tribunal that the Tribunal has rendered an award.[122] The Federal Reserve Bank then pays the claimant the amount awarded.

(b) United Nations Compensation Commission (UNCC)—claims relating to the 1990–1991 Gulf War

UNCC awards are paid out of a Compensation Fund established by the United Nations Security Council and administered by the Commission.[123] The Compensation Fund has been funded from the proceeds of Iraqi oil sales,

---

[119] The Claims Settlement Declaration, Article IV, paragraph 3, provides that "[a]ny award which the Tribunal may render against either government shall be enforceable against such government in the courts of any nation in accordance with its laws."

[120] General Declaration, paragraph 7.

[121] See Technical Agreement with De Nederlandsche Bank N.V., 17 August 1981, 1 Iran–U.S. C.T.R. 29.

[122] Iran–US CT Technical Agreement with N.V. Settlement Bank of the Netherlands, 17 August 1981, paragraph 1(e), 1 Iran–U.S. C.T.R. p. 38, at p. 41.

[123] UN Security Council Resolution 687 (1991) of 3 April 1991, U.N. Doc. S/RES/687 (1991) (8 April 1991), paragraph 18, in which the Council decided "to create a fund to pay compensation for claims . . . and to establish a Commission that will administer the fund." Resolution 692 (1991) of 20 May 1991, U.N. Doc. S/RES/692 (1991), paragraph 3, adopted recommendations by the UN Secretary-General for how to accomplish this.

which were permitted by the Security Council under the so-called "oil-for-food" arrangement, every six months, as an exception to the oil embargo.[124] (The arrangements described here relate only to the period before commencement in 2003 of war between the United States and its coalition partners and Iraq. Later arrangements are outside the scope of this book.)

UNCC Governing Council Decision 18 established the procedures for distributing payments, which are made from the Compensation Fund to the governments or international organizations that submitted the claims and that are responsible for distributing the funds to successful claimants within six months of receiving payment from the Fund.[125] Governments (or persons or bodies designated by the UNCC to submit claims on behalf of persons who are unable to have their claims submitted by a government) are required to report to the Commission on the distribution of the funds. Failing satisfactory reports, the UNCC Governing Council may suspend distribution of further funds to the governments or other bodies concerned.[126] Given the large number of claims and the complexity of the UNCC's payment procedures, the Secretariat put in place a computerized payment system to track payments and monitor their distribution by governments and international organizations to the claimants. Funds that are not distributed within twelve months, for whatever reason, are to be returned to the Secretariat of the Commission.[127]

Priority was given to the payment of the urgent claims of individuals (i.e., categories "A", "B" and "C").[128] All these claims have been paid in full.[129]

(c) Commission for Real Property Claims of Displaced Persons and Refugees (CRPC)—claims relating to the 1992–1995 war in Bosnia and Herzegovina

Annex 7 to the Dayton Peace Agreement did not grant the CRPC any enforcement or implementation powers. Instead, it imposed the responsibilities

---

[124] The initial ceiling of US$1 billion for such oil sales, which was later raised to US$5.256 billion, was eventually removed. See UN Security Council Resolution 1284 (1999) of 17 December 1999, U.N. Doc. S/RES/1284 (1999). Initially, 30% of the proceeds from Iraqi oil sales were paid into the Compensation Fund. Resolution 1284 (1999), Part C.

[125] UNCC Governing Council Decision 18 of 23 March 1994, *Distribution of Payments and Transparency*, U.N. Doc. S/AC.26/Dec.18 (1994) (24 March 1994).

[126] Ibid., section I, paragraphs 2 and 5, section II.

[127] UNCC Governing Council Decision 48 of 2 February 1998, *Decision Concerning the Return of Undistributed Funds*, U.N. Doc. S/AC.26/Dec.48 (1998) (3 February 1998), paragraph (a).

[128] See section 1.04(b) above for discussion of UNCC claims categories.

[129] For the initial allocation of funds see UNCC Governing Council Decision 17 of 23 March 1994, *Priority of Payment and Payment Mechanism—Guiding Principles*, U.N. Doc. S/AC.26/Dec.17 (1994) (24 March 1994). (Initially, awards on the larger claims of individuals and those of

for the implementation of the Commission's decisions upon the domestic authorities. The parties to Annex 7 (the Republic of Bosnia and Herzegovina, the Federation of Bosnia and Herzegovina, and the Republika Srpska) are required by the Agreement to respect and implement the CRPC's decisions expeditiously and in good faith, in cooperation with relevant international and non-governmental organizations having responsibility for the return and re-integration of refugees and displaced persons to Bosnia and Herzegovina.[130] In this connection, any title, deed, mortgage, or other legal instrument created or awarded by the Commission shall be recognized as lawful throughout Bosnia and Herzegovina.[131] This may require that local authorities take all appropriate action to enable the removal of inhabitants who had moved in after the refugees left, and to allow the lawful owners confirmed by the Commission to return to their properties.

According to the Commission's End of Mandate Report, "the domestic authorities actively failed to implement CRPC decisions and found numerous ways to obstruct the process until 2000."[132] The High Representative—the chief civilian peace implementation agency in Bosnia and Herzegovina desig-nated by the Dayton Peace Agreement to oversee the implementation of the civilian aspects of the Agreement on behalf of the international community—imposed specific laws setting forth concrete steps which the local authorities are expected to take when a claimant requests enforcement of a CRPC deci-sion. From 2000 onward, the CRPC, working closely with the international organizations involved in the area, achieved wide-spread implementation of its decisions.

By the end of its mandate, CRPC had delivered to claimants three fourths of the decision certificates it had issued, using its extensive network of regional offices and mobile teams. Any certificates not so delivered by the end of the Commission's mandate were made available to claimants in official archives of Bosnia and Herzegovina.[133]

(d) Claims Resolution Tribunal for Dormant Accounts in Switzerland (CRT-I)—first claims tribunal for assets deposited in Swiss banks

CRT-I awards, in any given case, were paid by the respondent Swiss bank holding the account of the claimant in question. There was no limit on the

corporations and governments would be paid in instalments as payments were received into the Compensation Fund.)

130 Dayton Peace Agreement, Annex 7, Article VIII.   131 Ibid., Article XII, paragraph 7.
132 CRPC End of Mandate Report, Executive Summary, p. 3.   133 Ibid., p. 2.

total aggregate amount that could be awarded against the banks.[134] Awards could be enforced in the same manner as any other Swiss arbitral awards. To facilitate any enforcement action that might be needed, each party receiving an award under the CRT-I Claims Process could request a certified copy of the award, which was deemed to comply with the requirements for enforcement of Article IV(1)(a) of the New York Convention.[135] The obligation of the Swiss banks to make payments was not secured and claimants relied solely on the credit of those banks.

(e) Claims Resolution Tribunal (CRT-II)—second claims tribunal for assets deposited in Swiss banks

The Settlement Agreement in the class action known as the Holocaust Victim Assets Litigation provides for the Swiss banks to pay a total settlement amount of US$1.25 billion into a Settlement Fund to cover claims for assets in Swiss bank accounts. Out of that amount, US$800 million was required to be allocated to claims in the Deposited Assets Class, the class which CRT-II is mandated to resolve.[136] No further enforcement mechanism is needed because awards approved by the supervising United States federal district court are paid out of the Settlement Fund. The Swiss banks are not obligated to make any payment in addition to the US$800 million, even if total awards and expenses of the Claims Process exceed that sum. In view of that circumstance, in cases where awards are based on presumptions established by the Governing Rules for claims in which the actual value of the account is unknown, an award paid in instalments is made, using value presumptions set forth in a schedule in the Rules.[137] Other awards are paid in full promptly after approval by the Court.

(f) Housing and Property Claims Commission (HPCC)—claims relating to the 1999 conflict in Kosovo

The Commission's decisions and eviction orders are executed by the Housing and Property Directorate (HPD) in coordination with one of the Commission's two Co-Registrars. Local law enforcement authorities are required to support

---

[134] Unlike the CRT-II Claims Process, governed by the Settlement Agreement in the Holocaust Victim Assets Litigation, section 5.2 of which provides that all such payments were to reduce the settlement amount.

[135] Convention on the Recognition and Enforcement of Foreign Arbitral Awards, New York, 10 June 1958, 330 U.N.T.S. 38. Article IV(1)(a) provides: "To obtain the recognition and enforcement mentioned in [Article III], the party applying for recognition and enforcement shall, at the time of the application, supply: (a) The duly authenticated award or a duly certified copy thereof."

[136] Plan of Allocation and Distribution, pp. 15 and 99.

[137] CRT-II Governing Rules, Article 29.

the Directorate in this function.[138] UNMIK Regulation 2000/60 contains detailed provisions on the procedures that the Directorate is to follow in executing such decisions and orders.[139]

As at 31 January 2006, regulatory action was pending to arrange for the payment of compensation in category "A" for claims where the property in question has been sold to a third party.[140]

(g) Mass Claims Processes administered by the International Organization for Migration (IOM)

German Forced Labour Compensation Programme (GFLCP)—claims against Germany and German industry for Nazi injustice

Under the German Foundation Act, the payment of compensation to eligible GFLCP claimants is carried out through the partner organizations from funds made available by the German Foundation for that purpose.[141]

The German Foundation has included provisions on necessary banking arrangements in its contracts with each of the partner organizations to ensure that payments will be effected in the appropriate manner. Payments to eligible claimants are made in two instalments, and each partner organization may pay out the second instalment only after it has completed the processing of all claims received by it.[142] Compensation payments for property losses, made pursuant to decisions of the Property Claims Commission, may only be made after all such claims have been processed by the Commission.[143] In addition, since the total funds available in this category were not sufficient to pay the full amount of the awards, a pro rata reduction had to be applied to all compensation payments.

A total amount of DM 50 million was allocated in the Foundation Act to cover all personal injury claims submitted to all of the partner organizations. Because this amount proved to be insufficient to pay the maximum amounts to all eligible claimants, only the claims in the priority categories (i.e., claims of victims of medical experiments and claims for injury or death of children in certain homes) were compensated; all claims for personal injury in lower

---

[138] UNMIK Regulation 2000/60, section 13.4.   [139] Ibid., section 13.

[140] See also section 1.05(f) above on remedies, and the rights of so-called "First Owners" to compensation.   [141] German Foundation Act, section 11, paragraph 4.

[142] Ibid., section 9, paragraph 9. Second installment payments may be made before conclusion of the appeals proceedings as long as the partner organization has set up a reserve of up to 5% of its *plafonds* (base allocation) for appeals.   [143] Ibid., section 9, paragraph 10.

priority categories were denied on the basis of lack of funds.[144] Additionally, the amount per compensated claim was capped based on the total funds available in this category.

Holocaust Victim Assets Programme (HVAP)—claims pursuant to 1999 class action Settlement

In the HVAP Claims Process, IOM makes compensation payments to eligible claimants after approval of the awards by the United States federal district court overseeing the class action known as the Holocaust Victim Assets Litigation, and from funds made available by the Court for that purpose from the Settlement Fund. Initially, it was envisioned that payments would be made in two instalments, and that the second payment would only be made after the processing of all claims received had been completed. This was to be done in order to ensure that all eligible claimants would receive some compensation— even if not the full amount to which they are entitled—before the funds would run out.[145] As it happened, the funds are sufficient, and full payments are made in one instalment.

(h) Eritrea–Ethiopia Claims Commission (EECC)—claims relating to the 1998–2000 war between Eritrea and Ethiopia

The two Government parties agreed in the 12 December 2000 Agreement to honor all decisions and to pay any monetary awards rendered against them promptly.[146] No other enforcement mechanism is provided for in the Agreement, and it does not provide for setting up a special fund to secure payments of awards.

(i) Humanitarian insurance Claims Process administered by the Jewish Claims Conference (JCC) for the International Commission on Holocaust Era Insurance Claims (ICHEIC)

Where a claimant in the ICHEIC Claims Process could not name the company that issued the policy against which the claim was made, or (in the case of the second phase of the Claims Process), where the claim could not be

---

[144] German Foundation Act, section 9, paragraph 3, and section 11, paragraph 1, sentence 3, number 5.   [145] See Plan of Allocation and Distribution, pp. 30, 34 and 38.
[146] Eritrea–Ethiopia Agreement of 12 December 2000, Article 5, paragraph 17; EECC Rules of Procedure, Article 18, paragraph 4.

matched with a known policy or where the named insurance company no longer exists and has no successor company, payments could be made from the special Humanitarian Fund established by ICHEIC. ICHEIC opened a bank account, and Humanitarian Fund monies were placed into that account to fund 8A1 Claim awards.

ICHEIC appointed a Senior Counselor to oversee the payment procedure. Each time the Senior Counselor authorized a batch—or *tranche*—of payments to be issued, the JCC Payment Operations Team paid the awards directly from the ICHEIC Humanitarian Fund.

(j) American Arbitration Association (AAA)—an illustrative case

As part of the Settlement Agreement in the illustrative case, the defendant insurance company agreed to the payment of all awards. The ultimate enforcement mechanism was the continuing authority of the United States federal district court seized of the underlying class action, which had retained oversight jurisdiction of the settlement.

Chapter 3

Starting the Claims Process

3.01 Outreach

How potential claimants are informed of the existence of the Claims Process, including the methods and extent of outreach.

Editors' Commentary

A Mass Claims Process has little practical value unless the potential claimants are aware of the opportunity to make claims and are given information on how to do so. No one method to accomplish this is appropriate for all Claims Processes; rather, the effectiveness of the method to be used depends on the particular circumstances involved. Thus, for example, the outreach can be quite precisely targeted if all of the claimants are expected to be from one country or region, speak one or two languages, and when the claims arise from relatively recent events that were well known and vividly remembered by the victims, such as losses of homes dealt with by the Commission for Real Property Claims of Displaced Persons and Refugees (CRPC) in Bosnia and Herzegovina, and the Housing and Property Claims Commission (HPCC) in Kosovo. In contrast, the outreach to potential claimants, and in some cases their heirs, is much more complex when claims arise from long-past events that affect persons in many countries who speak many different languages, as is the case with the Holocaust-related Claims Processes described in this book, i.e., the two Claims Resolution Tribunals for Dormant Accounts in Switzerland (CRT-I and CRT-II), the German Forced Labour Compensation Programme (GFLCP), the Holocaust Victim Assets Programme (HVAP), and the humanitarian Claims Process of the International Commission on Holocaust Era Insurance Claims (ICHEIC).

Designers of Mass Claims Processes and others must be particularly sensitive to the need to reach out to potential claimants where there are parties who stand to benefit from unclaimed assets in the Claims Process. In such situations, the credibility of the Claims Process depends on the public perception that the effort to find potential claimants has been vigorous and sincere.

In some Claims Processes, the only claimants are governments that extend to victims diplomatic protection, or something akin to it, as is the case with the United Nation Compensation Commission (UNCC) for claims arising out of the 1990–1991 Gulf War, and the Eritrea–Ethiopia Claims Commission (EECC). In such situations, the governments involved, not the staff of the Claims Process, typically perform the function of informing potential claimants of their opportunity to have claims made on their behalf. Designers of Mass Claims Processes in which governments are the sole or principal claimants may wish to consider including in the constituting instruments provisions describing the obligations of governments to inform potential claimants, and acceptable methods of doing so.

Annotations

(a) Iran–United States Claims Tribunal (Iran–US CT)—claims relating to the 1979 Islamic Revolution

The Iran–US CT did not itself establish any specific procedures to notify potential claimants of the existence of an opportunity for making claims, because it appeared that in the circumstances there was no need to undertake outreach procedures. Potential claimants—other than the two Government parties—were either nationals of the United States or Iran. Private claimants were well aware of the recent events of the Islamic Revolution in Iran, of the hostage crisis, and of the establishment of the Tribunal as a key element in resolving that crisis—all of which had been widely reported in the news media in both countries. In addition, during the hostage crisis, the United States Department of State had compiled a list of Americans who had suffered losses and, as was known to Iran, a number of such claims were pending in courts in the United States. The United States Department of State maintained contact with such claimants, and it also published material concerning the Tribunal in the Federal Register, the official journal for disseminating such information.[1] The two Governments were, of course, already aware of the provision of the Algiers Accords that established the jurisdiction of the Tribunal to consider

---

[1] See, e.g., Registration of Claims Against Iran with the Department of State and Submission of Claims to the Iran–United States Claims Tribunal; Time for Registration, Public Notice 749, 46 F.R. 19,893 (1 April 1981).

certain governmental claims. Given those circumstances, it is understandable that no provision for informing potential claimants appeared in the constituting instrument of the Tribunal, and that neither Government requested the Tribunal to establish any procedure to inform potential claimants.

(b) United Nations Compensation Commission (UNCC)—claims relating to the 1990–1991 Gulf War

Only governments or international organizations were allowed to submit claims to the UNCC, except in very limited circumstances that rarely occurred in practice.[2] Private applicants themselves did not generally have direct access to the Commission and therefore had to rely on their governments to submit claims on their behalf. Governments generally obtained and disseminated within their countries information on UNCC categories of claims. Some governments created an *ad hoc* administrative organ for this purpose,[3] while others utilized existing governmental mechanisms. The UNCC Secretariat advised governments and international organizations on questions regarding claims. With regard to refugees and potential stateless claimants—in particular Palestinians—who were not able to have claims submitted through their governments, various international organizations engaged in outreach programs, and numerous United Nations offices submitted claims for claimants where no government was able to do so.[4]

(c) Commission for Real Property Claims of Displaced Persons and Refugees (CRPC)—claims relating to the 1992–1995 war in Bosnia and Herzegovina

The CRPC Book of Regulations on Procedure provided for an "Executive Office and other offices of the Commission" to inform potential claimants of claims they might have and the procedures for filing those claims.[5] Specifically, the Regulations provided that:

"[p]otential claimants will receive information in the Commission offices orally or through written instructions, by media, by distribution of pamphlets, by direct participation of the Commissioners, the Executive Officer and other authorized persons on

---

[2] See UNCC Provisional Rules, Article 5, and discussion in section 1.04(b) above, on jurisdiction.

[3] E.g., The Kuwaiti Public Authority for Assessment of Compensation for Damages Resulting from the Iraqi Aggression; and The Jordanian Higher Compensation Commission.

[4] UNCC Governing Council Decision 5 of 18 October 1991, *Guidelines relating to paragraph 19 of the Criteria for Expedited Processing of Urgent Claims*, U.N. Doc. S/AC.26/1991/5 (23 October 1991).

[5] CRPC Book of Regulations on Procedure, Articles 6 and 7.

radio and TV programs or at meetings with representatives of potential claimants and in other appropriate ways."[6]

The CRPC also arranged for radio publicity spots and television advertisements informing the public of its role, and it sent out public notices to potential claimants concerning the deadlines for claims, as well as subsequent extensions of those deadlines. The notices contained detailed contact information.

(d) Claims Resolution Tribunal for Dormant Accounts in Switzerland (CRT-I)—first claims tribunal for assets deposited in Swiss banks

The Swiss Bankers Association (SBA) in 1997 published in newspapers throughout the world lists of 5,570 non-Swiss account holders whose accounts had been dormant since 1945. That list was also made available over the Internet. Following publication of the lists of dormant accounts, an information brochure and a form for filing claims were made available through the offices of an international accounting firm, ATAG Ernst & Young, in Basel, Switzerland, New York, Tel Aviv, Budapest, and Sydney. The firm was chosen because it had a network of multi-lingual offices in the many countries in which it was expected that potential claimants might be living. Claimants were invited to send their completed claim forms, along with supporting documentation, to one of those offices.

(e) Claims Resolution Tribunal (CRT-II)—second claims tribunal for assets deposited in Swiss banks

As CRT-II was established pursuant to the Settlement Agreement in the class action known as the Holocaust Victim Assets Litigation in the United States District Court for the Eastern District of New York, its outreach program was built upon an extensive notice plan carried out "to provide members of the Settlement Classes with notice of certification of the Settlement Classes, the terms of the Settlement Agreement, their rights with respect to the proposed settlement, and the deadline for submitting exclusion requests and objections."[7] The Plan of Allocation and Distribution approved by the District Court Judge provided for "not only direct mail, but worldwide publication, public relations ('earned media'), the Internet, and grass roots community outreach," that comprised "placement of the Court-approved Notice in paid publications, including 371 appearances in mainstream newspapers and 622

---

[6] CRPC Book of Regulations on Procedure, Article 7.
[7] Plan of Allocation and Distribution, p. 86.

appearances in Jewish publications, placed in 40 countries . . . [and] more than 1.7 million Notice packages [were] sent to potential Class members in 137 countries."[8] The Special Master appointed by the Court later reported that this massive notice program resulted in return of over 564,000 "Initial Questionnaires" from potential class members throughout the world.[9] After the Settlement Agreement was approved by the Court, the CRT-II Secretariat reviewed these Initial Questionnaires and sent packages of information, including claim forms, by direct mail to approximately 80,000 potential claimants whose responses to the Initial Questionnaire indicated that they had losses related to Swiss bank accounts. Names of approximately 21,000 account holders, compiled from Swiss bank records, who had "possible or probable" claims, were posted on the Internet and were published in several newspapers that did so without charge as a public service.

(f) Housing and Property Claims Commission (HPCC)—claims relating to the 1999 conflict in Kosovo

Outreach activities in the HPCC Claims Process are the responsibility of the Housing and Property Directorate (HPD), in cooperation with other institutions of the United Nations Interim Administration Mission in Kosovo (UNMIK). Outreach efforts were extended to Serbia and Montenegro on the basis, initially, of a Memorandum of Understanding between the United Nations Human Settlements Program (Habitat), and the Government of the State Union of Serbia and Montenegro.[10] The Directorate also set up a website to reach out to refugees and internally displaced claimants.[11] All claims in this Claims Process had to be filed in person by the claimant or by the claimant's family member or agent.

(g) Mass Claims Processes administered by the International Organization for Migration (IOM)

German Forced Labour Compensation Programme (GFLCP)—claims against Germany and German industry for Nazi injustice

The German Foundation made public information about the possibility of compensation under the German Foundation Act through the press and

---

[8] Plan of Allocation and Distribution, pp. 86–87.   [9] Ibid., p. 6, note 8, and p. 87.
[10] After August 2004, HPD operated under the auspices of the United Nations Office in Belgrade (UNOB). Like Habitat, UNOB has an agreement with the Government of the State Union of Serbia and Montenegro.   [11] See www.hpdkosovo.org.

through its website.[12] However, it was primarily the responsibility of the part-ner organizations implementing the GFLCP Claims Process to reach out to potential claimants within their respective jurisdictions.[13]

To this end, IOM ran several extensive and comprehensive information campaigns, using its worldwide network of field offices, and employing a whole range of techniques, including public service announcements, posters, brochures, press releases, newspaper advertisements, radio spots, and press conferences. IOM also maintains a special GFLCP website with relevant information and documents.[14] In addition, it has reached out with special campaigns to particularly disadvantaged claimant communities, and has issued information worldwide about filing deadlines and any extensions thereof.

Holocaust Victim Assets Programme (HVAP)—claims pursuant to 1999 class action Settlement

In the context of the Holocaust Victim Assets Litigation and its Settlement in the United States, extensive notice was carried out to potential members of the classes covered by the Settlement, including the distribution and collection of more than 600,000 "Initial Questionnaires." A summary of the Plan of Allocation and Distribution was mailed to all persons who had returned such Initial Questionnaires.

IOM used data collected in these outreach efforts to contact potential HVAP claimants within its jurisdiction and to send them claim forms. In addition, it employed similar methods as it did under GFLCP, including, for example, a special campaign for Roma communities. IOM also maintains a special HVAP website with relevant information and documents.[15]

(h) Eritrea–Ethiopia Claims Commission (EECC)—claims relating to the 1998–2000 war between Eritrea and Ethiopia

The 12 December 2000 Agreement does not address informing potential claimants of their eligibility under the EECC Claims Process. Responsibility for publicizing it rests with the two Government parties themselves. Each Government party was given one year (from the signing of the Agreement on 12 December 2000, until the deadline for filing claims, 12 December 2001) to

---

[12] www.stiftung-evz.de.   [13] German Foundation Act, section 10, paragraph 2.
[14] www.compensation-for-forced-labour.org.   [15] www.swissbankclaims.iom.int.

gather all claims. Thus it was up to each Government to disseminate news about the Claims Process to all potential claimants in their respective territories and elsewhere.

(i) Humanitarian insurance Claims Process administered by the Jewish Claims Conference (JCC) for the International Commission on Holocaust Era Insurance Claims (ICHEIC)

ICHEIC conducted an outreach campaign notifying potential claimants of the opportunity to file claims, by placing advertisements in both Jewish and non-Jewish press and media in areas (in the United States and elsewhere) where there was a significant population of Holocaust survivors. Claim forms were sent to community centers serving survivors. In addition, many state insurance regulators distributed claim forms among their constituencies and acted as liaisons with the Claims Process.

ICHEIC also maintains an online presence,[16] where contact information and printable application forms in a variety of languages were made available, and ICHEIC was later able to provide a searchable database of names of persons who might have had unclaimed wartime insurance policies. Thus, ICHEIC itself conducted most of the outreach and collected all the claim forms, some of which were later forwarded to the JCC for processing and review. The JCC did not conduct outreach, but for practical reasons, it served as a subsequent contact with claimants through the ICHEIC Call Center to answer questions and concerns.

(j) American Arbitration Association (AAA)—an illustrative case

The method for informing members of a class action in a United States court is ratified by the court overseeing the case, with the goal of reaching all potential class members. In the illustrative case, the class members were relatively easy to identify, as they had all purchased certain insurance products, during a certain period of time, from the same insurance company, which had maintained records with claimants' names and addresses. The news media also gave the lawsuit broad coverage. Moreover, when mail to a class member was returned as undeliverable, efforts were made by the Claims Process to find the actual insurance purchaser.

---

[16] www.icheic.org.

3.02 Claim Forms

Preparation of claim forms. In that connection, whether the claim forms include a waiver by which claimants agree to have their claims resolved only by the Claims Process and to forego recourse to national courts or other means.

Editors' Commentary

Almost all Claims Processes in which there are individual claimants develop a standard claim form for use in starting the Claims Process. Differences among these claim forms generally reflect differences in the nature of the claims the particular Claims Process is intended to resolve. Claim forms drafted in more recently established Processes have been designed to facilitate computer processing and analysis.[17]

The question of whether filing a claim has the legal effect of foregoing recourse to national courts or other means of dispute resolution is a fundamental issue. Regardless of whether the decision is that the particular Claims Process shall, or shall not, have exclusive jurisdiction, it is important that the question be answered directly and that the provision in the claim form be drafted clearly. Ambiguity on this point can create the potential for future litigation. Because claim forms are ordinarily drafted early in a Claims Process, drafters should be careful not to create contradictions between the forms and the rules of procedure, which are perhaps written concurrently with, or later than the forms. For example, if the rules of procedure deal with issues of confidentiality, or joinder of parties, a claim form which contradicts those provisions creates confusion and delay that could have been avoided.

Designers of Mass Claims Processes and others may find useful guidance in sub-section (b) below, on the claim forms used at the United Nations Compensation Commission (UNCC), and also in sub-section (h) below, on the work of the Eritrea–Ethiopia Claims Commission (EECC) in connection with the drafting of claim forms for the large numbers of claims that were initially expected to be filed in that Claims Process, although those EECC claim forms were not used (because it was later decided that claims of the individuals and juridical persons would be aggregated by their respective governments and submitted as Government-to-Government claims). Consequently, work on

---

[17] See also section 6.06 below, on computer facilities.

the claim forms was not completed, but a description of the analysis that was carried out is included below because it may provide insight for other Claims Processes.

The conduct of most Claims Processes requires, in addition to claim forms, the filing of notices, memorials, and other written communications. Those engaged in the Claims Process must know what procedures to follow to accomplish this and when delivery will be deemed to have been made. Designers of Mass Claims Processes and others should consider whether difficulties may arise due to the circumstances of a particular Claims Process. Thus, for example, the architects of the Iran–United States Claims Tribunal (Iran–US CT) anticipated that the practical problems that might arise might include uncertainty as to the current addresses of entities that had been nationalized, and difficulties in proving delivery in a continuing hostile environment. To address these problems, the constituting instrument of the Tribunal provided that "[e]ach government shall designate an Agent at the seat of the Tribunal . . . to receive notices or other communications directed to it or to its nationals, agencies, instrumentalities, or entities in connection with proceedings before the Tribunal."[18] This provision was implemented by detailed Tribunal Rules. For example, in order to guard against the possibility that a government might fail to designate an Agent, or that the Agent might be recalcitrant, the Tribunal Rules provide that documents shall be filed with the Registrar, and be deemed to have been delivered when physically received by the Registrar, who shall attempt to deliver copies to the Agents. The Agent, in turn, has the responsibility to transmit the document to the party in its country. The Tribunal Rules and the official Notes to them further regulate such related matters as signatures, required numbers of copies, and even the size of paper to be used.[19]

While detailed descriptions of such matters for all the Claims Processes described in this book are beyond its scope, the above-cited procedures relating to the Iran–US CT provide a comprehensive model, although not all of them are appropriate in all Claims Processes. For Claims Processes that accept electronic filings, it is necessary to decide, *inter alia*, when an electronic filing will be deemed to have been made, and to specify the electronic format(s) in which filings will be accepted, whether to issue receipts to claimants electronically or also on paper, and how to design an electronic archive to track the status of all communications.[20]

---

[18] Claims Settlement Declaration, Article VI, paragraph 2.

[19] See Iran–US CT Tribunal Rules, Article 2 and Notes to Article 2.

[20] See also section 6.03 below, on the role of the Registrars of the Claims Processes described in this book.

(a) Iran–United States Claims Tribunal (Iran–US CT)—claims relating to the 1979 Islamic Revolution

Except for the so-called "small claims" described below, no claim form was used at the Iran–US CT. Rather, claimants were required to prepare and submit a Statement of Claim containing information described in the Tribunal Rules.[21] Although the Tribunal Rules closely follow the UNCITRAL Arbitration Rules in many respects, the requirements for Statements of Claim differ from the UNCITRAL text in several ways. For example, the Tribunal Rules call for the Statement of Claim to include a number of particulars that are not required in the UNCITRAL text, such as reference to (i) the nationalities of the parties; (ii) the elements that bring the claim within the jurisdiction of the Tribunal as provided in the constituting instrument; (iii) various deadlines for submitting claims; and (iv) a provision that no priority for scheduling hearings shall be based on the date of filing the Statement of Claim.[22] Another difference between the UNCITRAL Arbitration Rules and the Tribunal Rules is that the Tribunal Rules state that it is "advisable," but not mandatory, that claimants annex documents that "will serve clearly to establish the basis of the claim, and/or [add a summary or quotation of] relevant portions of such documents" to the Statement of Claim.[23]

Claims for under US$250,000 (so-called "small claims") were presented by the United States Government on behalf of claimants. As to such claims, the United States itself prepared and circulated a claim form.

The Tribunal Rules contain no waiver by which claimants agree to forego recourse to national courts. Such waiver provisions were not necessary because interlocking provisions of the Tribunal's constituting instruments mandate that it has exclusive jurisdiction over claims that can be brought before it.[24]

(b) United Nations Compensation Commission (UNCC)—claims relating to the 1990–1991 Gulf War

The UNCC Provisional Rules required all claims to be submitted on standard forms prepared and submitted by the Secretariat.[25]

The Secretariat created the claim forms and distributed them to governments. There was a separate claim form for each of the six categories of claims

---

21 Iran–US CT Tribunal Rules, Article 18, paragraph 1.
22 Ibid., Article 18, paragraph 1 and Notes to Article 18.
23 Ibid., Article 18, paragraph 2. Compare UNCITRAL Arbitration Rules, Article 18.
24 General Declaration, General Principles B, quoted in section 2.02(a) above.
25 UNCC Provisional Rules, Article 6, paragraph 1.

recognized by the Claims Process (claims categories "A" through "F"), and a special claim form was designed later for the "*bedoun*" late claims program.[26] The claim form could be completed in any of the six official languages of the United Nations, although an English version had to be provided so that the form could be entered into the Commission's English-language computer database. In the case of urgent individual claims of persons forced to depart from Iraq or Kuwait (category "A"), forms had to be submitted in computerized format to facilitate mass processing of the most urgent claims. Claims and documents in all other categories were generally submitted in paper form with the option of submitting them also in computer format.[27] The Rules specified the computer programs with which claims and other electronic documents had to be compatible, but allowed as well for "such other format as may be agreed to by the Executive Secretary."[28] The claim forms contained no restriction on the right of claimants to pursue recovery in other fora, that being inappropriate as the UNCC is expressly a non-exclusive forum.[29] Accordingly, the claim forms contained no restrictions on that right.

The UNCC claim forms required disclosure of compensation from other sources, thereby assisting in determining the amount of compensation granted in decisions on claims. For example, insurance proceeds received by a claimant were set off from the amount that otherwise would have been granted as an award of compensation.[30]

(c) Commission for Real Property Claims of Displaced Persons and Refugees (CRPC)—claims relating to the 1992–1995 war in Bosnia and Herzegovina

The CRPC prepared its claim form in parallel to the development of software for computerized claims management. Although claim forms and accompanying evidentiary documents were submitted in paper form, the Book of

---

[26] See UNCC Governing Council Decision 225 of 2 July 2004, *Filing of "late" claims of the "bedoun"*, U.N. Doc. S/AC.26/Dec.225 (2004) (2 July 2004).

[27] UNCC Provisional Rules, Article 6, paragraph 1.   [28] Ibid., Article 7, paragraph 4.

[29] See Report of the Secretary-General of 2 May 1991, U.N. Doc. S/22559, paragraph 22.

[30] See UNCC Governing Council Decision 7 of 28 November 1991, as revised on 16 March 1992, *Criteria for additional Categories of Claims*, U.N. Doc. S/AC.26/1991/7/Rev.1 (17 March 1992), paragraph 25 ("Any compensation, whether in funds or in kind, already received from any source will be deducted from the total amount of losses suffered"). This rule was applied to set off insurance proceeds received by Kuwait Airways Corporation from the amount that would otherwise have been recommended as an award of compensation. *Report and Recommendations made by the Panel of Commissioners concerning the Fifteenth Instalment of "E4" Claims*, U.N. Doc. S/AC.26/2002/16 (20 June 2002).

Regulations on Procedure provided that staff members should enter the data registered on the claim form into the appropriate computer software.[31] For example, each action taken in the life of a claim—from the time it was received until it was decided—was logged in the CRPC's Claims Tracking Software. Thus, the claim form contained information that could be encoded by computer to enable an automated sorting of claims into different categories. The sorting criteria included, *inter alia*, the location of the claimed property, the type of claim, and the types of evidence submitted, which facilitated matching the data with information in public archives. The claim form was a component of the Book of Regulations on Procedure, and claims had to be submitted in person, and only on the forms provided.[32]

Filing a claim with CRPC did not constitute a waiver of legal rights in other legal fora, and hence the claim form included no such waiver provision.

(d) Claims Resolution Tribunal for Dormant Accounts in Switzerland (CRT-I)—first claims tribunal for assets deposited in Swiss banks

The CRT-I Claims Process required that each claimant submit a detailed claim form, on paper, which was made available in a number of different languages. The claim form included a provision that the claim was submitted to arbitration in Zurich under Swiss law. That arbitration clause thereby effectively gave the Tribunal exclusive jurisdiction that would be recognized by Swiss courts as well as courts in other countries that recognize and enforce foreign agreements to arbitrate pursuant to the New York Convention[33] or other governing law.

(e) Claims Resolution Tribunal (CRT-II)—second claims tribunal for assets deposited in Swiss banks

CRT-II issued a claim form which included an agreement that the submitted claim "be adjudicated by the Claims Resolution Tribunal according to its Rules of Procedure."[34] Claimants submitted claim forms on paper,[35] but the claim forms were designed for efficient electronic scanning and easy keyboard input of essential data.[36] In addition, in a significant step to simplify and expedite filing of claims, the Tribunal accepted, in place of its claim form, Initial

---

[31] CRPC Book of Regulations on Procedure, Article 28.   [32] Ibid., Articles 4 and 9.

[33] Convention on the Recognition and Enforcement of Foreign Arbitral Awards, New York, 10 June 1958, 330 U.N.T.S. 38 (New York Convention).

[34] CRT-II Claim Form, Question 30, available at www.crt-ii.org until the deadline for filing claims had passed.   [35] CRT-II Governing Rules, Article 15.

[36] See ibid., Introduction, Part II.

Questionnaires that were submitted in the class action known as the Holocaust Victim Assets Litigation, and that refer to a Swiss bank account.[37]

Persons covered by the Settlement Agreement in the class action in the United States District Court for the Eastern District of New York were precluded by it from bringing claims against the Swiss banks in any other forum.[38]

(f) Housing and Property Claims Commission (HPCC)—claims relating to the 1999 conflict in Kosovo

The Housing and Property Directorate (HPD) prepared standard claim forms, one for each of the three categories of claims that could be filed in the HPCC Claims Process.[39] Claimants filed their claims on the claim forms provided, signed and notarized, in paper form. As the Commission has exclusive jurisdiction over the types of claims that can be filed with it, claimants were not required to sign a waiver.

(g) Mass Claims Processes administered by the International Organization for Migration (IOM)

IOM used standard claim forms especially tailored to the GFLCP and HVAP Claims Processes, described below, designed to cover all the various categories of claims that could be made in each Claims Process. The claim forms were designed in parallel and consistent with the development of the software developed to support the processing of the claims. Thus, the claim forms contained information that could easily be entered into a database and that allowed computer-based searching, grouping, verification, and tracking of claims. The claim forms were made available in twenty languages for slave and forced labor and personal injury claims under GFLCP, in seven languages for property claims under GFLCP, and in ten languages under HVAP. The claim forms could be downloaded from the official IOM websites for the Claims Processes until the deadline for filing claims had passed.

Forms, signed by the claimant and notarized by official third parties, had to be submitted in paper form, but were scanned into IOM's computer network, allowing more than one person to review each claim simultaneously without ever having to extract the paper file and risk misplacing it. IOM retained a data-entry

---

[37] See section 3.01(e) above, on CRT-II Initial Questionnaires.

[38] See Holocaust Victim Assets Litigation Settlement Agreement, Article 12.

[39] The following claim forms were available from HPD: Category "A" (restitution claims based on discrimination), Category "B" (registration of informal real estate transactions), Category "C" (claims for repossession).

firm in the United States to scan every page of the claim forms manually, along with any accompanying documentary evidence, which was considered to be faster than doing it in-house. Each scanned form was then used by the claims processors to create an electronic profile on the claimant, indicating whether the claim was complete and what evidence was included. In many cases, this information was sufficient to submit a recommendation to the German Foundation for payment. For example, if the electronic profile showed that a GFLCP claimant had submitted a signed and notarized claim form before the deadline for filing claims, including proper evidence of having been held in a concentration camp, that triggered the presumption that the claimant had performed slave labor and qualified him or her for payment in the slave labor category, without the need to proceed with a further inquiry as to eligibility.

German Forced Labour Compensation Programme (GFLCP)—claims against Germany and German industry for Nazi injustice

For claimants participating in GFLCP, this Claims Process is the sole recourse against Germany or German entities. The signature page of the claim form contained a waiver stating that the claimant, upon receipt of a payment, is precluded from bringing any further claims against German and Austrian enterprises or government entities for slave or forced labor, property damage, or other claims in connection with Nazi injustice.[40]

The Supplemental Rules of the IOM Property Claims Commission provide that claimants must sign a waiver prior to receiving payment, waiving "any and all National Socialist era claims against German enterprises and the German Government, and all forced labour claims against Austrian enterprises or the Austrian Government."[41] This waiver does not, however, preclude a successful property claimant from receiving payments under the German Foundation Act for slave or forced labor or personal injury, from bringing insurance claims under the ICHEIC framework, or from bringing action against a German entity for return of art work stolen by the Nazis.[42]

Holocaust Victim Assets Programme (HVAP)—claims pursuant to 1999 class action Settlement

The members of the classes of claimants that are covered by the Settlement Agreement in the class action known as the Holocaust Victim Assets Litigation

---

[40] See German Foundation Act, section 16, paragraphs 1 and 2.
[41] IOM Property Commission Supplemental Rules, section 6.1.
[42] Ibid., section 6.2–6.4.

and who claim under HVAP have no other recourse available against Swiss entities that were party to the Settlement Agreement.[43] HVAP claim forms contained a similar waiver with respect to Swiss entities as the one with respect to German and Austrian entities on the GFLCP claim forms.

(h) Eritrea–Ethiopia Claims Commission (EECC)—claims relating to the 1998–2000 war between Eritrea and Ethiopia

In its preparatory work prior to December 2001—the deadline for filing claims—the EECC adopted several decisions and provisions in its Rules of Procedure aimed at permitting initial claims filings using mass claims procedures. In its Decision Number 2, the Commission authorized a mass claims procedure under which persons in specified categories could file claims for fixed-amount compensation. The Decision provided that "[t]he Parties shall prepare claims forms for all such claims, using forms to be established by the Commission."[44] Chapter Three of the Rules of Procedure (establishing procedures for handling mass claims) also refers to the use of claim forms. However, no such forms were adopted, due largely to the shortage of time under the one-year claims filing deadline.[45] The parties elected instead to file their claims as Government-to-Government claims.

The Commission envisioned that the design of claim forms would be a collaborative and iterative process involving the Commission, expert consultants, and the Government parties. "Notional" claim forms were prepared as a starting point for these discussions, but these were not assessed by technical experts and were of a preliminary and informal character. The system initially conceived would have been based on a general form identifying each natural or juridical person whose claims were filed. This form would have contained identifying information for *every* claim of a national, including those with claims for actual damages requiring individual consideration by the Commission. This basic form would have been accompanied by another form (or forms) with additional information regarding specific claims. Additional forms were envisioned for households claiming fixed amounts for wrongful expulsion or displacement, and for each claim for fixed amounts in claims Categories 1 to 5,

---

[43] See Settlement Agreement, section 12, and Final Order approving the Settlement, *In re Holocaust Victim Assets Litig.*, 105 F.Supp.2d 139, at pp. 142–143 (E.D.N.Y. 2000). See also section 2.02(g) above on Exclusivity of the Claims Process.

[44] EECC Decision Number 2: Claims Categories, Forms and Procedures, section B (24 July 2001), available at www.pca-cpa.org.

[45] EECC Rules of Procedure, Article 30, paragraph 3 provides: "Claims to be considered under Chapter Three shall be filed with the Commission on the claims forms approved by the Commission in both electronic and paper copies."

namely, for wrongful displacement, wrongful detention or mistreatment in detention, or for other types of loss or injury. Other forms were envisioned to submit additional evidence for claims for higher fixed amounts, for documented claims below US$100,000 for nationals not applying for fixed amounts, and for all other claims of nationals.

There was concern that claimants or their advisers might seek to use the claim forms to present legal arguments. Accordingly, a disclaimer was drafted, explaining that:

"Compensation can only be paid if there was a violation of international law. It will be the task of Governments to present legal arguments to show the Commission whether violations of international law took place. Do not use this form or other forms to make legal arguments."[46]

It was anticipated that the personal information requested on the basic form might include the claimant's citizenship (both presently and at the time the claim arose); ethnic identification; where the claimant currently lives, including country, region, zone, *werede*, *kebele*, and any street and number; and the name and location of someone who would know where to find the claimant. The proposed claim form for household claims included instructions to the claims collector aimed at ensuring that each person included on the form appeared before the claims collector to verify membership in a pre-existing household.

Subsequent technical consultations among the Commission, the Government parties, and experts from the International Organization for Migration (IOM), indicated that the design and implementation of an effective and reliable computer-based mass claims system utilizing these or any other forms would require significant financial resources and considerable time, more time than was available given the claims filing deadline of 12 December 2001. The Commission thereupon informed the parties that, in general, it anticipated bifurcating consideration of Government-to-Government claims, considering first liability and then damages in a second stage wherever liability was established. The Commission indicated that, in the second stage, it anticipated authorizing a party wishing to do so to utilize the mass claims procedures previously established for purposes of quantifying its claim for damages.

The Government parties filed their claims in both electronic and paper form, as authorized by the Commission's Rules, albeit not on special claim forms.[47] Given the nature of this Claims Process and the provisions on

---

[46] EECC non-published draft claim form.
[47] EECC Rules of Procedure, Article 30, paragraph 3.

exclusivity in the 12 December 2000 Agreement, the Commission did not consider including a waiver by which claimants agreed to forego recourse to national courts or other means.[48]

(i) Humanitarian insurance Claims Process administered by the Jewish Claims Conference (JCC) for the International Commission on Holocaust Era Insurance Claims (ICHEIC)

The ICHEIC claim form was made available in twenty-three languages and was amended from time to time. Prior to the establishment of the ICHEIC Claims Process, a variety of forms had been circulated by different state insurance regulators to potential claimants within the United States, but these were gradually replaced by a standardized ICHEIC form.[49] The forms were filled in by claimants on paper and later scanned into digital format for computer processing.

The ICHEIC claim form itself did not require the claimant to sign a waiver foregoing recourse to national courts, and for 8A1 Claims waivers were not required in order to receive a humanitarian 8A1 payment.[50] This differed from named or matched ICHEIC claims, where a waiver was required when an MOU Company made an offer to a claimant to settle a claim for a known insurance policy.

(j) American Arbitration Association (AAA)—an illustrative case

Standard forms were developed for handling all aspects of the Claims Process in the illustrative case. To the extent these forms were not already existing when the case was referred to the AAA for arbitration, the AAA assisted in the development of the forms, which were all designed to facilitate electronic transmission. All forms and all communications to claimants and to the reviewers had to be approved by a committee consisting of a representative of the plaintiffs, a representative of the defendant insurance company, and a representative of the state insurance regulators.

---

[48] The named parties in this Claims Process are the two Governments party to the Agreement of 12 December 2000, Article 5, paragraph 8, of which makes it clear that the Commission shall be the sole forum for adjudicating claims under its jurisdiction.

[49] In its review of 8A1 Claims, the JCC found many claims from 1998–1999 submitted on different state regulator forms. These had to be scored on the same basis as claims submitted on the ICHEIC claim form.

[50] However, there was a consent form allowing ICHEIC to direct the applications to necessary bodies, such as the MOU Companies, to comply with European Union privacy and data protection laws.

3.03 Deadlines for Submitting Claims

Whether there is a deadline for submitting claims and whether, and by whom, deadlines may be extended in special circumstances.

Editors' Commentary

The Mass Claims Processes described in this book typically establish and enforce deadlines for submitting claims. While resolute enforcement of deadlines is important in order to ensure an orderly proceeding, inflexible insistence on compliance with a deadline can be unfair in some circumstances. Therefore, those who design Mass Claims Processes and others may wish to consider the advisability of including an orderly method by which deadlines can be extended, or claims supplemented, in cases where there are legitimate showings of exceptional circumstances or hardships.

(a) Iran–United States Claims Tribunal (Iran–US CT)—claims relating to the 1979 Islamic Revolution

The constituting instrument of the Iran–US CT Claims Process, the Claims Settlement Declaration, provided that the deadline for submitting claims was "one year after entry into force of [the Claims Settlement Declaration] or six months after the date the President is appointed, whichever is later."[51] There was no provision for an extension of this period. The Registrar had the power to refuse to file claims that were not timely received, but the claimant could appeal such refusals to the Tribunal. As one authority on the Tribunal has noted, "[w]hile a few refusals were reversed on appeal, most were upheld."[52]

(b) United Nations Compensation Commission (UNCC)—claims relating to the 1990–1991 Gulf War

Deadlines were fixed by the UNCC's Governing Council for filing claims within each category of claims ("A" through "F"), and certain exceptions and

---

[51] Claims Settlement Declaration, Article III, paragraph 4.

[52] GEORGE H. ALDRICH, THE JURISPRUDENCE OF THE IRAN–UNITED STATES CLAIMS TRIBUNAL, AN ANALYSIS OF THE DECISIONS OF THE TRIBUNAL, at p. 412 (Clarendon Press 1996). See also CHARLES N. BROWER & JASON D. BRUESCHKE, THE IRAN–UNITED STATES CLAIMS TRIBUNAL, at p. 86 and note 385 (Martinus Nijhoff Publishers 1998).

extensions were issued for various categories depending on their differing degrees of urgency. The final deadline for the filing of claims in the individual claims categories ("A" through "D") was 1 January 1996. The filing deadline for claims in categories "E" and "F" (excluding "F4" environmental claims) was 1 January 1997. After 11 May 1998, the UNCC no longer accepted unsolicited supplements or amendments to previously filed claims in categories "E" and "F" (excluding environmental claims).

The deadline for filing "F4" environmental claims was 1 February 1998. There were separate deadlines for each "F4" instalment of claims for the filing of unsolicited supplements to the claim materials. The "F4" panel of Commissioners accepted results from monitoring and assessment studies that supported substantive claims according to a schedule designed to maximize the time available for claimants to conduct the studies, and for the Government of Iraq to provide comments, yet maintain the overall claims processing schedule.

The Governing Council extended the filing deadline for the claims of individuals for losses and personal injuries resulting from landmines or unexploded ordnance occurring after 1 January 1996, and for individuals whose detention in Iraq had prevented them from filing by the regular deadline.[53]

Having extended the original filing deadlines a number of times, the Governing Council was reluctant to accept late-filed claims, although under Article 12 of the UNCC's Provisional Rules, it reserved the ability to do so on a case-by-case basis. Requests for acceptance of "late claims" were considered in accordance with criteria established by the Council. Generally speaking, the Council required such claimants to show that they had attempted to file their claims within the relevant filing deadline but were unable to do so due to the existence of a war situation or civil disorder.[54] In other cases, the Council required claimants to demonstrate that they had been denied a full and effective opportunity to file claims within the relevant filing deadline (as, for example, in the Palestinian "late claims" program[55]).

In 2004, the Governing Council, noting that claims processing was drawing to a close, decided not to consider or accept any further requests for the late

---

[53] UNCC Governing Council Decision 12 of 24 September 1992, *Claims For Which Established Filing Deadlines Are Extended*, U.N. Doc. S/AC.26/1992/12 (25 September 1992).

[54] See, e.g., UNCC Governing Council Decision 101 of 28 September 2000, *223 claims of Bosnia and Herzegovina for departure from Iraq or Kuwait (Category "A" claims)*, U.N. Doc. S/AC.26/Dec.101 (2000) (29 September 2000).

[55] See UNCC Governing Council Decision 207 of 18 December 2003, *The first instalment of Palestinian late claims for damages up to USD 100,000 (Category "C" claims)*, U.N. Doc. S/AC.26/Dec.207 (2003) (18 December 2003).

filing of claims in any claims category.[56] The Council also established deadlines for the receipt of requests for correction under Article 41 of the Provisional Rules.[57]

(c) Commission for Real Property Claims of Displaced Persons and Refugees (CRPC)—claims relating to the 1992–1995 war in Bosnia and Herzegovina

There was initially no deadline for filing a claim with the CRPC for repossession of private property. However, after collecting a total of nearly 250,000 claims for approximately 320,000 properties and 360,000 claimants, claims collection activities were suspended as of 1 January 2002 because evidence indicated that substantially all the potential claimants had acted and the domestic authorities had begun accepting claims in an orderly fashion.[58]

There were, however, various deadlines for making claims for repossession of socially-owned apartments. For example, there was a 4 October 1999 deadline for filing claims for repossession of socially-owned apartments in the Federation of Bosnia and Herzegovina that was extended until 3 December 1999, and a deadline for filing such claims in the Republika Srpska expired on 19 June 2000.[59]

(d) Claims Resolution Tribunal for Dormant Accounts in Switzerland (CRT-I)—first claims tribunal for assets deposited in Swiss banks

The Rules of Procedure for CRT-I provided that "[t]he Sole Arbitrators or the Claims Panels shall set deadlines by indicating the date of expiry."[60] Furthermore, requests for extensions of a deadline had to be submitted before such deadline had expired.[61] The deadline for submitting claims passed in 1998, but some extensions were granted and some late claims were accepted.

(e) Claims Resolution Tribunal (CRT-II)—second claims tribunal for assets deposited in Swiss banks

The CRT-II Claims Process was triggered in February 2001 by the publication of the list of names of owners of approximately 21,000 accounts believed to

---

[56] UNCC Governing Council Decision 219 of 11 March 2004, *Requests for the late filing of claims*, U.N. Doc. S/AC.26/Dec.219 (2004) (11 March 2004).

[57] UNCC Governing Council Decision 196 of 26 June 2003, *Establishment of deadlines for the receipt of requests made pursuant to article 41 of the Provisional Rules for Claims Procedure*, U.N. Doc. S/AC.26/Dec.196 (2003) (26 June 2003).   [58] CRPC End of Mandate Report, p. 2.

[59] Some additional extensions of deadlines were granted.

[60] CRT-I Rules of Procedure, Article 19.   [61] Ibid.

have been owned by victims of Nazi persecution, and an initial claims filing deadline was established as 31 August 2001. The CRT-II Governing Rules indicate that the United States federal district court overseeing the class action known as the Holocaust Victim Assets Litigation can set further deadlines.[62] CRT-II received over 32,000 claims before the 31 August 2001 deadline expired. However, between 31 August 2001 and 31 December 2002, the Claims Process received close to 700 late claims. On 8 April 2003, the Court authorized CRT-II to accept late claims that were received before 31 December 2002, provided that they did not prejudice a timely filed claim.[63] In addition, the Court, in July 2001, ordered that some 40,000 of the Initial Questionnaires which potential class members had submitted to the Court in 1999 be treated as timely claims and processed as claim forms.[64]

On 13 January 2005, an additional list of approximately 2,700 names of Account Owners and 400 names of Power of Attorney holders was published (the "2005 List"). The deadline for filing new claims was 13 July 2005, which meant, according to the website of the Claims Process, that claim forms had to have been postmarked no later than 13 July 2005.

(f) Housing and Property Claims Commission (HPCC)—claims relating to the 1999 conflict in Kosovo

The original deadline for filing claims with the Housing and Property Directorate (HPD) was 1 December 2001, but the Special Representative of the Secretary-General of the United Nations extended it several times, ultimately fixing it as 1 July 2003. After that date, a claimant can no longer file a claim with the Directorate or any other related body for claims falling under HPCC's jurisdiction. The only possible recourse remaining for a claimant wishing to protect rights to property in Kosovo is to submit a "Request for Placing Property under HPD Administration."[65] The Directorate may then place the property under its administration and give the claimant an opportunity to demonstrate that he or she has a right to the property. If the claimant can make such a showing, the Directorate can release the property from its administration, although it will not actually certify the property right.

---

[62] CRT-II Governing Rules, Article 7.

[63] See Special Master's Report on the Claims Resolution Process of 30 June 2003, p. 3, available at www.crt-ii.org. [64] Ibid.

[65] See UNMIK Regulation 2000/60, section 12.2.

(g) Mass Claims Processes administered by the International Organization for Migration (IOM)

German Forced Labour Compensation Programme (GFLCP)—claims against Germany and German industry for Nazi injustice

Initial deadlines in the GFLCP Claims Process were set in the German Foundation Act for each partner organization's area of responsibility.[66] The Board of Trustees of the German Foundation later synchronized the deadlines of the various partner organizations, extending the filing deadline for all partner organizations to 31 December 2001 through an amendment to the German Foundation Act.[67]

Holocaust Victim Assets Programme (HVAP)—claims pursuant to 1999 class action Settlement

The initial deadline in the HVAP Claims Process corresponded to the initial deadline applicable for claimants in IOM's area of responsibility under GFLCP. The United States federal district court overseeing the class action known as the Holocaust Victim Assets Litigation later extended HVAP's deadline to make it consistent with the extended deadline of GFLCP.

(h) Eritrea–Ethiopia Claims Commission (EECC)—claims relating to the 1998–2000 war between Eritrea and Ethiopia

Pursuant to the 12 December 2000 Agreement, all claims submitted to the EECC had to be filed no later than 12 December 2001, one year after the Agreement was signed.[68] There is no provision for extension of this deadline, no requests for extensions were made, and all of the parties' claims were filed within the prescribed deadline.

(i) Humanitarian insurance Claims Process administered by the Jewish Claims Conference (JCC) for the International Commission on Holocaust Era Insurance Claims (ICHEIC)

ICHEIC set the final deadline for submitting claims at 31 December 2003, after conducting a global outreach campaign, and after offering general

---

[66] The initial deadlines were either eight or twelve months from the entry into force of the Act.

[67] German Foundation Act, section 14. See also IOM Property Commission Supplemental Rules, section 13.2, note 1, extending the deadline for filing property claims from 11 August 2001 to 31 December 2001.

[68] Eritrea–Ethiopia Agreement of 12 December 2000, Article 5, paragraph 8.

extensions on two previous occasions. Given the goals of the 8A1 humanitarian Claims Process, and considering the advanced age of the 8A1 claimants (most of whom were Holocaust survivors), it was important to process the claims quickly and send payments out as soon as possible.

In late 2003, ICHEIC decided that the 31 December deadline would apply only to the date by which claim forms could be requested. To allow claimants adequate time to receive and submit forms that might have been requested in the latter days of December 2003, the Commission extended the deadline for claims submission to 31 March 2004. The first payments in the 8A1 humanitarian Claims Process were made after the ICHEIC filing deadline expired.

(j) American Arbitration Association (AAA)—an illustrative case

Deadlines for filing claims in the illustrative case were published. As a matter of accommodation and good public relations, however, the deadlines were voluntarily extended by the defendant insurance company as the need arose.

3.04 Initial Screening

Whether there is a procedure for initially screening claims in order to eliminate claims that *prima facie* do not fall within the jurisdiction of the Claims Process or clearly lack merit. Whether there is a procedure by which claimants can appeal such initial screening determinations.

Editors' Commentary

Mass Claims Processes, by their nature, tend to attract large numbers of persons who may sincerely believe they have a valid claim but whose cases are not admissible under the constituting instruments or the rules of procedure. Therefore, special procedures may be needed to screen all claims at an early stage to eliminate those that are clearly ineligible, allowing the Claims Process to concentrate on claims properly before it. For this reason, all of the Mass Claims Processes described in this book have some form of initial screening procedure. In some, the initial screening is performed by those who decide the claims, as was the case at the first Claims Resolution Tribunal for Dormant Accounts in Switzerland (CRT-I), while in others they are conducted by the administrative staff, sometimes with the possibility of review by one or more decision-makers if the claimant objects to the administrative determination, such as at the Housing and Property Claims Commission (HPCC) in Kosovo. Other Claims Processes are aided by governments that provide an initial screening to weed out deficient claims, such as the United Nations Compensation Commission (UNCC) and the Eritrea–Ethiopia Claims Commission (EECC).

(a) Iran–United States Claims Tribunal (Iran–US CT)—claims relating to the 1979 Islamic Revolution

The Iran–US CT Tribunal Rules provide that the parties shall submit all documents to the Registrar, who screens them and may refuse to accept a document that is not received within the required time limit, or which does not comply with the constituting instruments or the Tribunal Rules, such as being a claim that is clearly one that the Tribunal has no power to consider. Refusals by the Registrar are subject to review by the Members of the Tribunal upon timely objection of the party concerned.[69]

(b) United Nations Compensation Commission (UNCC)—claims relating to the 1990–1991 Gulf War

The fact that claims to the UNCC had to be submitted by governments typically resulted in screening by the governments before they submitted claims. As for procedures conducted within the Claims Process after claims were received, the UNCC Provisional Rules required the Commission's Secretariat to perform a "preliminary assessment" of the claims received, to determine whether they fell within the Commission's jurisdiction, and whether formal filing requirements had been complied with, or whether there were deficiencies to be remedied.[70] If it was found that the claim did not meet formal requirements, the Secretariat was to notify the person or body that submitted the claim and give it sixty days from the date of that notification to remedy the defect.[71] In practice, however, the UNCC would review a claim with formal deficiencies "as is."

Under Article 34 of the Provisional Rules, the Secretariat also has provided assistance to the panels of Commissioners in obtaining additional information

---

[69] Iran–US CT Tribunal Rules, Article 2, paragraph 5. The objecting party must object within 30 days of notification of refusal.

[70] UNCC Provisional Rules, Articles 14 and 16. See also UNCC Governing Council Decision 1 of 2 August 1991, *Criteria for Expedited Processing of Urgent Claims*, U.N. Doc. S/AC.26/1991/1 (2 August 1991).　　　　　　　　　　　　[71] UNCC Provisional Rules, Article 15.

about the claims, and the Commissioners, when considering the claims, took into account the results of the preliminary assessment of claims made by the Secretariat in accordance with Article 14 of the Rules.[72] The Article 34 procedure enabled the Secretariat, under the direction of the panels of Commissioners, to send written interrogatories to the claimants and ask for additional documents and information in connection with claims in categories "D", "E" and "F". The Commission adopted a practice of notifying the governments concerned of any claims rejected by the Secretariat and providing six months for them to contact the claimants and invite them to remedy the deficiencies in the claim.[73] If the deficiency was not remedied within six months, the Commission would issue a formal sixty-day notice to remedy the defect pursuant to the Provisional Rules.[74] If the claimant did not remedy the claim within that sixty-day period, the claim was officially rejected.

In practice, the preliminary screening procedure has been an important part of the claims processing, particularly with respect to the less urgent categories of large individual claims, and claims by corporations, governments, and international organizations ("D", "E" and "F"). The Secretariat before submitting the claim to a panel of Commissioners has often used the Article 34 screening procedure to obtain additional information that might be needed in order to decide the claim, but which the Provisional Rules did not strictly require.

(c) Commission for Real Property Claims of Displaced Persons and Refugees (CRPC)—claims relating to the 1992–1995 war in Bosnia and Herzegovina

The CRPC Claims Process conducted initial screenings to ensure that claims were complete as filed. The Book of Regulations on Procedure provided that incomplete claims were not to be registered. Incomplete claims were those which did not contain "data on the claimant; data on the claimed real property; signature; [or] valid power of attorney."[75] If, as a result of error by the staff responsible for registration, an incomplete claim was registered, it was to be "supplemented or refused" in accordance with a "special instruction" in which the Commission set forth the requirements for rendering the claim complete.[76] In practice, however, no such special instruction was ever issued.

---

[72] UNCC Provisional Rules, Article 34, paragraphs 1 and 2.
[73] Report of the UNCC Executive Secretary, U.N. Doc. S/AC.26/1997/R.6 (23–24 June 1997), p. 6.　　　　　　　　　　　　　　　　　　　　　[74] UNCC Provisional Rules, Article 15.
[75] CRPC Book of Regulations on Procedure, Article 26, paragraph 3.
[76] Ibid., Article 26, paragraph 4.

(d) Claims Resolution Tribunal for Dormant Accounts in Switzerland (CRT-I)—first claims tribunal for assets deposited in Swiss banks

The published list of account holders eligible to file claims with CRT-I stated only the name of the account holder and his or her place of residence. To conform with Swiss bank secrecy laws, the published list did not include the name of the bank or the amount in the bank account. That information was disclosed to the claimant only if the bank agreed that the claimant might have a plausible claim to the account, or, when the bank did not agree, if the claim survived an initial screening procedure conducted by one or more of the Arbitrators.

If the bank refused to agree to disclose its name and the amount in the account, the file was sent for "Initial Screening" by a Sole Arbitrator.[77] According to the CRT-I Rules of Procedure, the Sole Arbitrator was to order disclosure unless he or she found, after reviewing the entire file, that "(i) the claimant has not submitted any information on his or her entitlement to the dormant account, or (ii) if it is apparent that the claimant is not entitled to the dormant account."[78] As a former Deputy Chairman of the Tribunal has stated:

"In short, the [Initial Screening] Procedure is an admissibility proceeding with a very low threshold. To survive it and move to [arbitration on] the merits, claimants merely have to provide some information indicating that they *might* plausibly be entitled. To be successful on the merits, however, claimants will have to show that it *is* plausible, applying [the relaxed standard of proof], that they are entitled to the account or a part thereof."[79]

If the claimant disagreed with the decision of the Sole Arbitrator, he or she could, within thirty days, re-submit the claim for further Initial Screening by a panel of three Arbitrators.[80] The panel then considered the case *de novo* and did not include the Sole Arbitrator who previously decided the matter.

(e) Claims Resolution Tribunal (CRT-II)—second claims tribunal for assets deposited in Swiss banks

The CRT-II Governing Rules provide that a claim is only admissible if the Tribunal determines, using the information submitted by the claimant on the claim form, that the claim meets five criteria listed in the Rules, thereby

---

[77] CRT-I Rules of Procedure, Article 10.   [78] Ibid.

[79] Thomas Buergenthal, *Arbitrating entitlement to Dormant Bank Accounts*, in Liber Amicorum Ibrahim F.I. Shihata, p. 79, at p. 83 (Schlemmer-Schulte & Tung eds., Kluwer Law International 2001) (emphasis in the original).   [80] CRT-I Rules of Procedure, Article 10.

establishing a "reasoned and satisfactory basis for further examination of the claim."[81] A decision of inadmissibility may be appealed, through the Special Masters, to the United States federal district court overseeing the class action known as the Holocaust Victim Assets Litigation, within ninety days of the date of the letter accompanying the decision.[82] However, appeals which are submitted "without either a plausible suggestion of error or relevant new evidence may be summarily denied."[83]

(f) Housing and Property Claims Commission (HPCC)—claims relating to the 1999 conflict in Kosovo

The Housing and Property Directorate (HPD) may reject a claim at any stage of the proceedings if it manifestly falls outside the Commission's jurisdiction. Such a decision is made in writing.[84] If the claimant disputes the Directorate's rejection, the Directorate will refer the matter to the Commission, which will then process the claim in accordance with its normal procedures.[85]

(g) Mass Claims Processes administered by the International Organization for Migration (IOM): *German Forced Labour Compensation Programme (GFLCP) for claims against Germany and German industry for Nazi injustice, and Holocaust Victim Assets Programme (HVAP) for claims pursuant to 1999 class action Settlement*

Formally, neither GFLCP nor HVAP has initial screening procedures for eliminating claims which *prima facie* do not fall within the jurisdiction of the relevant Claims Process or clearly lack merit. In practice, however, claims have been screened out that were easily identified in the electronic database as candidates for rejection because, for example, a deceased victim had died prior to 16 February 1999, or because membership in a group targeted for persecution

---

[81] CRT-II Governing Rules, Article 18, paragraph 1; the five criteria are listed in Article 18, paragraph 2, which provides that a claim is *inadmissible* if:

"(a) the Claimant has provided no plausible information indicating that the person he or she believes to be the Account Owner was a Victim, or (b) the claim is based essentially on a statement that the Claimant or his or her relative and the Account Owner have the same or similar last name, or (c) the Claimant has provided no relevant information and/or documentation regarding his or her relationship to the Account Owner, or (d) the Claimant has not asserted a relationship to the Account Owner that would justify an Award to the Account, or (e) it is apparent that the person the Claimant believes to be the Account Owner and the actual Account Owner are not the same person."

[82] CRT-II Governing Rules, Article 30, paragraph 1.   [83] Ibid., Article 30, paragraph 3.
[84] UNMIK Regulation 2000/60, section 10.3.   [85] Ibid., section 10.4.

was not asserted in an HVAP claim for compensation in Slave Labor Class I or the Refugee Class. IOM Secretariat staff also reviews claims for formal deficiencies that, if found, the claimants are invited to remedy. Finally, the claims database is used to match claims in order to identify and screen out duplicate claims.

The Supplemental Rules of the IOM Property Claims Commission provide that IOM is to perform an "initial review" of received property claims prior to submitting them to the Commission for review. This initial review consists of checking whether "(a) the claim form is duly completed; (b) the claim form, including the waiver clause, is duly signed; (c) the claim is accompanied by a Statement of Claim; and (d) documentary and other evidence is submitted with the claim."[86] If a claim did not meet these requirements, the claimant had an opportunity to remedy the deficiencies within a deadline set by IOM, after which the claim would be submitted to the Commission for review whether or not the deficiencies had been remedied.[87]

(h) Eritrea–Ethiopia Claims Commission (EECC)—claims relating to the 1998–2000 war between Eritrea and Ethiopia

The EECC has not established its own initial screening procedure. However, in its preliminary work on a possible mass claims procedure involving individual claimants, the Commission incorporated a mechanism intended to encourage the two Governments to scrutinize claims rigorously and to eliminate deficient ones. This mechanism linked the total amount of compensation to be paid in each mass claims sub-category to the proportion of those claims found to have insufficient evidence through random sampling. Thus, if twenty-five percent of the claims submitted by a party in a sub-category were to be found to have insufficient evidence, the total compensation awarded for all claims in that sub-category would be reduced by twenty-five percent.[88] This method was not put into practice, because the parties decided to file Government-to-Government claims rather than to attempt an individually-based mass claims procedure.

(i) Humanitarian insurance Claims Process administered by the Jewish Claims Conference (JCC) for the International Commission on Holocaust Era Insurance Claims (ICHEIC)

During the processing of the first phase of the humanitarian Claims Process, claims submitted to ICHEIC which did not name an insurance company and

---

[86] IOM Property Commission Supplemental Rules, section 15.1.   [87] Ibid., section 15.2.
[88] EECC Rules of Procedure, Article 32, paragraph 3.

could not be matched against either ICHEIC's internal research database or the records of a participating insurance company (unnamed and unmatched claims) were forwarded to the JCC. During the processing of the second phase, ICHEIC forwarded to the JCC any unnamed unmatched claims, as well as certain groups of named company claims that were not matched to policies, or where the named insurance company no longer exists and has no successor company. The JCC conducted no additional screening.

(j) American Arbitration Association (AAA)—an illustrative case

An initial screening process was used in the illustrative case to ensure that claimants made a *prima facie* case for inclusion in the Claims Process. This screening was done by pre-selected and trained insurance company representatives, with oversight by the plaintiffs' attorneys and the state insurance regulators.

3.05 Preparing Schedule

Whether there is a schedule showing the sequence of activities that need to be accomplished to resolve the claims, including a general time-frame, deadlines for particular actions, and a target date for winding up the Claims Process.

Editors' Commentary

As for any complex endeavor, planning is needed in order for a Mass Claims Process to conduct its work effectively and expediently. In general, little information is available concerning the extent to which each of the various Claims Processes described in this book engaged in such planning activities as preparing schedules showing: (i) the sequence of activities that need to be accomplished to resolve the claims, including establishing time-frames; (ii) deadlines for particular activities; (iii) a target date for winding up the Claims Process; and (iv) the changing staffing levels towards the end of the Process, when perhaps only complex cases, appeals, claims of heirs, and requests for review remain to be resolved. Planning has more often been done by persons in a position to administer or supervise the Claims Process rather than by arbitrators or other decision-makers. Some Claims Processes consider that planning is an internal matter and that plans should not be made public, except that

169

those Claims Processes which have deadlines for filing claims, and/or limited time periods for completing certain actions on claims or groups of claims, typically publish them. The discussion of each of the Claims Processes that follows describes those deadlines and time limits.

Those who design Mass Claims Processes might wish to consider preparation of plans and schedules covering the sequence of required activities with target dates for accomplishing each activity. This could be in the nature of a "master plan," it being understood that future modifications might be needed in the light of actual experience. Lessons may be learned from the experience of the United Nations Compensation Commission (UNCC) in establishing work programs for different types of claims before it. Similarly, the planning steps and consultations taken by the Eritrea–Ethiopia Claims Commission (EECC), described below, provide examples that may be of use to others.

In developing plans, it is necessary to take into account competing goals. Thus, for example, the principle that "justice delayed is justice denied" must be balanced against the need to allow sufficient time to assure due process; both must be realistically weighed against the scope and complexity of the task. Also, political considerations and the resources of the parties may be relevant.

(a) Iran–United States Claims Tribunal (Iran–US CT)—claims relating to the 1979 Islamic Revolution

The Iran–US CT has had no schedule of activities for resolving its claims or winding up the Claims Process. The General Declaration provides that the Security Account for paying awards to United States claimants is to be maintained until the President of the Tribunal certifies that all arbitral awards against Iran have been satisfied in accordance with the Claims Settlement Declaration, but neither Declaration imposes a specific deadline by which all awards must be satisfied.[89] The Tribunal's Internal Guidelines provide a deadline by which each claim is to be decided following the hearing of the case, but that provision has generally not been followed.[90]

(b) United Nations Compensation Commission (UNCC)—claims relating to the 1990–1991 Gulf War

The UNCC adopted work programs for various categories of claims which included, *inter alia*, schedules for carrying out and completing its tasks. These

---

[89] See General Declaration, paragraph 7, and Claims Settlement Declaration, Article IV, paragraph 2.
[90] Iran–US CT Internal Guidelines of the Tribunal, 1 Iran–U.S. C.T.R. p. 98.

schedules were driven by the decision of the Governing Council designating claims in categories "A", "B" and "C" as urgent claims requiring expedited processing for humanitarian reasons. Accordingly, the claims in categories "A" and "B", together with most of the claims in category "C", were processed prior to the claims in the other claims categories. The Secretariat devised a work program intended to resolve claims in categories "A", "B" and "C" as quickly as possible, having regard to the Council's guidance concerning the processing of these claims and the requirements of the mass claims processing techniques used to review them.[91] Within each of these claims categories, detailed work plans were prepared identifying the work to be done and the timetable for its completion. Claims in each of these categories were grouped into instalments and presented to panels of Commissioners, which were required to issue their reports and recommendations no later than 120 days from the date of submission of the claims to the panel.

Unlike the expedited claims categories, which were conducted using mass claims processing techniques, claims in categories "D", "E" and "F" required individual review. Claim development pursuant to Article 34 of the UNCC's Provisional Rules was often necessary in order to assist the panels of Commissioners in their review of these claims. These features influenced the scheduling of claims processing. Under the Rules, panels of Commissioners were required to complete their review of claims in these categories within 180 days from the date on which the claims were submitted to the panel. However, panels could designate claims requiring a more detailed review as "unusually large or complex," which had the effect of extending the time period for review to twelve months. Such designation could affect scheduling, as oral proceedings could then be held if the panel considered that they were warranted or if the claims met certain criteria established by the Governing Council.[92] Panels could also direct the Secretariat and external expert consultants to conduct on-site inspections and interviews as part of the claim development process, which also could have an impact on schedules.

Most claims in categories "D", "E" and "F" were designated as unusually large or complex, thus requiring panels of Commissioners to issue their reports and recommendations within twelve months of the date of submission to them of such claims. In the event that a panel was unable to complete

---

[91] See, in particular, UNCC Governing Council Decision 1 of 2 August 1991, *Criteria for Expedited Processing of Urgent Claims*, U.N. Doc. S/AC.26/1991/1 (2 August 1991), and Decision 10 of 26 June 1992, *Provisional Rules for Claims Procedure*, U.N. Doc. S/AC.26/1992/10 (26 June 1992).

[92] See UNCC Provisional Rules, Articles 36 and 38(d); UNCC Governing Council Decision 114 of 7 December 2000, *Review of current UNCC procedures*, U.N. Doc. S/AC.26/Dec.114 (2000) (7 December 2000).

its work within that time, it was granted up to a further six months to complete its work.[93]

The UNCC's work program for claims in categories "D", "E" and "F" rested on two key elements: (i) an operational framework identifying each step required in the processing of the claims and the roles and responsibilities of each of the panels of Commissioners, the Secretariat, external expert consultants, the claimants, and, where applicable, the Government of Iraq; and (ii) standard operating procedures prepared within the context of the Provisional Rules and other decisions of the Governing Council covering the fundamental aspects of the Claims Process, including the grouping of claims into instalments. Claims were grouped having regard to the date of receipt by the UNCC, geographic distribution, type of loss, type of industry, and common facts and issues. With these key elements in mind, an implementation schedule, including start and end dates for each instalment of claims, was prepared. Implementation of this work program required the creation of a number of new panels of Commissioners, the creation of new claims units within the Secretariat to support those panels, and the engagement of external expert consultants where necessary, to assist the panels of Commissioners with the verification and valuation of claims.

The UNCC work program was considered to be internal to the UNCC, although aspects relating to deadlines and other scheduling issues were communicated to claimant governments as needed. The resolution of claims in all claims categories was largely achieved in accordance with the relevant work program. Additional work programs were developed to deal with late claims and claims whose filing deadlines had been extended by the Governing Council.

The vast majority of the work of the panels of Commissioners was accomplished on or ahead of schedule. The schedule for a small portion of the UNCC's claims processing work was extended from mid-2003 until the end of 2004 in order to accommodate the complexity of the claims left to be resolved. A further brief extension was granted in respect of the fifth instalment of "F4" environmental claims in order to permit Iraq sufficient time to comment on the claims in that instalment. The "F4" panel of Commissioners signed its report and recommendations concerning the fifth instalment claims on 1 April 2005, and the Governing Council approved those recommendations at its fifty-sixth session in June 2005.[94]

---

[93] UNCC Governing Council Decision 35 of 13 December 1995, *Further Procedures for Review of Claims Under Article 38*, U.N. Doc. S/AC.26/Dec.35 (1995) (13 December 1995).

[94] See *Report and Recommendations made by the Panel of Commissioners Concerning the Fifth Instalment of "F4" Claims*, of 1 April 2005, U.N. Doc. S/AC.26/2005/10 (30 June 2005), and UNCC

In addition to the claims encompassed within the work program, the Governing Council approved a number of special "late claims" programs in accordance with its established criteria. These included the Palestinian late claims program (over 46,000 claims in categories "C" and "D"), the "*bedoun*" late claims program (approximately 32,000 claims for a fixed amount), and the categories "A" and "C" late claims program (approximately 4,100 claims). Also, claims filed pursuant to Governing Council Decision 12, most notably the claims in respect of approximately 600 Kuwaiti deceased detainees, had to be resolved.[95] Claims processing of these late and Decision 12 claims by panels of Commissioners continued until May 2005. The last of the panel reports and recommendations in connection with these claims were considered and approved by the Governing Council at its session in June 2005. Accordingly, UNCC claims processing concluded at the end of June 2005.[96]

Required work does not end when decisions are rendered by the Governing Council. Needed on-going activities include the payment of claims, correction of claims pursuant to Article 41 ("Correction of Decisions") of the Provisional Rules, the classification and archiving of records in accordance with the archiving policy approved by the Governing Council, the audit of UNCC activities, and the tracking of the expenditure of "F4" awards for monitoring and assessment activities by claimants. Such activities were still underway as of 31 January 2006. It is expected that, during the course of the 2006–2007 biennium, the question of the handover of any residual functions to a successor body will be addressed.

(c) Commission for Real Property Claims of Displaced Persons and Refugees (CRPC)—claims relating to the 1992–1995 war in Bosnia and Herzegovina

There was no provision in the constituting instruments that expressly addressed any time-frame for processing CRPC claims. CRPC was initially given a mandate to complete its work in five years (1996–2001). That mandate was extended by an additional three years. The work came to an end on 31 December 2003.

Governing Council Decision 248 of 30 June 2005, *Fifth Instalment of "F4" Claims*, U.N. Doc. S/AC.26/Dec.248 (2005) (30 June 2005).

[95] UNCC Governing Council Decision 12 of 24 September 1992, *Claims For Which Established Filing Deadlines Are Extended*, U.N. Doc. S/AC.26/1992/12 (25 September 1992).

[96] For further information concerning each of the late claims programs and Decision 12 Kuwait deceased detainee claims, see reports and recommendations of the "D1", "D2" and Palestinian "Late Claims" panels of Commissioners, available at www.uncc.ch, under categories "C" and "D".

(d) Claims Resolution Tribunal for Dormant Accounts in Switzerland (CRT-I)—first claims tribunal for assets deposited in Swiss banks

According to its Rules of Procedure, CRT-I was to "resolve all claims in an expedited procedure and . . . render its decision within six (6) months after submission of the claim . . . ."[97] In practice, it was envisioned that ownership of the dormant accounts would generally be resolved within a year in so-called "Ordinary" cases and, in "Fast Track" cases, within a month of submission. These deadlines proved to be unworkable, as the organizational tasks of establishing the Tribunal itself lasted through the summer of 1998. In 1999, the Tribunal adopted an internal schedule that called for the processing of a fixed target number of claims per week.

(e) Claims Resolution Tribunal (CRT-II)—second claims tribunal for assets deposited in Swiss banks

The CRT-II Governing Rules do not contain provisions regarding any official time-frame or deadline for processing claims, nor do such provisions appear in any other public documents, although some internal time-lines may have been adopted.

(f) Housing and Property Claims Commission (HPCC)—claims relating to the 1999 conflict in Kosovo

The HPCC Claims Process was formed in the summer of 2000. By the end of 2002, approximately 1,400 claims had been decided. At the end of 2003, the total number of claims decided was approximately 9,700. A target of resolving 1,000 decisions per month was reached in 2005, as was the goal of implementing 100 decisions monthly.[98] The deadline for receiving claims was extended until 1 July 2003, and after that extended deadline passed, a total of approximately 29,000 claims had been received. The Claims Process established a goal to complete substantially all cases by the end of 2005 and to hand over operations to local courts and municipalities in 2006.[99] As of 31 January 2006, the HPCC had resolved 99.7 percent of all claims filed before it, and the Housing and Property Directorate was actively preparing the hand-over to local authorities.

---

[97] CRT-I Rules of Procedure, Article 37.
[98] See, e.g., HPD/HPCC, *The Way Forward—Prospectus 2004 & 2005*, available at www.hpdkosovo. org.   [99] See ibid.

(g) **Mass Claims Processes administered by the International Organization for Migration (IOM):** *German Forced Labour Compensation Programme (GFLCP) for claims against Germany and German industry for Nazi injustice, and Holocaust Victim Assets Programme (HVAP) for claims pursuant to 1999 class action Settlement*

IOM has prepared detailed work plans and program schedules, including a general time-frame, for both GFLCP and HVAP, which have been submitted to the respective oversight bodies for these Claims Processes—the German Foundation for GFLCP, and the United States District Court for the Eastern District of New York for HVAP. In both cases, IOM fixed the target date for the completion of the claims processing as the end of 2004, but work on second installment payments, appeals, and issues relating to heirs continued through 2005. In fact, an amendment to the German Foundation Act adopted in the summer of 2004 requires payment efforts to continue to be made until September 2006 (in cases where payment has not been effected for reasons such as the death of the claimant, an unreported change of address, etc.). Hence, the Claims Process cannot be fully terminated until that date.

The Supplemental Rules of the IOM Property Claims Commission provide expressly that the Commission is to "endeavor to complete its review of and make its determinations on the compensability of the claims within a year after the expiration of the deadline for filing of claims [31 December 2001], subject to any extension of the filing deadline by the German Foundation."[100] In practice, a comprehensive work plan and schedule were prepared by the GFLCP Secretariat for the Commission's approval and use. The deadline of 31 December 2001 was not extended, but claims filed after that date in cases where an "informal claim" had been made before the deadline passed were accepted, as was also the practice for slave and forced labor claims. The first instance processing of property claims was completed in September 2004, the requests for reconsideration were decided by the end of 2004, and the payment of property claims was substantially completed by the fall of 2005.

(h) **Eritrea–Ethiopia Claims Commission (EECC)—claims relating to the 1998–2000 war between Eritrea and Ethiopia**

The constituting instrument of EECC, the 12 December 2000 Agreement, instructed the Commission to commence its work within fifteen days after

---

[100] IOM Property Commission Supplemental Rules, section 21.

being constituted, and to "endeavor to complete its work within three years of the date when the period for filing claims closes."[101] Within this broad framework, the Commission has the power to expedite particular claims or categories of concern to the parties, such that, upon application by either party, "the Commission may decide to consider specific claims, or categories of claims, on a priority basis."[102]

The Commission held several formal and informal meetings with the parties on organizational questions during 2001, leading to adoption of five procedural Decisions, completion of the Rules of Procedure, and clarification of many administrative matters. However, the actual volume of claims was not known until 12 December 2001, when both parties filed their claims. In the ensuing weeks, the Commissioners analyzed the claims and consulted with a view to identifying logical groupings of claims and a logical sequence for considering them. The Commission requested and received the parties' views on both matters.

Taking account of these comments, the Commission, in February 2002, established the broad outlines of its approach to planning its docket, providing for early consideration of claims that were significant to each Government party. This was implemented through a series of internal orders to the parties scheduling the filing of Statements of Defense, and then of Memorials and Counter-Memorials. The Commission was aided in organizing its docket by the fact that both parties' claims often invoked similar legal principles. The Commission scheduled filings and hearings in all of its claims with a view to meeting the three-year objective, staggering the tasks so that hearings regarding the first-briefed clusters of claims took place simultaneously with the parties' preparation of written submissions regarding the subsequent clusters, and so on. Careful scheduling notwithstanding, the Commission and the parties concluded that this could not be accomplished within the three-year mandate in the light of the unexpectedly large volume of cases and issues to be resolved, and they have extended the mandate of the Commission.[103]

---

[101] Eritrea–Ethiopia Agreement of 12 December 2000, Article 5, paragraph 12.

[102] Ibid., Article 5, paragraph 11.

[103] After hearings on prisoners of war in December 2002, both parties wrote to the Commission suggesting that it adjust the schedule for further proceedings. The Commission did so in February 2003, delaying its second set of hearings (on the Central Front claims) until November 2003 and its hearings on civilian claims until March 2004. Hearings on the merits of all remaining issues were combined in a single extended session of hearings in April 2005.

(i) Humanitarian insurance Claims Process administered by the Jewish Claims Conference (JCC) for the International Commission on Holocaust Era Insurance Claims (ICHEIC)

Decision-making related to all ICHEIC 8A1 eligible claims was completed in 2005, in accordance with a timeline of activities established by ICHEIC.[104] Review of the 8A1 Claims began prior to the expiration of the final (extended) claims submission deadline, as the Senior Counselor, who was appointed by ICHEIC to oversee the payment process and other aspects, wished to make it a priority to pay humanitarian claims as soon as possible. This allowed the first batch—or *tranche*—of payments to be issued immediately once the submission deadline passed. A fourth and final payment *tranche* was due in 2006.

Winding down the 8A1 Claims Process involves ICHEIC conducting follow-up work to ensure that humanitarian awards reach the appropriate recipients, investigating returned award letters, contacting claimants for their current address information, and investigating any remaining cases of heirs.[105]

(j) American Arbitration Association (AAA)—an illustrative case

Deadlines for all phases of the Claims Process in the illustrative case were fixed, and great effort was made to adhere to them. The goal for the AAA was to resolve all appeals within one year. Over ninety-five percent of the appeals were resolved in fifteen months. A thirty-day deadline was established for issuance of an award after a case had been heard. Due to the importance of adhering to this deadline, some claims reviewers were phased out of the Claims Process for untimely submission of awards.

---

[104] See www.icheic.org.
[105] See ICHEIC 2005 Meeting Report and Presentation, available at www.icheic.org.

Chapter 4

Appointing Those who will Make Decisions

4.01 Choice of Decision-Makers

Who makes decisions on claims and by whom such decision-makers are appointed. In that connection, whether any particular criteria, expertise, or other qualifications are specified. To what extent policy-making, executive, and adjudicative functions are differentiated and allocated to the decision-makers or to different bodies.

Editors' Commentary

Central to each of the Mass Claims Processes described in this book is a body that considers the merits of the claims. In some Claims Processes, such as the Iran–United States Claims Tribunal (Iran–US CT), the Eritrea–Ethiopia Claims Commission (EECC), and the American Arbitration Association (AAA) illustrative case, this body makes final decisions, while in others, such as the United Nations Compensation Commission (UNCC), it makes recommendations or rulings that are subject to approval by a supervisory organ.[1] These bodies are typically called either "Tribunal" (e.g., the Iran–US CT and the Claims Resolution Tribunals for bank accounts in Switzerland (CRT-I and CRT-II)) or "Commission" (e.g., UNCC, EECC, and the property claims commissions in Kosovo (HPCC) and in Bosnia and Herzegovina (CRPC)). These semantic differences reflect the preferences of the drafters and are unrelated to the legal characteristics of the particular Claims Process, such as whether decisions are final or subject to the approval of others. The individuals who comprise these bodies are variously called "Members" (as at the Iran–US CT), "Judge" or "Arbitrator" (also at the Iran–US CT and at CRT-I), or "Commissioner" (as at the UNCC, CRPC, HPCC, EECC, and the

---

[1] See section 2.05 above, on approval by another body.

International Organization for Migration (IOM) Property Claims Commission). For convenience, in this book, all of these individuals are generally referred to as "decision-makers," that term being appropriate even for those whose determinations are subject to approval by others inasmuch as, in practice, those determinations are almost always accepted by the supervisory organ.

The constituting instrument for each of the Mass Claims Processes described in this book includes provisions concerning how decision-makers will be appointed. Generally, one of two approaches is followed. In some Claims Processes, the parties each appoint an equal number of decision-makers and those party-appointed individuals then attempt to reach agreement on the remaining decision-makers, including a chairperson, failing which, those appointments are made by an appointing authority designated in the constituting instrument. This was the method followed, for example, at the Iran–US CT, the EECC, and the Property Claims Commission administered by IOM as part of the German Forced Labour Compensation Programme (GFLCP). Other Claims Processes abandon the practice of party-appointed arbitrators and choose instead to have all decision-makers appointed by a related body, as was done at the UNCC where they were appointed by the UNCC Governing Council upon nomination by the United Nations Secretary-General; at CRT-I where appointments were made by a separate Foundation; and at the HPCC in Kosovo, where a United Nations Special Representative makes the appointments. One Claims Process, CRPC in Bosnia and Herzegovina, combined both approaches and had party-appointed decision-makers who did not, however, participate in choosing the others, that being done instead by the President of the European Court of Human Rights. As can be seen from these examples, designers of Mass Claims Processes have a variety of options, all of which appear to work in practice.

Most Claims Processes include powers to fill the gap if a party entitled to appoint, or participate in appointing, a decision-maker refuses to cooperate in the designating procedure. Such provisions are vital to prevent delaying or frustrating the Claims Process (see, e.g., the provision of the Iran–US CT described in sub-section (a) below).

Constituting instruments do not typically identify specific professional qualifications that the decision-makers should have. Notable exceptions are the UNCC whose Provisional Rules state that Commissioners shall have expertise in a field such as finance, law, accounting, insurance, environmental danger assessment, oil, trade, or engineering; and the HPCC where Commissioners are to be experts in housing and property law. It is not unusual to find references to general characteristics such as experience, high moral standing, integrity, and competence to hold judicial office. Whether these qualifications are expressed or not, experience indicates that Mass Claims Processes can function best where the decision-makers are persons of wisdom, integrity, and experience, with a capacity and willingness to work hard.

Some Claims Processes regulate the nationality of the decision-makers who can be appointed. Thus, for example, the 12 December 2000 Agreement establishing the EECC requires that the Commissioners not be nationals or permanent residents of the party appointing them, and that the President of the Commission not be a national or permanent resident of either party.

In most Mass Claims Processes, the sole role of the decision-makers is to decide claims, with policy-making, executive, and administrative functions—including making budgets—being performed by others. At the Iran–US CT, however, the Members are responsible for all functions of the Tribunal. In addition to deciding claims, they appoint a Secretary-General who implements their instructions and carries out policies made by vote of a majority. Similarly, at the EECC, the Commissioners not only adjudicate claims but also determine administrative and financial matters. Some observers believe that centering responsibility for all functions of Claims Processes in the decision-makers who actually handle the cases results in more informed policies and more direct management. Others consider that it is a waste of time and a misuse of special talents to have the decision-makers engage in work better done by administrators. There is no obvious answer. One thing is clear, however: the scope of the function of the decision-makers should be carefully defined at the outset of a Claims Process in order to avoid the kinds of misunderstandings that arose, for example, when some Members of the Iran–US CT, who were accustomed to a system in which they had broad functions, were later appointed as Arbitrators at CRT-I and did not immediately recognize that they were expected to have far fewer responsibilities for the operation of that Claims Process.

Annotations

(a) Iran–United States Claims Tribunal (Iran–US CT)—claims relating to the 1979 Islamic Revolution

Pursuant to the terms of the constituting instrument, the Claims Settlement Declaration, within ninety days after the Declaration's entry into force, Iran and the United States were each required to, and did, appoint three "Members" of the Tribunal[2]—as the decision-makers of this Claims Process are called in the constituting instrument. (In practice, these Members are referred to as Judges.) Within thirty days after their appointment, those six Members were authorized to, and initially did, appoint the remaining three third-country Members, designating one of them President of the Tribunal.[3] The Tribunal Rules provide that if the party-appointed Members fail to agree on the three other Members and the President, they shall be named by an appointing authority designated by the Secretary-General of the Permanent Court of Arbitration (PCA) at The Hague.[4]

Replacements for Members who have died or resigned are appointed in the same way as the original Members.[5] To prevent delay or disruption of the work of the Claims Process, if one of the two Government parties fails to appoint a replacement, the other Government may request the appointing authority to appoint the Member. If the party-appointed Members fail to agree on the replacement for a third-country Member, such Member shall be appointed by the appointing authority. The same procedure applies for the replacement of a President of the Tribunal.[6]

In the interest of efficient operation, the Tribunal amended its Rules so that if a Member resigned it would not be necessary to repeat proceedings in any cases then pending before such Member. The amendment, known as the "Mosk Rule" because it was adopted at the time of the resignation of Richard M. Mosk, provided that:

"After the effective date of a member's resignation he shall continue to serve as a member of the Tribunal with respect to all cases in which he had participated in a hearing on the merits, and for that purpose shall be considered a member of the Tribunal instead of the person who replaces him."[7]

The provision followed the practices of the International Court of Justice and the European Court of Human Rights.

Claims are decided either by majority vote of a Chamber consisting of two party-appointed Members and a third-country Member who presides, or of the Full Tribunal of nine Members. Policy-making and adjudicative functions are exercised by the Members of the Tribunal. The President, acting pursuant

---

[2] The Claims Settlement Declaration, Article III, paragraph 1, first sentence, states that "[t]he Tribunal shall consist of nine members or such larger multiple of three as Iran and the United States may agree are necessary to conduct its business expeditiously." The two Governments did not agree on a number larger than nine.   [3] Ibid.

[4] Iran–US CT Tribunal Rules, Article 7, paragraph 2(b).   [5] Ibid., Article 13, paragraph 1.

[6] Ibid., Article 7, paragraphs 2 and 3.

[7] Ibid., Article 13, paragraph 5. See Charles N. Brower & Jason D. Brueschke, The Iran–United States Claims Tribunal, at p. 141 (Martinus Nijhoff Publishers 1998).

to powers granted to him in the Claims Settlement Declaration, issues orders that provide for the composition of the three Chambers, the assignment of cases to the Chambers, the transfer of cases among Chambers, and the relinquishment by Chambers of certain cases to the Full Tribunal.[8]

A Committee on Administrative and Financial Questions, composed of three Members, supervises and guides the administration of the Tribunal. A Secretary-General, appointed by the Tribunal, has the responsibility for supervising its administration, taking no part in deciding cases. The Agents of the two Governments attend meetings of the Committee and participate in discussions, but they do not vote on its decisions.

(b) United Nations Compensation Commission (UNCC)—claims relating to the 1990–1991 Gulf War

Policy-making, executive, and adjudicative functions were allocated to different bodies within the UNCC. The Governing Council sets the Commission's policy. Its membership is the same as that of the United Nations Security Council, of which it is a subsidiary organ. The Council's decisions are taken by a majority of at least nine of its Members; however, the right of veto, which in other matters is held by each of the five permanent Members of the Security Council, is expressly excluded with respect to the UNCC Governing Council.[9]

Claims were reviewed and amounts of compensation to eligible claimants were recommended by one of the three-person panels of Commissioners—the UNCC's quasi-judicial branch. Commissioners were appointed by the Governing Council upon nomination by the United Nations Secretary-General, on the basis of recommendations from the UNCC's Executive Secretary.[10] The main task of the Commissioners was to review the claims and recommend to the Governing Council whether or not they were compensable, and the amounts of compensation. Commissioners had the responsibility to ensure that due process was observed in the Claims Process. In addition to setting policy, the Governing Council determined whether to approve the reports and recommendations of panels of Commissioners on the claims, and on the Commission's budget.

---

[8] Claims Settlement Declaration, Article III, paragraph 1; Iran–US CT Tribunal Rules, Article 5. See also Iran–US CT Presidential Order No. 1 of 19 October 1981, 1 Iran–U.S. C.T.R. p. 95, paragraphs 3, 5 and 6.

[9] UNCC Governing Council guidelines, 25 July 1991, text not officially available.

[10] UNCC Provisional Rules, Article 18, paragraph 1. The recommendation also indicates the composition of the panels and who shall act as Chairperson.

A register of experienced decision-makers, for which the Secretary-General of the United Nations had invited nominations from United Nations Member States, is kept and updated by the UNCC's Executive Secretary. The Executive Secretary had power to draw on this register—but was not limited to it—when recommending candidates for Commissioners to the Secretary-General, who nominated them, whereupon the UNCC Governing Council appointed them for fixed terms.[11] In nominating and appointing the Commissioners, due regard was to be paid to the need for even geographical representation, professional qualifications, experience, and integrity, as well as to the nature of the claims assigned to them. The Provisional Rules provide that the Commissioners shall be independent experts in fields such as finance, law, accounting, insurance, environmental damage assessment, oil, trade, or engineering.[12] All Commissioners acted in their personal capacity, not as representatives of their governments.[13]

Under the Provisional Rules, the UNCC had the power to appoint as many panels as it considered necessary to process claims expeditiously.[14] Exercising that power, a total of nineteen panels of Commissioners were appointed. When panels were appointed, it was specified which claims or categories of claims were assigned to them by the Executive Secretary. All the claims were divided into categories and sub-categories designated in the Commission's work program.[15]

The Commissioners did not perform administrative functions. Rather, the Secretariat of the Commission—its executive branch—headed by an Executive Secretary appointed by the Secretary-General of the United Nations, provided administrative, technical, and legal support to the Governing Council and to the panels of Commissioners. The Secretariat also has administered the Compensation Fund out of which claims are paid. The functions that the Secretariat performs were set out in the Commission's work program and in its Standard Operating Procedures.[16]

(c) Commission for Real Property Claims of Displaced Persons and Refugees (CRPC)—claims relating to the 1992–1995 war in Bosnia and Herzegovina

As was provided in the constituting instrument, the Dayton Peace Agreement, the CRPC consisted of nine Commissioners. Initially, four were appointed by the Federation of Bosnia and Herzegovina and two by the Republika Srpska.

---

[11] UNCC Provisional Rules, Article 18, paragraph 2.

[12] Ibid., Article 19, paragraphs 1 and 2. [13] Ibid., Article 21, paragraph 1.

[14] Ibid., Article 20, paragraph 2.

[15] Ibid., Article 20, paragraph 3; UNCC Work Programme, U.N. Doc. S/AC.26/1997/WP.1, text not officially available. [16] Text of the Standard Operating Procedures is not officially available.

Three international Commissioners, among them the Chairman, were appointed by the President of the European Court of Human Rights.[17] The initial appointments for half of the national Commissioners were for three years, four years for the other half, and five years for the international Commissioners. In fact, the composition of the Commission remained the same throughout its eight years of operation, with the appointments being renewed at appropriate intervals. One of the national Commissioners, however, withdrew from the Commission in 2002 because of incompatibility with his other functions. The Dayton Peace Agreement provided that Commissioners were to be persons of recognized high moral standing.[18] The Agreement provided that, five years after its entry into force, responsibility for the financing and operation of the Commission would be transferred to the Government of Bosnia and Herzegovina. Commissioners appointed after the transfer are to be appointed by the Presidency of Bosnia and Herzegovina.[19]

The Commission performed both policy-making and adjudicative functions. Pursuant to the authority vested in it under Annex 7 to the Dayton Peace Agreement, the Commission, acting as a whole, promulgated the rules and regulations necessary to carry out its functions.[20]

(d) Claims Resolution Tribunal for Dormant Accounts in Switzerland (CRT-I)—first claims tribunal for assets deposited in Swiss banks

The Independent Claims Resolution Foundation (ICRF), which was set up to carry out the CRT-I Claims Process, is governed by a Board of Trustees. This Board of Trustees appointed the Arbitrators of CRT-I who resolved the claims. The seventeen Arbitrators were selected for their experience and judgement. No special professional qualifications were specified.

Claims were decided either by a Sole Arbitrator or by a claims panel composed of three Arbitrators. The appointment of Sole Arbitrators and of claims panels was made for each claim by the Chairman of the Tribunal, whose task it was to distribute the caseload fairly and equitably among the Arbitrators, taking into account the language of the claimants, and maintaining diversity of nationality between claimants and a majority of the Arbitrators.[21]

---

[17] Dayton Peace Agreement, Annex 7, Article IX, paragraph 1.

[18] Ibid., Article IX, paragraph 2.   [19] Ibid., Article IX, paragraph 4, and Article XVI.

[20] Ibid., Article XV and Article IX, paragraph 3. The regulations consist of the Book of Regulations on Confirmation of Occupancy Rights of Displaced Persons and Refugees, and the Book of Regulations on the Conditions and Decision Making Procedure for Claims for Return of Real Property of Displaced Persons and Refugees (Consolidated version, 8 October 2002), available at www.pca-cpa.org/MCP/index_MCP.htm "Links to Completed Mass Claims Processes."

[21] See CRT-I Rules of Procedure, Article 28(b).

After the initial adoption of the Tribunal's Rules of Procedure by the ICRF Board of Trustees, matters of importance to all claims were resolved and Internal Rules were issued by vote of all the Arbitrators on the Tribunal.[22] The Chairman administered the Tribunal in accordance with the Rules of Procedure and with Swiss law on international arbitration.[23] He was assisted in the performance of this function by the Secretary-General of the Tribunal, which was initially not a specific person, but rather a law firm appointed by the ICRF Board of Trustees, and later a named individual. A Secretariat, led by the Secretary-General, assisted the Arbitrators in the administrative arrangements for the proceedings, prepared the files, performed factual and legal research, prepared drafts for consideration by the Arbitrators, and attended meetings of the Arbitrators.[24]

(e) Claims Resolution Tribunal (CRT-II)—second claims tribunal for assets deposited in Swiss banks

The ultimate decision-maker in the CRT-II Claims Process is the presiding Judge of the United States federal district court acting pursuant to the Settlement Agreement in the class action known as the Holocaust Victim Assets Litigation. The Judge appointed Special Masters whose actions are subject to approval by the Court. The Special Masters, in turn, appointed individuals to consider specific cases and make recommendations with respect to them. Initially, larger cases were assigned to "Senior Claims Judges," and smaller cases to "Resident Claims Judges." The Senior Claims Judges at first consisted of the same persons as had been Arbitrators in the Claims Resolution Tribunal for Dormant Accounts in Switzerland (CRT-I), and the Resident Claims Judges were appointed from the senior staff of CRT-I. The Senior and Resident Claims Judges, in considering cases and making recommendations to the Special Masters, were expected to perform adjudicative functions, but policy-making, executive, administrative functions and the like were performed by the Special Masters, subject, as noted, to approval of the Court.

Later, the Court approved a reorganization of the Claims Process recommended by the Special Masters. Under the new arrangements, the mandate of the Senior Claims Judges terminated in late May 2002, and they had no part in the reorganization and acted in no cases after that time. The amended Governing Rules of CRT-II provide that the Claims Process "shall consist of a Secretariat, including attorneys, auditors, paralegals, researchers, clerical assistants, and other staff, as may be necessary to carry out its functions."[25]

---

[22] See CRT-I Rules of Procedure, Article 28(f). CRT-I unpublished Internal Rules.

[23] CRT-I Rules of Procedure, Article 28(e).   [24] Ibid., Article 30.

[25] CRT-II Governing Rules, Article 9. See also Article 16, which provides that Staff Attorneys shall prepare draft decisions.

The entire Claims Process is "organized under the direction of the Special Masters."[26] Throughout the Governing Rules, there are further provisions which establish reporting to, consultation with, or decision by, the Special Masters.

The Special Masters may furthermore "establish an Advisory Committee that may include persons drawn from Victims, the plaintiffs in Holocaust Victim Assets Litigation, Jewish organizations with experience in claims matters, organizations providing assistance to potential claimants, governmental entities, or other persons who can contribute to the administration of the claims resolution process."[27] As of 31 January 2006, the Special Masters have not exercised their authority to establish such an Advisory Committee.

(f) Housing and Property Claims Commission (HPCC)—claims relating to the 1999 conflict in Kosovo

With certain exceptions, such as the initial screening procedure performed by the Housing and Property Directorate (HPD),[28] adjudicative functions in this Claims Process are reserved exclusively to the Commission.

Commissioners of the HPCC are appointed by the Special Representative of the United Nations Secretary-General, who designates one Commissioner as the Chairperson. The Special Representative may also establish additional panels in consultation with the Commission, but the Commission has been composed of only one panel of one local and two international Commissioners, who are required to be "experts in the field of housing and property law and competent to hold judicial office."[29] Initial appointments are for one year, but the Commissioners can be re-appointed for one or more additional terms.[30]

Policy-making and legislative functions are exercised by the Special Representative, in cooperation with other parts of the United Nations Interim Administration Mission in Kosovo (UNMIK), whereas executive functions are largely the responsibility of the Directorate.

(g) Mass Claims Processes administered by the International Organization for Migration (IOM)

German Forced Labour Compensation Programme (GFLCP)—claims against Germany and German industry for Nazi injustice

Policy-making in the GFLCP Claims Process lies with the German Foundation, whereas executive functions are the responsibility of the partner

---

[26] CRT-II Governing Rules, Article 10, paragraph 1.   [27] Ibid., Article 47.
[28] See section 3.04(f) above, on Initial Screening.
[29] UNMIK Regulation 1999/23, section 2.2.   [30] UNMIK Regulation 2000/60, section 17.3.

organizations implementing the German Foundation Act. The Foundation's Board of Trustees, which is composed of twenty-seven persons representing the participants in the negotiations that led to the creation of the German Foundation and its partner organizations, decides on all fundamental matters having to do with the tasks of the Foundation, and it also establishes guidelines for the work of the partner organizations.[31]

With respect to slave and forced labor and personal injury claims, it is the task of IOM to implement the part of the Claims Process for which it is responsible, such as reviewing the claims and making decisions on eligibility for compensation. All claims for property losses in this Claims Process were decided by the Property Claims Commission administered exclusively by IOM. The German Federal Ministry of Finance and the United States Department of State each appointed one Commissioner, and those two Commissioners in turn chose a Chairperson.[32]

The Property Claims Commission had the power, at the request of IOM or another partner organization, to assign personal injury claims to arbitration and to appoint an independent arbitrator to determine such claims. Such arbitrator was required to be "knowledgeable and experienced in making [personal injury] determinations and . . . fluent in the language or languages in which the claims are made."[33] In practice, however, no such arbitrator was appointed.

Finally, considering the anticipated high number of appeals and the time pressures upon the IOM Appeals Body for Forced Labour Claims, IOM—in practice—required Members of that Body to be able to work in English, and to be able to communicate via electronic mail and fax between its meetings.

Holocaust Victim Assets Programme (HVAP)—claims pursuant to 1999 class action Settlement

The HVAP Claims Process is conducted pursuant to the Settlement Agreement in the same class action as described in section 4.01(e) above on CRT-II, the Holocaust Victim Assets Litigation, in the United States District Court for the Eastern District of New York. The presiding Judge in that class action is the ultimate decision-maker with respect to both policy-making and awarding compensation in the HVAP Claims Process.

The Court has entered into arrangements with IOM according to which the legal staff of IOM reviews the claims, applying criteria proposed by the Special

---

[31] German Foundation Act, section 5, paragraphs 5 and 7.   [32] Ibid., section 9, paragraph 6.
[33] IOM Property Commission Supplemental Rules, sections 28 and 29.1.

Masters and approved by the Court. The staff then makes recommendations to the Court, through the Special Masters, as to claimants' eligibility for compensation.

(h) Eritrea–Ethiopia Claims Commission (EECC)—claims relating to the 1998–2000 war between Eritrea and Ethiopia

The constituting instrument, the 12 December 2000 Agreement, provides that the EECC shall consist of five Commissioners, with the parties appointing two Commissioners each within forty-five days from the effective date of the Agreement (12 December 2000) by written notice to the United Nations Secretary-General. None of these four can be nationals or permanent residents of the party making the appointment.[34] The President of the Commission, who cannot be a national nor a permanent resident of either party, is then selected by the party-appointed Commissioners within thirty days after the last of them is appointed. If the four cannot agree, the appointment is to be made by the United Nations Secretary-General following consultation with the parties.[35]

The Commission itself sets policy, performs executive direction, and adjudicates the claims, and no such functions are allocated to different bodies. The Commission has agreed with the International Bureau of the Permanent Court of Arbitration (PCA) at The Hague for it to provide registry and support services on a part-time basis as required.

(i) Humanitarian insurance Claims Process administered by the Jewish Claims Conference (JCC) for the International Commission on Holocaust Era Insurance Claims (ICHEIC)

The Chairman of ICHEIC appointed a Senior Counselor to the 8A1 humanitarian Claims Process. The Senior Counselor approved the criteria by which claims were evaluated for humanitarian awards and oversaw the approval process.

The JCC 8A1 claims processing team was overseen by the Executive Vice-President and the Chief Operating Officer of JCC, and it was generally comprised of a Director, four supervisors, and approximately thirty claims analysts.

---

[34] Eritrea–Ethiopia Agreement of 12 December 2000, Article 5, paragraph 2.   [35] Ibid.

(j) American Arbitration Association (AAA)—an illustrative case

The Arbitrators in the illustrative case were selected in accordance with, and based on criteria set forth in, the Settlement Agreement. All Arbitrators had to be attorneys with arbitration experience. Experience with financial services disputes was also relevant, as was mediation experience. In addition, all potential Arbitrators had to verify their computer competency, access to computer equipment, willingness to follow the mandates of the Settlement Agreement, and a willingness to serve for a uniform hourly fee.

Representatives of the plaintiffs, of the defendant, and of the state insurance regulators were given over two thousand resumés of AAA commercial Arbitrators to review. From that group, each representative was free to eliminate any Arbitrator. After the lists of acceptable Arbitrators had been received from each representative, the Arbitrators who were acceptable on all three lists were informed that they were eligible to become reviewers in the Claims Process. Over five hundred and seventy Arbitrators eventually participated in the Claims Process, and about twenty resigned during the course of the Claims Process for various reasons. A few were removed for failure satisfactorily to complete the required three-day training program, conducted by AAA staff in cooperation with representatives of the plaintiffs' counsel and of the defendant insurance company. Arbitrators from every state in the United States participated in the appeals review process.

4.02 Impartiality

Whether procedures to assure that decision-makers are impartial and independent are included. Procedures for challenge, and the procedures followed in the event a challenge is successful, or if a decision-maker resigns or is unwilling to act. (Those procedures may be included in the procedural rules.)

Editors' Commentary

Confidence by the parties and the public in a Mass Claims Process depends on trust in the impartiality and independence of those who make decisions. Recognizing that fact, most of the Claims Processes described in this book contain requirements of independence and impartiality that are made effective by challenge procedures to remove decision-makers who fail to meet those standards. In some Mass Claims Processes, such provisions are set forth explicitly in the constituting instruments or rules of procedure; in others they are incorporated by reference to rules such as the UNCITRAL Arbitration Rules or the Permanent Court of Arbitration Optional Rules for Arbitrating Disputes between Two States (PCA Rules); and in others they may be considered to be implied terms. The approaches taken by various Claims Processes are described below. These provisions are largely based on ethical standards and challenge procedures typical in international commercial arbitration, even where the Claims Process is administrative, not arbitral. There is, however, a fundamental difference between, on one hand, Mass Claims Processes that handle a large number of cases with many different parties and must continue to function for an extended period of time until all of those cases are decided, and, on the other hand, commercial arbitral tribunals that usually have one case with two parties and disband when that case terminates. Designers of Mass Claims Processes and others should take account of the practical problems that may arise from this difference. Thus, for example, decision-makers in a Mass Claims Process might be successfully challenged because they have an investment in a company in one of the cases before them. While such persons would be disqualified from serving in that particular case, the disqualification need not apply to large numbers of continuing cases before them involving different parties in which they had no financial interest and where a challenge would not be brought. The Tribunal Rules of the Iran–United States Claims Tribunal (Iran–US CT) described below provide a useful example of how this problem was recognized and solved.

Challenges are, by their nature, sensitive and have the potential to poison the atmosphere of a Claims Process. Uncertainty and disputes over procedures can increase that tension. It is therefore prudent to establish in advance clear grounds and comprehensive procedures to govern possible challenges.

It is also useful to establish procedures to be followed in the event a decision-maker resigns or is unable or unwilling to act. These are found in some, but not all, of the Mass Claims Processes described below. The UNCITRAL Arbitration Rules contain a time-proven model for such provisions.[36] Where a constituting instrument refers to the UNCITRAL Arbitration Rules or the PCA Rules, it may be expected that the provisions on challenge in those rules are incorporated by reference in the rules of the Claims Process, including the provision that challenges shall be decided by the appointing authority agreed to by the parties, or designated by the Secretary-General of the PCA if the parties have not so agreed.[37]

[36] UNCITRAL Arbitration Rules, Article 13.

[37] Ibid., Article 11 on challenge procedures, and Articles 6 and 7 on the role of the PCA Secretary-General.

(a) Iran–United States Claims Tribunal (Iran–US CT)—claims relating to the 1979 Islamic Revolution

The requirement that all Tribunal Members of the Iran–US CT shall be impartial and independent flows from the provisions in the Tribunal Rules dealing with challenge and with the appointment of Members by the appointing authority. For example, the Rules state that, in appointing a Sole Arbitrator, the appointing authority shall have regard to "such considerations as are likely to secure the appointment of an independent and impartial arbitrator and . . . the advisability of appointing an arbitrator of a nationality other than the nationality of the parties."[38]

Further, the Tribunal Rules contain extensive provisions concerning the procedure in case of challenge of a Member for lack of independence or impartiality. As the Tribunal Rules are modeled on the UNCITRAL Arbitration Rules, it is not surprising that the challenge provisions are typical of those customarily followed in international commercial arbitration. First, prospective Members are required to disclose any circumstances likely to give rise to justifiable doubts as to their impartiality or independence.[39] Moreover, when a Member of the Tribunal obtains knowledge that a case involves circumstances likely to give rise to justifiable doubts as to his or her impartiality or independence with respect to that case, the Member shall disclose such circumstances and, if appropriate, shall disqualify himself or herself as to that case. Disclosure statements shall be made available to each party.[40]

The UNCITRAL Arbitration Rules were designed primarily to regulate proceedings in which there was one case, or at most a few related cases, with generally two parties. In contrast, the Iran–US CT has jurisdiction over many different parties in many separate cases. Provisions were added to the Tribunal Rules to respond to that fact. For example, the Tribunal Rules provide that the parties to a particular case may challenge a Member on the basis of the existence of circumstances that give rise to justifiable doubts as to the Member's impartiality or independence. A party in a particular case may make a challenge on grounds related only to that case, but challenges on general grounds which relate to many cases may only be made by one of the two Government parties.[41]

If a challenge is sustained with respect to a particular case, or if a Member withdraws, he or she shall continue as a Member for all other cases. If the case is before a three-Member Chamber, it is transferred to another Chamber. In a case before the Full Tribunal of nine Members, a substitute Member shall be

---

[38] Iran–US CT Tribunal Rules, Article 6, paragraph 4.   [39] Ibid., Article 9.
[40] Ibid., Note 6 to Articles 9–12.   [41] Ibid., Note 1 to Articles 9–12.

appointed for the purposes of that case in the same way as an original Member of the Tribunal was appointed.[42]

Notice, time periods, and formal requirements for challenges are regulated in detail.[43] A Member who withdraws after a challenge or whose challenge is sustained shall be replaced pursuant to the procedure that was used for the appointment of the replaced Member.[44] If the challenged Member does not withdraw, the decision on the challenge will be made by the appointing authority.[45]

In the event that a Member fails to act or in the event of the *de jure* or *de facto* impossibility of performing his or her functions, the procedure in respect of the challenge and replacement of a Member applies.[46] If the President of the Tribunal, after consultation with the other Members of the Full Tribunal, determines that the failure of a Member to act or impossibility to perform his or her functions is due to a temporary illness or other circumstances expected to be of a relatively short duration, the Member shall not be replaced but a substitute Member shall be appointed for the temporary period in the same way as an original Member of the Tribunal was appointed.[47]

(b) United Nations Compensation Commission (UNCC)—claims relating to the 1990–1991 Gulf War

The UNCC Provisional Rules provide that, in nominating and appointing the Commissioners of the UNCC, due regard be given, *inter alia*, to their integrity.[48] Before taking up their duties, all Commissioners were required to make a declaration to the effect that they would perform their duties and exercise their position "honourably, faithfully, independently, impartially and conscientiously."[49]

The independency requirement was elaborated further in several respects in the UNCC Provisional Rules. Commissioners, all of whom acted in their personal capacity, were not permitted to have financial interests in any of the claims submitted to them, and they could not be associated with or have financial interests in any corporations whose claims were submitted to them.[50] Commissioners also were not permitted to represent or advise any party or claimant concerning the preparation or presentation of their claims

---

[42] Iran–US CT Tribunal Rules, Notes 3–5 to Articles 9–12.
[43] Ibid., Article 11, paragraph 1, and Note 2 to Articles 9–12.
[44] Ibid., Article 11, paragraph 3, and Article 12, paragraph 2.
[45] Ibid., Article 12, paragraph 1.   [46] Ibid., Article 13, paragraph 2.
[47] Ibid., Article 13, paragraph 2.   [48] UNCC Provisional Rules, Article 19, paragraph 1.
[49] Ibid., Article 27.   [50] Ibid., Article 21, paragraph 1.

to the Commission during their service as Commissioner and for two years thereafter.[51]

Prospective Commissioners were required to disclose any prior or actual relationship with governments, corporations, or individuals, or any other circumstances likely to give rise to justifiable doubts as to their impartiality or independence. A Commissioner, once appointed, was further required to disclose any new circumstances giving rise to similar doubts.[52] When a Commissioner obtained knowledge that a particular claim before his or her panel involved such circumstances, he or she was obligated to disclose them and, if appropriate, disqualify himself or herself as to that case.[53] If a government, international organization, individual claimant, or Commissioner became aware of such circumstances, they were to be communicated no later than fifteen days after they become known.[54] The UNCC Executive Secretary would inform the Governing Council of the circumstances, and the Governing Council could determine whether the Commissioner in question should cease to act, either generally or with respect to a particular claim.[55]

In the event that a Commissioner failed to act, or in the event of his or her *de jure* or *de facto* impossibility to act, the Executive Secretary was to inform the Governing Council, which could decide to replace the Commissioner in accordance with the procedures for the appointment of Commissioners.[56] In practice, several Commissioners had to be replaced due to illness or their decision to leave the UNCC to accept judicial or ambassadorial appointments.

(c) Commission for Real Property Claims of Displaced Persons and Refugees (CRPC)—claims relating to the 1992–1995 war in Bosnia and Herzegovina

Annex 7 to the Dayton Peace Agreement provided that the CRPC was an independent body and that the Commissioners had to be of recognized high moral standing.[57] However, neither the Dayton Peace Agreement nor the Books of Regulations promulgated to implement it had provisions on impartiality or independence of the individual Commissioners, or on challenge, resignation, removal, and incapability, or on the procedures to be followed in such instances. These matters were dealt with in the Headquarters Agreement relating to

---

[51] UNCC Provisional Rules, Article 21, paragraph 2.
[52] Ibid., Article 22, paragraphs 1 and 2.   [53] Ibid., Article 22, paragraph 3.
[54] Ibid., Article 22, paragraph 4.   [55] Ibid., Article 22, paragraphs 5 and 6.
[56] Ibid., Article 25.
[57] Dayton Peace Agreement, Annex 7, Article VII and Article IX, paragraph 2.

the CRPC, which contained provisions regulating the appointment and termination of Commissioners.[58]

(d) Claims Resolution Tribunal for Dormant Accounts in Switzerland (CRT-I)—first claims tribunal for assets deposited in Swiss banks

Each CRT-I Arbitrator was required by the Tribunal's Internal Rules to be impartial and independent. The Chairman, who organized and administered the Tribunal, was at all times to respect the judicial independence of the Arbitrators in resolving claims. When accepting an appointment, each Arbitrator had to submit a written statement of impartiality and independence.[59]

If, during a proceeding, circumstances arose that might give rise to justifiable doubts as to an Arbitrator's impartiality or independence, the Arbitrator was required promptly to disclose such circumstances to the parties, to the Tribunal, and to the other Arbitrators. If this occurred during an initial screening procedure, the Arbitrator was required to disclose the circumstances and withdraw from the proceedings in that claim.[60]

Except as permitted by the Tribunal, no Arbitrator was allowed to have any *ex parte* communication with any party or with anyone acting on its behalf with respect to any matter of substance relating to the proceedings; this did not prohibit *ex parte* communications that concerned matters of purely organizational nature, such as the physical facilities, place, date, or time of the hearings.[61]

An Arbitrator could be challenged if circumstances existed that gave rise to legitimate doubts concerning his or her independence or integrity.[62] The challenge petition was to be submitted to the Chairman of the Tribunal immediately after the party making the challenge became aware of the relevant facts, and it was to specify the facts and circumstances on which it was based.

If the challenged Arbitrator withdrew, the Chairman of the Tribunal was to confirm the withdrawal without by so doing implying that the grounds for the challenge were valid.[63] If the challenge was contested, the Chairman was to submit the case to the Board of Trustees of the Independent Claims Resolution Foundation (ICRF) which finally decided on the challenge, and the

---

[58] Headquarters Agreement between CRPC and Bosnia and Herzegovina (full text not officially available), Article 2, paragraph 3, provides: "The members of the Commission can only be revoked on grounds which are applicable to Magistrates of the highest Court in their country and recognized by the Commission."   [59] CRT-I unpublished Internal Rules, Article 3.
[60] Ibid.   [61] Ibid.   [62] CRT-I Rules of Procedure, Article 8, paragraph 1.
[63] CRT-I unpublished Internal Rules, Article 4.

Chairperson was to communicate the Board's decision to the parties and the other Arbitrators.[64]

(e) Claims Resolution Tribunal (CRT-II)—second claims tribunal for assets deposited in Swiss banks

As explained in section 4.01(e) above, the ultimate decision-maker in the CRT-II Claims Process is the presiding Judge of the United States federal district court acting pursuant to the Settlement Agreement in the class action known as the Holocaust Victim Assets Litigation. Accordingly, matters relating to his impartiality and independence are governed by United States law applicable to judicial proceedings. For that reason, the Governing Rules of CRT-II contain no explicit provisions concerning the independence and impartiality of the staff attorneys who draft decisions subject to the Court's approval and who are named by the Special Masters appointed by the Court.

(f) Housing and Property Claims Commission (HPCC)—claims relating to the 1999 conflict in Kosovo

The UNMIK Regulations governing the HPCC Claims Process provide that the Commissioners may not take part in any proceedings on a claim in which they have a personal interest, or if they have been consulted by or are associated with a party to a claim, have been involved in any legal proceedings on the claim other than the proceedings before the Housing and Property Directorate (HPD) and the Commission, or if there are any other circumstances that may affect their impartiality. In case of any doubt regarding the impartiality of a Commissioner, the Chairperson shall decide, or in the event that the Chairperson's impartiality could be affected, the Vice-Chairperson shall decide.[65]

Before taking office, the HPCC Commissioners are required to make a solemn written declaration in which they declare that they will perform their duties and exercise their functions honorably, faithfully, impartially, and conscientiously.[66]

A Commissioner may be removed from office by the Special Representative of the United Nations Secretary-General, on the recommendation of a majority of the Commissioners, for failure to meet the qualifications for office or for persistent and unjustified refusal to perform the duties of office.[67]

---

[64] CRT-I unpublished Internal Rules, Article 4; CRT-I Rules of Procedure, Article 8, paragraph 3.
[65] UNMIK Regulation 2000/60, section 17.12.
[66] UNMIK Regulation 1999/23, section 2.3.
[67] UNMIK Regulation 2000/60, section 17.4.

(g) **Mass Claims Processes administered by the International Organization for Migration (IOM):** *German Forced Labour Compensation Programme (GFLCP) for claims against Germany and German industry for Nazi injustice, and Holocaust Victim Assets Programme (HVAP) for claims pursuant to 1999 class action Settlement*

There are no explicit provisions concerning impartiality, independence, challenge, resignation, or unwillingness or incapability to act in the constituting documents of either GFLCP or HVAP. The applicable IOM Staff Rules state that

"employees/officials shall exercise the utmost discretion in regard to all matters of official business. They shall not communicate to any person any information known to them which has not been made public, except in the course of their duties or by authorization of the Director General, nor shall they at any time use such information to private advantage. These obligations do not cease upon separation from the Organization."[68]

Neither the German Foundation Act nor the Supplemental Rules of the Property Claims Commission include any explicit requirements which Commissioners serving on that Commission must fulfill, nor provisions on challenge.

The IOM Appeals Body for Forced Labour Claims, including appeals from HVAP Slave Labor Class I first instance decisions, is an independent organ subject to no outside instruction.[69] The Members of the Appeals Body shall be appointed or removed by IOM in agreement with the German Foundation and shall be "persons of high moral character, impartiality and integrity."[70] Further, they shall not be members of the German Foundation's Board of Directors or of IOM's Executive Committee, or be involved in the processing of claims.[71] The Principles and Rules governing the appeals procedure further require that Members of the Appeals Body not have financial interests in the claims they consider, be associated with representatives who have submitted claims to them, or themselves represent or advise any party or claimant concerning appeals.[72] If a Member resigns or is unable to exercise his or her functions, he or she shall inform IOM so that a successor can be appointed.[73] The Members of the Appeals Body are subject to disclosure requirements substantially identical to those described in section 4.02(b) above, with respect to the United Nations Compensation Commission (UNCC).[74] Before taking up

---

[68] IOM Staff Rules and Regulations, available at www.iom.int.
[69] IOM Appeals Body Principles and Rules, Article 7, paragraph A.
[70] Ibid., Articles 8 and 9.   [71] Ibid., Article 9.   [72] Ibid., Article 11.
[73] Ibid., Article 10.   [74] Ibid., Article 12.

duties on the Appeals Body, the Members must make a declaration that they will perform their duties and exercise their position "independently, impartially and conscientiously."[75]

(h) Eritrea–Ethiopia Claims Commission (EECC)—claims relating to the 1998–2000 war between Eritrea and Ethiopia

The constituting instrument, the 12 December 2000 Agreement, states that the EECC is "neutral," and strict nationality requirements apply to all the Commissioners.[76] As the Commission's Rules of Procedure are based on the 1992 Permanent Court of Arbitration Optional Rules for Arbitrating Disputes between Two States (PCA Rules), the EECC provisions on challenge of decision-makers are very similar to those found in the PCA Rules,[77] except as they relate to the designation of appointing authority; under the EECC Rules, the Secretary-General of the United Nations, and not of the PCA, serves in that role.[78]

(i) Humanitarian insurance Claims Process administered by the Jewish Claims Conference (JCC) for the International Commission on Holocaust Era Insurance Claims (ICHEIC)

The Senior Counselor responsible for overseeing the 8A1 humanitarian Claims Process was appointed by the Chairman of ICHEIC on basis of his experience and public service record. The integrity of the Claims Process was maintained by closely supervising and reviewing the work of both claims analysts and their supervisors for impartiality, and by requiring all employees involved in the day-to-day review of claims to sign a non-disclosure agreement upon hire.

A delegate from the Senior Counselor's office came to the JCC's processing facility in New York to observe claims review procedures and conduct sample reviews of scored claims prior to the Senior Counselor's authorizing any 8A1 humanitarian award payments.

(j) American Arbitration Association (AAA)—an illustrative case

Arbitrators acting in the illustrative case were governed by the Code of Ethics for Arbitrators in Commercial Disputes, prepared jointly by the American Bar

---

[75] IOM Appeals Body Principles and Rules, Article 13.

[76] Eritrea–Ethiopia Agreement of 12 December 2000, Article 5, paragraphs 1 and 2.

[77] Ibid., Article 5, paragraph 7; EECC Rules of Procedure, Articles 5 and 6. See also PCA Rules, Articles 9–12.   [78] EECC Rules of Procedure, Article 6, paragraph 6.

Association and the AAA, which requires that Arbitrators be impartial and independent.[79]

In addition to requiring each Arbitrator to submit a conflict of interest form, the AAA conducted an initial check for obvious conflicts of interest. There was an obligation on each Arbitrator for continuing disclosure of conflicts of interest for the duration of the Claims Process. The AAA also monitored the amount of time spent on resolving each case and compared that to the average time of all the Arbitrators, eventually not reappointing Arbitrators who billed too much time on individual cases or failed to submit their awards in a timely manner.

4.03 Time Commitment

Time commitments expected of decision-makers (e.g., full-time, part-time, taking up residence at the location of the Claims Process).

Editors' Commentary

Those who decide claims in many of the Mass Claims Processes described in this book are engaged only part-time in the task and are not expected to take up residence at the location of the Claims Process. This might seem to be anomalous in Claims Processes overburdened with very large numbers of claims that must be resolved as quickly as possible. The explanation seems to be that Mass Claims Processes are like icebergs: there is a point at the top that is supported by a large infrastructure below. Those who make decisions are at the pinnacle, but much more work must be done by a full-time staff below in order for the decision-makers to perform their important, but less time-consuming, tasks. For example, in some Claims Processes, the staff analyzes claims, groups together similar claims, screens out cases that do not properly fall within the jurisdiction of the Claims Process, gathers evidence, prepares the files, performs legal research, and often prepares first drafts of awards and orders for consideration by the decision-makers.[80] The inclusion in some Claims Processes of factual presumptions that decision-makers must apply reduces or

---

[79] See AAA/ABA Code of Ethics for Arbitrators in Commercial Disputes, 1997, available at www.adr.org.   [80] See further section 6.03 below, on functions of Secretariat staff.

simplifies the remaining issues that need to be determined and thereby lessens the time needed for decision-making.[81] Similarly, the practice in some Claims Processes, such as the United Nations Claims Commission (UNCC), to employ accounting and loss adjusting firms to give certain advice and recommendations also reduces the time that decision-makers need to spend on each claim.[82]

Full-time decision-makers might find that they would be left sitting unoccupied while the staff and outside experts completed the tasks of preparing claims for consideration. Nevertheless, there may be circumstances in which having full-time decision-makers resident at the seat of the Claims Process will accelerate disposing of cases, and that it is worth the cost even if the decision-makers are not fully occupied at all times. This trade-off of higher cost for greater speed is an important issue that those who design and supervise Mass Claims Processes and others need to evaluate.

(a) Iran–United States Claims Tribunal (Iran–US CT)—claims relating to the 1979 Islamic Revolution

The appointment of the Members of the Iran–US CT is for a full-time position. They are therefore, in principle, required to take up residence at or near the seat of the Claims Process in The Hague. However, in view of changes in the workload in later years, that practice has been modified in the case of some new appointees who replaced earlier Members.

The Tribunal Rules authorize the Tribunal (i.e., the Full Tribunal of nine Members and the three-Member Chambers, respectively) to conduct the proceedings in such manner as it considers appropriate.[83] Thus, in practice, within the framework set by the Tribunal's Internal Guidelines and by Presidential Orders organizing the Tribunal's work, the Full Tribunal and the Chambers determine their own schedules.

(b) United Nations Compensation Commission (UNCC)—claims relating to the 1990–1991 Gulf War

Members of the UNCC Governing Council have dedicated part-time to their duties while retaining other duties in their respective governments. The UNCC Commissioners worked part-time, meeting at intervals of between one

---

[81] See, e.g., section 2.06(e) above, for examples of such presumptions in the Governing Rules of CRT-II.   [82] See section 2.01(b) above, on the Type of Process.

[83] Iran–US CT Tribunal Rules, Article 15, paragraph 1.

and two months.[84] Consequently, they were not required to take up residence at or near the seat of the Claims Process in Geneva.

Under the Commission's Provisional Rules, the Chairpersons of the panels of Commissioners organize the work of their respective panels.[85] In practice, a comprehensive schedule was prepared by the Secretariat for each panel within the framework of the Commission's work program, and was then agreed to by the panel.

(c) Commission for Real Property Claims of Displaced Persons and Refugees (CRPC)—claims relating to the 1992–1995 war in Bosnia and Herzegovina

The CRPC Commissioners worked part-time, meeting at intervals of between one and two months. Consequently, the Commissioners were not required to take up residence at the seat of the Claims Process in Sarajevo.

(d) Claims Resolution Tribunal for Dormant Accounts in Switzerland (CRT-I)—first claims tribunal for assets deposited in Swiss banks

The CRT-I Arbitrators worked part-time. Consequently, they were not required to take up residence at the seat of the Claims Process in Zurich. By accepting appointment, however, each Arbitrator was deemed to have undertaken to make available sufficient time to enable the proceedings to be conducted and completed expeditiously.[86]

(e) Claims Resolution Tribunal (CRT-II)—second claims tribunal for assets deposited in Swiss banks

Before the CRT-II Claims Process was reorganized to become an administrative rather than a quasi-judicial Claims Process, the Senior Claims Judges worked part-time. It was expected that their work would, to the extent practicable, be done at their homes or offices and they were therefore not required to take up residence at the seat of the Claims Process in Zurich. The Resident Claims Judges were employees of the Secretariat staff, as their title indicated, and were required to work full-time and to reside in Zurich.

---

[84] See UNCC Provisional Rules, Article 33, paragraph 2 ("meetings will be held to the extent deemed necessary"). [85] Ibid., Article 29.

[86] CRT-I unpublished Internal Rules, Article 3.

After the reorganization of this Claims Process, staff attorneys and Secretariat staff analyze and process the claims in Zurich and, beginning in 2004, also in New York. The presiding Judge in the class action known as the Holocaust Victim Assets Litigation, who is the ultimate decision-maker of this Claims Process, is a full-time member of the federal judiciary of the United States, works in New York, and performs a variety of duties unrelated to this Claims Process. The Special Masters appointed by the Judge work part-time and are not required to have residence in Zurich or in New York.

(f) Housing and Property Claims Commission (HPCC)—claims relating to the 1999 conflict in Kosovo

The HPCC Commissioners work part-time, meeting monthly or bi-monthly, and consequently they are not required to take up residence at the seat of the Claims Process in Pristina.

(g) Mass Claims Processes administered by the International Organization for Migration (IOM): *German Forced Labour Compensation Programme (GFLCP) for claims against Germany and German industry for Nazi injustice, and Holocaust Victim Assets Programme (HVAP) for claims pursuant to 1999 class action Settlement*

At the GFLCP and HVAP Claims Processes, senior administrative and legal staff who make recommendations on claims work full-time in Geneva, and they must be resident in Geneva. The Members of both the Property Claims Commission and the IOM Appeals Body for Forced Labour Claims have worked part-time and only needed to come to Geneva for meetings. When IOM sought candidates for the Appeals Body, it emphasized—considering the number of appeals and the time pressures upon the Appeals Body—that its Members be able to communicate by electronic mail and fax, and be available for a minimum number of days per month for work and meetings according to a schedule determined by the Appeals Body itself.

(h) Eritrea–Ethiopia Claims Commission (EECC)—claims relating to the 1998–2000 war between Eritrea and Ethiopia

The EECC Commissioners have worked part-time, although the amount of time required of them increased sharply as the Commission began hearings.

The Commissioners are, however, not required to take up residence at or near the seat of the Claims Process in The Hague.

In order to increase efficiency and productivity and to limit the expense and time required for frequent travel to and from The Hague, the Commissioners make heavy use of electronic mail for internal communications, deliberations, and drafting.[87] The parties' submission of correspondence addressing particular issues, requests, or suggestions to the Registry via electronic mail has proven particularly effective. Such submissions have been rapidly circulated to Commissioners and to the other party electronically, allowing prompt consideration and response, and reducing the need for travel between Africa, the United States, and The Hague.

(i) Humanitarian insurance Claims Process administered by the Jewish Claims Conference (JCC) for the International Commission on Holocaust Era Insurance Claims (ICHEIC)

The processing staff and supervisors who considered 8A1 humanitarian claims worked full-time for the JCC in New York, and many of them, including the Director of the Claims Process, were assigned exclusively to the 8A1 Claims Process for the whole duration of the claims review. The Executive Vice-President and the Chief Operating Officer of JCC oversaw other Claims Processes at the JCC at the same time.

(j) American Arbitration Association (AAA)—an illustrative case

Arbitrators in the illustrative case were requested to devote at least ten hours per week to the Claims Process. Since proceedings were conducted over the telephone and in several time zones, the actual hours could be in the early morning, the evening, or on weekends. Some Arbitrators voluntarily committed full-time to the Claims Process. These Arbitrators were given more cases to handle as the Claims Process progressed, and they were given preference for retention in the Claims Process when the volume of claims decreased.[88]

---

[87] EECC Rules of Procedure, Article 2, reflects the Commission's intention to make the greatest possible use of electronic communications.

[88] In subsequent Mass Claims Processes handled by the AAA, reviewers were requested to commit more time and to be available one evening or weekend day per week, to accommodate different scheduling needs.

Chapter 5

Procedures for Conducting the Claims Process

5.01 Procedural Rules

Whether an existing set of recognized procedural rules is incorporated by reference (for example, the appropriate Permanent Court of Arbitration Rules, which are based on the UNCITRAL Arbitration Rules), and where there is such incorporation, what changes, if any, are made to reflect the particular circumstances of the Claims Process. If an existing set of rules is not incorporated by reference, whether a set of respected rules is used as a guide.

Editors' Commentary

The constituting instruments of some Mass Claims Processes refer to an existing set of procedural rules, either incorporating them by reference or citing them as a basis or guide for drafting new rules. Reference to an established set of rules can facilitate the negotiation of the constituting instrument, save time in getting the Claims Process under way, and afford assurance that key elements of the text were drafted by an impartial international body and have been widely tested in actual practice. The rules referred to by the Claims Processes described in this book have been either the UNCITRAL Arbitration Rules, used by the Iran–United States Claims Tribunal (Iran–US CT), or the Permanent Court of Arbitration Optional Rules for Arbitrating Disputes between Two States (PCA Rules), used by the Eritrea–Ethiopia Claims Commission (EECC). Incorporating a set of rules by reference is usually accompanied by the granting of power to a named body to modify them in the light of needs and circumstances of the particular Claims Process.

A somewhat more flexible approach is to provide that, although a set of rules is not incorporated by reference, procedures may be "guided by" a set of existing rules, as was done by the United Nations Compensation Commission (UNCC) with respect to the UNCITRAL Arbitration Rules.[1]

Annotations

(a) Iran–United States Claims Tribunal (Iran–US CT)—claims relating to the 1979 Islamic Revolution

The constituting instrument of the Iran–US CT, the Claims Settlement Declaration, provides that "the Tribunal shall conduct its business in accordance with the [UNCITRAL Arbitration Rules] except to the extent modified by the Parties or by the Tribunal to ensure that [the Claims Settlement Declaration] can be carried out."[2] Once the Tribunal had been constituted and had begun its work, it conducted extensive deliberations to determine what modifications should be made to the UNCITRAL Rules in order to meet its particular needs and circumstances, such as the fact that it sometimes acts by a Full Tribunal of nine Members, but sometimes by Chambers of three Members each, and has cases in which either private parties or governments can be claimants. The Tribunal reached decisions on its Rules by majority vote, after consulting with the Agents of the two Government parties who had no vote. As a result of this procedure, the Tribunal issued its "Tribunal Rules" and later modified them to meet emerging needs.

The Tribunal Rules introduced a novel format, as explained in the Introduction to the Rules:

"— First, as to each Article, the text of the UNCITRAL Arbitration Rules is set forth.
— Second, as to each Article, the text of any modifications to the UNCITRAL Rules made by the Tribunal is set forth. . . .
— Third, various Articles include notes to indicate how the Tribunal will implement or interpret the UNCITRAL Arbitration Rules, as modified."[3]

This unique method of presentation made it easier to identify any modifications to the UNCITRAL text. Appending notes to various Articles assisted in application of the new Rules.

In addition, the Tribunal issued Internal Guidelines and Procedural Orders relating to certain procedural matters, some made by the President

---

[1] See Report of the Secretary-General of 2 May 1991, U.N. Doc. S/22559, paragraph 27; and UNCC Provisional Rules, Article 43.

[2] Claims Settlement Declaration, Article III, paragraph 2.

[3] Iran–US CT Tribunal Rules, Introduction and Definitions, paragraph 1.

acting alone pursuant to limited powers granted to him under the Tribunal Rules.[4]

(b) United Nations Compensation Commission (UNCC)—claims relating to the 1990–1991 Gulf War

The UNCC Governing Council was tasked with adopting the Commission's rules of procedure, and in its Decision 10, it adopted Provisional Rules of Procedure which have remained the rules of the Claims Process.[5] Under the Rules, the panels of Commissioners are authorized to rely on "the relevant UNCITRAL Rules for guidance" in making any additional procedural rulings that might become necessary in order for them to carry out their functions.[6] In practice, it was not necessary to refer to the UNCITRAL Rules.

(c) Commission for Real Property Claims of Displaced Persons and Refugees (CRPC)—claims relating to the 1992–1995 war in Bosnia and Herzegovina

The CRPC Books of Regulations were drafted by the Commission, and they were specifically tailored to the circumstances and mandate of the Claims Process. The rules or constituting instruments make no reference to any other existing set of procedural rules.

(d) Claims Resolution Tribunal for Dormant Accounts in Switzerland (CRT-I)—first claims tribunal for assets deposited in Swiss banks

The body that had the responsibility of establishing procedural rules for CRT-I, the Independent Claims Resolution Foundation (ICRF), adopted "Rules of Procedure for the Claims Resolution Process" without incorporating or referring to any existing set of rules. While the Arbitrators had no role in drafting the Rules and no power to amend them, they did have the limited authority "to enact such guidelines and procedures, consistent with these Rules, as are required to fill gaps in these Rules and to deal with unforeseen circumstances."[7]

---

[4] See, e.g., Iran–US CT Internal Guidelines of the Tribunal, 1 Iran–U.S.C.T.R. p. 98, and Iran–US CT Tribunal Rules, Article 31, paragraph 2, which is the same rule as Article 31 of the UNCITRAL Arbitration Rules.

[5] UNCC Governing Council Decision 10 of 26 June 1992, *Provisional Rules for Claims Procedure*, U.N. Doc. S/AC.26/1992/10.   [6] UNCC Provisional Rules, Article 43.

[7] CRT-I Rules of Procedure, Article 42.

The Arbitrators several times exercised this authority to supplement and interpret the Rules, but such interpretations and supplements were considered to be internal guidelines and the Chairman elected not to make them public.

(e) Claims Resolution Tribunal (CRT-II)—second claims tribunal for assets deposited in Swiss banks

The Governing Rules of the CRT-II Claims Process do not incorporate by reference any existing procedural rules. Nor do the constituting instruments require that any other rules be used as a guide.

(f) Housing and Property Claims Commission (HPCC)—claims relating to the 1999 conflict in Kosovo

The HPCC rules of procedure are contained in UNMIK Regulation 2000/60. They were designed to meet the particular needs of the Commission's mandate and do not officially incorporate or use any existing rules as guidelines. However, the designers of this Claims Process did look to the lessons of the Commission for Real Property Claims of Displaced Persons and Refugees (CRPC) in Bosnia and Herzegovina, especially as regards creating an effective enforcement mechanism.

(g) Mass Claims Processes administered by the International Organization for Migration (IOM)

While procedural rules and regulations for both the GFLCP and HVAP Claims Processes were tailored to their specific circumstances, they did draw upon the rules and experiences of other Claims Processes. A number of experiences from the United Nations Compensation Commission (UNCC), the Claims Resolution Tribunals for dormant accounts in Switzerland (CRT-I and II), and the Commission for Real Property Claims of Displaced Persons and Refugees (CRPC) in Bosnia and Herzegovina were taken into account.

German Forced Labour Compensation Programme (GFLCP)—claims against Germany and German industry for Nazi injustice

For slave and forced labor and personal injury claims under GFLCP, rules of procedure are not contained in one single constituting document, but rather in various provisions of the German Foundation Act, and also in the contract between the German Foundation and IOM, the decisions of the Foundation's Board of Trustees, and the legal circulars of the Foundation's Board of Directors. None of these instruments incorporates by reference or refers to any existing set of rules, although the architects of GFLCP, and in particular the

Property Claims Commission, looked for guidance to the procedures and practice of the United Nations Compensation Commission (UNCC).

Holocaust Victim Assets Programme (HVAP)—claims pursuant to 1999 class action Settlement

For the claims categories that IOM is responsible for resolving in HVAP, proposed rules of procedure were set out in the Plan of Allocation and Distribution adopted by the United States federal district court overseeing the class action known as the Holocaust Victim Assets Litigation. These proposed rules were to be further elaborated by IOM in consultation with the Court.[8] No existing rules are incorporated by reference or otherwise cited.

(h) Eritrea–Ethiopia Claims Commission (EECC)—claims relating to the 1998–2000 war between Eritrea and Ethiopia

The constituting instrument of the EECC Claims Process, the 12 December 2000 Agreement, provides that the Commission shall adopt its rules of procedure "based upon" the Permanent Court of Arbitration Optional Rules for Arbitrating Disputes between Two States (PCA Rules).[9] These in turn largely mirror the UNCITRAL Arbitration Rules. While generally modeled on the PCA Rules, the EECC Rules change the order of some provisions and amend some wording to reflect requirements contained in the 12 December 2000 Agreement, to provide further clarification, or to eliminate provisions that are not relevant to the circumstances of the EECC. A major structural departure from the PCA Rules was to divide the EECC Rules into three chapters: Chapter One applies to all proceedings, Chapter Two to procedures for individual claims, and Chapter Three to mass claims procedures.

(i) Humanitarian insurance Claims Process administered by the Jewish Claims Conference (JCC) for the International Commission on Holocaust Era Insurance Claims (ICHEIC)

The 8A1 humanitarian Claims Process did not incorporate by reference or use as a guide any existing rules. Rather, it was based on the experiences and resources developed from the other claims programs previously conducted by the JCC.

---

[8] Plan of Allocation and Distribution, pp. 164–167 (proposed rules for Slave Labor Class II) and pp. 176–179 (proposed rules for Refugee Class).

[9] Eritrea–Ethiopia Agreement of 12 December 2000, Article 5, paragraph 7; PCA Rules, available at www.pca-cpa.org.

The procedural rules that governed this Claims Process were set forth in the 8A1 Point Scoring System Guidelines implementing the ICHEIC 8A1 Point Scoring System.[10] That Point Scoring System, authorized by ICHEIC, to some degree converted narrative information into a point score by assigning a set number of points to each of twelve questions that had been developed, weighted, and tested on a random sampling of the 8A1 Claims. Each of the twelve questions could be given either a "yes" or "no" answer by a claims analyst reading through the information provided by a claimant. The final combined score of positive answers helped determine the likelihood of the claimant's entitlement to a humanitarian award. The JCC created the ICHEIC 8A1 Point Scoring System Guidelines,[11] with specific examples to guide the claims analysts in applying the Point Scoring System. This document was developed and revised by the JCC through training and testing phases, as well as through subsequent rounds of consultations. ICHEIC also from time to time issued additional guidelines and policy memoranda clarifying existing policies or setting forth additional ones.[12]

(j) American Arbitration Association (AAA)—an illustrative case

The procedural rules used in the illustrative case were created by the lawyers involved in the underlying class action suit. They did not make reference to any established rules of any organization.

5.02 Standards of Proof

Whether the constituting instruments or procedural rules include special provisions with respect to evidence and standards of proof.

Editors' Commentary

The extraordinary circumstances from which many Mass Claims Processes arise, such as wars, revolutions, and massive population movements, more often than not result in a dearth of available documentary evidence of each

---

[10] Text of the Point Scoring System not officially available.
[11] Text of the Point Scoring System Guidelines not officially available.
[12] Texts of ICHEIC Policy Memoranda not officially available.

claimant's loss. Problems in obtaining evidence are almost to be expected, and the quality of what little evidence the claimants can provide may be poor. This has led many Mass Claims Processes to design uniform methods for the assessment and valuation of evidence in all similar cases. Some Mass Claims Processes can justify reliance on such uniformity because the factual basis of the claims is often very similar: the losses have occurred in the same geographical area, within a defined time period, in the same market conditions, and often as a result of the same underlying wrong.

The pressure of processing and deciding many thousands—indeed, sometimes millions—of claims, coupled with the desire to speed payments of compensation and the difficulties that victims often face in finding documentary evidence, have led to major—one might say revolutionary—changes and simplification in the procedures of some Mass Claims Processes as compared with more traditional practices in arbitration and court litigation. For example, in some of the Claims Processes described in this book, lesser standards of proof have replaced strict evidentiary requirements, and there is reliance on certain presumptions applied to large groups of similarly situated claimants.

The most innovative legal contribution of Mass Claims Processes has been to introduce a new concept of "relaxed standards of proof" for finding facts, based on the test of what is "plausible" in place of traditional legal standards such as those by which facts are determined by a "preponderance of the evidence" or similar concepts.

It is noteworthy that lower standards of proof are applied not only in Claims Processes that are administrative in nature and which, accordingly, might be expected to be less legalistic, but also in those Claims Processes established as arbitrations, where strict evidentiary requirements might be anticipated. Indeed, the terms "relaxed standard of proof" and "plausible" appear first in the Rules of Procedure of the Claims Resolution Tribunal for Dormant Accounts in Switzerland (CRT-I), a Claims Process which all parties explicitly agreed was an arbitration governed by Swiss law.

The earliest Claims Process described in this book, the Iran–United States Claims Tribunal (Iran–US CT), has largely found facts on the typical legal basis of preponderance of the evidence. The trend away from that traditional standard began at the United Nations Compensation Commission (UNCC) in an effort to cope with the tremendous caseload of claims resulting from the 1990–1991 Gulf War. The UNCC pioneered the concept that the standard of proof required in a Mass Claims Process can be less demanding than the customary standard applied in a traditional arbitration. In certain categories of claims, it required only that a claimant submit evidence which "demonstrates satisfactorily" that it is eligible for compensation, a phrase intended to establish a lesser standard than the stricter requirement that "each party shall have the burden of *proving the facts* relied on to support its claim or defense" found in the UNCITRAL Arbitration Rules[13] and other typical arbitration rules. Next, CRT-I made the innovation concerning lesser standards of proof even more explicit and far-reaching by introducing the new wording "relaxed standards of proof" to describe the finding of facts based on the test of what is "plausible."[14] Other Claims Processes, as described in detail in the annotations below, have included what are, in essence, similar relaxed standards of proof, albeit sometimes expressed in different wording.

It may be that relaxed standards of proof that require plausibility rather than a preponderance of evidence are valuable not only in Mass Claims Processes, but that consideration could also be given as to whether they are a useful tool for simplifying and expediting some types of commercial and investment arbitration and other dispute resolution mechanisms.

Some Claims Processes undertake to collect evidence on their own where claimants are less able to do so. However, initiatives such as that of the Commission for Real Property Claims of Displaced Persons and Refugees (CRPC) in Bosnia and Herzegovina to gather evidence are most practical in Claims Processes where the evidence is available in official records located in a relatively small geographic area, and where the Claims Process has adequate resources—both in terms of staff and funding—to undertake to do so. They are more difficult in other Claims Processes, such as in the German Forced Labour Compensation Programme (GFLCP) and the Holocaust Victim Assets Programme (HVAP) at the International Organization for Migration (IOM), where many kinds of evidence have had to be sought in a wide variety of places.

(a) Iran–United States Claims Tribunal (Iran–US CT)—claims relating to the 1979 Islamic Revolution

The Iran–US CT Tribunal Rules adopt the text of the UNCITRAL Arbitration Rules, which provide that "[e]ach party shall have the burden of proving the facts relied on to support his claim or defence."[15] This has been recognized to be both a burden to present evidence and a burden to persuade the Tribunal of the truth of that evidence. The Rules go on to state that "[t]he arbitral tribunal shall determine the admissibility, relevance, materiality and weight of the evidence offered."[16] There is, however, no provision in the

---

[13] UNCITRAL Arbitration Rules, Article 24 (emphasis added).
[14] CRT-I Rules of Procedure, Article 22.
[15] Iran–US CT Tribunal Rules, Article 24, paragraph 1.   [16] Ibid., Article 25, paragraph 6.

Tribunal Rules concerning the standard of proof required with respect to the evidence offered—that matter being left to the discretion of the Full Tribunal or three-Member Chamber in each particular case, pursuant to its power to "conduct the arbitration in such manner as it considers appropriate."[17] In practice, the Tribunal has in most cases exercised its discretion to decide facts on the traditional basis of preponderance of the evidence. At times, however, the Tribunal has allowed simplified presentations of evidence, such as summaries by accountants. Conversely, it has required an "enhanced standard of proof" where the allegations were "particularly grave" such as where there were "implications of fraudulent conduct and intent to deceive."[18] Also, it has drawn inferences, including adverse inferences, in cases where it knew with reasonable certainty that a party had access to relevant evidence but failed to produce it.[19]

In weighing evidence, the Tribunal has taken into account the difficulty—sometimes impossibility—of finding and producing evidence due to revolutionary circumstances and unrest.

(b) United Nations Compensation Commission (UNCC)—claims relating to the 1990–1991 Gulf War

The pioneering Article relating to evidence in the UNCC Provisional Rules begins with the statement that "[e]ach claimant is responsible for submitting documents and other evidence which *demonstrate satisfactorily* that a particular claim or group of claims is eligible for compensation pursuant to the [relevant United Nations] Security Council resolution. . . ."[20] The phrase "demonstrate satisfactorily" establishes a lesser standard than the stricter requirement that "[e]ach party shall have the burden of *proving the facts* relied on to support his claim or defense," found in the UNCITRAL Arbitration Rules[21] and in various other typical arbitration rules.

UNCC Governing Council Decisions 1 and 7 established different verification procedures for the urgent individual claims (categories "A", "B" and "C") than for the larger individual ("D"), corporate ("E"), and government claims ("F"), and sometimes different standards applied for different amounts within

---

[17] Iran–US CT Tribunal Rules, Article 15, paragraph 1.

[18] *Vera-Jo Miller Aryeh, et al.* and *The Islamic Republic of Iran*, Award No. 581–842/843/844–1 (22 May 1997), 33 Iran–U.S.C.T.R. p. 272, at p. 317, paragraph 159.

[19] See Concurring Opinion of Judge Richard M. Mosk in *Ultrasystems Incorporated* and *The Islamic Republic of Iran, et al.*, Award No. 27–84-3 (4 March 1983), 2 Iran–U.S.C.T.R. p. 100, at p. 115.

[20] UNCC Provisional Rules, Article 35, paragraph 1 (emphasis added).

[21] UNCITRAL Arbitration Rules, Article 24, paragraph 1 (emphasis added).

a claims category. Thus, "simple and expedited procedures" were to be applied to processing the urgent claims in categories "A", "B" and "C,"[22] whereas more individualized verification was used for the additional categories, especially those that were "unusually large or complex."[23]

The standard of proof was lowered further for certain urgent claims by "guidelines" set forth in the Provisional Rules with respect to claims received under the criteria for expedited processing. Urgent claims for fixed amounts in the cases of forced departure and serious personal injury not resulting in death required the claimants to provide only "simple documentation" of the facts, and no documentation of the amount of loss.[24] Thus, in order for a claim to prevail in category "A", the fact and date of departure from Iraq or Kuwait needed to be shown with "simple documentation."[25] Because compensation for category "A" claims was set at fixed amounts,[26] no documentation concerning the actual amount of the loss was needed; the claimant was only required to show that he or she left Iraq or Kuwait during the relevant time period.[27] If it could be documented that the loss exceeded the fixed amount, a claim for the actual amount could be made under category "C" (or other appropriate category).

For claims in category "B", "simple documentation" of the fact and date of the injury or of the death and family relationship was sufficient; no documentation was needed of the actual amount of the loss.[28] Compensation for claims in category "B" was also fixed at an amount between US$2,500 and 10,000, depending on whether the claims were individual or family claims. If the claimant's loss exceeded that amount, the fixed amount was considered "interim relief" and a claim for actual amounts could be brought under category "C" (or other appropriate category).[29]

---

[22] UNCC Governing Council Decision 1 of 2 August 1991, *Criteria for Expedited Review of Urgent Claims*, U.N. Doc. S/AC.26/1991/1 (2 August 1991), paragraph 1.

[23] UNCC Governing Council Decision 7 of 28 November 1991, as revised on 16 March 1992, *Criteria for additional Categories of Claims*, U.N. Doc. S/AC.26/1991/7/Rev.1 (17 March 1992), paragraph 3.   [24] UNCC Provisional Rules, Article 35, paragraph 2(a) and (b).

[25] UNCC Governing Council Decision 1 of 2 August 1991, *Criteria for Expedited Review of Urgent Claims*, U.N. Doc. S/AC.26/1991/1 (2 August 1991) paragraph 11.

[26] Provision was made in category "A" for individual (US$2,500–4,000) and for family (US$5,000–8,000) claims; the fixed amount depended in each instance on whether claimants filed further claims in any of the other individual claims categories.

[27] In practice, claimants often did not even have to document their departure because the UNCC Secretariat had developed a database of arrival and departure records and was able to match claimants' computerized claim forms against this database to verify and award claims in the absence of additional documentation. See further section 5.06 below, on mass claims technologies.

[28] UNCC Governing Council Decision 1 of 2 August 1991, *Criteria for Expedited Review of Urgent Claims*, U.N. Doc. S/AC.26/1991/1 (2 August 1991), paragraph 12.   [29] Ibid.

Fixed amounts were generally not awarded for category "C" claims, and each claimant in this category was therefore required to support the claim with "appropriate evidence of the circumstances and amount of the claimed loss."[30] The Provisional Rules provide that, for claims of up to US$100,000 of actual losses, "[d]ocuments and other evidence required will be the *reasonable minimum* that is appropriate under the particular circumstance of the case. A lesser degree of documentary evidence ordinarily will be sufficient for smaller claims such as those below US$20,000."[31]

A common heightened standard of proof applied to the three categories of larger claims of individuals, corporations, and governments (categories "D", "E" and "F"). Claims in these categories had to be "supported by documentary and other appropriate evidence sufficient to demonstrate the circumstances and the amount of the claimed loss."[32] In a later decision, the Governing Council reiterated the requirement for a higher standard of proof, stating that "documents and other evidence must exceed the reasonable minimum that was required for claims in categories 'A', 'B' and 'C'" and "no loss shall be compensated by the Commission solely on the basis of an explanatory statement provided by the claimant."[33] Even in applying these heightened standards, however, Commissioners could take into account the extraordinary circumstances in which a claim arose, and exercise discretion in awarding compensation in instances where evidence fell short of demonstrating the amount of the loss with a reasonable degree of certainty.[34]

(c) Commission for Real Property Claims of Displaced Persons and Refugees (CRPC)—claims relating to the 1992–1995 war in Bosnia and Herzegovina

The CRPC Book of Regulations on Procedure contained detailed lists of the evidence required to prove ownership rights, lawful possession of property, and

---

[30] Ibid., paragraph 15(a); UNCC Provisional Rules, Article 35, paragraph 2(c).

[31] Ibid. (emphasis added).

[32] UNCC Governing Council Decision 7 of 28 November 1991, as revised on 16 March 1992, *Criteria for additional Categories of Claims*, U.N. Doc. S/AC.26/1991/7/Rev.1 (17 March 1992), paragraphs 8, 23 and 37. See also UNCC Provisional Rules, Article 35, paragraph 3.

[33] UNCC Governing Council Decision 46 of 2 February 1998, *Concerning Explanatory Statements by Claimants in categories "D", "E" and "F"*, U.N. Doc. S/AC.26/Dec.46 (1998) (3 February 1998).

[34] See *Report and Recommendations made by the Panel of Commissioners concerning Part One of the First Instalment of Claims by Governments and International Organizations (Category "F" Claims)*, U.N. Doc. S/AC.26/1997/6 (18 December 1997), paragraph 63.

occupancy rights to socially-owned apartments.[35] However, the Regulations provided that "if no relevant evidence is available to a claimant or if the evidence presented by the claimant is of doubtful credibility, the Commission will initiate evidence collection or evidence verification procedures"[36] using, *inter alia*, "the bodies and services where the records on real property, owners and possessors are kept."[37]

The CRPC also employed evidentiary presumptions including, for example, that claimants were not required to prove that they were displaced persons or refugees at the time of registering a claim; such status was presumed.[38] Also, it was presumed that persons who submitted claims were not in possession of the claimed real property, and no proof of those facts was required.[39] For example, in practice, the Commission accepted claims of claimants (e.g., claims of thousands of Serbs in Sarajevo Canton) who had fled their homes after the Dayton Peace Agreement was signed in 1995.

(d) Claims Resolution Tribunal for Dormant Accounts in Switzerland (CRT-I)—first claims tribunal for assets deposited in Swiss banks

A key Article in the CRT-I Rules of Procedure is headed "Relaxed Standard of Proof" and it states:

"The claimant must show that it is plausible in light of all the circumstances that he or she is entitled, in whole or in part, to the dormant account. The Sole Arbitrators or the Claims Panels shall assess all information submitted by the parties or otherwise available to them. They shall at all times bear in mind the difficulties of proving a claim after the destruction of the Second World War and the Holocaust and the long time that has lapsed since the opening of these dormant accounts."[40]

The terms "relaxed standard of proof" and "plausible" are not customary in other types of dispute resolution rules or legal texts. Therefore, to better understand them in this context, it may be useful to consult standard English dictionary definitions.[41] "Relaxed" has been defined as meaning "less strict, severe or rigid,"[42] and to be relaxed is "to make something such as a rule less

---

[35] CRPC Book of Regulations on Procedure, Articles 44 and 45.   [36] Ibid., Article 35.

[37] Ibid., Article 38.   [38] Ibid., Article 12.   [39] Ibid., Article 11.

[40] CRT-I Rules of Procedure, Article 22, paragraph 1.

[41] The official translations of the terms "relaxed standard of proof" and "plausible"/"plausibility" into other languages used at CRT-I may provide additional insight into their meaning. Some translations of those terms are: German *"erleichterter Beweis-standard"/"erleichterte Nachweispflicht"* and *"glaubhaft"*; French *"exigences de preuve"* and *"plausible"/"plausibilité"*; Italian *"criteri di prova agevolati"* and *"plausibile"/"plausibilità"*; Spanish *"relajación de las normas en materia de prueba"* and *"verosímil"/"verosimilitud"*.

[42] OXFORD ENGLISH DICTIONARY, see also WEBSTER's THIRD NEW INTERNATIONAL DICTIONARY—UNABRIDGED ("less rigid," "not strict," "not severe").

strict."[43] One dictionary defines "plausible" as "appearing likely to be true, usually in the absence of proof,"[44] while another includes in its definition of "plausible" the "appearance of reasonableness,"[45] and a third includes "superficially worthy of belief."[46]

The CRT-I Rules of Procedure provided the following guidelines to be followed in applying the plausibility standard:

"A finding of plausibility requires, inter alia,

(i) that all documents and other information have been submitted by the claimant regarding the relationship between the claimant and the published account holder that can reasonably be expected to be produced in view of the particular circumstances, including, without limitation, the history of the claimant's family and whether or not the published account holder was a victim of Nazi persecution; and

(ii) that no reasonable basis exists to conclude that fraud or forgery affect the claim or evidence submitted; or that other persons may have an identical or better claim to the dormant account."[47]

An even lower standard applied at the "initial screening" stage of a claim, when claims that had been filed by persons claiming to be related to listed account holders were sent to the relevant banks, but the claimants were as yet unaware of the identity of the bank. If the bank in question was unwilling to disclose its identity and the amount in the account, the Tribunal would, in an "initial screening" procedure, order disclosure unless the claimant had failed to submit "any information" regarding entitlement to the account, or if it was "apparent" that the claimant was not entitled to the account.[48]

Notwithstanding the emphasis on relaxed standards of proof, the Rules of Procedure included an exception for one type of issue deemed particularly sensitive. The exception provided that "the Sole Arbitrator or Claims Panel shall reject a claim if, by a *preponderance of the evidence*, it is established that [the claimant] was acting as an intermediary for the victim of Nazi persecution; and the assets deposited in the account were looted from victims . . . ,"[49] shifting the burden of proof to the banks, which did not benefit from the relaxed standard because they were likely to have had records available to them.

---

[43] ENCARTA WORLD ENGLISH DICTIONARY.   [44] Ibid.
[45] OXFORD ENGLISH DICTIONARY.
[46] WEBSTER'S THIRD NEW INTERNATIONAL DICTIONARY—UNABRIDGED.
[47] CRT-I Rules of Procedure, Article 22, paragraph 2.   [48] Ibid., Article 10.
[49] Ibid., Article 15 (emphasis added).

(e) Claims Resolution Tribunal (CRT-II)—second claims tribunal for assets deposited in Swiss banks

In CRT-II, as in CRT-I, the relaxed standard of proof is that "[e]ach Claimant shall demonstrate that it is plausible in light of all the circumstances that he or she is entitled, in whole or in part, to the claimed Account."[50] Here too, those who decide claims are instructed by the Governing Rules to "at all times bear in mind the difficulties of proving a claim after the destruction of the Second World War and the Holocaust and the long period of time that has elapsed since the opening of the account."[51] Unlike CRT-I, the CRT-II Governing Rules do not include guidelines as to how the plausibility test will be applied,[52] nor any exceptions to it.[53]

Closely related to the provisions on the standard of proof, the Governing Rules establish several presumptions—which apply in the absence of evidence to the contrary—including (i) a presumption that owners of a joint account have equal shares,[54] (ii) a presumption applicable to partial claims,[55] (iii) presumptions relating to claims to certain closed accounts,[56] and (iv) presumptions for establishing the value of accounts for which there is no evidence of the actual value.[57] In situations where such presumptions govern, no proof is required and therefore no standard of proof applies. Such presumptions greatly simplify the tasks of presenting and deciding claims in the actual circumstances to which they relate. Designers of Mass Claims Processes may wish to weigh the value of utilizing this technique against the need for greater accuracy in some cases.

(f) Housing and Property Claims Commission (HPCC)—claims relating to the 1999 conflict in Kosovo

At HPCC, the rules of evidence and proof are purposely flexible. This was necessary because of the effect of the conflict on public records. Cadastral records had in many instances been removed from Kosovo to Serbia, and those that remained were often outdated. Many street names had been changed—some more than once—and the displaced claimants were difficult to contact. Thus, the Commission's procedural rules, in UNMIK Regulation 2000/60, provide that "[t]he Commission may be guided but is not bound by the rules of

---

[50] CRT-II Governing Rules, Article 17, paragraph 1.   [51] Ibid., Article 17, paragraph 2.
[52] Compare CRT-I Rules of Procedure, Article 22, paragraph (i).
[53] Compare ibid., Article 22, paragraph (ii).
[54] CRT-II Governing Rules, Article 25, paragraph 1.
[55] Ibid., Article 25, paragraph 2.   [56] Ibid., Article 28.   [57] Ibid., Article 29.

evidence applied in local courts in Kosovo. The Commission may consider *any reliable evidence*, which it considers relevant to the claim. . . ."[58] The only evidentiary requirement is thus that evidence be "reliable." Further, if a party is able to present legally relevant evidence which the Commission did not consider in rendering a decision, such party may seek reconsideration of the claim within thirty days of being notified of the decision.[59]

(g) Mass Claims Processes administered by the International Organization for Migration (IOM)

German Forced Labour Compensation Programme (GFLCP)—claims against Germany and German industry for Nazi injustice

The German Foundation Act provides for a relaxed standard of proof: "Eligibility shall be demonstrated by the applicant by submission of documentation. The partner organization shall bring in relevant evidence. *If no relevant evidence is available, the claimant's eligibility can be made credible in some other way.*"[60] The legislative history of the Act confirms that this standard was chosen chiefly in view of the advanced age of the claimants, the long time that has elapsed since the events giving rise to the claims, and the difficulties of providing documentary proof for such events.

Heavy use is made of presumptions under GFLCP. For example, in order to establish a claim for slave labor, it is sufficient that a claimant show that he or she was held in a concentration camp, ghetto, or a comparable place of confinement;[61] the Claims Process will then assume that the claimant was made to perform slave labor, even if he or she was a small child at the time of confinement. Other presumptions used in GFLCP include: a presumption that, if claimant is of a certain nationality and was present in the German Reich during a certain time period, the claimant was deported; a presumption that, if claimant was in a certain concentration camp during a certain time period, claimant was forced to perform labor; a presumption that, if claimant was

---

[58] UNMIK Regulation 2000/60, section 21.1 (emphasis added).   [59] Ibid., section 14.1(a).

[60] German Foundation Act, section 11, paragraph 2 (emphasis added).

[61] The types of evidence that can establish that a claimant was interned in a concentration camp include, but are not limited to: matches between a claimant's wartime identification documents (issued by the Nazi authorities), such as "work books", or the number tattooed on a survivor's arm, with records kept by the camp administrators; matches between information on the claim forms and information contained in the archives of the International Tracing Service (ITS) in Bad Arolsen (www.its-arolsen.org), which contain files on millions of individuals and their fate and whereabouts in World War II. (The German Foundation accepts a positive ITS search result as sufficient evidence to establish eligibility for slave labor compensation.)

a victim of medical experiments, claimant suffered personal injury; and a presumption that, if claimant lost a certain type of property in a certain area during a certain time period, a German company was involved.

The Supplemental Rules of the Property Claims Commission provide that the Commission's decisions on compensation

"shall be based on relaxed standards of proof taking into account the lapse of time between the date the loss occurred and the date the claim was made; the circumstances in which the specific loss or types of losses occurred; the information available from other cases; and the background information available to the Commission regarding the circumstances prevailing during the National Socialist era and the Second World War and the participation of German enterprises in the commitment of National Socialist wrongs."[62]

According to the Supplemental Rules, a fact is considered established before the Property Claims Commission if it has been "credibly demonstrated," and a "claim cannot be rejected on the sole ground that it is not supported by official documentary evidence."[63]

The obligation of the partner organizations to assist the claimants in proving their claims, particularly by checking relevant archives in Germany and elsewhere, and the corresponding obligation of public archives to provide such information, is emphasized in a separate provision of the German Foundation Act.[64]

Holocaust Victim Assets Programme (HVAP)—claims pursuant to 1999 class action Settlement

For HVAP, the Plan of Allocation and Distribution adopted by the United States District Court for the Eastern District of New York in the class action known as the Holocaust Victim Assets Litigation, sets forth a standard of "plausibility."[65] In order to plausibly demonstrate slave labor, a claimant shall submit "a sworn statement (or the equivalent) explaining the nature of the slave labor performed by the Claimant, and all evidence, documentary and non-documentary, that the Claimant may reasonably be expected to possess in view of the circumstances and the years that have elapsed since World War II."[66]

Like GFLCP, the HVAP Claims Process also makes extensive use of presumptions. For example, if a claimant can show that he or she belongs to

---

[62] IOM Property Commission Supplemental Rules, section 22.1.   [63] Ibid., section 22.2.
[64] German Foundation Act, section 18.
[65] Plan of Allocation and Distribution, pp. 165–166.   [66] Ibid., p. 165.

a certain ethnic or other group targeted by the Nazis for persecution, and that he or she was detained in a certain camp during the war, the claimant will be presumed to have performed slave labor.

(h) Eritrea–Ethiopia Claims Commission (EECC)—claims relating to the 1998–2000 war between Eritrea and Ethiopia

The Commission's Rules of Procedure are based upon the Permanent Court of Arbitration Optional Rules for Arbitrating Disputes between Two States (PCA Rules), whose provisions on evidence are closely modeled on the UNCITRAL Arbitration Rules. In adapting the PCA Rules to carry out the goals of the 12 December 2000 Agreement, the Commission provided for increased flexibility in some significant areas, reflecting its possible need to consider large numbers of claims utilizing mass claims procedures. (The Rules were promulgated before claims were filed, so the Commission did not know at the time the nature of the caseload it would be required to administer.)

The provisions on evidence in the EECC Rules of Procedure are contained in Chapter One, which applies to all Commission proceedings. These general rules allow the Commission to "determine the admissibility, relevance, materiality and weight of the evidence offered;"[67] to "draw adverse inferences from any failure by a party to produce evidence" where circumstances warrant;[68] and to make the award based on the evidence before it "[i]f one of the parties, duly invited to produce documentary evidence, fails to do so within the established period of time, without showing sufficient cause for such failure."[69]

In an early decision dealing with evidence, the Commission emphasized that Article 5, paragraph 13, of the 12 December 2000 Agreement requires it to apply the relevant rules of international law and that it cannot make decisions *ex aequo et bono*.[70] The rules which the Commission must apply include those requiring evidence to prove or disprove disputed facts. It therefore urged the parties "to pay particular attention to matters related to evidence in the collection and preparation of claims; . . . to develop guidance for all personnel who collect or prepare claims, emphasizing the importance of evidence, and indicating the types of evidence potentially available."[71] The Commission also strongly encouraged both parties to harmonize such guidance.

The Commission indicated that either party may submit reasonably framed requests to the other for access to specific evidence believed to be located in the

---

[67] EECC Rules of Procedure, Article 14, paragraph 2. [68] Ibid., Article 14, paragraph 4.
[69] Ibid., Article 14, paragraph 5.
[70] EECC Decision Number 4: Evidence (24 July 2001), available at www.pca-cpa.org.
[71] Ibid.

other party's territory that is not otherwise available to the requesting party. If the requesting party does not obtain the cooperation it requests, the matter may be brought to the attention of the Commission.

The Commission also included significant provisions related to evidence in Chapter Three of its Rules of Procedure, regarding mass claims procedures. The most significant departure from traditional arbitration practice is a rule providing for evidence to be checked on a sample basis.[72] The Commission anticipated that, in mass claims procedures involving a sub-category of claims, it would first determine, based on the evidence and pleadings, whether "acts or omissions alleged to have been in violation of international law" have occurred, are attributable to the other party, and indeed violate international law. If any of these determinations cannot be made for lack of proof, the Commission must dismiss the claims in that sub-category. However,

"[i]f the Commission makes all of the [above-mentioned] determinations . . . , the claims in that sub-category for each of the two levels of compensation shall be subject to random sampling of their evidence to ascertain the percentage of such claims for which the evidence is inadequate to establish the claim. The compensation for all claims in that compensation level of that sub-category is automatically reduced by that percentage, and the Commission shall issue an award of such compensation for all claims in that sub-category."[73]

(i) Humanitarian insurance Claims Process administered by the Jewish Claims Conference (JCC) for the International Commission on Holocaust Era Insurance Claims (ICHEIC)

As explained in section 1.01(i) above, the test in the 8A1 humanitarian Claims Process was one of "likelihood"—not strict proof—that an insurance policy had existed. The 8A1 claims analysts read the claimants' submissions in the original language(s) in which they were provided, and, using twelve questions, they "scored" each claim using the Point Scoring System. When a claim reached a certain number of points, it was considered to establish a likelihood that a policy had indeed existed, and that the claimant was eligible to receive an award.

A first principle in evaluating an 8A1 Claim was that the evidence should be read in a light most favorable to the claimant. Claimants' assertions regarding details about the purchase of insurance policies were accepted as true.[74] This

---

[72] See further section 5.06(h) below, on mass claims techniques.

[73] EECC Rules of Procedure, Article 32.

[74] JCC has explained that its choice of questions used in "scoring" the 8A1 Claims was derived by it in part from its understanding of doctrines of sociology and observations about witness testimony

reflected the further recognition that the loss of documents was sometimes due to destruction or seizure, and the absence of archives was at times due to the fault of the issuing insurance companies.

Moreover, given the advanced age of the claimants and the difficulty of remembering traumatic events with accuracy, conflicting statements—even when mutually exclusive—were read to benefit the claimant. In short, the Point Scoring System was governed by the desire to elucidate and give credit to whatever scant memories remained to support a claim for a Holocaust era insurance policy.

(j) American Arbitration Association (AAA)—an illustrative case

In the illustrative case, a relatively low—or relaxed—standard of proof was applied, pursuant to the terms of the Settlement Agreement.[75] The burden of proof was relaxed in cases of claims by multiple individuals alleging an unauthorized sales practice involving a single agent of the defendant insurance company.

5.03 Languages

Whether the constituting instruments or procedural rules include special provisions with respect to the language(s) of the Claims Process, and, if applicable, how translation and interpretation services are provided (e.g., by an in-house language services department or contracted out in whole or in part). (See also section 6.01 on linguistic support.)

Editors' Commentary

The varying circumstances of different Mass Claims Processes have resulted in different provisions on translation. Designers of future Mass Claims Processes and others will wish to weigh the advantages of a translation requirement for key documents into the languages spoken by all potential claimants, against

---

in legal proceedings, to the effect that people are less likely to invent minor obscure details, and hence details and anecdotes can be indicia of truth. Similarly, the way in which assertions are phrased can give an indication as to whether a person is speaking from personal knowledge or mere belief.

[75] The terms of the Settlement Agreement are not officially available.

the practical realities of the difficulties and expense of having texts such as claim forms available in a large number of languages and scripts. One factor in this equation is the widespread use of computer databases for processing the claims received. In at least one Claims Process, language requirements had to be limited in order to meet the capability of the computer software. Thus, the United Nations Compensation Commission (UNCC) explained in its Provisional Rules that its working language had to be English because its "computerized software and database system, which is technically required for the processing of a large number of claims, has been designed in English."[76] The lesson for designers of Mass Claims Processes is that it is wise to consider the sophistication of available computer systems when drafting rules on translation and other procedures.

In many Mass Claims Processes, however, there will be no escaping the fact that effective outreach and consideration of fairness require making information available to potential claimants in a language which they can understand, and enabling them to submit inquiries and claims, preferably, in their native tongue. Some of the Claims Processes described in this book—although their official working language may be English—maintain portions of their websites in many different languages,[77] conduct publicity campaigns in different countries and communities in the local languages, set up call centers and regional field offices staffed by personnel who speak the claimants' languages and can answer questions and help fill out claim forms, and most importantly, allow claim forms and other documents to be filed in a number of different languages.

Creativity and resourcefulness are key to solving linguistic dilemmas quickly and early in a Mass Claims Process so as not to slow down or overly complicate the actual processing and evaluation of claims, while at the same time striving to keep costs low and data readily accessible. One solution which worked well both at the International Organization for Migration (IOM) and the Jewish Claims Conference (JCC) in processing Holocaust-related claims from all over the world, was to employ staff with the requisite language skills to process each claim in its original language and enter the information in English into a common database, rather than incurring high costs and losing precious time in translating the claims. Also, it was felt, this method captures nuances in the claims which might have been lost in translation in cases where, in the absence of documentary evidence, a claimant's personal statement formed the basis for certain evidentiary findings.

---

[76] UNCC Provisional Rules, Article 6, paragraph 2.

[77] See, e.g., www.swissbankclaims.iom.int; www.compensation-for-forced-labour.org; www.icheic.org; www.hpdkosovo.org.

(a) Iran–United States Claims Tribunal (Iran–US CT)—claims relating to the 1979 Islamic Revolution

A Note to the Iran–US CT Tribunal Rules records an agreement between the Agents of the two Government parties that "English and Farsi shall be the official languages to be used in the arbitration proceedings, and these languages shall be used for all oral hearings, decisions and awards."[78] The same Note also contains practical provisions listing the documents that are required to be submitted to the Tribunal in both languages.[79] A unique but very practical exception states that the Tribunal shall have discretion to determine what "documentary evidence and written evidence, or parts thereof" are required to be presented in both languages,[80] thereby providing discretion to relieve parties of the expense and effort of translating voluminous texts when not every word is needed (e.g., where technical notations on plans in complex construction projects are not at issue, or where the claim is based on thousands of invoices). The Claims Process provides translation services between English and Farsi for Tribunal Members and staff. At oral hearings before the Tribunal, simultaneous interpretation from English into Farsi, and vice versa, has been performed by professional interpreters employed by the Tribunal. A unique practical provision in the Tribunal Rules states that "[a]ny disputes or difficulties regarding translations shall be resolved by the arbitral tribunal."[81]

(b) United Nations Compensation Commission (UNCC)—claims relating to the 1990–1991 Gulf War

The language requirements of the UNCC are quite strict. The Provisional Rules specify that the "working language of the claims procedure before the Commission will be English" and explain that this is due to the fact that "the Commission's computerized software and database system, which is technically required for the processing of a large number of claims, has been designed in English."[82] Claim forms could be submitted in any of the six official languages of the United Nations,[83] but where the claim form was not in English, an English translation had to be provided by the claimant.[84] With respect to claims of corporations and other entities, as well as claims of governments and

---

[78] Iran–US CT Tribunal Rules, Note 2 to Article 17. Notwithstanding the reference to "Farsi" in the Tribunal Rules, the term "Persian" is used in some awards and other Tribunal documents.

[79] Ibid., Notes 3 and 4 to Article 17.   [80] Ibid., Note 4 to Article 17.

[81] Ibid., Note 5 to Article 17.   [82] UNCC Provisional Rules, Article 6, paragraph 2.

[83] The six official UN languages are: Arabic, Chinese, English, French, Russian, and Spanish.

[84] UNCC Provisional Rules, Article 6, paragraph 3.

of international organizations, "*all documents* . . . must also be submitted in English or be accompanied by an English translation."[85] The Secretariat notified each government as to the extent and time-limits of translations required.[86] Also, "[i]n the case of oral proceedings, the Executive Secretary [was to] arrange for interpretation as necessary into and from other official languages of the United Nations."[87]

Inasmuch as claims were submitted by governments which were able to arrange translation services, there was not the hardship which could have been created if individuals with small claims had been required to submit costly translations. Supporting documentation in the urgent claims categories was not required to be translated into English at the submission stage, as time was of the essence and supporting documentation often was not needed in order to render a decision.[88]

(c) Commission for Real Property Claims of Displaced Persons and Refugees (CRPC)—claims relating to the 1992–1995 war in Bosnia and Herzegovina

Bosnia and Herzegovina has three official languages spoken in different regions: Bosnian, Croatian, and Serbian. The official documents of the CRPC Claims Process (the Books of Regulations) were issued in all three languages, and the Decision Certificates recording the Commission's decisions were issued in the language of the claimant addressee. At CRPC sessions, the national Commissioners spoke their own language, whereas the international Commissioners all spoke English.

The Book of Regulations on Procedure, although it was issued in Bosnian, Croatian, Serbian, and English,[89] did not contain provisions on language of the proceedings, translation, or interpretation. In practice, the CRPC retained multi-ethnic lawyers and other staff who spoke the different languages of the affected population to collect claims and communicate with claimants. For example, successful claimants were given the choice of the language in which their Decision Certificate would be printed (Serbian (Cyrillic), Croatian, or Bosnian). The Commission hired its own translators who had some knowledge of property law. These translators translated documents from English into Bosnian, Croatian, and Serbian, and vice versa. They also acted as (non-simultaneous) interpreters during the Commission's sessions.

---

[85] UNCC Provisional Rules, Article 6, paragraph 5 (emphasis added).
[86] Ibid., Article 6, paragraph 5.   [87] Ibid., Article 6, paragraph 6.
[88] See section 5.02(b) above, on relaxed standards of proof at the UNCC.
[89] CRPC Book of Regulations on Procedure, Article 92.

(d) Claims Resolution Tribunal for Dormant Accounts in Switzerland (CRT-I)—first claims tribunal for assets deposited in Swiss banks

The CRT-I Rules of Procedure gave the Arbitrators the discretion to determine the language of the proceedings in each claim, but stated that, in doing so, they should take into account the languages spoken by the parties.[90] If there was no such determination, the language of the proceedings was English. Further emphasizing the policy of accommodating parties who might not speak English, the Procedural Rules required the Arbitrators to "provide, if necessary, the translation of documents and oral statements delivered in any language other than English into the language of the proceeding."[91]

(e) Claims Resolution Tribunal (CRT-II)—second claims tribunal for assets deposited in Swiss banks

The CRT-II Governing Rules state that the working languages of the Claims Process are English, French, German, Hebrew, and Spanish and that all communications addressed to the Tribunal must be in one of these languages.[92] Therefore, the Governing Rules do not provide for translation services. CRT-II has five working languages whereas CRT-I had one. An instruction sheet accompanying the claim form emphasized that this requirement would be applied rigidly, informing the claimants that the Tribunal could only communicate with them in English, French, German, Hebrew, or Spanish, and that it could only accept claims submitted in one of those five languages. It was thus recognized that some claimants would need to obtain translation assistance on their own.

(f) Housing and Property Claims Commission (HPCC)—claims relating to the 1999 conflict in Kosovo

The official languages of the HPCC Claims Process are Albanian, English, and Serbian. Although hearings are not in practice held, the rules of the Commission provide that the Chairperson may permit any Commissioner or person appearing before the Commission to speak in other languages.[93] The claim form and the Reply to a claim may be submitted in one of the official languages,[94] but the Housing and Property Directorate (HPD) may provide the parties with summaries in the language of their choice of any document

---

[90] CRT-I Rules of Procedure, Article 35. [91] Ibid., Article 35.
[92] CRT-II Governing Rules , Article 34. [93] UNMIK Regulation 2000/60, section 17.15
[94] Ibid., section 9.9.

presented by the other party.[95] In practice, the internal working language of the Commission and the Directorate is English. However, all documents issued by either body are translated into the three official languages.

In practice, since international staff members oversee the processing of claims, all statements and documentary evidence have to be translated. This has put a considerable strain on the resources of the Claims Process. The Directorate has its own in-house language services department which provides interpretation and translation services for both the Directorate and the Commission. UNMIK Regulation 2000/60 requires any interpreters employed by the Directorate or the Commission in connection with the proceedings to make a solemn declaration to perform their duties "faithfully, impartially, and conscientiously, and with full respect for the duty of confidentiality."[96]

(g) Mass Claims Processes administered by the International Organization for Migration (IOM)

Part of the translation of the initial standard claim forms in the German Forced Labour Compensation Programme (GFLCP) and the Holocaust Victim Assets Programme (HVAP), as well as most of the translation of the outreach and other information materials, was either performed by staff with the requisite language skills in IOM field offices, or it was outsourced. Subsequent standard decision and notification texts have been translated by staff in Geneva.

Considering, on the one hand, the large numbers of claims to be processed and decided and the many languages in which this had to be done, and, on the other hand, the limited time and budget resources available to these Claims Processes, it was decided that separate interpretation and translation was not feasible. Rather, IOM employs staff who, among them, cover all the languages in which claimants were allowed to file their claims (twenty languages for GFLCP and eleven for HVAP), and the work is organized in such a way that the processing, review, and drafting of the decisions on the claims is performed by staff with the relevant language skills. Appropriate quality control procedures to ensure linguistic consistency have been put into place. When required, the Secretariat staff members who have worked on the relevant files have been available to the Property Claims Commission and the IOM Appeals Body for Forced Labour Claims during meetings of those bodies.

---

[95] UNMIK Regulation 2000/60, section 9.7.   [96] Ibid., section 17.16

German Forced Labour Compensation Programme (GFLCP)—claims against Germany and German industry for Nazi injustice

The working language of the staff of GFLCP and the language of its computer database is English, but slave and forced labor and personal injury claims could be submitted in twenty different languages,[97] and property claims in seven languages.[98] While the constituting instruments do not require the use of all these languages, IOM agreed with the German Foundation that they be made available in order to make the Claims Process as claimant-friendly as possible. However, in order to avoid translating hundreds of thousands of claims from all the different languages into the working language—which would have been far too expensive and time-consuming given the mandate of the Claims Process to decide the claims quickly and efficiently—staff with relevant language skills were employed to read the claim forms and accompanying evidentiary documentation in the language in which they were submitted and enter all the claims data into a single English-language database. This avoided the additional step of retaining professional translators and has saved time and cost—bearing in mind that all expenses of this Claims Process are paid out of the overall Compensation Fund—and it promoted accuracy in that the person entering data into the computerized profiles was the same person who read what the claimant wrote in his or her own language.

Some written summaries in the working language are, however, unavoidable for the Property Claims Commission and the IOM Appeals Body for Forced Labour Claims, whose Members need to discuss the claims in a common language. The Rules of the Property Claims Commission provide that, "to the extent that the claim files are not in English or German, IOM will arrange for the translation of the files into one of these two languages."[99] The Rules also provide that, if evidence submitted by a claimant in support of a claim is not in English or German, it must be translated into one of those languages, or—if the claimant is an individual—it may also be translated into Czech, Hebrew, Hungarian, Polish, or Russian, as the case may be.[100] The decisions of the Property Claims Commission were communicated to the claimants in English and in the language in which the claim was filed.

---

[97] GFLCP slave and forced labor claims could be made in Albanian, Bosnian, Bulgarian, Croatian, Dutch, English, Finnish, French, German, Greek, Hungarian, Italian, Macedonian, Norwegian, Romanian, Serbian, Slovakian, Slovenian, Spanish, and Swedish.

[98] IOM Property Commission Supplemental Rules, section 8.2 provides that claim forms shall be accepted in "Czech, English, German, Hebrew, Hungarian, Polish and Russian." However, a claim form from a religious community or organization, or an individual claimant represented by counsel is expected to be submitted in English or German. Ibid.   [99] Ibid., section 16.

[100] Ibid., section 11.3.

At the IOM Appeals Body for Forced Labour Claims, the working language is English, and an appellant must submit the appeal in English or in the language in which the original claim was submitted.[101] The Rules of the Appeals Body provide that, "[a]s a rule, a decision shall be communicated to the appellant in the language in which the appeal was submitted. In some instances, a decision may be communicated in English, together with general information and a summary of the result of the decision in the language of the appeal submission."[102]

Holocaust Victim Assets Programme (HVAP)—claims pursuant to 1999 class action Settlement

The working language of the staff of HVAP is English. However, although the constituting documents do not prescribe this, claimants may file their claims in one of eleven specified languages,[103] with the corresponding need for IOM to employ staff with the requisite language skills to process the claims.

(h) Eritrea–Ethiopia Claims Commission (EECC)—claims relating to the 1998–2000 war between Eritrea and Ethiopia

English is the language to be used in EECC proceedings. The Commission's Rules of Procedure provide that any documents in other languages shall be accompanied by English translations, except as the Commission may otherwise permit.[104] Thus, the parties are responsible for submitting English translations of documents. The Rules also require interpretation into English of any oral statements made at a hearing.[105] If witnesses are to be heard, the parties must inform the Commission at least thirty days before the hearings of the languages required so that the Commission can make necessary arrangements for interpretation.[106] The Permanent Court of Arbitration, which acts as the Commission's Secretariat, does not have in-house language services, and in any case, the languages and dialects likely required (primarily Amharic and Tigrayan) would require the hiring of outside interpreters on a contract basis. However, in practice, problems regarding interpretation at hearings have been limited, as each party has provided interpreters for its witnesses whenever required, subject to possible comment or clarification by the other party. The

---

[101] IOM Appeals Body Principles and Rules, Article 15, paragraphs A and B.

[102] Ibid., Article 21, paragraph F.

[103] HVAP claims could be made in the following languages: in Slave Labor Category I: Czech, English, German, Polish, and Russian; in Slave Labor Category II: Dutch, English, French, German, Hebrew, Italian, Polish, and Russian; in the Refugee Category: English, French, German, Hungarian, Italian, Russian, and Slovak.   [104] EECC Rules of Procedure, Article 12.

[105] Ibid., Article 13, paragraph 2.   [106] Ibid.

parties have utilized sequential (rather than simultaneous) interpretation of testimony and cross-examination, which can sometimes significantly increase the time needed to examine a witness.

(i) Humanitarian insurance Claims Process administered by the Jewish Claims Conference (JCC) for the International Commission on Holocaust Era Insurance Claims (ICHEIC)

Complex language issues were at the heart of the 8A1 humanitarian Claims Process.[107] For example, a claims analyst might receive a claim form marked as "Hebrew"—his or her language of specialty—only to find attached supporting documents from all over the world, for example, immigration papers in Spanish or Brazilian Portuguese, deportation papers in Polish or German, and insurance or business documentation in French, German, or Italian. If the language diversity were judged by claim form submissions alone, German would be a less significant language—comprising less than 1,500 claims of the 36,000 reviewed in the first phase of 8A1 Claims. However, property lists in German appearing in claim forms written in other languages were often a crucial factor in granting awards.

Given the 8A1 team's experiences from the training phase, and the JCC's experience in other restitution projects, the choice was made not to allow partial scoring in one language and then handing the claim to another analyst to deal with material in another language, as this was seen as being too cumbersome. The Point Scoring System simplified the problem in some cases by providing a "passing" threshold: for example, if a claim passed (i.e., received a sufficient number of points) based on the evidence in the Hebrew and German, the information in the remaining languages was moot and did not need to be reviewed. Similarly, when necessary, if no regular 8A1 team member felt competent to read a less common language within this Claims Process (such as Estonian or Latvian), arrangements were made to find a JCC employee in another program to assist.

(j) American Arbitration Association (AAA)—an illustrative case

In the illustrative case, provisions were made for translation or interpretation if needed, as there was a consensus that the claimants should be given every opportunity to fairly present their cases. However, all claims were submitted, and virtually all proceedings were conducted, in English.

---

[107] See also section 6.01(i) below, on management and staffing.

5.04 Hearings

Whether the constituting instruments or procedural rules include special provisions with respect to oral hearings or decisions based on documents only.

Editors' Commentary

The practice of holding hearings and the opportunity of confronting witnesses, long considered an essential element of due process in many legal systems, has been modified in some Mass Claims Processes and abandoned in others. Indeed, a trend against holding hearings can be discerned. At the earliest Claims Process described in this book, the Iran–United States Claims Tribunal (Iran–US CT), each party has the right to a hearing at a reasonable stage of the proceeding if he or she so desires. In the Tribunal's practice, hearings—sometimes quite lengthy ones—have been held in all cases. In contrast, at the Claims Resolution Tribunal for Dormant Accounts in Switzerland (CRT-I), a right to a hearing existed in the Rules of Procedure, but hearings were not held in practice. This trend accelerated at the second Claims Resolution Tribunal (CRT-II), whose Governing Rules do not provide for hearings. The Rules of the United Nations Compensation Commission (UNCC) establish a hybrid system that provides for decisions to be made solely on the basis of documents in urgent and relatively small claims of individuals, but hearings may be held when the Commissioners desire them in larger and more complex cases.

(a) Iran–United States Claims Tribunal (Iran–US CT)—claims relating to the 1979 Islamic Revolution

The Tribunal Rules contemplate that claims may be decided either after a hearing or on written submissions only.[108] However, the Tribunal is required to hold a hearing if either party requests one for the purpose of "presentation of evidence by witnesses, including expert witnesses, or for oral argument."[109] In practice, hearings have been held in connection with disputes on the merits in substantially all cases. The Tribunal has interpreted its Rules to require holding hearings only at reasonable stages of the proceeding, as determined by the Tribunal, thereby providing a safeguard against dilatory or frivolous tactics.

---

[108] Iran–US CT Tribunal Rules, Article 15, paragraph 2.   [109] Ibid.

The Tribunal is free to determine the manner in which witnesses are examined.[110] Notes to the Tribunal Rules provide that, "when permitted by the arbitral tribunal, the representatives of the arbitrating parties in the case may ask questions, subject to the control of the presiding member," thus allowing for the possibility of both direct examination and cross-examination.[111] Witnesses may also be examined by the presiding Member and by the other Members of the Tribunal.[112]

(b) United Nations Compensation Commission (UNCC)—claims relating to the 1990–1991 Gulf War

The UNCC Provisional Rules provide that panels of Commissioners "normally" make their recommendations "on the basis of the documents submitted," but that they "may determine that special circumstances warrant holding an oral proceeding concerning a particular claim or claims."[113] The Provisional Rules also stipulate that unusually large or complex claims may receive detailed review, and grant the panels considering such claims the discretion to "ask for additional written submissions and hold oral proceedings."[114] In practice, oral hearings were occasionally held, but not in the urgent claims categories ("A" through "C"). One oral proceeding was held in the course of processing category "D" claims, and eight proceedings in respect of category "E" claims. There were oral proceedings in each of the five instalments of the "F4" environmental claims, and two oral proceedings were conducted in connection with "F3" claims of the Government of Kuwait. Oral hearings were not the only mechanism for gathering non-documentary evidence from claimants. Technical missions were conducted where warranted, and those missions could include interviews with claimants and other parties.

The Commissioners thus determined the degree of evidence needed in each case, as well as whether hearings and witness testimony were necessary. In practice, panels requested additional written submissions when needed, but oral hearings were relatively rare. When hearings were held, representatives of Iraq were allowed to attend for purposes of answering questions put by the Commissioners.

In December 2000, the UNCC Governing Council modified certain aspects of the Commission's procedures relating to the larger and more

---

[110] Iran–US CT Tribunal Rules, Article 25, paragraph 4. [111] Ibid., Note 6(b) to Article 25.
[112] Ibid. [113] UNCC Provisional Rules, Article 37(c). [114] Ibid., Article 38(d).

complex claims, instructing panels of Commissioners to hold oral hearings for each claim that had an asserted value of US$1 billion or more.[115]

(c) Commission for Real Property Claims of Displaced Persons and Refugees (CRPC)—claims relating to the 1992–1995 war in Bosnia and Herzegovina

The CRPC Book of Regulations on Procedure does not contain provisions on hearings, and none were conducted before the Commission.

(d) Claims Resolution Tribunal for Dormant Accounts in Switzerland (CRT-I)—first claims tribunal for assets deposited in Swiss banks

The CRT-I Rules of Procedure provided that the Arbitrators should, to the extent possible, conduct the proceedings as a documents-only arbitration, holding hearings, if necessary, at any place deemed appropriate to examine the parties, interview witnesses, and hear oral arguments.[116] While the Arbitrators thus had the discretion to order hearings, in practice, all claims were decided without hearings.

The Rules also provided that third persons, as well as the parties, could be heard either as unsworn witnesses or under oath. Where circumstances required it, or where the parties agreed, oral testimony could also be substituted by a sworn written statement (affidavit).[117]

(e) Claims Resolution Tribunal (CRT-II)—second claims tribunal for assets deposited in Swiss banks

The CRT-II Governing Rules are silent concerning hearings and none are held in practice. This Claims Process has been conducted on the basis of documents only.

(f) Housing and Property Claims Commission (HPCC)—claims relating to the 1999 conflict in Kosovo

According to the constituting instrument of the HPCC Claims Process, UNMIK Regulation 2000/60, the Commission shall "decide claims on the basis of written submissions, including documentary evidence," unless it invites a party to give oral evidence or argument before it.[118] Parties thus may

---

[115] UNCC Governing Council Decision 114 of 7 December 2000, *Decision concerning the review of current UNCC procedures*, U.N. Doc. S/AC.26/Dec.114 (2000) (7 December 2000), paragraph 12.
[116] CRT-I Rules of Procedure, Article 17, paragraph (iv).   [117] Ibid., Article 24.
[118] UNMIK Regulation 2000/60, section 19.1.

not give oral evidence or argument before the Commission unless invited by the Commission to do so.[119] The Commission may also consider written or oral submissions by any intergovernmental or governmental entity, or by an expert on any matter relevant to a claim.[120] The Commission may delegate to any one of its Commissioners to attend the hearing of oral evidence at any place, and report back to the Commission.[121]

In practice, however, formal hearings have not been held. On a few occasions, one of the Commissioners has been mandated by the Commission to hear oral testimony by parties. But this was considered fact-finding, and there was no cross-examination.

(g) Mass Claims Processes administered by the International Organization for Migration (IOM)

German Forced Labour Compensation Programme (GFLCP)—claims against Germany and German industry for Nazi injustice

Decisions on GFLCP claims are made on the basis of written materials only, including the claim files (i.e., the completed claim form and accompanying documentation, if any), the results of archive searches, or other information available in the claims or from other sources, such as historical research on the Holocaust. Neither the constituting documents nor the operating procedures of the Claims Process provide for hearings.

The Principles and Rules of the IOM Appeals Body for Forced Labour Claims explicitly state that "[t]here shall be no oral hearings of appellants or of third party representatives in relation to individual appeal decisions."[122] The Rules of the Property Claims Commission also do not provide for hearings. Given the number of claims, the fact that the Property Claims Commission's administrative costs had to be covered out of the limited Compensation Fund, and that the German Foundation Act stipulates that the Commission should complete its work within one year, the Commission did not hold hearings.

Holocaust Victim Assets Programme (HVAP)—claims pursuant to 1999 class action Settlement

Decisions on HVAP claims are made on the basis of the claim files, the results of archive searches, or matches against relevant lists of refugees. The Plan of

---

[119] Ibid., section 19.2.   [120] Ibid., section 19.3.   [121] Ibid., section 19.4.
[122] IOM Appeals Body Principles and Rules, Article 16, paragraph D.

Allocation and Distribution adopted by the United States District Court for the Eastern District of New York in the class action known as the Holocaust Victim Assets Litigation, provides that IOM may contact a claimant personally to obtain additional information or to clarify information previously submitted, but a claimant "shall not, under any circumstances, be required to travel to IOM's office" for this purpose, but rather "shall agree to a personal or telephonic interview."[123]

(h) Eritrea–Ethiopia Claims Commission (EECC)—claims relating to the 1998–2000 war between Eritrea and Ethiopia

The provisions on hearings are contained in Chapter One of the EECC Rules of Procedure and as such are generally applicable to all claims. Since the designers of this Claims Process considered that case-by-case hearings would not be feasible in connection with mass claims procedures, the Rules give the Commission discretion to decide whether to hold hearings in particular cases. It thus can decide "whether to hold hearings for the presentation of evidence by witnesses, including expert witnesses, or for oral argument, or whether the proceedings shall be conducted on the basis of documents and other materials."[124] In practice, hearings have been held on the merits of all the claims filed by the parties, all claims having been filed as Government-to-Government claims.

The Commission also incorporated into its Rules several provisions bearing on the conduct of hearings which were not in the PCA Rules upon which the EECC Rules are based.[125] Thus, any documents that a party is permitted to introduce at a hearing shall concurrently be given to the other party;[126] the Commission is required to take appropriate measures for the protection of the security and privacy of witnesses; and it can determine how witnesses are examined.[127] If a party fails to appear at a hearing without showing sufficient cause, the Commission may proceed with the hearing and decide the matter.[128] It may in exceptional circumstances decide, on its own motion or upon application, to reopen hearings at any time before the award is made.[129]

---

[123] Plan of Allocation and Distribution, pp. 166 and 178.
[124] EECC Rules of Procedure, Article 10, paragraph 2.
[125] Permanent Court of Arbitration Optional Rules for Arbitrating Disputes between Two States.   [126] EECC Rules of Procedure, Article 13, paragraph 4.
[127] Ibid., Article 13, paragraph 5.   [128] Ibid., Article 13, paragraph 8.
[129] Ibid., Article 13, paragraph 9.

(i) **Humanitarian insurance Claims Process administered by the Jewish Claims Conference (JCC) for the International Commission on Holocaust Era Insurance Claims (ICHEIC)**

No oral hearings were held for the 8A1 Claims. The humanitarian Claims Process was conducted on the basis of documents only.

(j) **American Arbitration Association (AAA)—an illustrative case**

Hearings in the illustrative case were conducted almost exclusively by conference telephone calls. At the request of the claimant, an on-site hearing could be arranged at a location convenient to the claimant. However, out of 63,000 appeals, fewer than twenty people requested an on-site hearing. Hearings with the parties in each other's physical presence were thus available, but were rarely if ever requested. There was no transcription of the hearings.

5.05 Communications

The extent to which various procedures are conducted by means other than in-person proceedings, including communications via telephone, fax, e-mail, etc. (See further section 1.06 on the location of the Claims Process, section 3.02 on claim forms, and section 6.06 on computer support and information technology.)

Editors' Commentary

Most modern Mass Claims Processes make use of the Internet in reaching out to potential eligible claimants and for posting claim forms and other information on how to make claims. Most Claims Processes post their procedural rules, constituting instruments, and the decisions they render, on their websites. Some Claims Processes allow claimants to file their claims in electronic form. Decision-makers and Secretariat staff often communicate with each other by electronic means, and some decision-making, such as on claims for fixed amounts or other simple forms of relief, preliminary decisions, or administrative decisions, have been made via telephone, fax, and e-mail. The American

Arbitration Association (AAA) decided claims in the illustrative case in telephone hearings, and in the 8A1 humanitarian Claims Process under the International Commission on Holocaust Era Insurance Claims (ICHEIC), claims were decided by scoring them according to a set system and entering points into computer software, which would indicate whether the claim "passed" or "failed." None of the Claims Processes discussed in this book, however, have conducted actual arbitrations online.[130]

(a) Iran–United States Claims Tribunal (Iran–US CT)—claims relating to the 1979 Islamic Revolution

At the time the Iran–US CT was established, in 1981, electronic means of conducting legal proceedings were not in common use and the Internet was not yet available. The Tribunal's procedures were therefore set in place without the use of electronic means, and they have not been changed to make use of such techniques as they have become available in recent years. No specific provision exists for conducting any part of the Tribunal's procedures electronically. The Tribunal has, however, launched its own website, containing the basic constituting documents and rules, the published decisions, and other essential information about the Claims Process.[131]

Also, fax and electronic communications are used in communicating among decision-makers and within the Secretariat, including exchanging drafts and comments, and reaching conclusions.

(b) United Nations Compensation Commission (UNCC)—claims relating to the 1990–1991 Gulf War

The panels of UNCC Commissioners, although they normally met at the Secretariat headquarters in Geneva, were required by the Provisional Rules to continue their work on the claims while away from the headquarters, "conducting the necessary communications among themselves and with the Secretariat."[132] In practice, much of this exchange of communications and conduct of deliberations was done through electronic mail, and on occasion, panel meetings were held by means of teleconference.

The UNCC maintains an official website with general information about the Claims Process, its procedures, panel reports and Governing Council

---

[130] For information on online arbitrations, see, e.g., website of the World Intellectual Property Organization, www.wipo.int, and its domain name dispute resolution mechanisms. See also Webfile process of the AAA, at www.adr.org.   [131] See www.iusct.org.

[132] UNCC Provisional Rules, Article 33, paragraph 2.

decisions, as well as status summaries of the claims processing, press releases, and a selected Mass Claims bibliography.[133]

(c) Commission for Real Property Claims of Displaced Persons and Refugees (CRPC)—claims relating to the 1992–1995 war in Bosnia and Herzegovina

At the outset of the CRPC Claims Process, claim forms and information on submitting claims were made available on the CRPC website, where the Commission's procedures and status reports were also posted and regularly updated.[134]

While computers and electronic communications were used extensively in claims processing at CRPC, management, and internal communications at the Claims Process, security concerns dictated that paper award certificates only be delivered in person to the claimant, or to an authorized representative of the claimant.[135]

(d) Claims Resolution Tribunal for Dormant Accounts in Switzerland (CRT-I)—first claims tribunal for assets deposited in Swiss banks

Claim forms and other necessary information on the CRT-I procedures were made available on the official website of the Claims Process.[136] CRT-I did not computerize any of the steps in its decision-making, except for some communications, storage of some information, and use of standard forms.

(e) Claims Resolution Tribunal (CRT-II)—second claims tribunal for assets deposited in Swiss banks

To assist potential CRT-II claimants in identifying account owners who had been victims or targets of Nazi persecution and who had accounts in Swiss banks during the period 1933–1945, the names of owners of approximately

---

[133] www.uncc.ch.

[134] The CRPC posted its decisions and other information on its activities on an official CRPC website, at www.crpc.org.ba. This website, however, was dismantled after the end of the Commission's mandate in 2003. Its former contents are now available at www.law.kuleuven.ac.be/ipr/eng/CRPC_Bosnia/CRPC%20bosnia.html, and via the website of the Permanent Court of Arbitration, at www.pca-cpa.org/MCP/index_MCP.htm "Links to Completed Mass Claims Processes."

[135] CRPC Book of Regulations on Procedure, Article 68.

[136] Available at www.crt-ii.org/_crt-i.

21,000 accounts were published on the Internet.[137] Claim forms and other necessary information on the CRT-II procedures were made available on the official website of the Claims Process.[138]

Information about 36,000 accounts classified as "probably or possibly" belonging to victims or targets of Nazi persecution is contained in an electronic database created by audit firms employed by the Independent Committee of Eminent Persons (ICEP). Those auditors also created computer databases of key information available on the approximately 4.1 million accounts that were open or opened during the 1933–1945 period.[139]

The CRT-II Governing Rules address the availability of this information. Names and information about the 36,000 "probable or possible" accounts are contained in so-called "Account History Databases" maintained at the CRT-II Zurich offices in secure facilities and consolidated into a single Account History Database for ease of use.[140] The Rules provide that one or more of the ICEP audit firms may be retained by the Special Masters to establish a "Total Accounts Database" out of the various databases containing information about the four million accounts from 1933–1945, and that the CRT-II will have access to these databases, which remain physically located at each bank, through a secure encrypted limited-access network.[141]

Much of the claims processing at CRT-II is conducted by performing computerized research and "matching" of claim forms against these various databases.[142]

(f) Housing and Property Claims Commission (HPCC)—claims relating to the 1999 conflict in Kosovo

Information about the HPCC Claims Process—its legal framework, decisions, claims statistics, etc.—is available and regularly updated on the official website of the Housing and Property Directorate (HPD).[143]

Under UNMIK Regulation 2000/60, the Commission may, in appropriate cases, decide to hold deliberations through electronic means.[144] Some of the Commission's sessions have been conducted via electronic communications.

---

[137] See CRT-II Governing Rules, Article 1. The 21,000 published victim accounts were made available on the website of the SBA (www.dormantaccounts.ch); the CRT-II website (www.crt-ii.org); and on the Holocaust Victim Assets Litigation website (www.swissbankclaims.com), searchable by each person's name or by city or country of residence.   [138] www.crt-ii.org.

[139] See CRT-II Governing Rules, Introduction, Part II.   [140] Ibid., Article 3.

[141] Ibid., Introduction, Part II, and Article 5.

[142] See section 5.06 below, on matching and other mass claims techniques.

[143] www.hpdkosovo.org; see also the UNMIK website at www.unmikonline.org.

[144] UNMIK Regulation 2000/60, section 17.8.

From 2005 onwards, use has been made of mobile telephone text messaging (SMS) to inform claimants that their claims have been decided.

(g) Mass Claims Processes administered by the International Organization for Migration (IOM): *German Forced Labour Compensation Programme (GFLCP) for claims against Germany and German industry for Nazi injustice, and Holocaust Victim Assets Programme (HVAP) for claims pursuant to 1999 class action Settlement*

At IOM, extensive use is made of electronic communications between internal departments and staff in processing the claim, and also between IOM headquarters and its various field offices; the different partner organizations; the German Foundation, and the United States District Court for the Eastern District of New York in the class action known as the Holocaust Victim Assets Litigation; and with official archives, data processing centers, banks, etc. A great number of standard computer forms, letters, memoranda, etc., are available to IOM staff to speed up the work and ensure uniformity. In practice, the Members of the Property Claims Commission and the IOM Appeals Body for Forced Labour Claims have exchanged communications and conducted deliberations through electronic means.

Given the advanced age, and often humble means, of the claimant population served by the GFLCP and HVAP Claims Processes, however, communication with claimants is conducted in writing or over the telephone. A special Call Center operates within the IOM Secretariat to respond to questions by claimants, as well as to contact claimants for supplemental information.

Once a group of similarly situated claims has been processed by IOM, the recommended decisions are sent electronically to the Foundation or the Court, as the case may be, for approval or denial.

(h) Eritrea–Ethiopia Claims Commission (EECC)—claims relating to the 1998–2000 war between Eritrea and Ethiopia

The EECC makes heavy use of e-mail, both for communication between the Commissioners themselves, as well as with the parties via the Registry. The Commission's Rules of Procedure state its intention "to utilize e-mail or fax to the greatest extent possible,"[145] and provide that "only those communications or documents that cannot reasonably be submitted to the Commission by fax

---

[145] EECC Rules of Procedure, Article 2, paragraph 1.

or e-mail are to be delivered to the Registrar in paper form, for circulation to the Commissioners and the other party by rapid and reliable means."[146]

In addition to facilities provided by the Permanent Court of Arbitration (PCA), the Commission also benefits from a secure electronic document "vault" made available by courtesy of the law firm of one of its Commissioners. This facility permits secure storage of documents, including internal deliberative memoranda, and easy online access by Commissioners utilizing passwords.

(i) Humanitarian insurance Claims Process administered by the Jewish Claims Conference (JCC) for the International Commission on Holocaust Era Insurance Claims (ICHEIC)

The 8A1 humanitarian Claims Process was conceived with electronic claims processing in mind, for reasons of advantages of cost and security. The JCC–ICHEIC Agreement provided that the JCC would develop the necessary software for processing the claims and for the interchange of data with ICHEIC's larger database system, which maintained information on all ICHEIC claimants, not just those in the 8A1 Claims Process. The claim forms which claimants had filled in by hand, and any accompanying documentation which they had submitted, were scanned into digital format by an outside contractor hired by ICHEIC, and ICHEIC submitted all 8A1 Claims electronically to the JCC. In order to review the claims using the Point Scoring System, the JCC developed software to work with the scanned images which ICHEIC provided.

The 8A1 Claims software provided the basic tools needed to evaluate a claim, and a claims analyst used it in the following manner to score each claim. First, the analyst selected his or her language of expertise from a menu on the screen, whereupon the computer brought up on the screen a scanned image of a claim from a queue of claims written in that language. In order to allow the claims analysts conveniently to view the claim form and the twelve questions of the Point Scoring System (which had to be answered with respect to each claim by ticking a "yes" or "no" box for each of them), the computer screen was divided in half, with the Point Scoring System questions appearing on the left half of the screen, and the scanned images of the claims themselves on the right half, along with some basic image manipulation tools.

When, based on the answers given, the number of points granted was sufficient to issue an award, the software program automatically marked the claim as "passing" and did not allow any further processing. This was done to shorten the processing time, as JCC claims analysts would not have to continue

---

[146] EECC Rules of Procedure, Article 2, paragraph 2.

searching through the submitted documentation to answer the remaining questions if a claim had already passed.

All work on the claims was stored in a central database that allowed for a complete review of each claim's history, viewable by a user with Administrator access rights using a special 8A1 Claims Processing Application. This Application also allowed for various administrative functions to be performed by a user with the necessary clearance, such as directly assigning a claim to a particular claims analyst, or clearing any previous scoring done on a claim. The claims database also provided information to a web-based interface to allow the Administrator to track employee efficiency, for example, to see whether a JCC claims analyst was spending too much or too little time, on average, on each claim, resulting in either reduced efficiency, or too superficial a review of the claim, as the case might be. Such defects could then be corrected.

(j) American Arbitration Association (AAA)—an illustrative case

In the illustrative case, all evidence was scanned into a common database maintained by the administrator for parties and neutrals, although special note was taken of a need for paper evidence where scanning technology proved ineffective. Basic data in the case was transmitted from the defendant insurance company to the AAA by a daily computer download. About one thousand cases were scheduled per day, and since there was an opportunity to adjourn hearings, rescheduling was frequent. Most communication was conducted via e-mail or fax, including simultaneous broadcast fax communications to all Arbitrators to answer frequently asked questions. Arbitrators received individualized case information on a CD-rom disc.

5.06 Mass Claims Techniques

The use of special mass claims processing methodologies such as grouping of claims, statistical modeling and sampling, computerized matching, and standardized valuation and verification methodologies.

Editors' Commentary

This section focuses on methodologies and techniques to facilitate the processing of very large numbers of claims as expeditiously as circumstances permit.

They do not derive from practices developed, or typical, in arbitral proceedings but, rather, evolved from mass tort litigation and large insurance cases as conducted in the United States, borrowing applications from other contexts such as use of statistics in the social sciences. These methodologies have the same goal of expediting resolution of claims as the case-management procedures for initial screening described in section 3.04 above, and the relaxed standards of proof discussed in section 5.02 above.

Most of the methodologies discussed here were not yet used at the Iran–United States Claims Tribunal (Iran–US CT). They can be said to have been pioneered by the United Nations Compensation Commission (UNCC) to meet the task of resolving approximately 2.6 million claims in less than eight years, and other later Claims Processes then benefitted from those innovations and learned from that experience, such as the Commission for Real Property Claims of Displaced Persons and Refugees (CRPC) in Bosnia and Herzegovina, which processed some 300,000 claims during an eight-year period. A striking illustration of this development can be seen from the fact that the Claims Resolution Tribunal for Dormant Accounts in Switzerland (CRT-I) made no use of techniques such as computer matching to verify claims, whereas those techniques are at the heart of the procedures of the second Claims Resolution Tribunal (CRT-II) created five years later to review similar claims.

Information technology (IT) has become the enabling factor of modern mass claims processing in cases where most, if not all, of the claims arose during the same time period and involved many of the same legal and factual issues. Such techniques as statistical sampling and modeling, grouping of similar claims, standardized verification procedures and valuation methods depend upon information technology and IT specialists.[147]

Statistical sampling and modeling

Statistical analysis allows Mass Claims Processes to extrapolate the results of certain decisions—such as a decision to use evidentiary presumptions—taken on the basis of a representative random sample, to all the remaining claims in the population from which the sample was taken, i.e., to all similarly situated claimants. The UNCC and the Eritrea–Ethiopia Claims Commission (EECC) are both expressly authorized to rely on statistical decision-making tools.

---

[147] See generally, Veijo Heiskanen, *Virtue out of Necessity: International Mass Claims and New Uses of Information Technology*, in REDRESSING INJUSTICES THROUGH MASS CLAIMS PROCESSES: INNOVATIVE RESPONSES TO UNIQUE CHALLENGES, p. 25 (Permanent Court of Arbitration ed., Oxford University Press 2006).

The basic method of statistical sampling and modeling is, first, to design a sample that is representative of the entire population constituting a similarly situated group of claimants; secondly, to analyze the claims of that sample group to answer the factual and legal questions that determine its eligibility for compensation; and, finally, to extrapolate or apply the results of the analysis of the sample to all other similarly situated claims.

One of the UNCC panels of Commissioners explained the legal justification for using statistical sampling as follows:

"[I]n situations involving mass claims or analogous situations raising common factual and legal issues, it is permissible in the interest of effective justice to apply methodologies and procedures which provide for an examination and determination of a representative sample of these claims. Statistical methods may be used to determine the size and composition of the sample claims and to apply the results of the review of the sample to the remaining claims."[148]

Matching

Some Claims Processes computerize the decision-making of large numbers of individual claims that can be resolved by determining relatively limited specific facts. This is done by computerizing both the claims data and the evidentiary data against which claims are checked. In other words, two databases are created—a claims database with information about the claims, and a verification database with information collected from sources such as banks, historical archives, or property registers. Custom-made computer software then processes the claims by "matching" the claims data (e.g., a personal bank account number) against the verification data (e.g., bank records). A computer-generated match may provide sufficient basis for resolving a claim, or it can provide a basis for further research to confirm the match. Matching of this sort has been used at the UNCC, CRPC, CRT-II, and the slave and forced labor compensation programs administered by the International Organization for Migration (GFLCP and HVAP). Some Claims Processes have also matched claims data against verification data outside their own databases, such as information in historical or contemporary archives.

Grouping and precedent-setting

For complex claims, such as large individual or, more frequently, corporate or government claims for damage to property or the environment, or for

---

[148] *Report and Recommendations Made by the Panel of Commissioners concerning the Fourth Instalment of Claims for Departure from Iraq or Kuwait (Category "A" Claims)*, U.N. Doc. S/AC.26/1995/4 (12 October 1995), paragraph 9.

commercial losses, matching may not be possible and the claims may need to be decided on an individual basis. Information technology can, however, aid the decision process by categorizing—or "grouping"—claims based on the similarity of their legal and factual issues. This is done by entering certain key data into a database, such as, for example, the types of losses claimed, the legal questions raised, the circumstances in which the losses occurred, and the types of evidence produced, to identify groups of similar claims. This enables the decision-makers to focus on resolving the principal legal and factual issues presented by a large number of claims, without having to consider each of them separately. This not only saves time and resources, but results in consistency of decisions. Grouping has been used at the UNCC, at the Housing and Property Claims Commission (HPCC) in Kosovo, and by IOM in administering the GFLCP and HVAP Claims Processes.

Grouping often goes hand-in-hand with a precedent-setting approach, whereby certain claims are singled out to be resolved early in the Claims Process due to common issues that they raise, in a "precedent-setting" decision, which can then be followed in all subsequent similar cases. This approach was used by the Iran–US CT in its forum selection clause cases, as is described in sub-section (a) below. Precedent-setting decisions allow some other Claims Processes to delegate later claims review to Secretariat staff, such as has been done at GFLCP, HVAP, CRT-II, HPCC, and in the 8A1 humanitarian Claims Process under the International Commission on Holocaust Era Insurance Claims (ICHEIC).

Standardized verification and valuation

Standardized verification and valuation are methods which address two problems common to many international Mass Claims Processes: (i) the poor quality, and even outright lack, of documentary evidence due to the extreme circumstances giving rise to the claims, and (ii) the need to avoid spending disproportionate amounts of time and resources for individualized verification and valuation. Technical experts, such as accountants and loss adjusters, have in many instances developed customized computer software to standardize the verification of claims and the calculation of the amount of awards. Because large numbers of claims in the Claims Processes described in this book arose out of the same incident or event, a dearth of evidence can be compensated for by using certain evidentiary presumptions justified by knowledge obtained from historical research or fact-finding about the event in question, to fill in gaps in the individual records. Moreover, because the losses tended to occur in the same market conditions, losses can be reasonably quantified through the use of standardized methods. These methods have been used at the UNCC, the Property Claims Commission at IOM, and CRT-II.

Awarding fixed amounts

Awarding fixed amounts of compensation or restitution is in some cases the most efficient way to expedite claims processing where losses are difficult to verify and quantify on a case-by-case basis, and where doing so would slow down the Claims Process and put a strain on resources. The way in which this works is that, once a claim has been verified as meeting the required minimum standard of proof, it is—without requiring actual proof of the amount of damages—automatically valued at the fixed amount, which ends the inquiry with respect to that claim.

**

The use of these and other methods has become so widespread that it is not surprising to find that a provision expressly authorizing them is included in the Eritrea–Ethiopia Peace Agreement of 12 December 2000, creating the Eritrea–Ethiopia Claims Commission. It states that,

"[i]n order to facilitate the expeditious resolution of these disputes, the Commission shall be authorized to adopt such methods of efficient case management and mass claims processing as it deems appropriate, such as expedited procedures for processing claims and checking claims on a sample basis for further verification only if circumstances warrant."[149]

Even without such provisions in their constituting instruments, however, other Claims Processes have based their authority to adopt such methodologies on their inherent power to determine how their proceedings can best be conducted.

(a) Iran–United States Claims Tribunal (Iran–US CT)—claims relating to the 1979 Islamic Revolution

The Iran–US CT did not provide for, or make use of, mass claims processing methodologies, except for making certain precedent-setting decisions that were then applied in later similar cases. One example of this approach involved the interpretation of a clause in the constituting instrument that defined its jurisdiction. There was a large number of cases (known as the "forum selection clause cases") in which that issue of interpretation arose and the effect of the clause depended on the particular facts of each case. Those facts fell into a number of different categories. The Tribunal selected nine cases, each of which was representative of one or more of those different categories. The jurisdictional issues in each of those cases were then heard and decided by the Full Tribunal

---

[149] Eritrea–Ethiopia Agreement of 12 December 2000, Article 5, paragraph 10.

at the same time.[150] This procedure was designed to create precedents for the rest of the cases that required interpretation of the jurisdictional clause and thereby expedite the work of the Tribunal. The effort was successful. This was done, however, without the aid of computers, and the remaining claims were not delegated to the Secretariat for standardized decision-making, but were decided by the Tribunal on a case-by-case basis, guided by the precedent that had been established.

Another example of the use of a precedent-setting decision was the Tribunal's award which held that, for purposes of jurisdiction, the nationality of a person having dual nationality shall be his or her "real and effective nationality."[151]

(b) United Nations Compensation Commission (UNCC)—claims relating to the 1990–1991 Gulf War

All of the methodologies described in the Editors' Commentary above have been used extensively at the UNCC. The work of the UNCC is described below in considerable detail because it has served as a model for mass claims techniques at many of the subsequent Mass Claims Processes discussed in this book. The Executive Secretary and the staff of the Commission's Secretariat were responsible under the Provisional Rules for developing and maintaining a computerized database of all claims received.[152] In all claims categories, claims with common or similar legal, factual, and valuation issues were categorized and processed together. The Rules assigned this task to the Secretariat so as to "facilitate the work of Commissioners and to ensure uniformity in the treatment of similar claims."[153] Thus, all urgent claims (categories "A", "B" and "C") were submitted to the panels of Commissioners in instalments prepared by the Secretariat, often consisting of tens of thousands of claims. The Provisional Rules further provided that panels should complete the review of urgent claims within 120 days from when the claims were submitted to them.[154] This would not have been feasible—even with as many as nineteen panels working simultaneously, as was the case at the height of the Claims Process—without the introduction of innovative claims review procedures.

Computerized matching and sampling were specifically mentioned in the Provisional Rules for the urgent individual claims (categories "A", "B" and "C"). Sampling was used for claims for forced departure from Iraq or Kuwait

---

[150] See cases cited in section 2.03(a) above.
[151] See section 1.04(a) above and cases cited therein.
[152] UNCC Provisional Rules, Article 34, paragraph 1.   [153] Ibid., Article 17.
[154] Ibid., Article 37(d).

(category "A"), which were then matched against external databases and departure records. Sampling was also used for individual claims for up to US$100,000 (category "C"), for which numerous loss elements were resolved by using profiling and statistical modeling.[155] The UNCC Secretariat, with the help of statisticians and experts in mass claims processing, developed both the verification database and the customized matching software. For claims that could not be completely verified through the database, if the volume of claims was large, the panel in question could check individual claims on the basis of a sampling with further verification only as circumstances warranted.[156]

A different kind of sampling—one based on case-by-case review—was applied to claims for serious personal injury, or the loss of a spouse, child, or parent, in category "B", whose number was relatively low (about 6,000 claims). The Secretariat grouped these claims into similar factual and legal categories, then analyzed the claims of each group, presenting samples representative of each group to the panels of Commissioners for review. Even for the bulk of larger individual claims for non-fixed amounts (category "C"), computerized statistical sampling and modeling were used, which helped eliminate the need for separate verification and valuation stages, as well as the need for oral hearings.

In the less urgent claims categories, where more individualized review and quantification of losses took place, claims were also grouped along common legal and factual issues and submitted to the panels of Commissioners in instalments. The Rules, however, provided a longer review period for these claims, namely 180 days rather than the 120 days allotted to the urgent categories.[157] The Rules expressly provided for grouping of the larger claims (categories "D", "E" and "F"): "Insofar as possible, claims with significant common legal and factual issues will be processed together."[158] Unusually large or complex cases could, however, receive detailed review, as appropriate.[159] The majority of the larger individual claims and of the corporate and government claims were also verified and valued through standardized methodologies.

---

[155] UNCC Provisional Rules, Article 37(a). The Secretariat is to "check individual claims by matching them, insofar as possible, against the information in its computerized database. The results of the database analysis may be cross checked by the panel." Ibid. For discussion of the matching methodology, see *Report and Recommendations Made by the Panel of Commissioners Concerning the First Instalment of Claims for Departure from Iraq or Kuwait (Category "A" Claims)*, U.N. Doc. S/AC.26/1994/2 (21 October 1994).　　　　　　[156] UNCC Provisional Rules, Article 37(b).

[157] See ibid., Article 38(c) and (d), allowing panels to complete the review of claims in the non-urgent categories in 180 days or, in the case of unusually large or complex claims, 12 months from the date claims were submitted to the panel.

[158] Ibid., Article 38(a).　　　[159] Ibid., Article 38(d).

(c) Commission for Real Property Claims of Displaced Persons and Refugees (CRPC)—claims relating to the 1992–1995 war in Bosnia and Herzegovina

The CRPC, which dealt with claims for individual real property, did not consider it appropriate to employ such mass claims techniques as statistical sampling and modeling. The CRPC did, however, develop a set of sophisticated computer programs and databases which allowed claims registration and decision-making to proceed more quickly.[160] The claim form was designed to allow for easy matching of claims against the CRPC's evidentiary databases, and such matching allowed legal advisors to prepare draft decisions for the majority of claims without the need to conduct additional verification or evidence collection in the field.[161]

(d) Claims Resolution Tribunal for Dormant Accounts in Switzerland (CRT-I)—first claims tribunal for assets deposited in Swiss banks

CRT-I did not use statistical sampling or modeling techniques, computer matching, or standardized valuation or verification of claims.[162] Claims were decided on a case-by-case basis in an arbitral procedure.

(e) Claims Resolution Tribunal (CRT-II)—second claims tribunal for assets deposited in Swiss banks

The electronic data resources available to CRT-II for claims verification purposes include computerized account data collected during the three-year investigation of Swiss banks by the Independent Committee of Eminent Persons (ICEP). This data is consolidated into an "Account History Database" which contains information about the approximately 36,000 accounts identified by the ICEP auditors as probably or possibly belonging to Holocaust victims.[163] The CRT-II Governing Rules also contemplate a "Total Accounts Database," that is to consist of key information about the approximately four million accounts that were open or opened during the 1933–1945 period.[164]

---

[160] CRPC created a cadastre database, allowing the Commission quickly to verify claims for property in 80% of pre-war municipalities; and a separate Integrated Property System database of all its claims, decisions, and repossessed properties.

[161] See CRPC End of Mandate Report, Annex E—*CRPC: A Mass Claims Body*, p. 2.

[162] In order to speed up decision-making, CRT-I did use an initial screening procedure, discussed in section 3.04(d) above, and a fast-track procedure, see CRT-I Rules of Procedure, Articles 11–13.

[163] CRT-II Governing Rules, Article 3.   [164] Ibid., Article 5.

The Account History Database is maintained at the offices of the Claims Process in Zurich. All claims are matched against the data contained in this database using a computerized matching program. If a computer-generated match between the name of a claimed account owner matches the name of an account owner in the Account History Database, the claim file and the account information are reviewed to determine whether the computer-generated match constitutes an actual identity match.[165]

(f) Housing and Property Claims Commission (HPCC)—claims relating to the 1999 conflict in Kosovo

HPCC developed a computerized claims database, and it is permitted by the governing UNMIK Regulation to use a wide range of mass claims processing techniques. Claims with a common legal and evidentiary basis are grouped and considered together.[166] Once the Commission has made a precedent-setting decision, the UNMIK Regulation expressly authorizes it to delegate the review of similar claims and evidence to the Registrar and the staff of the Housing and Property Directorate (HPD).[167] Computer databases, software programs, and other electronic tools are used to the extent the Commission considers appropriate to expedite its decision-making.[168] The use of methods such as statistical sampling and modeling, however, is not applicable in this Claims Process, as each claim is reviewed and verified individually.

The Commission is authorized to dispose of certain uncontested claims in a summary procedure[169] and to sign a single cover decision for many individual decisions in cases where the number of similar claims before it is high.[170]

(g) Mass Claims Processes administered by the International Organization for Migration (IOM): *German Forced Labour Compensation Programme (GFLCP) for claims against Germany and German industry for Nazi injustice, and Holocaust Victim Assets Programme (HVAP) for claims pursuant to 1999 class action Settlement*

For the verification of the slave and forced labor claims in both the GFLCP and HVAP Claims Processes, grouping, profiling, sampling and, in particular, computerized matching have been used. The large numbers of claims that the claimants are unable to support with documentary evidence are matched

---

[165] CRT-II Governing Rules, Article 20.
[166] UNMIK Regulation 2000/60, section 19.5(a).   [167] Ibid., section 19.5(b).
[168] Ibid., section 19.5(c) and (d).   [169] Ibid., section 23.   [170] Ibid., section 22.9.

against a range of historical archives in Germany and other countries. For some of these archive searches, the German Foundation has provided organizational assistance and funding. The German Foundation also assisted IOM with electronic matching against claims paid by German Foundation partner organizations and the Austrian Reconciliation Fund (ARF) for claims that had been submitted directly to IOM from countries outside IOM's geographical jurisdiction in the GFLCP Claims Process.

The Rules of the Property Claims Commission provide that, "to the extent possible, claims raising similar factual and legal issues shall be processed together."[171] The Commission used standardized verification methodologies, in particular with respect to questions of causation, as well as standardized valuation methodologies. Authority for this was derived in part from its relaxed standard of proof, which required the Commission to "take into account . . . the background information available to [it] regarding the circumstances prevailing during the National Socialist era and the Second World War and the participation of German enterprises in the commitment of National Socialist wrongs."[172]

(h) Eritrea–Ethiopia Claims Commission (EECC)—claims relating to the 1998–2000 war between Eritrea and Ethiopia

To facilitate the work of the EECC, its constituting instrument, the 12 December 2000 Agreement, authorizes it to "adopt such methods of efficient case management and mass claims processing as it deems appropriate, such as expedited procedures for processing claims and checking claims on a sample basis. . . ."[173] In its preparatory work during 2001, the Commission adopted various provisions intended to give the parties the option of filing claims utilizing mass claims procedures if they wished to do so.[174] The Commission's Rules of Procedure authorized mass claims filings in both electronic and paper form, on claim forms that would be approved by the Commission.[175] The intent was to permit the Commission to docket and then manage the processing of large numbers of claims filed in the mass claims procedure using

---

[171] IOM Property Commission Supplemental Rules, section 20.1.

[172] Ibid., section 22.1. See also section 17.2 ("The Commission shall make its determinations regarding causation pursuant to the terms of the German Foundation Act, these Rules and on the basis of respect for established principles of international law and practice regarding causation and directness of loss. In applying these principles, the Commission shall take into account the evidentiary standard set out in section 22").

[173] Eritrea–Ethiopia Agreement of 12 December 2000, Article 5, paragraph 10.

[174] See EECC Rules of Procedure, Chapter Three: "Mass Claims Procedures."

[175] Ibid., Article 30, paragraph 3.

computers and appropriate docket management software. For example, the Rules anticipated that sample mass claims would be selected in sub-categories where liability had been found, and that this would be done electronically, applying selection criteria identified by experts to ensure a representative sample. It was planned that the sufficiency of the evidence in the sample claims would then be screened in order to determine the level of compensation for the overall group. However, given the December 2001 deadline for filing claims, both parties decided to file traditional Government-to-Government claims rather than to utilize these procedures.

(i) Humanitarian insurance Claims Process administered by the Jewish Claims Conference (JCC) for the International Commission on Holocaust Era Insurance Claims (ICHEIC)

The Point Scoring System used in the 8A1 humanitarian Claims Process was in itself an innovation in mass claims processing. However, in advising ICHEIC on the development of the Point Scoring System, the JCC utilized its experience with similar programs, in particular a similar program it developed for the United States District Court for the Eastern District of New York for purposes of the class action known as the Holocaust Victim Assets Litigation.[176] The Point Scoring System provided a firm point-weighting system, a standard for establishing proof of any given criterion, and a methodology for processing the claims. The System generally awarded points to a claim depending on whether the information contained in the claim form and accompanying documentation yielded a "yes" or "no" answer to a finite number of questions. Because information in the claim forms included narrative, the Point Scoring System converted such information into a point score by asking the JCC claims analysts specific questions about key information contained in such narrative. The claims were grouped into different queues based on the language in which they had been submitted, and they were assigned to be reviewed by claims analysts who were fluent in that language.

The Point Scoring System was then further refined by the JCC using a sample of one hundred claims, and it was subsequently tested on a sample of seven hundred claims, in order to extrapolate administrative costs, schedules, and timetables.

---

[176] See generally sections in this book on the Holocaust Assets Victim Programme (HVAP) administered by the International Organization for Migration (IOM), and the second Claims Resolution Tribunal for accounts in Swiss banks (CRT-II).

(j) American Arbitration Association (AAA)—an illustrative case

In the illustrative case, a claims review team grouped claims by shared characteristics, including the quality of evidence, and then established remedies in a grid system. The AAA also used grouping techniques in its administration of the appeals process, consolidating similar cases and sending them in batches to individual Arbitrators.

5.07 Coordinating Decisions

If the Claims Process involves different decision-makers acting as, e.g., Sole Arbitrators or in a number of separate panels or chambers, whether there are internal procedures for coordinating and harmonizing the work to avoid inconsistent results. (See also section 2.04 on *stare decisis*.)

Editors' Commentary

Maintaining a high degree of consistency in substantive decisions or explaining the reasons for differing results are important elements in establishing public confidence in a Mass Claims Process. For example, members of a similarly situated claimant group may often be able to compare their results with those of other members of the same group, such as refugees or internally displaced persons returning to their homes in the same community after having been expelled or forced to flee under the same circumstances. Neighbors in such a community would be quick to notice unexplained inconsistencies in treatment of their claims and some would perceive the results as unfair.

In Claims Processes in which all claims are decided by the same persons, such as the Eritrea–Ethiopia Claims Commission (EECC), it is more likely that decisions will be consistent than if a number of different Sole Arbitrators or separate panels of Commissioners decide large numbers of claims. Given the high volume of claims to be decided in a relatively short period of time in many Mass Claims Processes, some designers of such Claims Processes have built into the procedures methods for ensuring consistent application of those procedures. That has been accomplished with varying results in some, but not all, of the Claims Processes described in this book.

Some of these methods rely on initiatives and vigilance of the decision-makers themselves, while others incorporate assistance by the Secretariat or oversight by another body. The simplest method is for each decision-maker to be aware of what the others have done. While that, perhaps, goes without saying, it cannot occur without establishing an administrative mechanism for—at a minimum—promptly circulating copies of all decisions. The task is further facilitated in Claims Processes where decisions are published, because there the parties have the opportunity to point out what they consider to be similarities among cases. In some Claims Processes, the Secretariat has the function of informing decision-makers of other cases in which the same issues have been addressed and/or resolved, and in others, an oversight body reviews decisions before they become effective in order to avoid unexplained inconsistencies.

(a) Iran–United States Claims Tribunal (Iran–US CT)—claims relating to the 1979 Islamic Revolution

Decisions by the Iran–US CT are made by the Full Tribunal of nine Members or by Chambers of three Members. The nine Members are assigned to three Chambers. Some cases, particularly those involving disputes between the two Government parties, are heard by the Full Tribunal of nine, while many more are heard by one of the Chambers of three.[177] The Full Tribunal and the three Chambers have generally maintained a high level of consistency of jurisprudence.[178]

To promote consistency, a 1981 Presidential Order provided that "[i]f the preliminary or main issues in two or more cases before different Chambers are similar, the President may determine that they shall be assigned to the same Chamber."[179] Further, the same Presidential Order stated that "[w]here a case pending before a Chamber raises an important issue the Chamber may, at any time prior to the final award relinquish jurisdiction in favour of the [Full Tribunal of nine Members]."[180] Also, where a case pending before a Chamber raises a particularly important issue that may arise in a number of cases, the Chamber may relinquish jurisdiction in favor of the Full Tribunal.[181] In addition, a Chamber may decide to relinquish jurisdiction to the Full Tribunal when the resolution of an issue might result in inconsistent decisions or awards

---

[177] Claims Settlement Declaration, Article III, paragraph 1.

[178] See, however, section 5.11(a) below, on awarding interest, where each Chamber had a distinct approach and line of precedent in dealing with interest.

[179] Iran–US CT Presidential Order No. 1 of 19 October 1981, 1 Iran–U.S. C.T.R. p. 95 [hereinafter Iran–US CT Presidential Order No. 1], paragraph 5(a).   [180] Ibid., paragraph 6(a).

[181] Ibid.

by the Tribunal.[182] The Full Tribunal may either retain jurisdiction over the whole case or may, after deciding the issue in question, transfer the case back to the Chamber for the remaining part of the case.[183]

Another harmonizing measure is that the Tribunal may make orders to coordinate and expedite cases that raise important issues, including, but not limited to, (i) transferring cases from separate three-Member Chambers to the Full Tribunal of nine Members, thereby eliminating the possibility of inconsistency among Chambers; (ii) providing that such issues be heard separately and prior to the hearing of the remaining issues; and (iii) coordinating the scheduling of hearings. The Tribunal may authorize parties to "give, through a single designated representative, common explanations on similar issues arising out of different cases, without [it] resulting in consolidation or joinder."[184]

All awards of the Claims Process are circulated among all the Members as soon as they are filed. Thus, the Members of the Tribunal know about past decisions and can act consistently, and awards are also published, which gives the parties opportunity to point out similarities with other cases. Thus, publication has assisted the harmonization of the Tribunal's procedures.

(b) United Nations Compensation Commission (UNCC)—claims relating to the 1990–1991 Gulf War

As the different panels of UNCC Commissioners decided on different categories of claims, there was generally harmonization of decisions within each panel. In all claims categories, claims with common or similar legal, factual, and valuation issues were categorized and processed together. The Provisional Rules assigned this task to the Secretariat in order to "facilitate the work of Commissioners and to ensure uniformity in the treatment of similar claims."[185] Thus, all urgent claims (categories "A", "B", and "C") were submitted to the panels of Commissioners in instalments prepared by the Secretariat, often consisting of tens of thousands of claims. This practice facilitated uniformity and consistency of decisions of claims within each claims category. The Secretariat provided significant support to the panels of Commissioners in ensuring consistency both within and among claims categories.

Another means of achieving consistency arose from the role of the UNCC Governing Council in approving recommendations of the panels of Commissioners. A panel submitted reports of its recommendations to the

---

182 Iran–US CT, Presidential Order No. 1, paragraph 6(b).   183 Ibid., paragraph 6(c).
184 Iran–US CT Internal Guidelines of the Tribunal, 1 Iran–U.S. C.T.R. p. 98, paragraph 1.
185 UNCC Provisional Rules, Article 17.

UNCC Governing Council in each category of claims regarding the amount to be awarded to each claimant. Those reports were subject to approval by the Governing Council, which could refer the report back to the Commissioners for further consideration. This ensured a certain consistency among the work of the different panels of Commissioners. However, by virtue of the fact that all reports were subject to approval of the Council, monitoring consistency was built into the claims processing and was addressed by the Commissioners well before the reports reached the Governing Council level.

In a further effort to achieve consistency, the Chairpersons of all the panels of Commissioners met once every year to discuss and coordinate issues facing several or all panels. In addition, panels concerned met on an as-needed basis to discuss and coordinate issues of particular importance facing them. The Secretariat regularly brought common issues to the attention of the panels affected by them.

The Secretariat has further developed computerized databases containing information on all the claims, the texts of all Commissioner panel reports, and Governing Council decisions, an index of the panel reports and Governing Council decisions, and an index of the legal, factual, and valuation issues raised by the claims and of those addressed by the reports and decisions.[186] The Secretariat staff also has provided administrative, technical, and legal support to the Commissioners in the form of conducting research, preparing claims summaries and valuation materials, and drafting briefs and decisions. Secretariat staff has regularly attended panel deliberations and coordinated support among different panels so as to identify common issues and promote consistency.[187]

For the large number of urgent individual claims for relatively small amounts of compensation where Iraq's liability was established by United Nations Security Council Resolution 674 (1990),[188] a detailed, individual review of the amount of each claim was considered to be neither warranted nor feasible. Rather, the Commission employed a range of standardized mass claims processing techniques, ranging from computerized matching of claims and verification information, to sampling and statistical modeling. Here, the role of the panels of Commissioners was primarily to ensure the soundness of the various methodologies and their consistent application.[189]

---

[186] The parts of the database available to the public include texts of panel reports and Governing Council decisions, as well as the index of same.   [187] UNCC Provisional Rules, Article 34.

[188] UN Security Council Resolution 674 (1990) of 29 October 1990, U.N. Doc. S/RES/674 (1990) (29 October 1990), paragraph 8.

[189] See further section 5.06 above, on mass claims techniques.

The Secretariat also has coordinated the work of expert consultants, such as accountants, actuaries, loss adjusters, and asset valuation experts, to ensure consistent results and equal treatment of the claimants. A special unit within the Claims Processing Division of the Secretariat, the so-called Verification and Valuation Support Branch (VVSB), was devoted to this task. Members of the VVSB supported panels of Commissioners, as did members of the Legal Services Branch, and staff members from the two branches worked very closely together.

(c) Commission for Real Property Claims of Displaced Persons and Refugees (CRPC)—claims relating to the 1992–1995 war in Bosnia and Herzegovina

At the CRPC, elaborate procedures for preparing awards led to a high degree of uniformity and consistency of decisions. First, the Legal Department reviewed a batch of similar claims and prepared draft decisions. Those drafts were then presented to a "Legal Working Group" of Commissioners for consideration and discussion. Based on the instructions given by the Legal Working Group, the legal staff reviewed the claims again, assessed the evidence, and proposed a large batch of decisions to the Commission for accepting the claims, rejecting them, or declaring them inadmissible.[190] The staff of the Executive Office then reviewed the claims and assessed the evidence upon which the draft decision was based, and, after reviewing the claim, proposed to the Commission a decision by which a claim was either refused as inadmissible, accepted, or rejected.[191] The Legal Working Group regularly reviewed draft decisions in order to ensure that they were in accordance with the Book of Regulations on Procedure.[192] Then, the Commission, in plenary session, would make decisions on claims for return of real property based on the proposal of the Executive Office.[193] The Commission could (i) completely accept the decision proposals; (ii) partly change or amend the decision proposals; or (iii) send the proposals back to the Legal Working Group for supplementing.[194]

The effect of applying these procedures consistently to all claims promoted harmony among the work of different claims reviewers.

(d) Claims Resolution Tribunal for Dormant Accounts in Switzerland (CRT-I)—first claims tribunal for assets deposited in Swiss banks

In order to promote consistent procedures for all claims submitted to the CRT-I Claims Process, the Sole Arbitrators and panels of Arbitrators were

---

[190] CRPC Book of Regulations on Procedure, Article 53.   [191] Ibid., Articles 54–56.
[192] Ibid., Article 57.   [193] Ibid., Article 58.   [194] Ibid., Article 59.

permitted to call issues to the attention of the Chairman. If necessary, the Chairman could coordinate the adoption of a new Internal Rule for the issue in question, thereby ensuring that it be dealt with in a consistent manner.[195]

(e) Claims Resolution Tribunal (CRT-II)—second claims tribunal for assets deposited in Swiss banks

Claims at CRT-II are processed in an administrative procedure by many different claims reviewers. All decisions are prepared in draft form by staff attorneys and submitted to the Special Masters appointed by the United States federal district court overseeing the class action known as the Holocaust Victim Assets Litigation. The Special Masters review the draft decisions before certifying them to the Court for approval.[196] This review, in addition to detailed provisions on claims admissibility criteria,[197] matching of claims and accounts,[198] criteria for making awards,[199] and presumptions to be applied to certain classes of claims,[200] assists in maintaining consistency among different claims reviewers.

(f) Housing and Property Claims Commission (HPCC)—claims relating to the 1999 conflict in Kosovo

The UNMIK Regulation governing the HPCC Claims Process provides that the Commission shall either sit in plenary session or in such panels as may be established under UNMIK Regulation 1999/23.[201] The Commission has only convened as one single panel, and thus no special efforts are necessary for maintaining consistency of procedure among different decision-makers. UNMIK Regulation 2000/60 further provides that "[t]he Registrar, in consultation with the Chairperson of the plenary Commission, shall determine the order in which claims will be considered by the Commission, and shall [if there is more than one Panel] allocate claims between the Panels, taking into account the desirability of developing a consistent practice."[202]

Also, if there is more than one panel, in case of doubt, "[a] Panel or the Chairperson of a Panel may refer specific issues relating to a claim to the plenary session of the Commission for guidance."[203] The Commission may also group together any claims raising common legal and evidentiary issues so that these may be reviewed all at once, which promotes consistency.[204]

---

[195] CRT-I unpublished Internal Rules, Article 6. [196] CRT-II Governing Rules, Article 16.
[197] Ibid., Article 18. [198] Ibid., Articles 19–21. [199] Ibid., Article 22.
[200] Ibid., Articles 28 and 29. [201] UNMIK Regulation 2000/60, section 17.1.
[202] Ibid., section 17.14. [203] Ibid., section 20.4. [204] Ibid., section 19.5(a).

(g) Mass Claims Processes administered by the International Organization for Migration (IOM): *German Forced Labour Compensation Programme (GFLCP) for claims against Germany and German industry for Nazi injustice, and Holocaust Victim Assets Programme (HVAP) for claims pursuant to 1999 class action Settlement*

Claims review and decision recommendations at both the GFLCP and HVAP Claims Processes are coordinated by Secretariat legal staff. Each class or category of claims is handled by a team of claims processors, led by a staff attorney as "team leader" who monitors their work and conducts quality control checks to ensure that they are applying uniform claims processing methods established by IOM. For example, claims processors must identify the types of evidentiary documentation—such as proof of detention in a concentration camp—which can, without further review, establish a claimant's eligibility for slave labour compensation.[205] The GFLCP team leaders coordinate among each other and consult with the office of the legal director and the German Foundation on an on-going basis as to the application of the Foundation Act to the facts of the claims as they emerge.

IOM also coordinates with the other partner organizations working on different claimant populations to share data and methods and harmonize the overall Claims Process. The German Foundation periodically conducts sample audits of the decisions on each group of claims recommended by IOM and the other partner organizations before it approves any awards of compensation. This further promotes consistency.

The teams working on HVAP claims must certify draft decisions to the United States federal district court overseeing the class action known as the Holocaust Victim Assets Litigation for approval. The Plan of Allocation and Distribution, approved by the Court, and various Court orders, set out the procedures that IOM is to follow. This arrangement leads to consistency and uniformity of working methods.

The only organs in the IOM Claims Processes that have had Commissioners making decisions are the Property Claims Commission and the IOM Appeals Body for Forced Labour Claims. The decisions of the Property Claims Commission tended to be consistent because all its decisions were rendered by the same panel of three Commissioners. Consistency was furthermore enhanced by the rule that the IOM Secretariat was required to perform an initial

---

[205] See section 5.02(g) above regarding the types of proof that could establish eligibility.

review of all property claims prior to their submission to the Commission, including checking documentary and other evidence submitted by the claimant, and carrying out inquiries to ascertain the information required to verify a claim.[206] IOM also submitted the claims to the Commission in installments, ensuring, to the extent possible, that claims raising similar factual and legal issues were processed together.[207]

Similarly, for the three Members of the IOM Appeals Body for Forced Labour Claims, appeals that present similar situations or circumstances are grouped together for efficient consideration and consistent decisions.[208]

(h) Eritrea–Ethiopia Claims Commission (EECC)—claims relating to the 1998–2000 war between Eritrea and Ethiopia

The five Commissioners of the EECC act together as a single panel in deciding all claims. Hence, no internal procedures are needed to harmonize the work of separate groups of decision-makers. Although not required by its Rules of Procedure, until 31 January 2006, all of the Commission's decisions had been unanimous. However, it is recognized that, should the Commission decide to utilize experts to assist it in assessing damages, measures to ensure quality control and consistency may become necessary.

All claims are submitted to the EECC by counsel for each of the two Government parties who, in their submissions, address legal issues common to large groups of claims. These lawyers thus perform much of the organizational work which in other Claims Processes—where individual claimants file their own claims—is carried out by the Secretariat of the Claims Process.

(i) Humanitarian insurance Claims Process administered by the Jewish Claims Conference (JCC) for the International Commission on Holocaust Era Insurance Claims (ICHEIC)

In order to ensure consistent and uniform application of the Point Scoring System Guidelines across a team of thirty claims analysts, several tests were conducted before live recorded scoring of the 8A1 Claims began. Given the complexities inherent in evaluating a wide variety of written personal statements and evidence using a finite number of questions, the JCC focused in on certain general ways in which claimants responded to the claim form questionnaire and conferred with ICHEIC on how the claims analysts should rate—or

---

[206] IOM Property Commission Supplemental Rules, section 15.1 and 15.3.
[207] Ibid., section 20.l.
[208] IOM Appeals Body Principles and Rules, Article 19, paragraph C.

"score"—such responses. Much of the first month of processing consisted of a training phase in which the instructions to claims analysts were refined and adjusted. Certain patterns were identified among the claims and were reflected in adjustments made to the Point Scoring System Guidelines. Thus, once actual live scoring began, it rarely occurred that a claims analyst would not have a model on which to base a decision.

During the training phase, groups of three or four analysts scored the same batch of claims. After completing their review, the analysts gathered to discuss any inconsistencies among their individual scores. The results of each claims analyst were available through intranet web tools to the analysts' supervisor and to the program Director, allowing them to monitor any wide discrepancies and address their underlying causes—such as an unclear instruction or ambiguity within the Point Scoring System Guidelines. (These types of issues, rather than any individual claims analyst's misunderstanding, were the cause of most scoring discrepancies.) The Point Scoring System software also enabled the program Director to gather statistics on claims analysts' performance and identify anyone whose performance substantially diverged from what was expected, based on average claim passing rate, speed of review, and other aspects.

The testing period was important for several reasons. It was critical for testing the 8A1 Application software and the database that recorded analysts' scoring. Also, because formal training was held only on claims written in English, whereas claims had to be scored in over twenty different languages, certain phrases and nuances which were accepted as anecdotal evidence in English did not necessarily have a corresponding meaning in all the other languages. The testing period allowed the analysts to develop a common understanding of what the Point Scoring System meant in any one of the languages used by 8A1 claimants. The testing period aided the ongoing development of the Point Scoring System Guidelines by identifying common patterns and exceptional cases. Based on this experience, scoring rules were implemented as examples with commentary in the Guidelines. The Guidelines continued to be adjusted and updated once live scoring commenced, whenever a circumstance arose which all claims analysts should address in the same manner. Notice of such updates was given to the analysts via e-mail, while the most current copy of the Guidelines was kept in a directory on the JCC's computer network accessible to all members of the 8A1 team. Any substantive changes to the Guidelines were cleared with ICHEIC.

(j) American Arbitration Association (AAA)—an illustrative case

In the illustrative case, the AAA could cease giving cases to an Arbitrator on the ground that he or she was rendering awards that were disproportionately higher or lower than those issued by other decision-makers in the Claims Process. This was one way of maintaining consistency among a great number of decision-makers.

The defendant insurance company also monitored the Claims Process on a daily basis, frequently having staff present at the AAA offices in order to do so without causing delay.

5.08 Due Process

The extent to which the Claims Process includes elements to assure due process, including the right to present claims and defenses, the right for all sides to be represented and assisted by persons of their choice, the right to confront witnesses, etc.

Editors' Commentary

The twin requirements common to all Mass Claims Processes are swift justice and due process. The special challenge of each Claims Process is therefore how to reconcile these requirements in its unique circumstances. The large numbers of claims and the complexity of the issues involved call for a thorough review, while the individual claimants and their families have often suffered greatly and depend on a swift resolution of their claims in order, for example, to move back into their homes, afford medical treatment, and resume their lives after a major disruption. It is often said with respect to such claimants that "justice delayed is justice denied."

The designers of all of the Mass Claims Processes described in this book were aware of the need for the parties and the public to accept that the procedures include the elements necessary to assure due process. They recognized and, for the most part, incorporated the core concepts of due process, and the principles akin to them known in some legal systems as "natural justice." These principles are typically found in other international dispute resolution mechanisms, including equal rights to present claims and defenses, the rights to choose representatives, and to question witnesses. Such due process procedures are incorporated in several Mass Claims Processes by governing instruments that refer to the UNCITRAL Arbitration Rules, and they are similarly incorporated in the procedures of Claims Processes that refer to the Permanent Court of Arbitration Optional Rules for Arbitrating Disputes between Two States (PCA Rules), which include due process procedures substantially similar to those in the UNCITRAL Arbitration Rules. But the requirement of due process can be said to exist even when not expressly stated in the applicable rules.

Even if a Mass Claims Process does not include provisions expressly mandating due process or describing norms of fair procedures in detail, such requirements can be implied based on the theory that they are an inherent part of all systems of international justice. Nevertheless, designers of Mass Claims Processes may find it prudent to state those requirements expressly in order to avoid contentious ambiguities that may arise from cultural differences.

An interesting mechanism to facilitate representation of all views in a Mass Claims Process was provided in the Marshall Islands Nuclear Claims Tribunal, established in 1988 to compensate citizens of the Marshall Islands for loss or damage to property and person resulting from atmospheric nuclear testing by the United States in the Pacific Ocean. The United States provided a US$150 million financial settlement for the damages, which was used to create a special fund intended to generate US$270 million for distribution over a fifteen-year period. Compensation awarded by the Tribunal was to be paid from this fund, and the parties had an interest that the fund be used properly. To afford representation of that interest, the constituting instrument created an independent "Office of the Defender of the Fund,"[209] a function not included in any of the Claims Processes described in this book.

(a) Iran–United States Claims Tribunal (Iran–US CT)—claims relating to the 1979 Islamic Revolution

The Iran–US CT Tribunal Rules include the text of all of the due process provisions of the UNCITRAL Arbitration Rules and thus expressly repeat the full panoply of those protections to assure fair and equal treatment of the parties and their rights to present their cases. For example, the Tribunal Rules include provisions based on the UNCITRAL Arbitration Rules that state that the proceedings must assure that "the parties are treated with equality and that at any [appropriate] stage of the proceedings each party is given a full opportunity of presenting his case."[210] Further, the Tribunal Rules contain a number of

---

[209] See Agreement Between the Government of the United States and the Government of the Marshall Islands for the Implementation of Section 177 of the Compact of Free Association, section 2, available at www.nuclearclaimstribunal.com.

[210] Iran–US CT Tribunal Rules, Article 15, paragraph 1. Although the word "appropriate" does not appear in this context in the original text of UNCITRAL Arbitration Rules, Article 15, paragraph 1, the provision has been widely interpreted to include that common-sense qualifier.

detailed procedures to effectuate that requirement, including enumerating basic rights to assure fairness, such as the right of parties to be "represented or assisted by persons of their choice;"[211] to receive copies of documents filed;[212] and to be given advance notice of oral hearings.[213] The Tribunal Rules provide that parties shall be informed of the identity of witnesses who will testify and be given an opportunity to question them, which encompasses the right to confront witnesses.[214]

While the Tribunal Rules state that the parties may be represented or assisted by persons of their choice, they, like the UNCITRAL Arbitration Rules, do not include procedures for authenticating the authority of such persons.[215]

An interesting feature of this Claims Process is the contribution of the Agents of the United States and Iran in providing representation for the parties. In this regard, the role of the Agents was unique among government representations at the Mass Claims Processes described in this book. The Agents carried out several functions, including: arguing cases in which their Governments had positions, by oral and written presentations on legal, procedural, jurisdictional, and administrative issues; consulting with attorneys for private parties in order to advise on Tribunal jurisdiction, procedures, and the Tribunal Rules; negotiating with each other and with the Tribunal Members and staff on general procedural and administrative matters; negotiating with officials of the Netherlands Ministries of Foreign Affairs and Justice, and the Netherlands Central Bank concerning Tribunal matters such as the application of Dutch law, privileges and immunities, payment mechanisms, etc.; and attending hearings, pre-hearing conferences, and meetings of the Committee on Administrative and Financial Questions.

(b) United Nations Compensation Commission (UNCC)—claims relating to the 1990–1991 Gulf War

The provisions of the UNCC relating to due process may be considered in the light of a statement in a Report of the United Nations Secretary-General issued pursuant to paragraph 19 of Security Council Resolution 687 (1991):

"The Commission is not a court or an arbitral tribunal before which the parties appear; it is a political organ that performs an essentially fact-finding function of examining

---

[211] See Iran–US CT Tribunal Rules, Article 4 and Notes 2 and 3 to Article 4, defining "a representative" as a person having power to bind a party and to receive notices on its behalf, in contrast to a person who "assists" in presenting a case without power to act in place of a party.

[212] Ibid., Article 2, paragraph 2.   [213] Ibid., Article 25, paragraph 1.

[214] Ibid., Article 25, paragraph 2 and Note 6(b) to Article 25.   [215] Ibid., Article 4.

claims, verifying their validity, evaluating losses, assessing payments and resolving disputed claims. It is only in this last respect that a quasi-judicial function may be involved. Given the nature of the Commission, it is all the more important that some element of due process be built into the procedure. It will be the function of the commissioners to provide this element."[216]

The Secretary-General's Report listed recommendations for how this due process might be achieved while balancing the pressing need to resolve expediently a very large number of claims. It took the position that traditional arbitration methods were probably not suitable for resolving the very large number of claims against Iraq arising out of its invasion, and that, in the circumstances, approaches which might not be acceptable in the case-by-case traditional arbitration model were justified and necessary. For example, the Commissioners would be given discretion to determine the degree of evidence needed in each case, as well as whether hearings and witness testimony were required.[217]

Iraq, although technically not a party to each case before the Commission, was assured an opportunity to express its views in the Claims Process through operation of Article 16 of the UNCC Provisional Rules, which charged the Executive Secretary with making periodic reports to the Governing Council concerning the claims received. Such reports—known as "Article 16 Reports"—were required to include certain statistical and other information about the claims, such as the eligible parties that submitted claims, the categories of claims submitted, the number of claimants in each consolidated claim, the total amount of compensation sought in each consolidated claim, as well as the "significant legal and factual issues raised by the claims, if any."[218] These Reports were promptly communicated to Iraq and to all States and organizations submitting claims so that they might present "additional information and views concerning the report to the Executive Secretary for transmission to [the competent] panels of Commissioners. . . ."[219] The Article 16 procedure, in practice, became Iraq's chief avenue for participating in UNCC

---

[216] Report of the Secretary-General of 2 May 1991, U.N. Doc. S/22559, paragraph 20. Although the quoted text appears in Part II of the Report, which was not adopted by the UN Security Council in Resolution Resolution 692 (1991) of 20 May 1991, creating the Commission, U.N. Doc. S/RES/692 (1991) (20 May 1991), the Security Council in paragraph 5 of that Resolution directed the Governing Council to take Part II "into account" when implementing Resolution 687 (1991) of 3 April 1991, deciding to create the Commission, U.N. Doc. S/RES/687 (1991) (8 April 1991), paragraph 18,

[217] See generally section 5.02(b) above, on evidentiary standards at the UNCC.

[218] UNCC Provisional Rules, Article 16, paragraph 1.

[219] Ibid., Article 16, paragraphs 2 and 3.

proceedings, as oral hearings were held only in exceptional circumstances. Iraq took full advantage of the procedure and regularly submitted its arguments and views on the issues contained in the Reports.

In addition to the Article 16 procedure, claims files for those claims designated by panels of Commissioners as "unusually large or complex," claims in which the situs of the loss was Iraq, or claims involving an Iraqi party, were transmitted to Iraq for comments. (A slightly modified procedure obtained for category "D" claims —i.e., individual claims in excess of US$100,000— due in part to the need for keeping confidential the names of individual claimants.) Any comments received were presented to the panels of Commissioners and were taken into consideration when making findings and recommendations. In addition, for some of the "F4" claims for environmental damage, a special program was implemented which enabled Iraq to retain technical assistance for the environmental and public health claims for the purpose of providing written and oral submissions to the "F4" panel of Commissioners.

On the matter of representation, the Provisional Rules provide that,

" . . . except in cases where a specially authorized representative is designated by a Government and notified to the Executive Secretary, the head of the Permanent Mission [in Geneva] of a Government shall be considered as its representative before the Commission. Governments that do not maintain Permanent Missions in Geneva and international organizations shall notify the name of their duly authorized representatives to the Executive Secretary."[220]

(c) Commission for Real Property Claims of Displaced Persons and Refugees (CRPC)—claims relating to the 1992–1995 war in Bosnia and Herzegovina

Claims for return of real property were submitted to the CRPC by the claimants themselves or by their authorized representatives.[221] An authorized representative was required to present a valid power of attorney when submitting a claim, and such power of attorney had to have been verified by one of the relevant authorities listed in the CRPC Book of Regulations on Procedure.[222]

As no hearings were held before the Commission, the issue of confronting witnesses did not arise.

---

[220] UNCC Provisional Rules, Article 9.
[221] CRPC Book of Regulations on Procedure, Articles 8 and 14.
[222] Ibid., Articles 15 and 16.

(d) Claims Resolution Tribunal for Dormant Accounts in Switzerland (CRT-I)—first claims tribunal for assets deposited in Swiss banks

The CRT-I claim form included an agreement which the claimants had to sign, agreeing that their claims would be decided by arbitration under Swiss law. This agreement incorporated into the CRT-I Claims Process all of the fairness safeguards in Swiss law. In addition, the Rules of Procedure established procedures to assure fairness. Thus, in the CRT-I proceedings, the claimant and the responding bank each had the opportunity to address the submissions made by the other. The Rules of Procedure provided that, if the Members deemed appropriate, they could invite other persons—such as other heirs of the account holder, intermediaries, or beneficiaries—to participate in the proceedings.[223]

As far as representation in the Claims Process, the CRT-I Rules provided that "[a]ny party may be represented and assisted in the [Claims Resolution Processes] by persons of their choice, including counsel provided by voluntary organizations."[224] The Tribunal also informed potential claimants that:

"It is not necessary to hire a lawyer. The arbitrators are responsible to determine the facts and the law that apply to your claim and to assist you in submitting relevant information. Of course, you may have a lawyer or another person assist and represent you in the claims procedure at your own expense."[225]

In practice, few claimants employed lawyers to assist them in the Claims Process. As hearings were not held in any cases at CRT-I, the issue of confronting witnesses did not arise.

(e) Claims Resolution Tribunal (CRT-II)—second claims tribunal for assets deposited in Swiss banks

The CRT-II Claims Process is conducted pursuant to the Settlement Agreement reached in a class action in a United States federal district court and, accordingly, the due process safeguards of United States law apply. Further, the Court adopted the CRT-II Governing Rules, which include procedures intended to promote fair handling of the claims. It is not necessary for CRT-II claimants to employ lawyers to assist them in the Claims Process. The Rules do, however, allow claimants who wish to be represented by a person of their choice to do so, provided that they submit a power of attorney in a form provided by CRT-II.[226]

---

[223] CRT-I Rules of Procedure, Article 21. See also Article 24 on Statements by the Parties and Third Persons.   [224] Ibid., Article 39.

[225] CRT-I Information Brochure, "Frequently Asked Questions," p. 10.

[226] CRT-II Governing Rules, Article 35.

No hearings are held at CRT-II, and the issue of confronting witnesses therefore does not arise.

(f) Housing and Property Claims Commission (HPCC)—claims relating to the 1999 conflict in Kosovo

The UNMIK Regulations governing the HPCC Claims Process contain detailed provisions on the rights of the parties to present a claim and be represented in proceedings before the Commission and the Housing and Property Directorate (HPD). Notice of claim is to be given to the current occupant of the claimed property and any parties having a legal interest in the claim, and such parties are given the right to submit a Reply to Claim, in which a current occupant may request that his or her housing needs be taken into consideration.[227] A party with a legal interest in the claim who did not receive notification may be admitted as a party at any later point in the proceedings up until final adjudication of the claim.[228]

UNMIK Regulation 2000/60 provides that a "claimant or a party to a claim may be represented by an authorized person with a valid and duly executed power of attorney. In exceptional cases, where the provision of a power of attorney is problematic, the Directorate may certify an alternative document authorizing representation of a claimant."[229]

Although hearings before the Commission are provided for in the Regulations, none are held in practice. (Occasional evidentiary hearings have, however, been held before a single Commissioner.) The issue of confronting witnesses therefore does not generally arise.

(g) Mass Claims Processes administered by the International Organization for Migration (IOM)

German Forced Labour Compensation Programme (GFLCP)—claims against Germany and German industry for Nazi injustice

Due process includes the right to present a claim. Given the advanced age of most of the claimant population in this Claims Process, and the difficulty of presenting evidence so long after the events giving rise to it took place, the exercise of this right is given practical assistance by the IOM Secretariat's helping the claimants to substantiate their claims by, for example, pointing out specific deficiencies of their claims and indicating possible corrections. IOM

---

[227] UNMIK Regulation 2000/60, section 9.1, 9.5 and 9.6.   [228] Ibid., section 9.2.
[229] Ibid., section 7.3.

also conducts archive searches and historic research on claimants' behalf, to verify evidence and supplement gaps in the evidentiary record.

Claimants may be represented by counsel or other representatives whom they retain at their own cost. There are no hearings or oral examinations of witnesses held for slave or forced labor claims, or before the Property Claims Commission or the IOM Appeals Body for Forced Labour Claims.

*Holocaust Victim Assets Programme (HVAP)—claims pursuant to
1999 class action Settlement*

The exercise of the right to present a claim in the HVAP Claims Process is facilitated through the same types of claimant assistance, archival searches, and historic research as are noted in the preceding section on the German Forced Labour Compensation Programme, and as are permitted under the Settlement Agreement reached in the class action known as the Holocaust Victim Assets Litigation, in the United States District Court for the Eastern District of New York.

(h) Eritrea–Ethiopia Claims Commission (EECC)—claims relating to the 1998–2000 war between Eritrea and Ethiopia

The EECC Rules of Procedure provide that the Commission shall conduct its arbitration so that the parties are treated with equality and given full opportunity to present their cases in accordance with the Rules.[230] The Rules grant the Commission discretion to determine whether hearings will be held.[231] This differs from both the UNCITRAL and PCA Rules that give the parties a *right* to a hearing[232] and was intended to take account of the possible simplification and compression of proceedings potentially required in mass claims procedures. In applying its Rules, the Commission, after

---

[230] EECC Rules of Procedure, Article 10, paragraph 1.

[231] Ibid., Article 10, paragraph 2, provides that "[t]he Commission shall decide whether to hold hearings for the presentation of evidence by witnesses, including expert witnesses, or for oral argument, or whether the proceedings shall be conducted on the basis of documents and other materials." Article 13 contains detailed notice requirements for hearings, including, if witnesses are to be heard:

"at least thirty days before the hearing, each party shall communicate to the Commission and to the other party the names and addresses of the witnesses it intends to present, and the subject upon and the languages in which such witnesses will testify . . . .

5 . . . . The Commission may require the retirement of any witness during the testimony of other witnesses. The Commission is free to determine the manner in which witnesses are examined and shall take appropriate measures as required for the protection of the security and privacy of witnesses."

[232] See section 5.04(h) above, on oral hearings at the EECC.

consultation with the parties, did schedule extensive hearings in the first phase (liability), where witnesses were heard and questioned by both sides and by the Commission.

The practice of the EECC demonstrates how the right of the parties to present their cases has been effectuated. Pursuant to the Rules, each side has submitted not only Statements of Claim against the other, and Statements of Defense responding to the Statements of Claim,[233] but also detailed legal Memorials and Counter-Memorials.[234]

The EECC Rules further provide that each party shall appoint an Agent (and if they so desire, a Co-Agent), and that the parties may be assisted by counsel or other persons of their choice.[235] Both Government parties have been represented, throughout the Claims Process and during hearings, by counsel.

(i) Humanitarian insurance Claims Process administered by the Jewish Claims Conference (JCC) for the International Commission on Holocaust Era Insurance Claims (ICHEIC)

The 8A1 award constituted a humanitarian payment; it served as recognition of injustice and was not a settlement for lost insurance policies. Given the symbolic nature of the award, the 8A1 Claims Process was conducted based on submitted documentation only. Assertions and documentation were accepted on their face, and ambiguities were resolved in favor of the claimant.

(j) American Arbitration Association (AAA)—an illustrative case

The Settlement Agreement in the illustrative case gave both sides the right to counsel, with the defendant paying all attorneys' fees. The claimants were represented by counsel who were available for consultation before and during the telephone hearings. Parties could request an in-person hearing in lieu of a telephone hearing, but this was rare in practice. Both sides had equal access to participate in the hearings, question parties, cross-examine witnesses, and present evidence.

---

[233] EECC Rules of Procedure, Articles 24 and 25.

[234] Ibid., Article 28 provides that "[t]he Commission shall decide which further written statements, in addition to the Statement of Claim and the Statement of Defense, shall be required from the parties or may be presented by them and shall fix the period of time for filing such statements. The Commission may seek the views of the parties in this regard."   [235] Ibid., Article 3.

5.09 "Voice" for Claimants

Whether there is a means by which thousands of claimants who may lack funds and legal sophistication can be provided with assistance and have a "voice" in the Claims Process, in addition to the right to be represented by their own counsel. Whether to allow *amicus curiae* briefs or similar submissions on claimants' behalf.

Editors' Commentary

In Claims Processes involving masses of claimants, there will often be non-governmental organizations and advocates' groups that wish to assist victims in gaining access to the Claims Process and receiving fair treatment by it. Designers of Mass Claims Processes and others may therefore wish to consider procedures that allow and regulate some form of participation by such advocates—in addition to permitting counsel to be employed in individual cases—as they can often facilitate the overall work of the Claims Process. This not only relates to evidence gathering, but also to making certain that the Claims Process is sufficiently transparent;[236] that outreach efforts are working effectively; that claimants understand their rights and the steps to take; and, most importantly, that the rights of thousands of claimants who by necessity are not physically present before the Tribunal or Commission in question will be adequately represented.

Some have suggested that each Mass Claims Process should provide an "ombudsman" or similar independent official to assist claimants and to give them a voice in the Claims Process. Although they generally do not expressly provide for an ombudsman, the Claims Processes described in this book tend to include opportunities for some assistance through the governments involved, or the staff of the Claims Process. For example, the Commission for Real Property Claims of Displaced Persons and Refugees (CRPC) in Bosnia and Herzegovina had a Claimant Query Response Team which provided information to assist claimants during the claims collection phase and responded to queries throughout the life of the Claims Process, and a claimant assistance program providing free legal aid. The American Arbitration Association (AAA) illustrative case also utilized a "claimants' representative" nominated by the plaintiffs' class action counsel, in the role of an ombudsman for the duration of the Claims Process.

---

[236] See section 8.01 below, on issues of transparency and reporting.

(a) Iran–United States Claims Tribunal (Iran–US CT)—claims relating to the 1979 Islamic Revolution

The Iran–US CT Tribunal Rules allow each of the two Governments—or, in special circumstances, any other person who is not an arbitrating party in a particular case—to submit oral or written statements that are "likely to assist the tribunal in carrying out its task."[237] This practice is tantamount to submission of an *amicus curiae* brief to a national court.

No provisions are otherwise made for a "voice" in the Claims Process by persons other than, on one hand, the Government parties and their representatives, and, on the other hand, United States persons having claims of less than US$250,000 whom the Government represented and assisted with claims preparation (so-called "small claims").[238]

(b) United Nations Compensation Commission (UNCC)—claims relating to the 1990–1991 Gulf War

No provision was made in the UNCC Provisional Rules or the practice of the Commission for claimants as a group to have a "voice" in the Claims Process, other than through a lawyer or other representative.

Certain groups of claimants, however, who were not in a position to have a government submit claims on their behalf because they were stateless persons or refugees, had their claims submitted by certain international organizations pursuant to appointment by the UNCC Governing Council.[239]

(c) Commission for Real Property Claims of Displaced Persons and Refugees (CRPC)—claims relating to the 1992–1995 war in Bosnia and Herzegovina

Although the CRPC Book of Regulations on Procedure did not contain specific provisions on a "voice" for claimants in the Claims Process, it did contain explicit safeguards meant to ensure that the claimant was making informed decisions in the Claims Process:

"Before claims registration takes place, an authorized staff member is obliged to inform the potential claimant as to how to submit a claim, about evidence and other information relevant for submitting a claim. The authorized staff member is also obliged to

---

[237] Iran–US CT Tribunal Rules, Note 5 to Article 15.

[238] See Claims Settlement Declaration, Article III, paragraph 3.

[239] UNCC Governing Council Decision 5 of 18 October 1991, *Guidelines Relating to Paragraph 19 of the Criteria for Expedited Processing of Urgent Claims*, U.N. Doc. S/AC26/1991/5 (23 October

ensure that the potential claimant has expressed his free will regarding the disposal of the claimed real property."[240]

In 1999, CRPC established a Claimant Query Response Team (CQRT) to answer a large number of questions from claimants and non-governmental organizations concerning the Commission's procedures and other information. The CQRT consisted of four Public Information Officers who had been trained on the property laws and procedures, and who responded by telephone, written replies, and in person to tens of thousands of actual and potential claimants.[241] Furthermore, through a claimant assistance program, the CRPC legal advisors provided free legal advice and advocacy to claimants. CRPC intervened on behalf of thousands of claimants in cases of non-enforcement of its decisions.[242]

Finally, it is also worth noting that Annex 6 of the Dayton Peace Agreement established a Commission on Human Rights consisting of two parts: the Office of the Ombudsman and the Human Rights Chamber to address alleged or apparent violations of human rights.[243] Article 90 of the CRPC's own Book of Regulations provides that, in order to help monitor enforcement, the Executive Office will distribute summaries of CRPC decisions to, *inter alia*, the Office of the Ombudsman and the Human Rights Chamber on a monthly basis.[244]

(d) Claims Resolution Tribunal for Dormant Accounts in Switzerland (CRT-I)—first claims tribunal for assets deposited in Swiss banks

In the CRT-I Claims Process, parties could not only be represented and assisted by persons of their choice, but also by "counsel provided by voluntary organizations."[245]

There were no specific provisions on *amicus* briefs or other outside "voices" in the Claims Process.

(e) Claims Resolution Tribunal (CRT-II)—second claims tribunal for assets deposited in Swiss banks

Except for the role of counsel acting for the plaintiffs in the class action known as the Holocaust Victim Assets Litigation that resulted in the Settlement

---

1991). UNCC Governing Council Decision 1of 2 August 1991, *Criteria for Expedited Processing of Urgent Claims*, U.N. Doc. S/AC.26/1991/1 (2 August 1991), paragraph 19.

[240] CRPC Book of Regulations on Procedure, Article 25.
[241] See CRPC End of Mandate Report, pp. 15–16.   [242] Ibid., p. 25.
[243] Dayton Peace Agreement, Annex 6, Chapter 2, Part A, Article II.
[244] CRPC Book of Regulations on Procedure, Article 90.
[245] CRT-I Rules of Procedure, Article 39.

Agreement, CRT-II does not provide a specific mechanism by which claimants can have an advocate or "voice" in the Claims Process. Numerous victims advocacy groups have taken an active interest in the litigation. For example, they have made proposals, in response to the Court's solicitation, for how to distribute possible unclaimed residual funds of the US$1.25 billion Settlement Fund among needy Nazi victims.[246]

(f) Housing and Property Claims Commission (HPCC)—claims relating to the 1999 conflict in Kosovo

The UNMIK Regulation governing the HPCC Claims Process provides that the Housing and Property Directorate (HPD), in addition to itself investigating claims and obtaining relevant evidence from public records, companies, or private individuals, may cooperate with and receive information from "any intergovernmental, governmental or non-governmental entity." Also, it may "delegate any of its functions to the responsible municipal service . . . as it considers appropriate."[247] This broad power in some cases results in claimants' causes being supported by organizations external to the Claims Process.

(g) Mass Claims Processes administered by the International Organization for Migration (IOM)

German Forced Labour Compensation Programme (GFLCP)—claims against Germany and German industry for Nazi injustice

The system set up to implement the GFLCP Claims Process does not provide a specific means by which claimants can have an advocate and a "voice" in the Claims Process. In practice, however, IOM receives information from various advocates and organizations active in certain victim communities and keeps such channels of communication open, as those advocates and organizations can often help in gathering evidence and reaching out to claimants. In fact, IOM has institutionalized this practice through periodic meetings with a steering group of the associations representing the most affected victims.

Holocaust Victim Assets Programme (HVAP)—claims pursuant to 1999 class action Settlement

Throughout the class action suit in the United States District Court for the Eastern District of New York, known as the Holocaust Victim Assets

---

[246] See section 1.05(e) above, on remedies. See also proposals for use of residual funds, available at www.swissbankclaims.com.   [247] UNMIK Regulation 2000/60, section 15.

Litigation, numerous victims' advocacy groups have taken an active interest in the Claims Process, submitting information and proposals to the Court, as well as offering assistance to IOM and the Jewish Claims Conference (JCC) in evaluating the claims. For example, many organizations that provide service to needy elderly Nazi victims (in Israel, the former Soviet Union, the United States, and elsewhere), responding to an invitation of the Court, submitted proposals for how best to allocate possible residual funds of the US$1.25 billion Settlement Fund among the most needy Holocaust survivors.[248]

(h) Eritrea–Ethiopia Claims Commission (EECC)—claims relating to the 1998–2000 war between Eritrea and Ethiopia

No provisions in the 12 December 2000 Agreement or in the EECC Rules of Procedure establish an "ombudsman" or other similar agency. Similarly, no provisions give claimants falling under any part of the Rules access to the Claims Process independently of the two Government parties, which remain solely responsible for gathering and filing all claims. Various international aid organizations and advocacy groups active in the afflicted region do provide information and assistance to the two Governments, but not to the Commission directly.

(i) Humanitarian insurance Claims Process administered by the Jewish Claims Conference (JCC) for the International Commission on Holocaust Era Insurance Claims (ICHEIC)

ICHEIC maintains several means by which all claimants, including the 8A1 claimants, can seek information about the Claims Process and voice their concerns. ICHEIC contracted with the JCC to provide a Call Center to answer questions or help claimants with problems relating to the submission of their claims or the status of their payment. Significantly, ICHEIC maintained an in-house position of a Claimant Advocate who was available as an ombudsman to resolve claimant concerns.

In addition, various other concerned parties made their services available to claimants, such as the Holocaust Claims Processing Office (HCPO) of the New York State Banking Department and the state insurance regulators from California, Florida, and other states with large numbers of Holocaust survivors.

---

[248] See, e.g., Special Master's Recommendations for Allocation of Possible Unclaimed Residual Funds (16 April 2004), available at www.swissbankclaims.com, and proposals on the same website for use of residual funds.

(j) American Arbitration Association (AAA)—an illustrative case

In the illustrative case, a Claimants' Representative closely monitored the entire Claims Process. The Claimants' Representative was designated by plaintiffs' counsel in the underlying class action, with the approval of the defendant insurance company and the United States federal district court overseeing the Settlement. The group of lawyers designated as Claimants' Representative then hired many other lawyers to assist in the Claims Process. Each claimant was thus assigned a Claimant Representative lawyer to help prepare his or her case and to be present on the telephone during the teleconference hearing.

5.10 Costs

By whom costs of parties in the Claims Process are paid, and, if parties do not bear their own costs, how the amounts are determined. (For matters relating to the costs of running the Claims Process itself, see section 7.03.)

Editors' Commentary

In Claims Processes whose procedural rules are based on the UNCITRAL Arbitration Rules or on the Permanent Court of Arbitration Optional Rules for Arbitrating Disputes between Two States (PCA Rules), the Claims Process in question may award the costs of the successful party as defined in those rules, including reasonable fees of lawyers.[249]

In contrast, the rules, or governing instruments, of some other Mass Claims Processes provide that the parties shall bear their own costs. Still, other rules and governing instruments are silent on the subject, leaving this often vexing issue to be faced at a later stage.

(a) Iran–United States Claims Tribunal (Iran–US CT)—claims relating to the 1979 Islamic Revolution

The Iran–US CT Tribunal Rules define "costs" as including only:

> "(a) The costs of expert advice and of other special assistance required for a particular case by the arbitral tribunal;

---

[249] See UNCITRAL Arbitration Rules, Articles 38–40; PCA Rules, Articles 38–40.

(b)   The travel and other expenses of witnesses to the extent such expenses are approved by the arbitral tribunal;

(c)   The costs for legal representation and assistance of the successful party if such costs were claimed during the arbitral proceedings, and only to the extent that the arbitral tribunal determines that the amount of such costs is reasonable."[250]

The Rules specify that the "costs of arbitration . . . shall in principle be borne by the unsuccessful party," but that the Tribunal "may apportion each of such costs between the parties if it determines that apportionment is reasonable, taking into account the circumstances of the case."[251] The Tribunal also decides which party shall bear the costs of legal representation, or it may also apportion such costs as it deems reasonable.[252]

In practice, some awards have included costs and attorneys' fees[253] and some have awarded a standard amount bearing no relationship to actual costs incurred,[254] while others have not awarded any costs to the prevailing party.[255]

(b) United Nations Compensation Commission (UNCC)—claims relating to the 1990–1991 Gulf War

Parties before the UNCC bear their own costs. UNCC Governing Council Decision 1 provided that no compensation would be paid to a party for attorneys' fees and other expenses of claims preparation under category "C".[256] The Commission issued decisions clarifying, for example, that governments could offset their costs of processing claims on behalf of claimants by deducting a small fee from payments ultimately made to those claimants, as long as the governments provided explanations satisfactory to the Governing Council for any processing costs so deducted, and as long as such fees were commensurate with the actual expenditure of the governments.[257]

---

[250] Iran–US CT Tribunal Rules, Article 38, paragraph 1.

[251] Ibid., Article 40, paragraph 1.   [252] Ibid., Article 40, paragraph 2.

[253] See, e.g., *Vera-Jo Miller Aryeh, et al.* and *The Islamic Republic of Iran*, Award No. 581/842/843/844-1 (22 May 1997), 33 Iran–U.S. C.T.R. p. 272 (award of $20,000 in arbitration costs).

[254] See, e.g., *George E. Davidson (Homayounjah)* and *The Government of the Islamic Republic of Iran*, Award No. 585–457–1 (5 March 1998), 34 Iran–U.S. C.T.R. p. 3 (award of $20,000 in arbitration costs).

[255] See, e.g., *Starrett Housing Corporation, et al.* and *The Government of the Islamic Republic of Iran, et al.*, Final Award No. 314–24–1 (14 August 1987), 16 Iran–U.S. C.T.R. p. 112, at p. 235, paragraph 372. But see Concurring Opinion of Judge Howard M. Holtzmann for discussion of reasons why costs, including attorneys' fees, should be awarded to the prevailing party. Ibid. at pp. 254–255.

[256] UNCC Governing Council Decision 1 of 2 August 1991, *Criteria for Expedited Processing of Urgent Claims*, U.N. Doc. S/AC.26/1991/1 (2 August 1991), paragraph 16.

[257] UNCC Governing Council Decision 18 of 24 March 1994, *Distribution of Payments and Transparency*, U.N. Doc. S/AC.26/Dec.18 (1994), Part I, paragraph 1. This fee may not exceed 1.5% of awards payable in expedited claims categories, and 3% of awards in additional claims categories.

If a government that had deducted a processing fee for claims of States in category "F" (government claims) later received compensation for such costs, it was then required to reimburse to claimants those fees deducted.[258] This applied equally to the distribution of payments by any person, authority, or body designated by the Commission to collect and submit claims on behalf of persons who were not in a position to have their claims submitted by a government.[259]

In 2005, the Governing Council took a decision regarding claim preparation costs in categories "D", "E", and "F" (for individual claims in excess of US$100,000, corporate claims, and government claims, respectively). In that decision, the Council, after noting that certain claimants had requested awards in respect of such costs, but noting also the imminent completion of the Claims Process and the unavailability of adequate funds, decided "not to give any further consideration to claims preparation costs."[260]

(c) Commission for Real Property Claims of Displaced Persons and Refugees (CRPC)—claims relating to the 1992–1995 war in Bosnia and Herzegovina

The CRPC Book of Regulations on Procedure did not contain any provision on awarding fees and expenses to claimants. In practice, no such fees or expenses which they incurred were awarded.

(d) Claims Resolution Tribunal for Dormant Accounts in Switzerland (CRT-I)—first claims tribunal for assets deposited in Swiss banks

The CRT-I Rules of Procedure provided that "[e]ach party shall bear at its own expense all costs, including fees and expenses of lawyers, accountants and other professionals, incurred in connection with such representation."[261] However, in the case of needy claimants, or in complex cases requiring special efforts by a claimant to prove his or her entitlement, a claims panel or Sole Arbitrator could award a claimant up to US$5,000 for costs and expenses.[262]

---

[258] UNCC Governing Council Decision 18 of 24 March 1994, *Distribution of Payments and Transparency*, U.N. Doc. S/AC.26/Dec.18 (1994), Part I, paragraph 1. [259] Ibid., Part II.

[260] See UNCC Governing Council Decision 250 of 30 June 2005, *Claims Preparation Costs*, U.N. Doc. S/AC.26/Dec.250 (2005) (30 June 2005). [261] CRT-I Rules of Procedure, Article 39.

[262] Ibid. An information brochure for claimants issued by CRT-I, stated, in answer to "Frequently Asked Questions," p. 10, that, "as a general matter you will be responsible for the cost of any lawyers, accountants or other professionals you may choose to retain. Under certain limited

(e) Claims Resolution Tribunal (CRT-II)—second claims tribunal for assets deposited in Swiss banks

The CRT-II claimants themselves bear any costs they may incur in pursuing and presenting their claims.[263]

(f) Housing and Property Claims Commission (HPCC)—claims relating to the 1999 conflict in Kosovo

The rules of the HPCC Claims Process provide that "[n]o party may recover any costs from any other party in connection with proceedings before the [Housing and Property] Directorate or Commission."[264] Parties thus bear their own costs, if any.

(g) Mass Claims Processes administered by the International Organization for Migration (IOM): *German Forced Labour Compensation Programme (GFLCP) for claims against Germany and German industry for Nazi injustice, and Holocaust Victim Assets Programme (HVAP) for claims pursuant to 1999 class action Settlement*

Claimants in both the GFLCP and HVAP Claims Processes were advised—on the claim forms and on the official websites of the Claims Processes—that they did not need to retain a lawyer to assist them with their claims. Claimants who nevertheless chose to employ legal counsel or incurred other costs in relation to submitting their claims do not receive any reimbursements for such costs.

(h) Eritrea–Ethiopia Claims Commission (EECC)—claims relating to the 1998–2000 war between Eritrea and Ethiopia

As of 31 January 2006, all claims before the EECC alleging damages both to natural and juridical persons had been presented as Government-to-Government claims in accordance with the alternate procedure described in section 1.04(h) above. There had not yet been any decisions or agreements on whether a Government that thus presents such claims may seek to recoup some

---

circumstances, you may be awarded up to 5,000 US$ as a full or partial reimbursement of your cost and expenses."

[263] CRT-II Governing Rules, Article 36.   [264] UNMIK Regulation 2000/60, section 22.4.

of its costs—costs being one of the issues remaining to be addressed in the damages phase of the Claims Process.

(i) Humanitarian insurance Claims Process administered by the Jewish Claims Conference (JCC) for the International Commission on Holocaust Era Insurance Claims (ICHEIC)

The 8A1 Claim Process was funded by the ICHEIC Humanitarian Fund, a fund created through contributions of the signatories of the ICHEIC Memorandum of Understanding (MOU Companies) and the German Foundation "Remembrance, Responsibility and Future." While not required, some claimants did have representatives, including lawyers, submit claims on their behalf. All payments of humanitarian awards were made directly to the actual claimant, and not through any intermediary. There were no provisions for payment of costs of claimants of making their claims.

(j) American Arbitration Association (AAA)—an illustrative case

The Settlement Agreement in the illustrative case provided that all costs, including provision of attorneys for claimants and all fees of the AAA, as well as the fees of the Arbitrators, were to be paid by the defendant insurance company. Hence, there was no cost to claimants.

5.11 Awarding Interest

Whether awards of compensation pursuant to the Claims Process include interest. If so, how the interest rate is determined, for what period it is paid, and whether simple or compound interest is awarded.

Editors' Commentary

Awarding interest is an established legal principle in international arbitration and court litigation.[265] Some Mass Claims Processes have awarded interest, even where the constituting instrument or rules of procedure include no

---

[265] See, e.g., *The Islamic Republic of Iran* and *The United States of America*, Decision No. DEC 65-A19-FT (30 September 1987), 16 Iran–U.S.C.T.R. p. 285, at pp. 289–290 ("it is customary for

express provision concerning interest, on the ground that the governing law that the Tribunal or Commission should apply provides for interest. Interest awarded has been simple interest, and none of the Claims Processes described in this book has thus far awarded compound interest.[266]

The rules governing the two Claims Resolution Tribunals for dormant accounts in Switzerland (CRT-I and CRT-II) provide that awards shall be adjusted upward for interest lost and bank fees charged, and they include formulas for computation. The constituting instruments and rules governing other Mass Claims Processes are either silent on the subject of interest or state that interest may be paid, but include no provisions on the rate of interest or method of calculation.

(a) Iran–United States Claims Tribunal (Iran–US CT)—claims relating to the 1979 Islamic Revolution

The Iran–US CT Tribunal Rules do not specifically provide for awarding interest to parties. However, the Tribunal has considered it appropriate that interest be paid.[267] Rulings as to whether to award interest, and the amount of interest actually awarded, have been made on a case-by-case basis. Some Chambers have generally decided the rate of interest by applying a formula established by Chamber One that takes into account that interest rates vary both upward and downward during the period for which interest is granted.[268] In other cases, interest has been granted at a rate considered fair, but without using a fixed formula.[269]

(b) United Nations Compensation Commission (UNCC)—claims relating to the 1990–1991 Gulf War

Pursuant to a decision by the UNCC Governing Council, interest was to be awarded "from the date the loss occurred until the date of payment, at a rate

arbitral tribunals to award interest as part of an award for damages, notwithstanding the absence of any express reference to interest in the *compromis*").

[266] But see arguments that compound interest should be awarded in *Starett Housing Corporation* and *The Government of the Islamic Republic of Iran et al.*, Concurring Opinion of Judge Howard M. Holtzmann, Final Award No. 314–24–1 (14 August 1987), 16 Iran–U.S.C.T.R. p. 112, at pp. 251–254.

[267] See, e.g., *The Islamic Republic of Iran* and *The United States of America*, Decision No. DEC 65-A19-FT (30 September 1987), 16 Iran–U.S. C.T.R. p. 285, at p. 290, paragraph 12.

[268] See, e.g., *Sylvania Technical Systems, Inc.* and *The Government of the Islamic Republic of Iran*, Award No. 180–64–1 (27 June 1985), 8 Iran–U.S. C.T.R. p. 298, pp. 320–322.

[269] See, e.g., *McCollough & Company, Inc.* and *The Ministry of Post, Telegraph and Telephone, et al.*, Award No 225–89–3 (22 April 1986), 8 Iran–U.S. C.T.R. p. 3, at pp. 26–31.

sufficient to compensate successful claimants for the loss of use of the principal amount of the award."[270] In the light of the limited funds available, the Governing Council determined that interest would only be paid after the principal amount of all awards had been paid out, and it postponed decision on the methods of calculation and payment of interest.[271]

It was left to the panels of Commissioners deciding cases in the six different categories of claims to determine the dates when losses occurred and from which interest—provided that funds would be sufficient to award interest—began to accrue in the respective categories. For example, three panels deciding urgent claims of individuals decided that 2 August 1990, the date of the Iraqi invasion of Kuwait, was the date on which interest began to accrue.[272] A panel deciding claims of States and international organizations determined that, because the claimed losses arose fairly regularly throughout the period of the occupation, the midpoint of the occupation period, 16 November 1990, was the date of loss for the purpose of interest calculation.[273] A panel deciding claims by corporate and public sector enterprises determined, in the case of a certain oil well blowout control claim, that interest had begun to accrue during the period from October 1990 until the end of July 1992, during which the relevant loss occurred. It therefore fixed a midpoint, 15 October 1991, as the date the loss occurred for purposes of interest calculation.[274]

The question of when interest ended was left for decision by the Governing Council. In 2005, the Council, having given "consideration to the issue of the

---

[270] UNCC Governing Council Decision 16 of 18 December 1992, *Awards of interest*, U.N. Doc. S/AC.26/1992/16 (4 January 1993), paragraph 1.   [271] Ibid., paragraphs 2 and 3.

[272] See *Report and Recommendations made by the Panel of Commissioners Concerning the First Instalment of Claims for Departure from Iraq or Kuwait (Category "A" Claims)*, 15 September 1994, U.N. Doc. S/AC.26/1994/2 (21 October 1994), p. 23 (section IV.C.3); *Report and Recommendations made by the Panel of Commissioners Concerning the First Instalment of Individual Claims for Damages up to US$100,000 (Category "C" Claims)*, 2 September 1994, U.N. Doc. S/AC.26/1994/3 (21 December 1994), p. 33 (section II.G); *Report and Recommendations made by the Panel of Commissioners Concerning Part One of the First Instalment of Individual Claims for Damages above US$100,000 (Category "D" Claims)*, 6 October 1997, U.N. Doc. S/AC.26/1998/1 (3 February 1998), p. 20, paragraph 65; and *Report and Recommendations made by the Panel of Commissioners Concerning Part Two of the First Instalment of Individual Claims for Damages above US$100,000 (Category "D" Claims)*, 5 February 1998, U.N. Doc. S/AC.26/1998/3 (12 March 1998), p. 17, paragraph 68.

[273] *Report and Recommendations made by the Panel of Commissioners Concerning Part One of the First Instalment of Claims by Governments and International Organizations (Category "F" Claims)*, 23 September 1997, U.N. Doc. S/AC.26/1997/6 (18 December 1997), p. 27, paragraphs 103 and 104.

[274] *Report and Recommendations made by the Panel of Commissioners Appointed to Review the Well Blowout Control Claims (The "WBC" Claim)*, 15 November 1996, U.N. Doc. S/AC.26/1996/5/Annex (18 December 1996), pp. 65–66, paragraph 229.

methods of calculation and of payment of interest," and taking into account "all relevant circumstances, in particular the unavailability of adequate funds and the imminent completion of the [Claims Process]," decided "to take no further action with respect to the issue of awards of interest."[275]

(c) Commission for Real Property Claims of Displaced Persons and Refugees (CRPC)—claims relating to the 1992–1995 war in Bosnia and Herzegovina

The CRPC Books of Regulations did not contain any explicit provisions for awarding interest. The constituting instrument, the Dayton Peace Agreement, did provide that any claimants found by the Commission to be the lawful owners of the property in question could, in lieu of return of their real property, be awarded "just compensation" as determined by the Commission.[276] There were never any funds available, however, for compensation payments by the CRPC, and the issue of interest therefore did not arise.[277]

(d) Claims Resolution Tribunal for Dormant Accounts in Switzerland (CRT-I)—first claims tribunal for assets deposited in Swiss banks

In the CRT-I Claims Process, victims of Nazi persecution, in cases where the amount in a dormant account was known, were entitled to receive the amount of the deposit, adjusted upward to compensate for unpaid simple interest lost since 1945, not compounded.[278] An additional upward adjustment was made to compensate for bank fees deducted from the account during that period. These adjustments were not available to account holders who had not been victims of Nazi persecution.[279]

The Board of Trustees of the Independent Claims Resolution Foundation (ICRF) commissioned a panel of international experts to establish guidelines on interest, and for adjustment of bank fees, that the Arbitrators were required to apply.[280] Using such guidelines on interest and fees to be awarded simplified the awarding of interest and facilitated administration.

---

[275] UNCC Governing Council Decision 243 of 10 March 2005, *Awards of Interest*, U.N. Doc. S/AC.26/Dec.243 (2005) (10 March 2005), p. 1.

[276] Dayton Peace Agreement, Annex 7, Chapter 2, Article XII, paragraph 2.

[277] See CRPC End of Mandate Report, Annex B—*Annex 7 Compensation Fund Unrealised*.

[278] CRT-I Interest Guidelines, Article 4A, available at www.crt-ii.org/_crt-i.

[279] Ibid., Article 4B.

[280] See CRT-I Rules of Procedure, Article 16, and CRT-I Interest Guidelines, available at www.crt-ii. org/_crt-i.

(e) Claims Resolution Tribunal (CRT-II)—second claims tribunal for assets deposited in Swiss banks

The CRT-II Governing Rules provide that the amount of its awards shall be the amount in the claimed bank accounts, as established by bank records or by a schedule set forth in the Rules,

" . . . adjusted by (a) reducing the Awards by the amount of any interest paid to the Accounts for which the Awards are being made, (b) increasing the Awards by the amount of any fees and charges deducted from such Accounts, and (c) multiplying the resulting account by [a factor] to bring the Awards up to current value."[281]

(f) Housing and Property Claims Commission (HPCC)—claims relating to the 1999 conflict in Kosovo

The issue of interest has not arisen at the HPCC with respect to claims for compensation of damage to, or destruction of, real property, nor has it been deemed relevant in circumstances where compensation is awarded in lieu of moving back into socially-owned property. Compensation is set at the present market value of the property, taking into account possible subsidization at the time of purchase.

(g) Mass Claims Processes administered by the International Organization for Migration (IOM)

German Forced Labour Compensation Programme (GFLCP)—claims against Germany and German industry for Nazi injustice

The GFLCP Claims Process awards fixed-amount compensation, except in the case of claims for property losses decided by the Property Claims Commission. No interest is payable on awards of fixed amounts.

The Property Claims Commission determines individual amounts of compensation for property losses. It does not award interest, nor do the Rules of the Commission expressly mention interest.

Holocaust Victim Assets Programme (HVAP)—claims pursuant to 1999 class action Settlement

Awards in the HVAP Claims Process are exclusively fixed amounts of money that do not include interest. No interest is paid, or payable, on the awards.

---

[281] CRT-II Governing Rules, Article 31, paragraph 1. The current value adjustment factor is reviewed and reestablished annually in accordance with a formula established by the Special Masters and approved by the Court seized of the class action known as the Holocaust Victim Assets Litigation.

(h) Eritrea–Ethiopia Claims Commission (EECC)—claims relating to the 1998–2000 war between Eritrea and Ethiopia

The constituting instrument, the 12 December 2000 Agreement, and the EECC Rules of Procedure provide that interest may be awarded for individual claims, but no detailed provisions are included on matters such as the rate of interest, the period for which interest should be paid, whether simple or compound interest should be awarded, and so on.[282] These questions are left for determination by the Commission once its proceedings have progressed to the point of determinations of damages.

(i) Humanitarian insurance Claims Process administered by the Jewish Claims Conference (JCC) for the International Commission on Holocaust Era Insurance Claims (ICHEIC)

ICHEIC set the 8A1 humanitarian award at US$1,000 (or the equivalent in another currency) per claimant. Because this amount was fixed by ICHEIC as a symbolic payment and did not constitute compensation for specific insurance policies, the issue of interest did not arise in this Claims Process.

(j) American Arbitration Association (AAA)—an illustrative case

The amount of the monetary awards in the illustrative case was pre-determined, based on qualifying criteria, in the Settlement Agreement. It did not include interest as such, although interest may have been part of the overall negotiations in determining the amounts due at each level of claims.

5.12 Settlement

Inclusion of provisions dealing with settlement and/or withdrawal of claims.

Editors' Commentary

Many Mass Claims Processes provide in their procedural rules a mechanism whereby a claimant may withdraw a claim or settle it independently with the respondent. Some Claims Processes are designed to promote settlement, such

---

[282] Eritrea–Ethiopia Agreement of 12 December 2000, Article 5, paragraph 14; EECC Rules of Procedure, Article 29.

as the Housing and Property Claims Commission (HPCC) in Kosovo, in order to reduce the total number of claims and expedite the recovery of amounts owed. The use of mediation in the American Arbitration Association (AAA) illustrative case also had the effect of promoting settlements that were suited to claimants' needs and still acceptable to the defendant. The Mass Claims Processes described in this book do not typically include safeguards to ensure that claimants who consider settlement have the opportunity to make an informed choice, and that they not be coerced, due to an uneven bargaining situation, to accept unfavorable terms. Furthermore, there are not typically provisions for notifying any interested third persons who might be affected by a withdrawal, or who should be party to settlement discussions. Designers of future Mass Claims Processes and others might wish to consider adding explicit protections for parties and third persons in such situations.

Claims Processes that have Rules based on the UNCITRAL Arbitration Rules or the Permanent Court of Arbitration Optional Rules for Arbitrating Disputes between Two States (PCA Rules) permit awards on agreed terms to be issued to effectuate settlement of claims.

(a) Iran–United States Claims Tribunal (Iran–US CT)—claims relating to the 1979 Islamic Revolution

The Iran–US CT Tribunal Rules include a provision to govern if the parties agree to settle a claim. In that event, the Tribunal can issue an order terminating the case. As under the UNCITRAL Arbitration Rules, the Tribunal has the discretion to refuse to do so if it considers settlement inappropriate in the circumstances of a case. A settlement of a dispute can also result in an arbitral award on agreed terms.[283]

The Notes to Article 15 of the Tribunal Rules provide that the Tribunal may order parties to appear for a pre-hearing conference,[284] and in that conference, the Internal Guidelines of the Tribunal provide that it may inquire concerning the status of any settlement discussions.[285]

(b) United Nations Compensation Commission (UNCC)—claims relating to the 1990–1991 Gulf War

The UNCC Provisional Rules provided that a government or entity that submitted a claim to the Commission could at any time withdraw it. Furthermore,

---

[283] Iran–US CT Tribunal Rules, Article 34, paragraph   [284] Ibid., Note 4 to Article 15.
[285] Iran–US CT, Internal Guidelines of the Tribunal, 1 Iran–U.S. C.T.R. p. 98, paragraph 2(c).

in any case where a claim had already been paid, settled, or otherwise resolved, it was to be withdrawn.[286]

(c) Commission for Real Property Claims of Displaced Persons and Refugees (CRPC)—claims relating to the 1992–1995 war in Bosnia and Herzegovina

The CRPC Book of Regulations on Procedure included a provision that claimants before the Commission were entitled to amend, supplement, or withdraw their claims at any time until such time as decision had been rendered. The withdrawal of a claim had to be explicit, in writing, and signed by the claimant, and a regional office that received a withdrawal was required to immediately inform the Executive Office.[287]

(d) Claims Resolution Tribunal for Dormant Accounts in Switzerland (CRT-I)—first claims tribunal for assets deposited in Swiss banks

In certain cases at CRT-I, if a respondent bank made an offer of settlement, the claim could be submitted for "Fast Track Review." The payment to settle offered by the bank had to comply with the CRT-I Interest Guidelines,[288] and the Arbitrator was required to investigate the matter and determine the plausibility of the claimant's entitlement. The Arbitrator was also required to satisfy himself or herself that the settlement offer was fair and equitable in view of the fact that most of the claimants in this Claims Process were elderly, often spoke only another language, and were typically not represented by legal counsel.

(e) Claims Resolution Tribunal (CRT-II)—second claims tribunal for assets deposited in Swiss banks

The Plan of Allocation and Distribution in the class action known as the Holocaust Victim Assets Litigation, and the CRT-II Governing Rules, contain no specific provision for settlement and/or withdrawal of claims.

(f) Housing and Property Claims Commission (HPCC)—claims relating to the 1999 conflict in Kosovo

One of the core functions of the Housing and Property Directorate (HPD) is to seek to settle claims amicably through agreements between the parties. The

---

[286] UNCC Provisional Rules, Article 42.

[287] CRPC Book of Regulations on Procedure, Article 31.

[288] See section 5.11(d) above, on interest at CRT-I, and see CRT-I Rules of Procedure, Articles 11 and 12.

Directorate may take whatever steps it sees fit to facilitate such settlement and may develop standardized forms of settlement agreements for use by the parties, as well as certify such agreements once they have been signed.[289] Claims which the HPD cannot resolve successfully through mediation are referred to the Commission for decision.[290] Any withdrawals are recorded by the Directorate.

(g) **Mass Claims Processes administered by the International Organization for Migration (IOM):** *German Forced Labour Compensation Programme (GFLCP) for claims against Germany and German industry for Nazi injustice, and Holocaust Victim Assets Programme (HVAP) for claims pursuant to 1999 class action Settlement*

Neither the GFLCP nor the HVAP Claims Process has specific provisions dealing with settlement or withdrawal of claims.

(h) **Eritrea–Ethiopia Claims Commission (EECC)—claims relating to the 1998–2000 war between Eritrea and Ethiopia**

Under the constituting instrument, the 12 December 2000 Agreement, the two parties may agree at any time to settle outstanding claims—individually or by categories—through direct negotiation or by referring them to another mutually agreed settlement mechanism.[291] The EECC Rules of Procedure explain the effect of a settlement in language drawn from the PCA Rules.[292] If the parties agree to settle a claim or group of claims before the Commission makes its award, the Commission shall either terminate the relevant proceedings or, if the parties so request and the Commission agrees, record the settlement as an arbitral award on agreed terms.[293]

(i) **Humanitarian insurance Claims Process administered by the Jewish Claims Conference (JCC) for the International Commission on Holocaust Era Insurance Claims (ICHEIC)**

Generally, 8A1 Claims had passed through a matching process in which the MOU Companies searched their relevant archives and passed the claims on to

---

[289] UNMIK Regulation 2000/60, section 10.1.
[290] UNMIK Regulation 1999/23, section 1.2.
[291] Eritrea–Ethiopia Agreement of 12 December 2000, Article 5, paragraph 16.
[292] PCA Rules, Article 34.
[293] EECC Rules of Procedure, Article 20, paragraph 1. An award on "agreed terms" is enforceable in States adhering to the Convention on the Recognition and Enforcement of Foreign Arbitral Awards, done at New York, 10 June 1958, 330 UNTS 38 (New York Convention).

the 8A1 humanitarian Claims Process only after no match was found. In rare cases, ICHEIC would locate a policy with an MOU Company after it had been sent to the JCC for evaluation for a humanitarian award. In such cases, ICHEIC informed the JCC of the settlement offer in the named company process, and instructed the JCC to withdraw the claim from the 8A1 Claims Process and not to issue the humanitarian payment.

(j) American Arbitration Association (AAA)—an illustrative case

In the illustrative case, settlement was available at every stage, from the time of the initiation of the claim onward. The use of a separate mediation conference resulted in a significant number of claims being resolved and not proceeding to arbitration. Claims were withdrawn only upon request of the claimant or upon settlement of a claim.

5.13 Appeals

Whether the rules include provisions for review or appeal of decision within the Claims Process itself. (See section 2.04 on the final and binding nature of decisions.)

Editors' Commentary

One of the chief attributes of international Mass Claims Processes is that they are *ad hoc* regimes whose decisions are to be final and binding.[294] Therefore, to the extent appeals are allowed, they are normally handled within the system itself. Most Claims Processes provide at a minimum for correction of any errors in an award or decision, and some also allow claimants or interested third parties to request that the decision-makers reconsider a decision if new evidence is discovered which might have altered the outcome of the claim had it been known earlier. However, where applicable national laws provide automatic rights of review of such claims, the right of review may not need to be written into the governing documents of a Claims Process. This was the case at the Claims Resolution Tribunal for Dormant Accounts in Switzerland (CRT-I), which was governed by Swiss law. It may be prudent in other international

---

[294] See note in section 2.03(g) above, on special regimes.

Mass Claims Processes to alert parties, who may not be familiar with the particular national law that applies, of any automatic right of review that may apply.

It is of interest to note the rule of the Appeals Body of the German Forced Labour Compensation Programme (GFLCP) that, because the overall purpose of the Claims Process is to compensate victims of the Holocaust for serious harms and losses, the decisions of the IOM Appeals Body can only alter an initial decision in the claimant's favor; the claimant cannot be made worse off by lodging an appeal of the initial decision.[295]

(a) Iran–United States Claims Tribunal (Iran–US CT)—claims relating to the 1979 Islamic Revolution

The constituting instrument of the Iran–US CT, the Claims Settlement Declaration, provides that "[a]ll decisions and awards of the Tribunal shall be final and binding."[296] Thus, there is no possibility of appeal or substantive review within the Claims Process. However, the Tribunal Rules, like the UNCITRAL Arbitration Rules, provide that a party may request the Tribunal to (i) correct any "errors in computation, any clerical or typographical errors, or any errors of similar nature;"[297] (ii) "make an additional award as to claims presented in the arbitral proceedings but omitted from the award;"[298] or (iii) "give an interpretation of the award."[299] An interpretation forms part of the award in question. Strict time limits are established for making and granting all such requests.

(b) United Nations Compensation Commission (UNCC)—claims relating to the 1990–1991 Gulf War

Under the UNCC Provisional Rules, the UNCC Governing Council could increase or reduce an award recommended to it by a panel of Commissioners.[300] It could also return a claim or group of claims to the panel that made the recommendation for further review.[301] In practice, however, the Council has approved all panel recommendations by consensus.

A decision of the Governing Council approving a panel report with respect to a claim or group of claims is final and not subject to appeal or review on

---

[295] See section 5.13(g) below. [296] Claims Settlement Declaration, Article IV, paragraph 1.
[297] Iran–US CT Tribunal Rules, Article 36, paragraph 1.
[298] Ibid., Article 37, paragraph 1. [299] Ibid., Article 35, paragraph 1.
[300] UNCC Provisional Rules, Article 40, paragraph 1. [301] Ibid., Article 40, paragraph 2.

procedural, substantive, or other grounds.[302] The Provisional Rules provide that computational, clerical, typographical, or other errors brought to the attention of the Executive Secretary will be reported to the Governing Council, and if the Council determines that a correction must be made, it will direct the Executive Secretary as to the proper method of correction.[303]

(c) Commission for Real Property Claims of Displaced Persons and Refugees (CRPC)—claims relating to the 1992–1995 war in Bosnia and Herzegovina

The CRPC Book of Regulations on Procedure contained extensive and detailed provisions on reconsideration by the Commission of decisions at the request of claimants or other persons having a legal interest in the property in question. Decisions issued by the CRPC contained a clause which stated that, although the decision was final, it could exceptionally be reconsidered by the Commission. This was the case, for example, when a claimant or an interested party presented new evidence that could have had a substantial influence on the outcome of the original decision.[304] Such requests had to be made within sixty days of discovering new evidence which could have materially affected the outcome of the original decision.[305] The Regulations required the Commission to consider such requests, along with any further evidence submitted, and authorized it to invite any party to provide further information in writing, if appropriate, or undertake investigations as it saw fit.[306] The Commission was to examine the request as soon as practicable and could "(a) refuse to admit the request as being inadmissible, not submitted within due time or as submitted by an unauthorised person; (b) reject the request as being unfounded; [or] (c) accept the request, revoke its previous decision and issue a new certificate."[307]

The Commission furthermore had the power to correct any errors or obvious mistakes in a decision by issuing a separate decision on correction.[308]

(d) Claims Resolution Tribunal for Dormant Accounts in Switzerland (CRT-I)—first claims tribunal for assets deposited in Swiss banks

There was no provision of appeal of a CRT-I award within the Claims Process itself, but under Swiss law—which the parties agreed governed the Claims

---

[302] UNCC Provisional Rules, Article 40, paragraph 4.
[303] Ibid., Article 41, paragraph 2.
[304] See CRPC Book of Regulations on Procedure, Article 76.
[305] Ibid., Chapter VIII "Reconsideration of Decisions" and Article 64(e).
[306] Ibid., Articles 82 and 83.
[307] Ibid., Articles 84 and 85.   [308] Ibid., Articles 73–75.

Process—a claimant had the right to challenge the award of the Arbitrators on certain limited grounds within thirty days.[309] The Tribunal had the authority to adjust awards to take into account interest and bank charges.[310]

(e) Claims Resolution Tribunal (CRT-II)—second claims tribunal for assets deposited in Swiss banks

The CRT-II Governing Rules provide for appeal of decisions in two separate circumstances: if their claims (i) have been ruled inadmissible by CRT-II, or (ii) have been awarded by CRT-II but subsequently denied enforcement by the United States federal district court seized of the class action known as the Holocaust Victim Assets Litigation. In either case, the appeal must be made through the Court-appointed Special Masters and within ninety days of the date of the letter accompanying the decision.[311] If appeals are submitted without a plausible suggestion of error or relevant new evidence, they may be denied summarily.[312]

The Governing Rules also allow the participating banks to appeal certain CRT-II decisions to the Court. If a bank believes that the Tribunal has inappropriately matched and researched a claim against the bank's total accounts database, the bank, through the Special Masters, may request the Court to review that decision.[313] The Special Masters shall ascertain the facts concerning the review request and report their recommendations to the Court.[314]

(f) Housing and Property Claims Commission (HPCC)—claims relating to the 1999 conflict in Kosovo

The UNMIK Regulation governing the HPCC Claims Process provides that a party to a claim, or a person having an interest who can show good cause why he or she did not participate as a party to the claim, may submit to the Housing and Property Directorate (HPD) a request for reconsideration of a decision of

---

[309] CRT-I Information Brochure, Answer to "Frequently Asked Questions," p. 11.

[310] See section 5.11(d) above, on interest at CRT-I.

[311] CRT-II Governing Rules, Article 30, paragraphs 1 and 2.

[312] Ibid., Article 30, paragraph 3.

[313] Ibid., Article 21, paragraph 1, provides that the conditions for matching a claim are that, "[f]or Claims that are determined to be Admissible and eligible for Matching under [the Rules] based on, among other things, a claim that the Account Owners gave Swiss addresses to the banks holding their Accounts, but for which no match to a Probable or Possible Account is determined . . . or for which a match to a Probable or Possible Account has been disconfirmed by the CRT, then such claim shall . . . be matched by the CRT with all the Accounts in the Total Accounts Databases of the Participating Banks, provided that a reasoned and satisfactory determination is made to proceed with such Matching and Research."   [314] Ibid., Article 21, paragraph 6(b).

the Commission within thirty days of being notified of such decision "(a) upon the presentation of legally relevant evidence, which was not considered by the Commission in deciding the claim; or (b) on the ground that there was a material error in the application of the [UNMIK] regulation."[315]

Any interested person who was not a party to the original claim and who can show good reasons for why he or she did not participate as a party thereto, may also request reconsideration within thirty days of learning of the decision, but he or she may not do so later than one year from the date of the decision.[316] If an eviction order from housing is pending when a reconsideration request is lodged, such eviction order shall be stayed until the Commission has decided on the request.[317]

(g) Mass Claims Processes administered by the International Organization for Migration (IOM)

German Forced Labour Compensation Programme (GFLCP)—claims against Germany and German industry for Nazi injustice

The German Foundation Act requires each partner organization implementing the Act—including IOM—to establish an internal appeals organ for slave and forced labor claims to which claimants can appeal if they disagree with the initial decision of the organization in question.[318] Pursuant to this, IOM created a three-Member Appeals Body that is independent and not subject to any outside instruction. Its rules of procedure are set out in a document entitled IOM Appeals Body for Forced Labour Claims: Principles and Rules of Appeals Procedure, and it applies to "appeals against initial IOM eligibility decisions on compensation claims for slave and forced labour or claims for personal injury that were submitted to IOM under Section 19 of the Foundation Act."[319] Eligible to submit appeals are (i) persons whose claims of compensation were denied, in whole or in part, by the initial decision; (ii) heirs of victims who died after having submitted claims to IOM but whose claims were denied; and (iii) lawyers and other representatives of claimants or their heirs.[320] Applications must be submitted in writing and mailed to the IOM no later than one hundred days from the date of the issuance of the initial decision.[321] The

---

[315] UNMIK Regulation 2000/60, section 14.1.   [316] Ibid., section 14.2.

[317] Ibid., section 14.3.   [318] German Foundation Act, section 19.

[319] IOM Appeals Body Principles and Rules, Article 2.   [320] Ibid., Article 4.

[321] Ibid., Article 5, paragraph D. If an appeal has been timely submitted, and if within six months after the death of the appellant no eligible heir has notified IOM of such death, the appeals procedure will terminate and the eligibility for award expire. Ibid., paragraph E.

appeals process is free of charge to the applicant, but costs incurred by the applicant in pursuing the appeal are not reimbursed by the Claims Process.[322]

The IOM Appeals Body applies the Foundation Act, decisions of the Foundation's Board of Trustees, and other official Foundation Directives, and it is also bound by IOM's guidelines concerning sub-categories of claims and the application of the "opening clause" in the Foundation Act.[323] The Appeals Body holds no oral hearings of claimants or third parties, and its work is confidential.[324] The Appeals Body makes decisions by majority vote, taking into account:

"(i)   the initial IOM decision and its rationale;
(ii) the statements and all material submitted by the appellant during the initial procedure;
(iii) the statements and all material submitted by the appellant during the appeals procedure;
(iv) information obtained from archives or other sources on the circumstances and facts relevant to the claim;
(v)   historic background information available to the Appeals Body regarding the circumstances prevailing during the National Socialist period."[325]

The Appeals Body can also solicit additional information, evidence, or clarification as it deems necessary for the appropriate and efficient consideration of appeals.[326] For efficient consideration and decision, the Appeals Body can group together any appeals that present similar facts or issues.[327] A decision of the Appeals Body is final and has the effect of either granting or denying an appeal, in whole or in part, setting forth the reasons for the decision. In no circumstances, however, will initial decisions on claims be changed to the disadvantage of the claimant.[328]

Decisions of the IOM Property Claims Commission are not subject to appeal to any other body. Claimants have the right to request reconsideration by the Commission itself of its decisions, but the only grounds for such reconsideration are (i) manifest error, or (ii) new evidence that was unavailable to the claimant at the time of submission of the claim or its supplements.[329] A request for reconsideration had to be received by the IOM Secretariat in Geneva within three months of the date of the Commission's initial decision,

---

[322] IOM Appeals Body Principles and Rules, Article 6.
[323] Ibid., Article 18. On the opening clause, see section 1.05(g) above.
[324] Ibid., Article 16, paragraph D, and Article 17.   [325] Ibid., Article 19, paragraphs A and B.
[326] Ibid., Article 20.   [327] Ibid., Article 19, paragraph C.
[328] Ibid., Article 21, paragraphs A–C and E.
[329] IOM Property Commission Supplemental Rules, section 25.1 and 25.2.

and the Supplemental Rules of the Commission list in detail the information which claimants were required to include in their request.[330]

Holocaust Victim Assets Programme (HVAP)—claims pursuant to 1999 class action Settlement

Different review or appellate mechanisms have been established for the separate classes of claims under the HVAP Claims Process. For Slave Labor Class I, appeals are decided by the same Appeals Body as reviews slave and forced labor appeals in the GFLCP Claims Process described in the preceding section, except that the HVAP appeals are subject to the further supervision of the United States federal district court overseeing the class action known as the Holocaust Victim Assets Litigation.[331] The reason for this arrangement is that the legal and evidentiary criteria for HVAP Slave Labor Class I claims are very similar to those which apply to slave and forced labor claims under GFLCP. Consequently, the Court concluded that appeals of Slave Labor Class I decisions should be dealt with by the IOM Appeals Body for Forced Labour Claims.

Different criteria apply to HVAP Slave Labor Class II claims, and the Special Master proposed in the Plan of Allocation and Distribution that decisions denying claims in Slave Labor Class II, upon request by a claimant, be reviewed by an independent Review Officer designated by IOM.[332] As for claims not recommended for payment during their initial evaluation, a different Review Officer—appointed by the Court and independent of IOM—will review such claims upon request by the claimant.[333]

Finally, with respect to the claims in the HVAP Refugee Class, which are governed by yet another set of criteria, a common appeals procedure applies for IOM and the Jewish Claims Conference (JCC), because both process claims in the Refugee Class—the JCC for Jewish claimants and the IOM for non-Jewish claimants.

(h) Eritrea–Ethiopia Claims Commission (EECC)—claims relating to the 1998–2000 war between Eritrea and Ethiopia

The two Government parties agreed that the EECC's decisions and awards shall be final and binding.[334] There are no provisions for appeal within or

---

[330] IOM Property Commission Supplemental Rules, section 25.3 and 25.5.
[331] Plan of Allocation and Distribution, p. 155.   [332] Ibid., p. 166.   [333] Ibid., p. 175.
[334] Eritrea–Ethiopia Agreement of 12 December 2000, Article 5, paragraph 17; EECC Rules of Procedure, Article 18, paragraph 4.

outside the Claims Process, but it has provisions for interpretation or correction modeled on the UNCITRAL Arbitration Rules. Thus, either party may, within sixty days after receiving an award, ask the Commission to give an interpretation of the award. Such interpretation is given in the sole discretion of the Commission, and any interpretation will form part of the award. The parties may request correction of errors (computational, clerical, or typographical) in an award. They may also petition the Commission for an additional award as to claims presented in the arbitral proceedings that were omitted from an award.[335]

(i) Humanitarian insurance Claims Process administered by the Jewish Claims Conference (JCC) for the International Commission on Holocaust Era Insurance Claims (ICHEIC)

The 8A1 humanitarian Claims Process provided no means for appeal. As noted in section 1.01(i) above, awards were offered strictly on a humanitarian basis and not pursuant to a legal right.

(j) American Arbitration Association (AAA)—an illustrative case

In the illustrative case, the Arbitrators' decisions were final and binding, but provisions were made for correcting computational and typographical errors in the awards.

---

[335] EECC Rules of Procedure, Article 21, paragraph 1.

Chapter 6

Administration, Facilities, and Computer Support

6.01 Management and Staffing

Legal, administrative, technical, and linguistic support required to implement the Claims Process. The organizational and management structure created to execute the identified functions. The type and level of expertise of the required personnel, and the corresponding job descriptions.

Editors' Commentary

An early and on-going task of the architects of each Mass Claims Process is to analyze and determine the level of administrative and technical support that it will require to perform its functions. Factors that are typically considered include: (i) the anticipated workload, based in the starting stages largely on the extent to which it is possible to estimate the number of claims that will be made; (ii) any deadlines established by the constituting instruments or mutually desired by the parties; (iii) whether the proceedings will be conducted and documents submitted in more than one language, thus requiring multi-lingual staff and/or translators; (iv) the extent to which hearings are anticipated that would require services of interpreters as well as translators,[1] and, if so, whether interpretation would be simultaneous (as at the United Nations), requiring interpreters with that special training and necessary equipment; (v) the volume of exhibits, memorials, and other written materials that will have to be filed and how they will be stored and distributed; (vi) whether the staff will be expected to perform legal and factual research, prepare background memoranda and analyses for those who decide the

---

[1] "Translators" express in writing a written text from one language into another; "interpreters" express orally an oral statement spoken in another language.

claims, and prepare drafts of decisions, orders or awards; and (vii) last but not least, whether the staff should include information technology specialists and other technical experts, such as statisticians, to develop customized software programs and databases, and generally to manage the technological aspects of the Claims Process. It should be recognized that this is not an exhaustive list and that the amount and nature of the needed support may have to be adjusted upward or downward on the basis of experience and the stage of the particular Claims Process.

While no single format or formula can be used to determine the administrative needs and organizational structure of all Mass Claims Processes, examples illustrating what has been done at the various Claims Processes described in this book are presented below, together with statistical information on size and characteristics of the staff, in order to provide context in determining whether the infrastructure that is described for a particular Claims Process is appropriate for another.

Annotations

(a) Iran–United States Claims Tribunal (Iran–US CT)—claims relating to the 1979 Islamic Revolution

The Tribunal had, at its peak, a support staff of over one hundred to aid the nine Members. Headed by a Secretary-General, the staff consisted of legal assistants to the Members, Registry personnel, interpreters and translators, and administrative support staff, all located in The Hague, the Netherlands. The policy is to employ staff personnel from Iran and the United States, as well as from a number of other countries. The Secretary-General is from neither Iran nor the United States. The Registry is headed by two Co-Registrars, one from Iran and one from the United States.

Although the Secretary-General is the chief administrative and financial officer of the Tribunal, a Committee on Financial and Administrative Questions, consisting of three Members (one from Iran, one from the United States, and one from a third country), makes recommendations to the Tribunal with respect to administrative and financial matters that require the Tribunal's approval, including the annual budget.

The Secretary-General is assisted in his work by a Deputy-Secretary-General (who also functions as special assistant to the President of the Tribunal in relation to pending cases), a Finance Officer, and a secretarial staff. The Finance Officer prepares the annual budget estimates, maintains the accounting records, and is responsible for the overall administration of the Tribunal's funds. The Administrative Officer is responsible for the administration of the Tribunal's Staff Rules, for the administration of the Tribunal's group health and social insurance schemes (in collaboration with the Finance Officer), and for the supervision of the General Services Staff.

The value of including legal assistants in the staff of the Tribunal has been widely recognized. Each Member is assisted by one legal assistant whom she or he recruits, chooses, and supervises. The President of the Tribunal, in addition to having one legal assistant, is also aided by the Deputy-Secretary-General. Each Member determines the role and scope of activities of his or her legal assistant, which may vary among different Members. The work which a Member and a legal assistant conduct together is respected as being confidential. Functions typically performed by legal assistants include assisting their Member by writing memoranda summarizing the allegations of the parties and the factual and legal issues in the case; researching choice of law issues and the terms of the governing law, which may include Iranian, United States, and international law; and preparing drafts of orders, awards, and opinions. Legal assistants generally attend hearings and deliberations. A Member sometimes delegates to a legal assistant the task of conferring with other legal assistants working on the same case to explore possible solutions to particular problems. Notwithstanding the valuable contributions of legal assistants, the responsibility of making decisions is vested only in Members, as required by the Tribunal Rules.[2] For administrative purposes, the legal assistants are considered to be part of the Secretariat.

The two Co-Registrars, of Iranian and United States nationality, respectively, are the heads of the Tribunal's Registry. They are responsible for the important work of receiving and filing incoming documents, as well as ensuring appropriate distribution thereof. In addition, they maintain and produce a Quarterly Index of relevant statistics. The Co-Registrars are assisted in their work by two Registry clerks.

English and Farsi are the Tribunal's two official languages.[3] The Tribunal's Language Services Division is responsible for translating into English or Farsi, as the case may be, all official documents generated by the Tribunal. The Language Services Division is also responsible for arranging for simultaneous interpretation into Farsi and English during Tribunal hearings. At some stages of the Tribunal's work, translation and interpretation have been performed by full-time in-house Tribunal staff, and at other times, in whole or in part, by outside individuals employed for particular purposes. At its peak, the Tribunal employed several translators and revisers as full-time staff members, as well as

---

[2] Iran–US CT Tribunal Rules, Article 31.
[3] See note in section 5.03(a) above, on the use of the terms "Farsi" and "Persian".

two in-house interpreters. The Tribunal began downscaling the Language Services Division in the early 1990s due to changes in the scheduling pattern and volume of the Tribunal's work. As of 31 January 2006, the Language Services Division consists of one in-house translator and one reviser, with outside freelance interpreters employed when needed.

(b) United Nations Compensation Commission (UNCC)—claims relating to the 1990–1991 Gulf War

The UNCC has received support from the United Nations Office at Geneva (UNOG) in the recruitment of staff and procurement of services. The UNCC Secretariat is the Commission's executive branch. At its height, it had at one time approximately three hundred professional and general services staff in Geneva, Switzerland. These included legal staff, accountants, loss adjusters, statisticians, information technology specialists, and administrative support staff from a number of different countries. The staff provided support to the Governing Council and to as many as nineteen panels of Commissioners.

The UNCC Secretariat is organized into: (i) the Office of the Executive Secretary; (ii) the Claims Processing Division, consisting of a legal services branch, support staff for verification and valuation of claims, and a claims registry; (iii) the Support Services Division, whose functions include payments of claims and the administration of the Compensation Fund, and an information systems section; (iv) the Executive Office, as part of the Support Services Division, responsible for personnel and budget matters; and (v) the Governing Council Secretariat.[4]

(c) Commission for Real Property Claims of Displaced Persons and Refugees (CRPC)—claims relating to the 1992–1995 war in Bosnia and Herzegovina

The CRPC had approximately 320 staff working in the Executive Office in Sarajevo and in a network of regional offices. A large Information Technology Department (of approximately thirty members) was set up to convert land records into a user-friendly computer database for quick reference by the lawyers preparing draft decisions, and a large Legal Department (of approximately sixty members) was staffed with experienced professionals, most of

---

[4] See UNCC Provisional Rules, Article 34, paragraph 1, which provides that "[t]he Executive Secretary and the staff of the Secretariat will provide administrative, technical and legal support to the Commissioners, including the development and maintenance of a computerized database for claims and assistance in obtaining additional information."

them nationals of Bosnia and Herzegovina. A special effort was made to recruit staff from the three relevant ethnic groups, Bosnian, Croat, and Serb. Both departments were headed, however, by an "international" staff member (i.e., not a national of Bosnia and Herzegovina). Hiring requirements depended on the position: for international staff members, the minimum requirements were to have had experience working abroad and, if possible, a familiarity with international organizations. For national staff, requirements depended on the position but required in many cases a working knowledge of English. Hiring was done on the basis of interviews. The more essential the function, the higher the level of the staff members who conducted the interview.

The Secretariat supporting the Commission was headed by an Executive Officer appointed by the Commission. The staff was required to be professionally competent and experienced in administrative, financial, banking, and legal matters.[5] The respective functions of the Commission and the Secretariat were carefully delineated, and details of the functions that the Secretariat performed were set out in the Book of Regulations on Procedure. Pursuant to it, authorized members of the staff conducted the claims registration;[6] the Executive Office, through its staff, reviewed the claims and assessed the evidence on the basis of which it prepared draft decisions;[7] a Legal Working Group within the Executive Office reviewed the prepared decisions, ensured that they conformed with the Book of Regulations, and presented decision proposals to the Commission.[8]

The analysis and assessment of legal, administrative and technical support was constantly evolving throughout the life of the Claims Process.

(d) Claims Resolution Tribunal for Dormant Accounts in Switzerland (CRT-I)—first claims tribunal for assets deposited in Swiss banks

The CRT-I Secretariat was designed to support a Tribunal composed of a Chairman, a Vice Chairman, and up to fifteen Arbitrators.[9] The Secretariat consisted of legal, technical, and administrative staff from different countries. At its peak, the Secretariat reached the staffing level of approximately fifty-five. Over the lifetime of the Claims Process, some 125 persons from more than twenty-five different countries served on its staff.[10] The specific

---

[5] Dayton Peace Agreement, Annex 7, Article X, paragraph 1.
[6] CRPC Book of Regulations on Procedure, Articles 24 and 27.
[7] Ibid., Articles 54 and 55.   [8] Ibid., Articles 53 and 57.
[9] CRT-I Rules of Procedure, Article 25.
[10] See Final Report on the Work of the Claims Resolution Tribunal for Dormant Accounts in Switzerland (CRT-I), 5 October 2001, available at www.crt-ii.org/_crt-i, "Progress Report."

responsibilities of the Secretariat staff assigned in each case were set out in the Tribunal's Internal Rules.

Many of the staff had the ability to communicate in the languages of the bank documents submitted, as well as in the languages of some of the countries in which it was expected that significant numbers of claimants resided.

The Chairman, in addition to acting as an Arbitrator under Swiss law, was charged with a number of administrative functions, including distributing the caseload fairly and equitably among the Arbitrators; submitting monthly written reports to the Board of Trustees of the Independent Claims Resolution Foundation (ICRF) on the activities of the Tribunal; administering the Tribunal's financial planning and submitting a quarterly budget to the Board of Trustees; and generally fulfilling all functions assigned to him by the Board.[11]

(e) Claims Resolution Tribunal (CRT-II)—second claims tribunal for assets deposited in Swiss banks

The original CRT-II Governing Rules provided that the Claims Resolution Tribunal should consist of (i) a Chairperson, (ii) a Vice Chairperson, (iii) Senior Judges, who would serve both as Senior Claims Judges and as Senior Appeals Judges, (iv) Resident Claims Judges, and (v) a Secretariat, including attorneys, paralegals, researchers, clerical assistants, and other staff as necessary to carry out the functions of the Claims Process.[12] As amended, the Governing Rules provide that "[t]he CRT shall be organized under the direction of the Special Masters" appointed by the United States District Court for the Eastern District of New York in the Holocaust Victim Assets Litigation.[13] The Special Masters "may promulgate guidelines and procedures necessary for the fair and expeditious functioning of the CRT and consistent with [the] Rules."[14] The Special Masters appoint all Secretariat attorneys and may remove them.[15] Under the supervision of the Special Masters, CRT-II is to

"(a) administer the [Claims Process];
 (b) submit to the Special Masters a monthly written report on the activities and the conduct of the [Claims Process];
 (c) supervise the financial planning and financial controls of the [Process] and submit to the Special Masters a quarterly financial report and periodic budgets of the [Claims Process];

---

[11] CRT-I Rules of Procedure, Article 28.
[12] CRT-II Governing Rules, unamended, Article 9.
[13] Ibid., as amended, Article 10, paragraph 1.   [14] Ibid., Article 10, paragraph 2.
[15] Ibid., Article 11.

(d) exercise all other functions provided for under [the] Rules or assigned by the Special Masters."[16]

The CRT-II Secretariat carries out the functions set forth in the Governing Rules and in any guidelines or procedures issued by the Special Masters, assists the Special Masters, and performs all other functions assigned to it by the Special Masters.[17] CRT-II employs approximately twenty lawyers in Zurich and approximately thirty-five supporting staff members, including paralegals, information technology specialists, translators, and administrative assistants. In addition, the Claims Process employs close to fifty staff members at the Jewish Claims Conference (JCC) in New York. The CRT-II staff attorneys review the claims and are responsible for making recommendations of decisions. They are supported by administrative assistants. Paralegals and other administrative staff handle mail received from the claimants, perform research for staff attorneys, and answer telephone-calls from claimants in the Call Center. There is also a "pre-processing" team responsible for creating claim files.

Appended to the Governing Rules are Rules concerning the "Data Librarian," who shall be responsible for "a Data Library consisting of the Account History Database, the Account Dossiers, and the Total Accounts Databases" which CRT-II is to use in resolving claims of victims or their heirs to Swiss bank accounts from the 1933–1945 period.[18] The Data Librarian is selected from among independent accounting firms, resident in Switzerland, and is retained and mandated by the Special Masters and reports to them and to the Swiss Federal Banking Commission (SFBC).[19] The Special Masters also retain an audit firm authorized to audit banks in Switzerland to perform matching and research on behalf of the Tribunal, using the applicable databases in the office space of the Data Librarian at CRT-II in Zurich.[20]

(f) Housing and Property Claims Commission (HPCC)—claims relating to the 1999 conflict in Kosovo

Under an initial arrangement between the United Nations Interim Administration Mission in Kosovo (UNMIK) and the United Nations Centre for Human Settlements (Habitat), the latter was responsible for the administration of the Commission and the Housing and Property Directorate (HPD),

---

[16] Ibid., Article 12. See also section 4.01(e) above, on the appointment of CRT-II decision-makers.
[17] Ibid., Article 13.   [18] Ibid., Appendix A, paragraph 1.
[19] Ibid., Appendix A, paragraph 2.   [20] Ibid., Appendix A, paragraph 9(a).

which also serves as the Commission's Secretariat.[21] Subsequently, in 2002, the administration of the Commission and the Directorate was transferred to UNMIK pursuant to an exchange of letters between UNMIK and Habitat.[22] In this connection, an advisory body, consisting of representatives of UNMIK and Habitat, was created to advise the Special Representative of the United Nations Secretary-General.

Over time, the Directorate has grown to include some 250 staff members, including lawyers, paralegal assistants, information technology experts, translators, and administrative support staff. The overwhelming majority of staff (over ninety percent) are local; the rest are from other countries. It is reported that funding challenges have caused this Claims Process to be under-staffed, and staff turnover is said to have been high due to the use of short-term contracts and the resulting uncertainty among staff members.

The HPCC staff was designed to support the Commission, which consists of one panel of two international and one local Commissioner,[23] as well as a Registry and related personnel. While the governing regulation, UNMIK Regulation 2000/60, provides that additional panels may be added, the initial panel ("Panel 1"), appointed in August 2000 by the chief executive of UNMIK, the Special Representative of the United Nations Secretary-General, has been able to handle the caseload, and it is unlikely that additional panels will be appointed, considering the advanced stage of the Claims Process.[24]

(g) Mass Claims Processes administered by the International Organization for Migration (IOM)

The two Claims Processes described below are operated as independent projects within IOM, under a common management, but with different

---

[21] UNMIK Regulation 1999/23, section 3.

[22] UN-HABITAT was invited to manage HPD by UNMIK through an exchange of letters; UN-HABITAT proposed the project, and in 2002 it was agreed through a "Letter of Understanding" that the management of HPD should be handed back to UNMIK when specified conditions were met. In November 2002 these conditions were met and an "implementation agreement" was signed to implement the "Letter of Understanding" for the Kosovo operations of HPD, hence the hand-over on 4 November 2002. For operations outside Kosovo, UNMIK had no legal agreement with Serbia and Montenegro and UN-HABITAT continued supporting UNMIK. In August 2004 UNMIK implemented (unilaterally) the "Letter of Understanding" for operations outside Kosovo by an exchange of letters. None of the above documents are published, nor are they officially available.

[23] The composition of the panel is regulated by UNMIK Regulation 1999/23, section 2.2, which requires the Members to be "experts in the field of housing and property law and competent to hold judicial office."   [24] The HPCC is scheduled to complete its work in 2006.

functional teams. The fact that an experienced core team was assembled quickly when the Claims Processes began allowed for an early assessment of the type and level of expertise required for the overall staff, and for an efficient establishment of the organization of the Claims Processes and the techniques they employ. Additional staff was then recruited to work full-time on the two programs, as IOM could not devote its existing staff to work exclusively on the Claims Processes, and because special skills were required for many of the functions. However, since claims collection and registration had to be conducted all over the world, a support structure with corresponding facilities, systems, and procedures needed to be in place at the very beginning of the Claims Processes. The availability of IOM's existing worldwide network of field offices was instrumental in achieving this and saved significant start-up time.

All claims (other than property claims filed with the Property Claims Commission) are processed and decided by members of the IOM Secretariat, which means that the full range of legal, administrative, and technical functions had to be established before claims could be decided. Further, procedures had to be established for claims processing. Other initial needs included legal, historical, and linguistic expertise, as well as management, financial, and administrative staff. An important and integral part of the Secretariat is a group of specialized information technology (IT) support staff. However, for reasons of efficiency and cost, a number of functions were outsourced, in particular the electronic scanning of claims files, data entry of claims information, printing and mailing of decisions and notices, as well as the generation and mailing of checks for compensation payments.

German Forced Labour Compensation Programme (GFLCP)—claims against Germany and German industry for Nazi injustice

GFLCP had, at its peak, approximately 250 staff members. These included almost one hundred legal, technical, and administrative support staff from different countries working at IOM's headquarters in Geneva, and about 150 staff stationed in almost sixty IOM field offices worldwide who worked for the Claims Process during outreach, claim forms distribution, claims intake and registration, and during the initial screening of claims. In addition to processing and resolving slave and forced labor and personal injury claims, the Secretariat staff in Geneva has served as support to the three-Member Property Claims Commission, and to the three-Member Appeals Body for Forced Labour Claims.

*Holocaust Victim Assets Programme (HVAP)—claims pursuant to
1999 class action Settlement*

HVAP has approximately forty legal and claims processing staff from different
countries—including shared IT and administrative support staff with GFLCP.
The majority of staff are based at IOM's headquarters in Geneva. They process
and resolve the slave and forced labor and refugee claims and provide support
to the HVAP appeals structures (i.e., the IOM Appeals Body for Forced Labour
Claims and two Independent Review Officers).

(h) Eritrea–Ethiopia Claims Commission (EECC)—claims relating to the 1998–2000 war between Eritrea and Ethiopia

The EECC is comprised of five jurists experienced in international mass claims
work who devote their efforts to the Claims Process on a part-time basis. The
constituting instrument, the 12 December 2000 Agreement, empowers the
Commission to employ such professional, administrative, and clerical staff as
it deems necessary to accomplish its work, including establishing a Registry.
The Rules of Procedure provide that the Commission shall have a Registrar to
maintain its archives and act as a channel of communication between the parties and the Commission.[25] The Commission has retained the International
Bureau of the Permanent Court of Arbitration (PCA) to serve as its Registry.
The PCA as Registry stores and catalogs the EECC pleadings and correspondence, acts as conduit for communications, maintains the Commission's docket,
and is available for legal research and general administrative support.

The Commission may also retain consultants and experts,[26] and early in its
work, the Commissioners and the parties consulted with technical experts from
the International Organization for Migration (IOM) in Geneva on a possible
computer-based system for collecting and processing mass claims. However,
given the limited financial resources of the parties, the Commission has
worked to limit its expenses. While it has greatly benefitted from support provided by the PCA, it directly employs no full-time staff, and the parties and
Commissioners make heavy use of e-mail and electronic document transmission
to limit travel and other costs.

In advance of the December 2001 filing deadline for claims, the
Commissioners and the Registrar confirmed that the PCA would have legal

---

[25] EECC Rules of Procedure, Article 9.
[26] Eritrea–Ethiopia Agreement of 12 December 2000, Article 5, paragraph 6.

and paralegal staff available to devote time to the Claims Process, and that it could offer sufficient storage capacity—physical and electronic—to safely archive and permit quick retrieval of a potentially large number of documents. Prior to the initial filing of claims, it was necessary to consider such issues as secure storage and the system for numbering the pleadings to avoid confusion as further pleadings were filed. As this is a Claims Process where two sides file claims against each other and submit documents and evidence in response to specific claims of the other side on the same dates, confusion could easily arise in cataloging and keeping track of the claims. Designing a numbering system, filing-stamps, color-coded folders, filing cabinets, and receipts ahead of time, and rehearsing the filing procedure prior to the first filing day, proved useful.[27]

(i) Humanitarian insurance Claims Process administered by the Jewish Claims Conference (JCC) for the International Commission on Holocaust Era Insurance Claims (ICHEIC)

The processing of claims in the 8A1 humanitarian Claims Process was overseen by the JCC's Executive Vice President and Chief Operating Officer. Day-to-day operations were supervised by the Director of the Claims Process. A team was recruited, hired, and trained to meet the processing needs of the 8A1 Claims Process. Persons who were hired to be supervisors of the team were all bilingual or multilingual with managerial backgrounds. The team of claims analysts was comprised of individuals who possessed advanced university degrees in various fields, many of whom had worked on translating documents, particularly hand-written documents. During the hiring interview, claims analysts were asked about their interest or previous experience in Holocaust-related matters.

In total, the 8A1 Claims Process employed one Director, four supervisors, approximately thirty claims analysts, one database administrator, one software programmer, and one office manager. In addition, payment approval and issuance procedures required the assistance of the JCC Payment Operations Team.

During the first phase of processing the 8A1 Claims, the JCC decided to add a night shift of claims analysts at its existing claims processing center in Manhattan, New York; it was less expensive to add a later shift at this facility than to lease additional accommodations and outfit a location with the

---

[27] For example, the simple facts that Eritrea and Ethiopia both begin with the letter "E" and would be submitting documents on the same dates throughout the Claims Process had to be taken into account when devising a numbering system.

resources necessary for electronic claims processing. The night shift ran for eight hours, from 6 p.m. to 2 a.m. As the night shift was established, support staff to meet the demands of the hour was needed. A night-time office manager handled the logistics of feeding over twenty people and transporting them home safely late at night at the lowest cost feasible. As the JCC information technology (IT) support and development staff was unavailable into the later hours of the night, support was provided by a single IT administrator, but this support was limited to basic hardware issues, as the 8A1 Claims database and application developer was on call at home during most of the night shift.

During the second phase of processing the 8A1 Claims, the JCC had a greater amount of daytime office space available, and the bulk of the processing operations were conducted during a 9 a.m. to 5 p.m. shift. This daytime shift was staffed by the Director, three supervisors, and approximately twenty-five claims analysts. The JCC also employed a second but smaller evening shift from 5:30 p.m. to 10:30 p.m., staffed by one evening supervisor and approximately five claims analysts. During the second phase of the Claims Process, the general JCC daytime infrastructure for all JCC programs provided the needed office management and IT support.

As is explained in section 5.03 above on languages, it is critical in some Mass Claims Processes to hire claims processing staff with linguistic abilities that correspond proportionally to the languages in which the claims are written. In the 8A1 Claims Process, by identifying the languages in which the highest concentration of claims was filed, the JCC was able to determine the specific skills which the team and its supervisors needed to possess in order to manage and review the work. The magnitude of the task can be seen from the following breakdown of the languages of the claims received in the first phase of the Claims Process:

English:	15764	Spanish:	439
Hebrew:	6694	Serbian:	280
Russian:	6484	Portuguese:	155
Hungarian:	2054	Dutch:	127
Romanian:	2025	Swedish:	64
Czech:	1649	Italian:	48
German:	1545	Yiddish:	44
Polish:	1120	Bulgarian:	14
French:	517	Greek:	5

In all, the thirty claims analysts, and the four supervisors who directly reviewed their work, were able to cover, in varying degrees of proficiency, each of these eighteen different languages, with an average of nearly three languages per individual. All claims analysts had to be fluent in English, the working language of the Claims Process.

(j) American Arbitration Association (AAA)—an illustrative case

The illustrative case involved full-time AAA staff of approximately fifty persons in one location, and the participation of at least ten AAA headquarters staff at various locations, on a half-time basis. About ten highly skilled information technology staff were involved in the Claims Process. During the training of the Arbitrators, four additional AAA staff members were required, three days a week, for five months.

For most of the cases, an AAA staff lawyer served as the "manager." Remaining staff consisted of non-legal personnel. About thirty were college graduates hired from a temporary employment agency. Approximately ten were secretarial and data-entry staff. The temporary employees scheduled the hearings and kept the cases flowing by each maintaining contact with a designated group of Arbitrators.

6.02 Infrastructure

Whether the Claims Process creates its own staff, facilities, and administrative organization, or uses an existing institution to provide all or part of such infrastructure.

Editors' Commentary

Each Mass Claims Process has the choice of either building its own staff, facilities, and organization, or turning to an existing outside institution to provide the infrastructure needed to support its activities. Some of the Claims Processes described in this book have chosen to establish in-house their own physical facilities and support staff, designed in the light of their particular circumstances, as was the case, for example, with the Commission for Real Property Claims of Displaced Persons and Refugees (CRPC) in Bosnia and Herzegovina. Others have turned for assistance to an existing institution that already has the physical premises, equipment, and people in order to be up-and-running more quickly and thereby meet deadlines imposed by urgent circumstances or by their constituting instruments. For example, the use of temporary staff in the insurance policies case allowed the American Arbitration Association (AAA)—an organization which maintains its own sizable staff—to increase and reduce staff levels quickly to meet caseload needs and minimize expense. This has also been the case for the German Forced Labour Compensation Programme (GFLCP) and the Holocaust Victim Assets Programme (HVAP) at the International Organization for Migration (IOM). Alternatively, there have been solutions that have combined elements of both approaches. Thus, some Claims Processes have relied on outside institutions in their early phases and later organized in-house capabilities, such as, for example, the Iran–United States Claims Tribunal (Iran–US CT). Another way of combining approaches is to establish an in-house infrastructure but to contract out some specialized functions to others, as has been done extensively at the United Nations Compensation Commission (UNCC), as described in section 6.03(b) below, and at the International Commission on Holocaust Era Insurance Claims (ICHEIC) humanitarian Claims Process.

If an existing institution is used, the benefits of doing so are to be balanced against the need to observe that institution's staff rules, recruitment practices, salary and benefits expectations, and working procedures. Additionally, if the chosen institution is an international organization with many member States, there may be the possibility that conflicts of interest exist or will arise.

(a) Iran–United States Claims Tribunal (Iran–US CT)—claims relating to the 1979 Islamic Revolution

The treaty that created the Iran–US CT established deadlines for accomplishing certain initial activities[28] and provided that the seat of the Tribunal was to be in The Hague. At the time the treaty was written, however, the Tribunal had no staff, no place to meet or conduct business, and no equipment or other infrastructure. In the circumstances, the United States and Iran sought and were granted the assistance of the International Bureau of the Permanent Court of Arbitration (PCA) in The Hague, which was, pursuant to the 1907 Hague Convention for the Peaceful Settlement of Disputes, authorized to make its offices and staff available "for the use of any Special Board of Arbitrators," such as the Iran–US CT.[29] As a result, the Tribunal was provided with the use, at the

---

[28] Claims Settlement Declaration, Article III, paragraph 1.
[29] 1907 Hague Convention for the Pacific Settlement of International Disputes, Article 47 reprinted in PERMANENT COURT OF ARBITRATION, BASIC DOCUMENTS (Secretary-General and

PCA's premises in the Peace Palace, of offices, conference rooms, space for receiving and archiving claims, and for temporary storage of files of claims as they were received, as well as basic office equipment. The Secretary-General of the PCA and members of his International Bureau staff assisted the Tribunal on a part-time basis. The International Bureau also temporarily employed translators and clerical personnel.

Subsequently, as the Tribunal grew and proceedings in thousands of cases began, the Tribunal built its own administrative staff and moved to a compound in The Hague that was provided rent-free by the Government of the Netherlands.

(b) United Nations Compensation Commission (UNCC)—claims relating to the 1990–1991 Gulf War

The UNCC created its own staff and also utilized support provided by another body, the United Nations Office in Geneva (UNOG). The UNCC Secretariat staff expanded from five persons initially to approximately three hundred persons at the height of claims processing. In making staffing decisions, the UNCC took into account that its work progressed in phases, initial planning being focused on the development and dissemination of claim forms in claims categories "A", "B" and "C" (designated by the Governing Council as urgent humanitarian claims requiring expedited processing). Adjustments to infrastructure, staffing, the appointment of Commissioners, and the engagement of external experts were made on an on-going basis as claims were received and as claims processing expanded to cover all of the claims categories and the "late claims" programs established by the Governing Council.[30]

The UNCC relied on administrative support provided for a fee by UNOG in the areas of procurement, financial services (including accounts, treasury, banking, and payroll), conference servicing (including the provision of interpreters and translators) and, in the initial stages, staff administration. The UNCC later became largely independent of UNOG in the areas of recruitment and staff administration, although, as a United Nations entity, it has followed all of that organization's rules and regulations. The benefit of UNOG's provision of administrative support is that the UNCC has been able to utilize

International Bureau of the Permanent Court of Arbitration, eds.), p. 17, at p. 29. Also available at www.pca-cpa.org.

[30] See sections 3.03(b) above, on deadlines for submitting claims to UNCC, and 3.05(b) above, on scheduling.

UNOG's existing systems. However, such reliance can increase the time required to adapt to meet changing needs.

(c) Commission for Real Property Claims of Displaced Persons and Refugees (CRPC)—claims relating to the 1992–1995 war in Bosnia and Herzegovina

CRPC had its headquarters in Sarajevo, Bosnia and Herzegovina. It always employed its own staff, as it would not have been feasible to use other institutions within Bosnia and Herzegovina to perform the work of the CRPC, or parts thereof—all institutions in the country being either overburdened by their own work at the time, and/or funded for a particular purpose and thus not allowed to assume other assignments. In its first two years of operations, CRPC relied, however, upon the International Organization for Migration (IOM) in Geneva for the administration of its finances and other logistical support. After that initial period, the CRPC administered its own finances and bookkeeping.

To carry out its mandate under Annex 7 to the Dayton Peace Agreement, the constituting instrument of this Claims Process, CRPC was supposed to receive space for its operations provided by the Government of Bosnia and Herzegovina. Attempts made at the very beginning to obtain office space from the Government were not fruitful. For the first year of operations, CRPC had much less room than it required, but after receiving more funding from donors in the second year, adequate space was obtained. The infrastructure of CRPC evolved over time, with the basic components being the Administration Department, the Legal Department, and the Information Technology Department. It took one year to put these departments in place.

(d) Claims Resolution Tribunal for Dormant Accounts in Switzerland (CRT-I)—first claims tribunal for assets deposited in Swiss banks

Pursuant to the CRT-I Rules of Procedure, the Board of Trustees of the Independent Claims Resolution Foundation (ICRF) appointed a Zurich- and Geneva-based law firm to serve as the Secretariat of the Claims Process and to provide staff and facilities.[31] Initially, it was expected that, in addition to the lawyers of the firm designated to work for the Tribunal, only a small number of seconded lawyers from foreign law firms would be needed to form the necessary staff. However, as the number of claims filed was significantly higher than expected, the Secretariat staff had to be increased. By 1998, when it became clear that the Claims Process would last longer and require higher staffing levels than anticipated, CRT-I began to recruit and employ its own staff directly.

---

[31] See CRT-I Rules of Procedure, Article 30.

The Tribunal continued to operate out of the law firm's Zurich and Geneva offices until 2000, when the decision was made to move the Secretariat out of the firm's offices to a separate office building, and to centralize all activities in Zurich. (That decision was linked to the completion of the CRT-I Claims Process and its transformation into CRT-II, as described in the section which follows.)

(e) Claims Resolution Tribunal (CRT-II)—second claims tribunal for assets deposited in Swiss banks

CRT-II, which was established after CRT-I had largely completed its work, took over the CRT-I staff and offices.

Initially, all work was carried out in Zurich. In 2001, additional technical assistance and, later, claims processing was provided by the Jewish Claims Conference (JCC) in New York. The claims are decided in Zurich and in New York, but most administrative work is carried out in Zurich. In addition, the final checking of all decisions recommended in the Claims Process, before they are submitted to the Special Masters, takes place in Zurich.

(f) Housing and Property Claims Commission (HPCC)—claims relating to the 1999 conflict in Kosovo

The Commission and the Housing and Property Directorate (HPD) form part of the United Nations Interim Administration Mission in Kosovo (UNMIK). All legislative and executive authority with respect to Kosovo, including the administration of the local judiciary, is vested in UNMIK and exercised by the Special Representative of the United Nations Secretary-General.[32] It is thus UNMIK which provides the entire administrative framework and physical facilities for HPCC until the local Kosovo judiciary is able to assume its functions.

(g) Mass Claims Processes administered by the International Organization for Migration (IOM): *German Forced Labour Compensation Programme (GFLCP) for claims against Germany and German industry for Nazi injustice, and Holocaust Victim Assets Programme (HVAP) for claims pursuant to 1999 class action Settlement*

While GFLCP and HVAP Claims Processes are projects within IOM with their own staff and other resources, they rely on administrative support by

---

[32] UNMIK Regulation 1999/1 *On the Authority of the Interim Administration in Kosovo*, U.N. Doc. UNMIK/REG/1999/1 (25 July 1999), section 1.

IOM headquarters, particularly with respect to the recruitment of staff, the procurement of services, worldwide telecommunications, and office facilities. This reduced the start-up time significantly. IOM charges the Claims Processes a standard overhead fee for these services.

(h) Eritrea–Ethiopia Claims Commission (EECC)—claims relating to the 1998–2000 war between Eritrea and Ethiopia

In an effort to limit administration and overhead expenses, the EECC has utilized support drawn from an existing organization rather than create its own staff and infrastructure. It has entered into an agreement with the International Bureau of the Permanent Court of Arbitration (PCA) in The Hague, which is, pursuant to the 1907 Hague Convention for the Peaceful Settlement of Disputes, authorized to make its offices and staff available "for the use of any Special Board of Arbitrators," such as the EECC.[33] Under the agreement, the PCA provides Secretariat support and Registry services on a reimbursable basis. Among other services, the PCA arranges for conference and hearing facilities in the Peace Palace in The Hague when required. The PCA has responded flexibly and fully to the Commission's needs, permitting the Commission to avoid making expensive long-term commitments for personnel and facilities that might have been excessive to its eventual needs. PCA support was particularly valuable during the Commission's initial organizational phase, because it was not clear until claims were actually filed in December 2001 how much administrative support would be needed. For all these reasons, it has made particular sense in the circumstances of this Claims Process to utilize an experienced existing institution to provide support infrastructure.

(i) Humanitarian insurance Claims Process administered by the Jewish Claims Conference (JCC) for the International Commission on Holocaust Era Insurance Claims (ICHEIC)

ICHEIC chose to contract the tasks of designing and administering the 8A1 humanitarian Claims Process to an outside organization, rather than expanding its operations in-house. It chose the Conference on Jewish Material Claims Against Germany ("Jewish Claims Conference" (JCC)), in New York City, which has had extensive experience since 1951 in handling damages for Holocaust-related suffering.[34]

---

[33] 1907 Hague Convention for the Pacific Settlement of International Disputes, Article 47 reprinted in PERMANENT COURT OF ARBITRATION, BASIC DOCUMENTS (Secretary-General and International Bureau of the Permanent Court of Arbitration, eds.), p. 17, at p. 29. Also available at www.pca-cpa.org.   [34] For information about JCC, see www.claimscon.org.

The 8A1 Claims were processed in New York City, at the JCC's existing claims processing center in Manhattan, where all necessary administrative infrastructure, support staff, telecommunications, and computer equipment was already in place, and only a relatively small number of additional staff needed to be recruited for processing the 8A1 Claims. ICHEIC was able to have all relevant documentation scanned into digital media and submit it electronically for review by the JCC, without having to physically move and store large amounts of paper records. ICHEIC eventually also delegated to the JCC the payment processing of the 8A1 humanitarian awards.

(j) American Arbitration Association (AAA)—an illustrative case

When the Claims Process began in the illustrative case, it was anticipated that it would be completed within eighteen months. Therefore, pre-existing office space, with furniture and a telephone system in place, was leased for full-time staff, with an option to renew for an additional six months. Computers, fax-machines, and copiers were leased. Staff were provided by an outside company experienced in temporary staffing that was able to increase or decrease the personnel as the Claims Process required. The outside company received a fee to handle all staff hiring, scheduling, and salary payments. The remaining infrastructure was provided by already existing AAA facilities and staff.

6.03 Secretariat Functions

The relationship between Secretariat staff and the decision-makers. Defining their respective powers and functions. What role, if any, Secretariat staff has in conducting research, drafting orders and decisions, and whether the task of deciding certain claims is delegated to staff members.

Editors' Commentary

Each Mass Claims Process described in this book comprises two elements: (i) those who decide claims, and (ii) those who administer the Claims Process. Some Claims Processes also include a third element consisting of a body that oversees and supervises in greater or lesser detail. The hierarchy of the powers of these elements and their relationships with each other differ among

317

Claims Processes. At one end of the spectrum are those in which the Judges or Arbitrators not only decide claims but also exercise ultimate control over organization and administration, such as the Iran–United States Claims Tribunal (Iran–US CT), which decides such matters unless both Government parties mutually agree otherwise. At the other end of the spectrum are Claims Processes in which the function of Judges or Arbitrators is limited to deciding particular claims assigned to them—or even merely reviewing decisions made by staff attorneys applying standardized review criteria established by Judges or oversight bodies—with organizational and administrative functions being largely left in the hands of others. Examples of this are the Holocaust Victim Assets Programme (HVAP) and German Forced Labour Compensation Programme (GFLCP) at the International Organization for Migration (IOM). In between the two extremes are a variety of hybrid arrangements. In most of the Claims Processes described in this book, all decisions on claims—large and small—were made by the Judges, Arbitrators, Commissioners or Tribunal Members. In some later Claims Processes, in an effort to expedite the resolution of very large numbers of claims, some or most claims decisions have been delegated to staff members, usually in cases where the amount claimed is relatively small and the rules provide that only a fixed amount of damages can be awarded.

Confusion can be avoided by carefully defining the powers, functions, and relationships of the elements that comprise a Claims Process. This is important because participants typically have different backgrounds and experiences and, consequently, may have different expectations.

Another area in which expectations and functions may differ relates to the role of a Secretariat in performing research and drafting orders and decisions. In some of the Claims Processes described in this book, such as the United Nations Compensation Commission (UNCC), staff members have a major responsibility in this respect. In others, they do not. In some, assistance to the decision-makers is provided by legal assistants, as at the Iran–US CT.[35]

The many options that may be considered by designers of Mass Claims Processes can best be understood by examining actual practice at a number of different Claims Processes, particularly where innovative arrangements have been made to meet existing circumstances or to expedite the resolution of very large numbers of claims.

(a) Iran–United States Claims Tribunal (Iran–US CT)—claims relating to the 1979 Islamic Revolution

The Iran–US CT is one of the Claims Processes described in this book in which the Members of the Tribunal themselves control not only decision-making on

---

[35] See section 6.01(a) above, on legal assistants at the Iran–US CT.

claims, but all aspects of the organization, administration, and staff support. The Secretary-General, who heads the staff, is chosen by the Members, reports to them, and is supervised by them. While, in practice, the Secretary-General has broad latitude in organizing and directing the staff, his authority is subject to the Members who operate by majority vote of nine Members, or through power delegated to a three-Member Committee on Administrative and Financial Questions, or by the President of the Tribunal exercising power delegated to him with respect to certain matters.

Legal assistants, hired as part of the Secretariat, provide assistance to the Members by conducting research and, in some cases, helping to draft awards and orders, as described in section 6.01(a) above.

(b) United Nations Compensation Commission (UNCC)—claims relating to the 1990–1991 Gulf War

Although it has no official decision-making authority, the UNCC Secretariat, as the only UNCC body whose staff works on a full-time basis at the Commission's headquarters in Geneva, in practice came to carry out most of the Commission's daily functions. Given the large volume of claims, the technical and administrative complexity of the issues involved, and the need for outside expertise and sophisticated computer support, the Secretariat played a major role in developing and drafting policies, rules, recommendations, and decisions, and in maintaining the consistency of the Commission's jurisprudence.[36]

The fact-finding nature of this Claims Process also enhanced the role played by the Secretariat and led to its retaining outside experts and consultants in areas such as accounting, loss adjusting, engineering, insurance, and environmental damage assessment. It was considered impracticable to attempt to establish an expert verification team of such scope in-house. Reliance on outside experts became a distinctive characteristic of the UNCC's procedures. Although it has outsourced the work, however, the Secretariat has exercised oversight and coordination of the work of the various outside consultants.

(c) Commission for Real Property Claims of Displaced Persons and Refugees (CRPC)—claims relating to the 1992–1995 war in Bosnia and Herzegovina

The CRPC did not have a "Secretariat" in the proper sense of that term, but rather a large administrative staff that was headed by the Executive Officer.

---

[36] See section 5.07(b) above, on harmonizing procedures at the UNCC.

Neither the Executive Officer nor the administrative staff had any actual decision-making power. Their major function was to receive claims from refugees, register them electronically, research the title rights on CRPC's database of land records, and to propose draft decisions to the Commission, which ultimately rendered a final decision.

The Head of the CRPC Executive Office and the claims registration staff were responsible for the registration of claims.[37] Verification of evidence could be conducted through the Executive Office, its regional offices, or an international or non-governmental organization.[38] The Book of Regulations on Procedure contained detailed provisions on the decision-making process, which proceeded from draft decisions written by the Legal Department, considered by the Legal Working Group, and reviewed by expert staff in the Executive Office. The Executive Office then prepared final draft decisions that it proposed to the Commission.[39]

The Chief Executive Officer and the heads of the various departments provided policy research and opinion papers that were discussed in meetings of the Commission. Moreover, they represented the Commissioners' positions at various meetings at the government level and within the international community.

(d) Claims Resolution Tribunal for Dormant Accounts in Switzerland (CRT-I)—first claims tribunal for assets deposited in Swiss banks

At CRT-I, the relationship between the Arbitrators and the Secretariat was established in the Rules of Procedure of the Claims Process, pursuant to which the Secretariat staff assisted the Chairman, the Sole Arbitrators, and claims panels in the administrative arrangements for the proceedings, including "preparation of a file for use in the [Claims Process] and factual and legal research on behalf of the Sole Arbitrators and Claims Panels."[40] The Secretariat was subject to supervision and direction by the Board of Directors of the Independent Claims Resolution Foundation (ICRF).

The support provided by the Secretariat included drafting of awards and orders, subject to approval of the Sole Arbitrator or claims panel in the case. It handled correspondence with the parties (i.e., claimants and the banks), and was involved in advising parties on the claims procedures, conducting legal and

---

[37] CRPC Book of Regulations on Procedure, Article 27.   [38] Ibid., Article 36.
[39] Ibid., Articles 53 and 54.   [40] CRT-I Rules of Procedure, Article 30(a) and (b).

factual research, coordinating the exchange of drafts and correspondence between the Arbitrators, drafting legal memoranda regarding procedural and substantive legal issues, and reviewing translations of documents submitted by the parties.

(e) Claims Resolution Tribunal (CRT-II)—second claims tribunal for assets deposited in Swiss banks

At CRT-II, paralegals perform research for staff attorneys. There is also a "pre-processing" team responsible for creating files for claims and administering mail received from the claimants. The staff attorneys are responsible for drafting decisions on claims submitted to them, but they are allowed to consult other staff attorneys, team leaders, or the management of the Claims Process in more complicated cases. Drafted decisions undergo a checking process before they are submitted by the Special Masters for approval by the United States federal district court overseeing the Settlement in the class action known as the Holocaust Victim Assets Litigation.

(f) Housing and Property Claims Commission (HPCC)—claims relating to the 1999 conflict in Kosovo

The relationship between the Commission and the Housing and Property Directorate (HPD) is complex, and serving as the Commission's Secretariat is only one of the many functions of the Directorate. Under the constituting instrument, the Directorate's tasks include: (i) policy-making and advisory functions for the purpose of providing overall direction on property rights in Kosovo; (ii) giving guidance to the United Nations Interim Administration Mission in Kosovo (UNMIK) and other international organizations present in Kosovo on specific issues related to property rights; and (iii) conducting research for development of policies and legislation concerning property rights.[41] In practice, however, the processing of claims for the purpose of their referral to the Commission has been the Directorate's principal function.

The Directorate's support functions *vis-à-vis* the Commission include the preparation of referral reports, which summarize the claim referred and the evidence provided, explain the notification and verification process undertaken by the Directorate, and make a recommendation to the Commission for the resolution of the claim.[42] The Directorate's verification function is particularly

---

[41] UNMIK Regulation 1999/23, section 1.1.
[42] UNMIK Regulation 2000/60, section 10.4.

important, as it involves not only the verification of documents submitted by the claimants, but also independent searches that it makes for records with public authorities and private entities.[43]

The Commission has its own Registry, which is under its exclusive control. The Registrar's functions include review of HPD referrals pursuant to guidelines provided by the Commission, drafting of decisions, and overseeing their implementation. The Registrar also acts as the Commission's on-site representative between sessions of the Commission, which generally take place on a bi-monthly basis. The Registrar is furthermore authorized to correct any textual errors in a Commission decision, as long as such corrections do not materially affect the rights of any party, and provided the Chairperson of the Commission agrees.[44]

The relationship between the Directorate and the Commission's Registrar is somewhat fluid: in practice, staff members of the Directorate also participate in the drafting of decisions, as a consequence of resource constraints in the Registry, and the function of the Registrar has often been exercised on an acting basis by a staff member of the Directorate.

The Directorate also has its own independent decision-making powers with respect to certain claims. For example, under the UNMIK Regulations, the Directorate has jurisdiction to reject a claim that manifestly falls outside the Commission's jurisdiction. The Directorate may also seek amicable settlement of claims between the parties.[45]

Pursuant to UNMIK Regulation 2000/60, the Commission "may . . . delegate to the Registrar and the staff members of the Directorate assigned to service the Commission certain claims review and evidentiary functions, subject to the supervision of the Commission."[46] The Commission has exercised its authority under this provision by delegating the review of certain uncontested claims to the Registrar pursuant to guidelines established by the Commission. The delegation of such review functions has taken place only after the Commission has rendered a precedent-setting decision on the legal, factual, and evidentiary issues raised by the types of claims whose review functions are to be delegated. The Commission oversees and controls the exercise of the delegated functions by reviewing samples of claims falling under the delegated function during each of its sessions.

---

[43] UNMIK Regulation 2000/60, section 10.2, provides that HPD may "investigate a claim, and obtain evidence relevant to a claim from any record held by a public body, corporate or natural person. The Directorate is entitled to free access without charge to any records in Kosovo relevant to the settlement of a claim or for any other verification purposes." HPD also has access to relevant records in Serbia.   [44] Ibid., section 22.11.

[45] Ibid., section 10.1 and 10.3. A party whose claim has been rejected by the Directorate on this basis may challenge the decision, which is then referred to the Commission for determination.

[46] Ibid., section 19.5(b).

(g) Mass Claims Processes administered by the International Organization for Migration (IOM): *German Forced Labour Compensation Programme (GFLCP) for claims against Germany and German industry for Nazi injustice, and Holocaust Victim Assets Programme (HVAP) for claims pursuant to 1999 class action Settlement*

Both GFLCP and HVAP are Claims Processes in which claims review and recommendations on decisions are, in effect, all assigned to Secretariat staff: teams of claims processors review the claim forms and the accompanying evidence, enter the information into a database, creating an electronic profile for each claim which indicates whether basic showings of slave or forced labor have been made, according to criteria—including certain evidentiary presumptions—developed by IOM and approved, in the case of GFLCP, by the German Foundation and, in the case of HVAP, by the United States federal district court overseeing the class actions known as the Holocaust Victim Assets Litigation. If certain basic showings have been met, a claim will automatically be recommended for payment; if not, historians and attorneys serving as team leaders of the different teams of claims processors will review the claim and make a recommendation for its resolution. They will also provide guidance to the claims processors on how to process similarly situated claims in the future. Once a group of similar claims has been resolved, the proposed decisions affecting all claimants in that batch are submitted to the German Foundation or the Court, respectively, for approval or denial. The attorneys acting as team leaders also oversee quality control of the claims review, and coordinate with the information technology department to continuously adjust the claims software as more historic detail surfaces and precedent-setting decisions are made by the oversight bodies.

The relationships between the Secretariat and the Property Claims Commission and the IOM Appeals Body for Forced Labour Claims, respectively, are defined in the respective sets of procedural rules.[47] In view of the large numbers of claims and appeals on the one hand, and the limited time and other resources available to the Commission and the Appeals Body on the other, the Secretariat has reviewed the claims and appeals, conducted extensive research, and prepared and drafted the decisions, which in almost all cases are accepted. Thus, as a practical matter, the main function of these two decision-making bodies is the development of standard review methodologies and criteria, and a quality control of the work of the Secretariat.

---

[47] See generally IOM Property Commission Supplemental Rules and IOM Appeals Body Principles and Rules.

(h) Eritrea–Ethiopia Claims Commission (EECC)—claims relating to the 1998–2000 war between Eritrea and Ethiopia

The EECC Commissioners themselves draft their own orders and decisions. The Commission has to date relied upon the International Bureau of the Permanent Court of Arbitration (PCA) to provide administrative support and some legal assistance, such as research.

The PCA staff also performs the function of Registrar which, under the EECC Rules of Procedure, is to "maintain the archives of the Commission for further disposition as the Commission may direct, and . . . act as a channel of communication between the parties and the Commission as directed by the Commission."[48]

(i) Humanitarian insurance Claims Process administered by the Jewish Claims Conference (JCC) for the International Commission on Holocaust Era Insurance Claims (ICHEIC)

The decision-making in the 8A1 humanitarian Claims Process is described in section 4.01(i) above.

(j) American Arbitration Association (AAA)—an illustrative case

Support staff in the illustrative case performed purely ministerial functions and did not draft opinions or conduct legal research. Senior staff facilitated the resolution of day-to-day problems that might arise and provided continuous coordination of the many Arbitrators and oversight of the Claims Process.

6.04 Facilities

The facilities needed to implement the Claims Process (e.g., physical premises, copying and other office equipment and supplies, computers, telephone lines, etc.). What facilities need to be in place at the outset in order to handle claims as they are received.

Editors' Commentary

At the start-up phase of a Mass Claims Process, what is needed at a minimum is an address and place for receiving claims, a telephone and fax number and

---

[48] EECC Rules of Procedure, Article 9.

a postal or e-mail address for use by potential claimants to inquire about submitting claims, and a website and/or brochure containing information about the Claims Process for purposes of outreach and publicity. Although the use of websites and electronic mail has become increasingly prevalent, consideration will need to be given to the extent to which the expected claimant population for the particular Claims Process is likely to have access to, and be familiar with, the use of computers.

Once basic procedures and staffing estimates have been made, however, it is essential that adequate office space be secured for conducting the actual Claims Process.

In planning the facilities, certain characteristics of Mass Claims Processes are relevant. These Claims Processes are *ad hoc* institutions, set up to perform certain tasks as quickly as possible and with low overhead costs. Most of the Claims Processes described in this book rent their offices and equipment on a short-term basis with options for renewal. There may be phases in the life of a Claims Process which require more activity and staff than others. Thus, for example, the outreach and claims collection activities may require that satellite offices be established, and later dismantled once they are no longer needed. Similarly, once the bulk of the claims has been registered, processed, and paid out, it may be advantageous to reduce space as operations wind down and the only remaining tasks are to decide a relatively few remaining claims, as well as appeals and requests for reconsideration. The different phases should factor into the negotiation of leases and overall planning. As with other administrative aspects, it may be beneficial to begin a Claims Process by taking over space and equipment from an earlier Claims Process that has already run its course—as was the case with the second Claims Resolution Tribunal (CRT-II) in Zurich taking over facilities from the Claims Resolution Tribunal for Dormant Accounts in Switzerland (CRT-I)—or by performing initial functions under the auspices of a permanent existing institution in order to be able to begin without delay and defer other decisions until the actual scope of the Claims Process is known (see, for example, the arrangement between the Eritrea–Ethiopia Claims Commission (EECC) and the Permanent Court of Arbitration (PCA)). However, if a Claims Process outgrows the facilities provided by a host organization, as was the case with the German Forced Labour Compensation Programme (GFLCP) and Holocaust Victim Assets Programme (HVAP) at the International Organization of Migration (IOM), it can be disruptive to have to relocate staff, equipment, and records once claims processing and decision-making is underway.

There is usually a great urgency to get a Mass Claims Process off to a quick start and, often, to perform all, or substantially all, of the work within a relatively short period. Certain staff, such as Commissioners or other decision-makers, may work part-time and thus not require individual offices. Full-time staff, however, need to be provided with a work environment that meets recognized health and safety standards.

Despite advances in the use of electronic document management and data storage, most Mass Claims Processes—due to the number of claimants and the corresponding volume of evidentiary documentation—are very paper-intensive, requiring ample archive capacity with room for expansion, and large copying capacity, in addition to traditional office equipment and supplies. All of this needs to be taken into account when selecting the physical facilities. Some of the Claims Processes described in this book have used scanning technology to create digital files for review by claims processors and decision-makers, and for digital storage of documents.

Also, claimants in the types of Mass Claims Processes described in this book are often asked to submit highly personal information, such as bank records or descriptions of abuses they suffered, and a Claims Process must be able to store such information securely to protect the privacy and safety of those who are to benefit from it. Secure buildings, selective access to records, computer fire-walls, and strict confidentiality rules should be considered.

Last, but not least, modern Mass Claims Processes and "mass claims technologies" are increasingly reliant on information technology. These methods require most, if not all, staff members to have an individual computer workstation at their disposal, with network, e-mail and Internet access, in addition to the use of a printer, photocopier, and telephone. It is essential to choose office facilities that can support the necessary computer servers and are capable of being wired for digital communications.

The discussion in this section of some of the Claims Processes, particularly the Iran–United States Claims Tribunal (Iran–US CT), includes somewhat detailed descriptions of physical facilities. This information is included because it gives concrete examples of the infrastructure that is needed. This excursion into mundane detail may be useful in reminding designers of Mass Claims Processes that they must not only take account of legal issues, but must also consider that the staff will need offices, equipment, and a place to park their cars or access to public transportation.

(a) Iran–United States Claims Tribunal (Iran–US CT)—claims relating to the 1979 Islamic Revolution

As noted in section 6.01 above, the Iran–US CT began its operations in borrowed space in the Peace Palace in The Hague, with the assistance of a few members of the staff of the Permanent Court of Arbitration (PCA). Quite soon, however, the Tribunal employed its own staff and more extensive facilities were needed. To meet those growing needs, a compound owned by the Government of the Netherlands was converted to meet the Tribunal's needs. This included a four-story office building, several smaller adjacent buildings, and a parking lot. Space was provided for two hearing rooms equipped for simultaneous interpretation, individual offices for each Tribunal Member, for the Secretary-General and other Secretariat officials, as well as for a Registry and archive storage, a Language Services Department, and extensive copying facilities. Offices for use by the Agents of the Governments of the United States and Iran were provided. There was also an Islamic prayer room, a cafeteria, and a library.

Until 2004, hearings in cases between the two Governments and of claims requiring the participation of large numbers of lawyers and witnesses were held in one of the courtrooms in the Peace Palace. In 2004, however, a larger hearing room was constructed in the Tribunal's own building with a view to eliminating the need to go to the Peace Palace.

In 1981 when the Tribunal began its operations, facilities of this type were not typically designed for extensive use of computers, and the Internet was not yet in common use. The Tribunal had word processors in English, but the software for word processing in Farsi was not yet available; it was added a few years later.

(b) United Nations Compensation Commission (UNCC)—claims relating to the 1990–1991 Gulf War

The UNCC, having begun with five staff members, ultimately employed approximately three hundred individuals (not including Commissioners) at the height of its claims processing operations at three locations in Geneva (approximately 7,250 square meters of office space). The Office of the Executive Secretary, Governing Council Secretariat, and Support Services Division were housed in two different buildings on the grounds of the United Nations complex in Geneva, the *Palais des Nations*. The Claims Processing Division was housed in a commercial office building near the airport, having the very large secure storage capacity required for the claim files (in total, the UNCC required approximately 2,600 square meters for the storage of claim files). In addition to the space needed for offices, workrooms, and file storage, conference rooms were required for informal meetings of the Working Group of the Governing Council, meetings of the panels of Commissioners, and meetings with delegations from claimant governments. Formal meetings of the Governing Council and oral proceedings convened by panels of Commissioners were held in large conference rooms having simultaneous interpretation facilities in the *Palais des Nations*.

Equipment required by the UNCC included file and database servers (and the infrastructure necessary to support the computer hardware and a very large

UNCC database), individual computer workstations and telephone lines, printers, high speed photocopiers, high quality scanners (to scan claim forms and other documents), facsimile machines, teleconferencing facilities, office furniture, filing cabinets, shelving, secured disposal bins, labeling machines, trolleys, office supplies, and claim file folders and storage containers.

With the commencement of the winding down of the UNCC as claims processing drew to a close, physical space was relinquished on an incremental basis. As of 31 January 2006, the Claims Processing Division, except for the Registry, had been relocated to the two buildings in the grounds of the *Palais des Nations*.

(c) Commission for Real Property Claims of Displaced Persons and Refugees (CRPC)—claims relating to the 1992–1995 war in Bosnia and Herzegovina

During the start-up phase of CRPC, it was impossible to determine what facilities it would come to require. However, by 1999, a complete analysis had been conducted to determine the Commission's needs with regard to telephones, computers, and office equipment. The required facilities included headquarters in Sarajevo, and rented regional offices inside and outside Bosnia and Herzegovina where claims could be collected. All offices needed to be equipped with computers to log the received claims and forward them on to Sarajevo. The Claims Process also needed automobiles for on-site visits and property surveys, and for the mobile teams that collected claims in remote areas and among displaced populations, and who later distributed decision certificates in person to successful claimants.

Due to the eventual expansion of the Claims Process, CRPC continued to have to rent more office space in Sarajevo. By 1999, its staff was working from four different locations in the city; one for administration and finance, one for information technology, one for legal staff, and one for claims processing. These offices were interconnected by e-mail through a low-cost antenna radio frequency system, which allowed for smooth and seamless operations.

(d) Claims Resolution Tribunal for Dormant Accounts in Switzerland (CRT-I)—first claims tribunal for assets deposited in Swiss banks

CRT-I used the facilities of the Swiss law firm which had been designated to serve as the Tribunal's Secretariat. The facilities provided by the law firm included office space, office equipment, and computer support. Given this arrangement, CRT-I was able to gear up and become functional relatively quickly.

As the Claims Process grew in scope, it became necessary to rent additional office space outside the law firm's Zurich office. Part of the Tribunal remained in the firm's Zurich office until the whole Tribunal moved into a new rented office in preparation for the launch of the CRT-II Claims Process described in the section which follows.

(e) Claims Resolution Tribunal (CRT-II)—second claims tribunal for assets deposited in Swiss banks

The CRT-II Claims Process has an office in Zurich. The office was rented and furnished by the Secretariat of the CRT-I Claims Process, described in the preceding section. CRT-II uses software developed for the purposes of the Claims Process and the necessary infrastructure, such as servers, individual computer work-stations, and standard office equipment. The Claims Process also operates a Call Center which claimants and other persons interested in the Claims Process can contact toll-free.

Since 2001, some processing of claims in categories involving unnamed or unmatched bank accounts has taken place in New York, at the offices of the Conference on Jewish Material Claims Against Germany ("Jewish Claims Conference" (JCC)).

(f) Housing and Property Claims Commission (HPCC)—claims relating to the 1999 conflict in Kosovo

The Housing and Property Directorate (HPD) is housed in several locations in Kosovo and elsewhere in the former Yugoslavia. The headquarters of the HPCC Claims Process and the Pristina regional office are located in Pristina (the capital of Kosovo), and one in Serbia proper (in Belgrade). In addition to the Pristina office, there are four additional regional offices in Kosovo. Field offices, which serve as claims intake centers and points of contact with claimants but do not conduct claims processing functions, have been established in minority enclaves inside Kosovo, throughout Serbia, in Montenegro (with permanent offices in Podgorica), and the former Yugoslav Republic of Macedonia (Skopje). After claims intake was concluded, a number of offices remained operational in order to maintain a channel of communications with the claimants (Belgrade, Kragojevac, and Nis (in Serbia proper), Podgorica, Skopje, and three minority areas inside Kosovo). These locations were still operating as of 31 January 2006, with full-time staff.

Adequacy of office space, equipment and supplies has been an issue throughout this Claims Process. However, since 2004, the Claims Process has provided a Call Center for communication with claimants, with two daily shifts, seven days a week. Since 2005, use has also been made of mobile telephone text messaging (SMS) to inform claimants of decisions on their claims.

(g) **Mass Claims Processes administered by the International Organization for Migration (IOM):** *German Forced Labour Compensation Programme (GFLCP) for claims against Germany and German industry for Nazi injustice, and Holocaust Victim Assets Programme (HVAP) for claims pursuant to 1999 class action Settlement*

The GFLCP and HVAP Claims Processes use a full range of IOM office facilities (premises, equipment, utilities, etc.). In a great number of countries, they were able to rely on existing IOM field offices for the outreach and claims collection phase. The work performed in Geneva was initially hosted inside IOM's head-quarters building, which allowed for speedy commencement of operations during the intake of claims and their registration. However, when the claims processing and review operations expanded in scope and the bulk of the work became centralized in Geneva, the Claims Processes outgrew their space at the IOM headquarters so that separate commercial office space had to be rented nearby, and equipped, with a lease until the projected end of operations.

(h) **Eritrea–Ethiopia Claims Commission (EECC)—claims relating to the 1998–2000 war between Eritrea and Ethiopia**

The EECC has used the physical premises, address, telephone and fax numbers, office facilities, and equipment of the Permanent Court of Arbitration (PCA) in The Hague, which acts as Registry to the Commission. This obviated the need for installing expensive facilities "from scratch"—a course which would have added greatly to the cost and complexity of organizing the work of the Commission, particularly given the limited time allotted to it for completing its work.

In addition, each of the Commissioners has utilized his or her own personal computer and communication facilities to transact Commission business, much of which has been carried out utilizing e-mail.

(i) **Humanitarian insurance Claims Process administered by the Jewish Claims Conference (JCC) for the International Commission on Holocaust Era Insurance Claims (ICHEIC)**

The 8A1 humanitarian Claims Process was conducted in the existing JCC facilities in New York City, which minimized infrastructure costs to ICHEIC. Workstations for claims analysts were already in place, as were computer servers, network, and telecommunications equipment. The JCC did purchase one extra computer network server to handle the data storage and processing functions of the 8A1 claims processing.[49]

ICHEIC handled the intake of claims and contracted with a scanning company to create electronic images of the claim forms. The JCC processed the 8A1 Claims using only these scanned images and did not need large archives in which to store voluminous paper documents.

(j) American Arbitration Association (AAA)—an illustrative case

A centralized infrastructure, with supporting computer equipment, was used until the last few months of the Claims Process in the illustrative case, whereupon the claims staff moved into a pre-existing AAA facility, to save on costs.

In establishing the needed infrastructure, it took approximately two months to find the physical office space, hire initial staff, and order initial equipment. It took an additional four months to complete staff hiring, purchase equipment, and to establish sufficient telephone lines for the proceedings that were conducted over the telephone.

6.05 Satellite Offices

If relevant in view of the geographic distribution of the claimant population, the various options and facilities available, including satellite offices, for reaching potential claimants, receiving and registering claims, and other functions.

Editors' Commentary

As stated at the outset of the Editors' Commentary in section 3.01 above, "[a] Mass Claims Process has little practical value unless potential claimants are aware of the opportunity to make claims and are given information on how to do so." While section 3.01 focuses on the methods for accomplishing such outreach (e.g., publication of notices in newspapers, direct mail, the Internet), this section 6.05 describes facilities that a Claims Process may establish to facilitate outreach (e.g., satellite offices, offices of affiliates, and mobile teams).

---

[49] This server had a processing capability of 3GHz, a memory capacity of 4GB RAM, and a storage capacity of 700 GB.

As in the case of outreach methods, no one type of facility "is appropriate for all Claims Processes; rather, the effectiveness of the [facility] to be used depends on the particular circumstances involved."[50] Most of the Claims Processes described in this book operate solely from central headquarters, such as the Iran–United States Claims Tribunal (Iran–US CT). Others employ another institution to perform some, or all, of its administrative tasks and utilize affiliated offices of that institution, such as the Claims Processes administered by the International Organization for Migration (IOM). Still others open satellite field offices and/or organize mobile teams to go to where potential claimants live, such as the Commission for Real Property Claims of Displaced Persons and Refugees (CRPC) in Bosnia and Herzegovina. Going to where claimants live is not only a personal convenience for them, but also—and perhaps most importantly—puts a human face on the Claims Process that may enhance community satisfaction and help heal wounds.

(a) Iran–United States Claims Tribunal (Iran–US CT)—claims relating to the 1979 Islamic Revolution

The Tribunal has no facilities outside its headquarters in The Hague.

(b) United Nations Compensation Commission (UNCC)—claims relating to the 1990–1991 Gulf War

The UNCC has had no permanent offices outside its headquarters in Geneva. Communication between the Commission and claimants who are located at a distance takes place through their government representatives based in Geneva.

(c) Commission for Real Property Claims of Displaced Persons and Refugees (CRPC)—claims relating to the 1992–1995 war in Bosnia and Herzegovina

CRPC had its headquarters in Sarajevo. It was authorized by its constituting instrument to have offices at other locations as it deemed appropriate.[51] Pursuant to that authority, it utilized five regional offices elsewhere in Bosnia and Herzegovina, three offices in Yugoslavia, and two in Croatia, and claims registration could occasionally be conducted away from these offices if the

---

[50] See Editors' Commentary to section 3.01 above, on Outreach.
[51] Dayton Peace Agreement, Annex 7, Article VII.

Executive Director so approved.[52] CRPC had offices in Denmark (Copenhagen), Germany (Berlin, Duisburg, Freiburg), the Netherlands (Utrecht), and Norway (Oslo).

In addition to its regional offices, CRPC also used mobile outreach teams to reach more isolated areas in Bosnia and Herzegovina, Serbia, and Croatia. The mobile teams consisted of two to five staff members, depending on the population density in the areas they covered. The teams traveled throughout the country and collected claims at fixed dates at specific locations, registering claims using laptop computers. Later, these mobile teams also distributed the Commission's decision certificates to any claimants who failed to pick up their certificate at the nearest regional CRPC office. The mobile teams proved to be both cost effective and highly dependable.

(d) Claims Resolution Tribunal for Dormant Accounts in Switzerland (CRT-I)—first claims tribunal for assets deposited in Swiss banks

CRT-I had its headquarters in Zurich. At an early stage of the Claims Process, it also maintained an additional office in Geneva to assist the Arbitrators for whom Geneva was a more convenient location, but that practice was discontinued when it was decided to centralize all staff in Zurich. Although it had one central office, CRT-I was supported in its work by volunteer assistance organizations in various parts of the world which provided information and aid to claimants.

In addition, an international auditing firm, ATAG Ernst & Young, served as central contact office for the claimants and banks.[53] It had offices for the filing of claims in Basle, Budapest, New York, Sydney, and Tel-Aviv, the Basle office serving as the central contact office.

(e) Claims Resolution Tribunal (CRT-II)—second claims tribunal for assets deposited in Swiss banks

Claims submitted to the CRT-II Claims Process were sent to an office in the United States where they were registered and scanned. The main offices of the Claims Process are at its headquarters in Zurich, and some CRT-II claims are also processed at the facilities of the Jewish Claims Conference (JCC) in New York City.

---

[52] CRPC Book of Regulations on Procedure, Article 21.
[53] CRT-I Rules of Procedure, Article 4(ii).

(f) Housing and Property Claims Commission (HPCC)—claims relating to the 1999 conflict in Kosovo

The Rules of the Commission and the Housing and Property Directorate (HPD) provide that the Directorate "shall register claims . . . at offices established for this purpose in Kosovo and in such other locations as it sees fit."[54]

The Directorate has made use of this authority and, in addition to the Claims Process headquarters in Pristina, has established five regional offices and a number of field offices for claims intake purposes. In total, twenty-two offices were involved in claims intake. Many of these were located in Serbia, and one in Skopje, Macedonia. Several of these (in Belgrade, Kragojevac and Nis (in Serbia proper), Podgorica (Montenegro), Skopje (Macedonia), and three minority areas inside Kosovo) continued to operate beyond the claims intake phase.

The HPD also employed mobile teams to reach claimants residing outside major population centers. Some of these teams operated outside Kosovo, in Serbia, Montenegro, and Macedonia. Claims intake missions by the Directorate's staff were also made to various locations in Western Europe.

(g) Mass Claims Processes administered by the International Organization for Migration (IOM)

German Forced Labour Compensation Programme (GFLCP)—claims against Germany and German industry for Nazi injustice

The GFLCP Claims Process—the part of the German Foundation Act implementation for which IOM is responsible—is based in Geneva where the management and coordination of the Claims Process and the substantive decision-making take place. The Property Claims Commission and the IOM Appeals Body for Forced Labour Claims have also met in Geneva for deliberations. In order to provide the most claimant-friendly set-up, and in view of the worldwide distribution of potential claimants, outreach, distribution of claim forms, assistance to claimants, claims intake and registration, and the initial screening of claims, were performed in over sixty countries—mostly at IOM field offices already existing in those countries. While this approach greatly helped the claimants in obtaining information about the Claims Process and in the filing of claims, and although the field offices were already part of the

---

[54] UNMIK Regulation 2000/60, section 7.1.

IOM network of operations, it did present considerable communication and coordination challenges to the management of the incipient Claims Process.

Holocaust Victim Assets Programme (HVAP)—claims pursuant to
1999 class action Settlement

The HVAP Claims Process—the part of the Settlement Agreement implementation for which IOM is responsible in the class action known as the Holocaust Victim Assets Litigation—is based at IOM's offices in Geneva. For outreach and claim form distribution, the Claims Process made extensive use of IOM field office support.

(h) Eritrea–Ethiopia Claims Commission (EECC)—claims relating to the 1998–2000 war between Eritrea and Ethiopia

The two Governments party to the EECC are themselves responsible for all claims intake and evidence gathering in the Claims Process.

The Commission's work has been centered in The Hague, although it also had some meetings with the parties elsewhere. It has not established any presence or carried out any activities in either Eritrea or Ethiopia, although the 12 December 2000 Agreement and the Rules of Procedure both allow for such arrangements if they are deemed necessary at any time.[55]

(i) Humanitarian insurance Claims Process administered by the Jewish Claims Conference (JCC) for the International Commission on Holocaust Era Insurance Claims (ICHEIC)

ICHEIC contracted with relevant companies to conduct all claimant outreach and to collect all claims. It sent all claim forms and evidence falling within the 8A1 humanitarian Claims Process electronically to the JCC for processing and evaluation. There was no need for the JCC to set up satellite offices outside of New York. The JCC did have contact with claimants through its operation of ICHEIC's toll-free Call Center, and checks of award payments were mailed directly from New York to each eligible claimant's place of residence. In connection with issuing awards to claimants located in certain countries where the safe receipt of payment might be uncertain due to political considerations or

---

[55] Eritrea–Ethiopia Agreement of 12 December 2000, Article 5, paragraph 5; EECC Rules of Procedure, Article 11, paragraph 1.

local banking systems, the JCC relied upon local affiliate offices or agents to help deliver the funds directly to the claimants.

(j) American Arbitration Association (AAA)—an illustrative case

All potential claimants in the illustrative case were in the United States. The appealed cases which the AAA was responsible for resolving did not involve any "claims collection" or other activities requiring satellite offices; the appeals were sent from the defendant insurance company via computer directly to the AAA at the administration site. If a claimant prevailed on appeal, the award was paid directly by the insurance company, obviating the need for any field teams to reach the claimants as in some of the international Claims Processes described in this book.

6.06 Information Technology

How computers are used to facilitate the Claims Process. Whether information technology (IT) specialists are part of the initial Claims Process design team. Computer databases, systems, applications, hardware, network, and telecommunications facilities needed to provide the required level of computer support. The design of claim forms to enable and facilitate the creation of a computerized claims database. (For procedures conducted electronically and mass claims techniques, see sections 5.05 and 5.06.)

Editors' Commentary

The earlier Mass Claims Processes described in this book made relatively little use of information technology (IT), but later Claims Processes have increasingly taken advantage of the constant evolution of systems using computers. Thus, in the more recent Claims Processes, computerization of claims and certain evidentiary data have become the first steps taken, followed by the development of claims management and claims tracking systems. Many of the later Claims Processes described in this book have established their own in-house IT departments to provide ongoing computer support to claims processing and resolution.

The compatibility of the computer software and systems used by certain parties, on the one hand, and by the Claims Process, on the other, has been an issue in some Claims Processes. At the Commission for Real Property Claims of Displaced Persons and Refugees (CRPC) in Bosnia and Herzegovina, for example, the often out-dated software in use for local land records databases presented a challenge when developing the Commission's own software.

Problems may also arise if the designers of a Claims Process proceed with the computerization effort too early, or before they are given the appropriate technical specifications by the actual decision-making body. Inasmuch as Mass Claims Processes depend on harmonized procedures to achieve consistent results, it is difficult to change or adapt the software once claims processing has begun. This highlights the importance of timely planning and foresight, and of using standardized technologies wherever possible. For example, the International Organization for Migration (IOM) used Internet-based technologies to collect over 300,000 slave and forced labor claims from all over the world. Similarly, the Claims Resolution Tribunal (CRT-II) uses a web-based interface that allows off-site parties to access its database in Zurich through the Internet. Finally, it is essential that the software used by a Mass Claims Process be functional and easy to use, so that the staff working on the claims processing does not have to spend valuable time on procedures that are built into the software but that are not necessary for the work.

All of the Claims Processes described below have had their own websites, or have utilized the website of a hosting or supporting organization, for posting various information about the Claims Process, such as claims statistics and periodic reports, the procedural rules, and constituting instruments. Some have also included the decisions rendered. One must be cautioned, however, that some websites may be out of date, or may even be dismantled after the mandate of a Claims Process terminates.[56] Similarly, while the IT procedures and the software of various Claims Processes may provide useful lessons and examples for others, procedures that are initially useful may become quickly obsolete.

(a) Iran–United States Claims Tribunal (Iran–US CT)—claims relating to the 1979 Islamic Revolution

When the Iran–US CT was established in 1981, electronic means of conducting legal proceedings were not in common use and the Internet was not yet available.

---

[56] In an effort to preserve the information about completed Mass Claims Processes and continue, the Permanent Court of Arbitration, as of February 2006, has created a permanent archive on its own

Thus, no information technology specialists were consulted during the initial design of the Claims Process and the Tribunal's procedures were not computerized, nor have they been significantly altered to make use of new technologies as they have become available during the life of this Claims Process. Computers are used at the Tribunal typically for word-processing and for financial, budgetary, and accounting purposes. In addition, the Registry uses computers for generating and maintaining a Quarterly Index of relevant claims statistics,[57] and its decisions are available on its website and on electronic legal databases.

(b) United Nations Compensation Commission (UNCC)—claims relating to the 1990–1991 Gulf War

The UNCC has maintained a large in-house IT department and has relied heavily on computer support in all aspects of its operations, including the registration of claims, document management, cross-checks, the verification and valuation of claims, generation of reports, payment of awards, general information management, and the archiving of records. The UNCC's large claims database is highly integrated into its general claims processing and claims payment systems. It performs a range of information management functions and the IT department has developed a number of software applications to facilitate the operations mentioned above.

The UNCC worked with IT specialists early in the design of the claim forms in order to capture information in a manner best suited to its subsequent electronic analysis and management. In the UNCC's experience, it is important to have the input of such specialists prior to the finalization of claim forms. Claims were tracked electronically from their receipt by the UNCC. Documents submitted by claimant governments and other submitting entities on behalf of claimants—including claim forms, statements of claim, supporting documentation, and correspondence—were registered electronically on docket sheets that became part of the claim files. In certain instances, claims were submitted to the UNCC in electronic rather than hard copy form.

Computers were central to the development of mass claims processing techniques and other claims review procedures or methodologies to assist panels of Commissioners and the UNCC Secretariat. This included the development and application of software capable of performing a range of statistical analyses, including correlation and regression analyses, and of automatically gener-

---

website where such information will be stored and made available to the public, with permission of the relevant decision-makers. See www.pca-cpa.org/MCP/index_MCP.htm.

[57] The Tribunal's website is www.iusct.org.

ating preliminary recommendations with respect to awards of compensation for various loss types. Data in respect of each claim in the UNCC's database was used to match claims electronically (with manual follow-up) in order to identify and screen out duplicate claims. Computer applications also facilitated the management of documents and the archiving of records. A separate jurisprudence database was also created. Claimant governments and other submitting entities have been able to access certain information remotely in respect of the claims they filed.

The UNCC maintains a website on which is posted, *inter alia*, information about the Commission, Governing Council decisions, and the reports and recommendations of panels of Commissioners once they have been approved by the Governing Council.[58]

(c) Commission for Real Property Claims of Displaced Persons and Refugees (CRPC)—claims relating to the 1992–1995 war in Bosnia and Herzegovina

Early on in the CRPC Claims Process, the determination was made that the Commission could only rely upon land records as evidence. Therefore, a large IT department was required in order to put those records into a user-friendly computer database for quick reference by the staff attorneys preparing draft decisions. An extensive IT department (headed by an international staff member and consisting of some thirty programmers, database administrators, and network administrators who supported over 290 work stations) was created to register the claims and check the databases to verify claims. It developed, in-house, cadastre land survey databases into which collected data was entered. Using these databases allowed CRPC to verify claims for property in eighty percent of pre-war municipalities.[59] Sophisticated software was developed to enable the collection and storage of claims throughout Bosnia and Herzegovina (BiH) and other refugee-hosting countries. Much of the claims collection and registration was also conducted by mobile teams equipped with laptop computers.

In 2001, CRPC completed the design of a Repossessions Tracking Database to track and follow-up on repossessions throughout BiH. This database included over 186,700 registered repossessions at the end of 2003. As an extension of this database, in 2002, CRPC established the Integrated Property System, a database that integrated CRPC's claims and decision database and CRPC's Repossessions Tracking Database (both of which covered the entire BiH) with thirty-nine

---

[58] www.uncc.ch.   [59] See CRPC End of Mandate Report, Executive Summary, p. 2.

municipal claims and decisions databases. At the time of the hand-over of the Claims Process to the BiH Ministry of Human Rights and Refugees at the end of 2003, the Integrated Property System contained all relevant data on property claims, establishing a framework which domestic authorities could use to take over the implementation of Annex 7 to the Dayton Peace Agreement.[60]

The computer databases, systems, applications, hardware, network, and telecommunication facilities evolved over time to address the changing needs of the Claims Process. The decision-making procedures and the claim form were, however, determined at the outset after elaborate discussions between the Executive Officer, the heads of the Legal and IT Departments, and the computer programmers. The claim form had to request all information necessary in order to make a legal decision. Once designed, the claim forms did not change.

(d) Claims Resolution Tribunal for Dormant Accounts in Switzerland (CRT-I)—first claims tribunal for assets deposited in Swiss banks

CRT-I initially relied upon the computer support system of the Swiss law firm serving as the Tribunal's Secretariat, the firm's computer programs being adapted for use by the Claims Process. For reasons of confidentiality, separate servers were used for the Claims Process Secretariat and the law firm's own work. ATAG Ernst & Young, which served as a contact office with the claimants, employed its own computer system, as did the participating banks. The three systems were not compatible with each other.

CRT-I eventually developed its own computer support system, which was similar to those commonly used by law firms. The system was essentially a claims cataloging system consisting of filing and reporting functions, including the generation of statistical data. Actual claims data was not computerized and there was no electronic claims database. CRT-I did not develop a computerized database or a claims and processing status tracking system. Given the comparatively low number of claims (as compared to some other Claims Processes described in this book)—9,918 in total—and the traditional arbitration procedures that were employed to decide the claims, extensive computer support was not considered necessary.

(e) Claims Resolution Tribunal (CRT-II)—second claims tribunal for assets deposited in Swiss banks

CRT-II uses a complex database that was designed and created especially for the Claims Process and covers all aspects of the claims processing. This database

[60] See CRPC End of Mandate Report, pp. 25–26.

replaced an earlier one which had been designed from the point of view of individual adjudication of claims and did not meet all the needs of the Claims Process as envisioned in the amended Governing Rules. As revised, the database includes scanned images of the claim forms, information extracted from the claims, data from bank records entered by auditors, images of the bank records themselves, decisions issued on the claims, and correspondence with the claimants.

CRT-II employs its own IT team. Some of the IT specialists work on the database development, and others administer software and hardware.

Information about CRT-II, including the text of its decisions and amounts of payments to claimants, is posted on the official website of the Claims Process.[61]

(f) Housing and Property Claims Commission (HPCC)—claims relating to the 1999 conflict in Kosovo

The Rules of the HPCC and the Housing and Property Directorate (HPD) do not envisage a computerized processing of the claims, and IT experts were not involved in the initial design of the Claims Process. The Rules do provide, however, that the Commission "may . . . use computer databases, programs and other electronic tools in order to expedite its decision-making."[62]

For a number of reasons, inadequacy of computer support was for a long time one of the principal challenges of this Claims Process. In the absence of a computerized claims database and claims tracking system, the productivity of the Commission suffered. The problem was eventually resolved when an in-house IT service was created within the Directorate. Computer support played an important role in the turnaround of the Claims Process in 2002–2003, when the number of resolved claims at each session of the Commission increased significantly.

The Claims Process is supported by a computer system that includes a claims database and basic claims and processing status-tracking functions. The system has been developed essentially in-house by the Directorate's own IT service.

The database maintained by the Directorate reflects the structure of the claim forms used in the Claims Process. The system has been described as not being particularly sophisticated, but it meets the basic functional requirements of the Claims Process. The Directorate has access to the computerized records of the Kosovo Cadastre Agency, an electronic version of which is kept with the Directorate. Claimed properties are checked against this database as appropriate.

---

[61] See www.crt-ii.org.
[62] UNMIK Regulation 2000/60, section 19.5(c).

The Directorate's regional offices (except those located outside Kosovo) have access to the central database via an intranet. Given the decentralized nature of the claims verification procedures and the critical role that the regional offices play in this Claims Process, off-site access to the database is considered to be mission-critical.[63]

In view of the degraded state of the telecommunications infrastructure in Kosovo at the time of the launch of the Claims Process in 1999, the creation of a distributed claims processing system can be considered an achievement in and of itself.

(g) Mass Claims Processes administered by the International Organization for Migration (IOM): *German Forced Labour Compensation Programme (GFLCP) for claims against Germany and German industry for Nazi injustice, and Holocaust Victim Assets Programme (HVAP) for claims pursuant to 1999 class action Settlement*

For both the GFLCP and HVAP Claims Processes, the processing of claims, their review and verification, the generation of the decision texts and their notification to the claimants, as well as the payments, management, reporting and audit needs, all require extensive computer support. This includes worldwide telecommunications and networks, large claims databases, claims registration, processing, tracking, reporting and notification applications, imaging, matching and profiling software, and financial and payment tools. Hardware includes personal computers, servers, printers, scanners, copiers, network, and communications equipment. Claims data and images can be accessed by multiple users working in each of the Claims Processes, and documents are exchanged via e-mail with the Members of the Property Claims Commission and the IOM Appeals Body for Forced Labour Claims.

Several IT specialists formed part of the initial core team recruited for the two Claims Processes. The team performed an initial analysis of the procedures and shortly thereafter drafted the first user specifications. However, the Claims Processes have continued to evolve, and new computer applications or modifications of existing ones are constantly needed. This, as well as the maintenance of the existing systems and applications, requires the continued availability of specialized IT staff.

---

[63] The verification function involves checking property records in the appropriate public authorities and private entities, depending on where the property is located.

In both GFLCP and HVAP, claim forms were designed for the various claims categories in such a way that maximum use could be made of the information collected on them through computerized claims databases. This included an early assessment of the methods by which the claims were likely to be processed and verified, the information needed to apply these methods, the information likely to be available to claimants, and the information needed for the grouping and processing of the claims in groups. The questions on the forms were formulated and numbered in a consistent manner, and they were, to the extent possible, organized so as to facilitate the filling out of the forms, and entering the information contained (in different languages) on the forms into the respective databases. Bar-coding and unique numbering were used at the intake and registration stages to allow digital scanning of all claims documentation into the respective networks of the Claims Processes.

(h) Eritrea–Ethiopia Claims Commission (EECC)—claims relating to the 1998–2000 war between Eritrea and Ethiopia

For the initial design of the EECC, the main IT planning concerned, on the one hand, what sort of database should be used for general document management and, on the other hand, the electronic processing of eventual claim forms for fixed-sum compensation claims under Chapter Three of the Commission's Rules of Procedure governing mass claims procedures. The EECC is authorized under the 12 December 2000 Agreement and its Rules of Procedure to employ consultants and experts to advise it,[64] and it did consult with mass claims experts from the International Organization for Migration (IOM) regarding data collection, analysis, and sampling techniques in the months before the deadline for filing claims.

The EECC Commissioners and the Registry have utilized e-mail and fax for most internal communications between the times of their face-to-face meetings. Many communications between the Commission and the parties likewise occur through the conduit of e-mails channeled through Permanent Court of Arbitration (PCA) personnel providing Registry services. The Claims Process has been able to rely on the hardware and applications already in use by the PCA, using standard commercial software and e-mail applications, including a commercial database for document management. In addition, one of the Commissioners has made available through the support of her law firm a secure electronic document vault for storage of important documents in a fashion remotely accessible by all five Commissioners.

---

[64] Eritrea–Ethiopia Agreement of 12 December 2000, Article 5, paragraph 6; EECC Rules of Procedure, Article 16.

If, during the damages stage of the proceedings, the parties file a large mass of information related to the situations of numerous individuals, more advanced IT support may well be required, which means that the Commission needs to revisit the issue early enough for the system to be operational by the necessary date.

(i) Humanitarian insurance Claims Process administered by the Jewish Claims Conference (JCC) for the International Commission on Holocaust Era Insurance Claims (ICHEIC)

The 8A1 humanitarian Claims Process was conceived with electronic claims processing in mind, and the JCC–ICHEIC Agreement provided that the JCC would develop the software necessary for processing the claims, and for the interchange of data with ICHEIC's larger database system. The completed claim forms and accompanying evidentiary documentation were scanned into digital format and submitted electronically to the JCC. The JCC developed software to work with the scanned images and employed, as part of its 8A1 Claims team, one of its regular in-house database developers to handle software development and information management. Access to the electronic records was strictly controlled through fire-walls to protect the privacy of individual claimants.

The 8A1 team included one database administrator and one software programmer. For the first phase night shift, IT support was provided by a single IT administrator, but this support was limited to basic hardware issues, as the 8A1 Claims database and application developer was at home, though on call, during most of the night shift. During the second phase of claims processing, the JCC was able to rely upon similar levels of IT support from the JCC general pool of IT staff, during their regular daytime office hours.

The 8A1 software provided the basic tools needed for claims analysts to evaluate a claim, working with the computer screen divided in half, with the Point Scoring System questions shown on the left half of the screen, and the scanned images of the claims themselves on the right half, along with some basic image manipulation tools.

All work on the claims was stored in a central database that allowed for a complete review of each claim's history, viewable by a user with Administrator access rights using a special 8A1 Claims Processing Application. This Application also allowed for various administrative functions to be performed by a user with the necessary clearance. Aside from the 8A1 Application's Administrator mode, the claims database provided information to a web-based interface to allow the Administrator to track employee efficiency.

(j) American Arbitration Association (AAA)—an illustrative case

In the illustrative case, an IT team had been hired by the defendant insurance company for over a year before the appeals process began, and it was available on a daily basis for consultation. This team was part of the initial Claims Process design team, but most of the IT work was done as the Claims Process developed by the AAA's own IT staff in cooperation with the defendant's IT team, with much trial and error.

All Arbitrators in the illustrative case were required to have at their disposal a personal computer, printer, and fax equipment, and to be personally capable of operating this equipment, although this expectation was not always met in practice. All such equipment had to be compatible with the equipment being used by the defendant insurance company. All parts of the Claims Process were governed by prepared claim forms, which were designed to operate within a computerized database, and all evidence was digitized through the use of scanning technology.

Chapter 7

Funding the Claims Process

7.01 Budgeting

The costs of running the Claims Process, other than compensation payments to claimants, such as salary structure for staff, fees and expenses of decision-makers, infrastructure, and other overheads.

Editors' Commentary

The expenses of a Mass Claims Process include personnel costs of staff, fees and expenses of decision-makers such as the Arbitrators or Judges, occupancy costs of offices, purchases and maintenance of equipment, supplies, telephone and other communication costs, amounts paid for outsourced services, and a myriad of other items. Some of those costs, such as recruiting, relocation expenses of newly hired individuals, and purchases of equipment, must be paid at an early stage of the Claims Process. Others are continuing costs that can be expected to increase as the Process evolves, and to decline as it completes its mission and winds down. Many of these expenses tend to be relatively high because of urgent pressures to accomplish tasks as quickly as possible and to complete the mandate of the Claims Process by a fixed deadline.

Although the circumstances of the Mass Claims Processes described in this book vary widely, information concerning their expenses may nevertheless be helpful to those who seek to estimate the costs of future Claims Processes. Some Claims Processes make such financial information publicly available, others do not. Accordingly, the description of each of the Claims Processes below either includes the amount of its total annual expenses for a representative period, or states that the figures are not publicly available. The total expense figures for various Claims Processes that appear below are not comparable in a strict accounting sense because of the different circumstances of those Processes. For example, some Claims Processes use, in whole or part, staff and facilities of another organization and the methods of accounting for such costs may differ. Another factor that makes it difficult to compare costs is that some Claims Processes can use relatively large numbers of local staff, whereas others, particularly when the claimants come from many different countries, must recruit, transport, and house multi-lingual staff from many locations. A further difference is that, in at least one Claims Process—the Iran–United States Claims Tribunal (Iran–US CT)—the Members serve full-time and are expected to take up residence at the place where the Tribunal is located, while in other Claims Processes, decision-makers work part-time and do not establish such residences.

One element of costs is the fees and expenses of those who decide the claims. These, however, are only a relatively small amount of the total costs of the Claims Processes. Decision-makers in some Claims Processes receive annual fees ranging from US$150,000 (plus a per diem for each day of hearings) to approximately US$225,000 (including expenses for living abroad). Some fees are free of certain taxes by virtue of diplomatic privileges and immunities. In setting fees, some Claims Processes are guided by fee practices of other international organizations; for example, one Claims Process follows United Nations compensation scales, and another refers to amounts paid to Judges of the European Court of Human Rights. Some Claims Processes, rather than paying decision-makers an annual fee, compensate them on an hourly basis, generally somewhat lower than the rate those persons would receive in an international commercial arbitration. Many senior decision-makers accept lower compensation than they would earn in their other professional activities because of the public interest nature of international mass claims work.

Annotations

(a) Iran–United States Claims Tribunal (Iran–US CT)—claims relating to the 1979 Islamic Revolution

The Claims Settlement Declaration provides that "[t]he expenses of the Tribunal shall be borne equally by the two governments."[1] For the fiscal year 2001–2002, the Tribunal's annual expenses were US$4,569,575; in 2002–2003, they were US$5,047,027; in 2003–2004, US$6,260,013; and in 2004–2005, US$7,917,058 (subject to audit).

At the request of the two Governments, the Tribunal adopts its annual budget several months prior to the date when the Governments' contributions

---

[1] Claims Settlement Declaration, Article VI, paragraph 3.

are due. The possibility of significant currency-rate fluctuations, however, have made such budget forecasting difficult and created potential budgeting problems. As an additional consequence of currency-rate fluctuations, the Tribunal until 2005 paid exchange adjustment allowances to the Members of the Tribunal and to those staff members whose salaries, health benefits, and separation pay were paid in United States dollars. The Tribunal then shifted to a Euro-based budget, which has ameliorated some of the difficulties caused by currency fluctuations.

The Iran–US CT has its own facilities and staff, and its expenses reflect that. To the extent that it used a hearing room in the Peace Palace at The Hague from time to time, it paid a charge to the Permanent Court of Arbitration (PCA), but the Tribunal, in a move aimed at reducing costs, constructed a new courtroom on its premises, where hearings in the remaining large government cases will be held.[2] The Government of the Netherlands accorded the Members of the Tribunal and its staff tax exemptions and immunities comparable to those accorded to other intergovernmental organizations.

(b) United Nations Compensation Commission (UNCC)—claims relating to the 1990–1991 Gulf War

Since the autumn of 1991, the UNCC has implemented seventeen separate claims programs established by the Governing Council, each with different types of claims, differing factual and legal issues and different claims review procedures developed by panels of Commissioners. There have been nineteen panels of Commissioners, and the Secretariat has employed a total of over six hundred individuals during the UNCC's existence. Notwithstanding these numbers, the overall administrative costs of the UNCC have been comparatively low, largely due to the application of mass claims processing techniques whenever appropriate.

The yearly expense figures for the operation of the UNCC are not public. The UNCC's administrative expenditures from its inception in 1991 to May 2005 totaled US$362.6 million. Expressed as percentages of the value of claims, compensation awarded, and compensation paid until May 2005, respectively, that figure represents: 0.10 percent of the asserted value of the claims filed; 0.69 percent of the amount of compensation awarded; or 1.89 percent of the amount of compensation paid to successful claimants until May 2005.

---

[2] See section 6.02(a) above, on the Tribunal's facilities.

The Commission's expenses, including those of the Governing Council, the Secretariat, and the Commissioners, have in principle been covered by the Compensation Fund.[3] In effect, the expenses of the Claims Process, in addition to awards of compensation, have thus been paid by Iraq. The expenses of the UNCC take into account that it has its own staff and facilities, except that certain limited administrative services are provided to it by the United Nations Office in Geneva. Commissioners and staff have been paid by the United Nations on that organization's salary scale, and they have enjoyed United Nations privileges and immunities.

(c) Commission for Real Property Claims of Displaced Persons and Refugees (CRPC)—claims relating to the 1992–1995 war in Bosnia and Herzegovina

The total expenses of the CRPC for the period from 1997 to 2003 were US$33,492,500. In 1999, the annual expenses of the Claims Process were US$6,551,000; in 2000, approximately US$6 million; in 1998 and 2001, approximately US$ 5 million; in 2002, approximately US$4 million; and in 1997 and 2003—the first and last year of operations—approximately US$3.5 million. These expenses include the costs of the Commission's own staff and facilities.

The constituting instrument, the Dayton Peace Agreement, accorded to Members of the Commission and their families, who were not citizens of Bosnia and Herzegovina, "the same privileges and immunities as are enjoyed by diplomatic agents and their families under the Vienna Convention on Diplomatic Relations."[4]

(d) Claims Resolution Tribunal for Dormant Accounts in Switzerland (CRT-I)—first claims tribunal for assets deposited in Swiss banks

The total costs of the CRT-I Claims Process amounted to CHF 32 million, which were incurred over a period of three-and-a-half years.

CRT-I's expenses reflected the fact that, although it initially used facilities and services of a law firm in Zurich, in later years it had its own staff and facilities.[5] CRT-I did not enjoy tax-free status in Switzerland.

---

[3] See section 2.07(b) above, on the creation of the UNCC Compensation Fund. The Report of the Secretary-General of 2 May 1991, U.N. Doc. S/22559, Part II, paragraph 29, although not actually binding on the Governing Council, provides that "[t]he expenses of the Commission, including those of the Governing Council, the commissioners and the secretariat, should in principle be paid from the Fund."   [4] Dayton Peace Agreement, Annex 7, Article X (3).

[5] See sections 6.01(c), 6.02(c), and 6.04(c) above, on administration, infrastructure, and facilities at CRPC.

(e) Claims Resolution Tribunal (CRT-II)—second claims tribunal for assets deposited in Swiss banks

The amount of the costs of conducting the CRT-II Claims Process are not readily available.

The staffing, infrastructure, and facilities of CRT II are described in Chapter 6 above.[6] The Tribunal is an association under Swiss law and, as such, it is in principle subject to taxation in Switzerland.

(f) Housing and Property Claims Commission (HPCC)—claims relating to the 1999 conflict in Kosovo

The annual budget of the HPCC for 2005 was approximately US$5.2 million, not including compensation payments. The administrators of the Claims Process consider that it is underfunded.

Both the HPCC and the Housing and Property Directorate (HPD) form part of the administration of the United Nations Interim Administration Mission in Kosovo (UNMIK), and all international and national staff employed by the Claims Process are therefore covered by the relevant privileges and immunities granted to United Nations staff.

(g) Mass Claims Processes administered by the International Organization for Migration (IOM): *German Forced Labour Compensation Programme (GFLCP) for claims against Germany and German industry for Nazi injustice, and Holocaust Victim Assets Programme (HVAP) for claims pursuant to 1999 class action Settlement*

Specific budgetary and administrative cost figures for the GFLCP and HVAP Claims Processes are not publicly available. To give an indication, however, the IOM estimates that the total cost for the first instance processing of the 330,000 slave and forced labor claims, and the processing of the 30,000 appeals in this category, all together over a period of close to six years, will be approximately Euro 40 million. The expenses of both GFLCP and HVAP reflect that, although they rely to a certain extent on support from IOM's headquarters and field offices, they have their own staff and facilities.

---

[6] See sections 6.01(e), 6.02(e), and 6.04(e) above, on Management and Staffing, Infrastructure, and Facilities of CRT-II.

GFLCP and HVAP staff, as well as the Property Claims Commissioners and Members of the IOM Appeals Body for Forced Labour Claims, have been paid by IOM according to IOM salary scales, and they have enjoyed the same privileges and immunities as other employees of IOM. Fees of Commissioners have been comparatively low because they do not work full-time. On average, they have met two to three days per month in Geneva and done their remaining work away from Geneva.

(h) Eritrea–Ethiopia Claims Commission (EECC)—claims relating to the 1998–2000 war between Eritrea and Ethiopia

The EECC reimburses the Permanent Court of Arbitration (PCA) at established hourly rates for staff time and other resources provided by the PCA. The EECC budget is quite modest, and the Commission's largest item of expenditure has been the compensation of the individual Commissioners. The five Commissioners serve for a fixed annual honorarium, the rate of which was established following consultation with the parties and with their approval. The staff of the PCA provide part-time support for EECC Secretariat work. There are some hearing expenses (e.g., transcripts, travel expenses, and hearing room rentals).

The expense figures of the EECC Claims Process have not been made publicly available.

(i) Humanitarian insurance Claims Process administered by the Jewish Claims Conference (JCC) for the International Commission on Holocaust Era Insurance Claims (ICHEIC)

At the time of the signing of the JCC–ICHEIC Agreement, a budget and a financial reporting system for the 8A1 humanitarian Claims Process were agreed. The Agreement is not a public document, and the expense figures were not made public.

(j) American Arbitration Association (AAA)—an illustrative case

Specific budgetary and administrative cost figures in the illustrative case are not publicly available, as the Settlement Agreement was confidential. The AAA was paid on a per-case basis for its services, including overhead, staff salaries, information technology costs, equipment costs, and other administrative costs. The AAA also received an up-front payment for setting up the Claims Process.

In comparing the expenses of this Claims Process with the international Claims Processes described in this book, it should be borne in mind that each of the claims was relatively small and the issues were limited. Reflecting this, the Arbitrators were each paid US$150 per hour spent working on the case. They were required to submit time-sheets recording their hours of work. The defendant insurance company forwarded to the AAA a fixed amount of money on a regular basis, from which Arbitrators' expenses and fees were paid. Most cases were resolved in an average of five hours of billable time.

Costs for claimant and defendant counsel were separate and paid directly by the defendant insurance company, and claimants' counsel were given an up-front payment to cover all expenses of their representation of claimants in the Claims Process.

7.02 Budget Process

The roles, if any, which Secretariat staff and decision-makers play in establishing periodic budgets.

Editors' Commentary

Typically, two basic questions arise with respect to the budget process of a Mass Claims Process. The first is who prepares the budget, and the second is who has the power to approve, modify, or reject the budget. As is described in the sections below, the answers to these questions can differ widely.

(a) Iran–United States Claims Tribunal (Iran–US CT)—claims relating to the 1979 Islamic Revolution

The Tribunal establishes the budget of the Claims Process unless the two Government parties mutually agree otherwise.[7] To assist in performing that function, the Tribunal established a Committee on Administrative and Financial Questions, comprised of one Iranian Member of the Tribunal, one United States Member, and one third-country Member. The Tribunal's

---

[7] See Iran–US CT Tribunal Rules, Article 41, and Claims Settlement Declaration, Article III, paragraph 2, which provides that the Rules may be modified by the parties. Thus, Iran and the United States could by agreement between them take control over the budget. In practice, however, the Tribunal has controlled the budget of the Claims Process.

Secretary-General and the United States and Iranian Agents attend meetings and are consulted on budgetary matters, but they have no vote.

(b) United Nations Compensation Commission (UNCC)—claims relating to the 1990–1991 Gulf War

The UNCC Secretariat prepares the budgets of the Claims Process, subject to review and approval by the Governing Council. Expenses of the UNCC and awards for compensation are paid out of the Compensation Fund described in section 2.07(b) above. That Fund has been administered by the Secretariat in accordance with the United Nations Financial Regulations and Rules, and under the financial oversight of the United Nations Secretariat in New York.

The UNCC Governing Council also established a Committee on Administrative Matters, stating that it "will review and provide guidance on major administrative and budgetary matters presented to it by the Executive Secretary, including the annual administrative budget."[8]

(c) Commission for Real Property Claims of Displaced Persons and Refugees (CRPC)—claims relating to the 1992–1995 war in Bosnia and Herzegovina

CRPC established the total amount of its annual budget and had discretion in making expenditures. It made an annual report to justify its expenditures. Annual contributions were made by the signatory States to the Dayton Peace Agreement and the European Union based on projected activities and past achievements. In the initial years of operation, contributions were made on an *ad hoc* basis, and in later years donors supported CRPC in accordance with a fixed contribution formula.

(d) Claims Resolution Tribunal for Dormant Accounts in Switzerland (CRT-I)—first claims tribunal for assets deposited in Swiss banks

The CRT-I Rules of Procedure provided that the Chairman of the Tribunal was to administer financial planning and control, prepare a quarterly financial statement on costs and expenses, and submit a quarterly budget to the Board of Trustees of the Independent Claims Resolution Foundation (ICRF).[9] The Board of Trustees ultimately controlled the budget of the Claims Process.

---

[8] UNCC Governing Council Decision 14 of 18 December 1992, *Establishment of the UNCC Committee on Administrative Matters*, U.N. Doc. S/AC.26/1992/14 (4 January 1993).
[9] CRT-I Rules of Procedure, Article 28(g).

(e) Claims Resolution Tribunal (CRT-II)—second claims tribunal for assets deposited in Swiss banks

The CRT-II Governing Rules state that "[t]he CRT shall under the supervision of the Special Masters: . . . supervise the financial planning and financial controls of the CRT and submit to the Special Masters a quarterly financial report and periodic budgets of the CRT."[10] The Special Masters control the budget subject to the ultimate control of the United States District Court for the Eastern District of New York in the class action known as the Holocaust Victim Assets Litigation.

(f) Housing and Property Claims Commission (HPCC)—claims relating to the 1999 conflict in Kosovo

The Members of the HPCC have no role in establishing the budget of either the Commission or the Housing and Property Directorate (HPD). That control lies with the United Nations Interim Administration Mission in Kosovo (UNMIK).

(g) Mass Claims Processes administered by the International Organization for Migration (IOM): *German Forced Labour Compensation Programme (GFLCP) for claims against Germany and German industry for Nazi injustice, and Holocaust Victim Assets Programme (HVAP) for claims pursuant to 1999 class action Settlement*

The IOM Secretariat prepares the periodic budgets for both the GFLCP and HVAP Claims Processes. The budgets for GFLCP must be approved by the Board of Directors of the German Foundation; those for HVAP are reviewed by the Special Masters and submitted for approval to the United States District Court for the Eastern District of New York in the class action known as the Holocaust Victim Assets Litigation.

(h) Eritrea–Ethiopia Claims Commission (EECC)—claims relating to the 1998–2000 war between Eritrea and Ethiopia

The EECC is a comparatively small Claims Process and its budget reflects this. The budget is relatively low and stable, and the expenses of running the Claims

---

[10] CRT-II Governing Rules, Article 12(c).

Process can be accurately estimated in advance. The President of the Commission monitors the expenditure of funds, based on periodic accountings by the Registrar, such as of the time spent by staff of the Permanent Court of Arbitration (PCA) on EECC Secretariat work. The President sets the budget in collaboration with the PCA and sends letters to the Government parties requesting additional cash contributions as required.

(i) Humanitarian insurance Claims Process administered by the Jewish Claims Conference (JCC) for the International Commission on Holocaust Era Insurance Claims (ICHEIC)

The JCC–ICHEIC Agreement provided that ICHEIC would reimburse the JCC for its actual expenses incurred in running the 8A1 humanitarian Claims Process. The JCC provided ICHEIC with an estimated budget at the start of the 8A1 Claims Process, pursuant to which ICHEIC provided funding for the project on a quarterly basis. As claims processing commenced, the JCC submitted to ICHEIC periodic reports of actual expenses incurred, pursuant to which a reconciliation of estimated funding to actual costs was made.

(j) American Arbitration Association (AAA)—an illustrative case

The AAA fulfilled the tasks of a Secretariat in the illustrative case and was involved, along with the parties, in preparing periodic budgets and monitoring costs. The Arbitrators submitted bills for their work, but they had no role in establishing the budget of the Claims Process.

7.03 Funding

The source(s) of funds to pay for the expenses of the Claims Process as a whole.

Editors' Commentary

The sources of the funds for payment of the expenses of the Claims Processes described in this book vary widely. There are also substantial differences as to whether the amount each source is obligated to pay is open-ended or fixed. These elements are typically established in the constituting instrument of each

Claims Process. Each arrangement is largely the result of political circumstances, as well as the relative financial abilities and bargaining strengths of the parties funding the particular Process. This has led to a number of different approaches, as illustrated by the examples below.

Thus, for example, at the Iran–United States Claims Tribunal (Iran–US CT), the constituting instrument provides that the two Governments will each pay half of the expenses without any limitation on the total amount to be paid. A quite different arrangement exists at several other Claims Processes where the expenses are paid from a settlement funded by one side whose obligation is limited to the amount it has paid into a settlement account to cover both claims and expenses, such as the second Tribunal for dormant Swiss bank accounts (CRT-II), the Claims Processes administered by the International Organization for Migration (GFLCP and HVAP), and the American Arbitration Association (AAA) illustrative case. Elements of both approaches are combined at the first Tribunal for Dormant Accounts in Switzerland (CRT-I), where one side—the Swiss banks—paid all of the expenses and there was no limit on the amount of their obligation. At the United Nations Compensation Commission (UNCC) for claims relating to the 1990–1991 Gulf War, one side—Iraq—is obligated to pay all the expenses but its required payments are limited not by a settlement amount but by a complex formula based on sales of oil. A further variation occurred at the Commission for Real Property Claims of Displaced Persons and Refugees (CRPC) in Bosnia and Herzegovina, where the funding of expenses was augmented by contributions of non-governmental bodies that wished to assist.

Two ethical challenges may arise with respect to funding of expenses. The first is when one side which is a respondent pays all the expenses, as at CRT-I and in the AAA illustrative case. While funding by one side is welcome and appropriate in the circumstance of some Claims Processes, it is important that one side not have, or appear to have, a controlling or disproportionate influence on the budget. That places upon the paying party a responsibility to exercise restraint, and on the Claims Process and its Secretariat to maintain vigilance, to avoid any appearance, or actuality, of purse-string influence by the paying party that might be seen to affect the independence of the Claims Process. This is important because decisions on how much a Claims Process can spend, and for what purposes, could affect its operations and, consequently, the quality of justice it provides.

A second source of possible ethical tension arises from the possibility of conflict of interest between claimants and institutions that participate in the Claims Process. Thus, for example, in CRT-II, if there is money remaining in the Settlement Fund after all awards and expenses have been paid, a portion of that remainder may be allocated by the United States federal district court overseeing the Holocaust Victim Assets Litigation to institutions for cultural, memorial, or educational purposes. Thus, some institutions could have a conflicting interest *vis-à-vis* the claimants because every payment made to claimants reduces the potential amount available to the institutions.

Designers of Mass Claims Processes should be aware of these two potential ethical issues and either include provisions to safeguard against them or satisfy themselves that they can rely on the good faith of the parties to resolve them. Other observers of Mass Claims Processes should also be aware of these issues.

(a) Iran–United States Claims Tribunal (Iran–US CT)—claims relating to the 1979 Islamic Revolution

The Governments of the United States and Iran are the source of funds for paying the expenses of the Iran–US CT Claims Process in accordance with the provision of the constituting instrument, that "[t]he expenses of the Tribunal shall be borne equally by the two governments."[11]

The amount of those expenses is determined by majority vote of the Members of the Tribunal, acting pursuant to the power under the Tribunal Rules which state that "[t]he Full Tribunal shall fix the fees and expenses of the Tribunal . . . "[12] and, having done so, "[d]uring the course of its proceedings the Full Tribunal may from time to time . . . request each of the two Governments to deposit equal amounts as advances for such costs."[13] The two Governments are required to make equal quarterly payments.

Although the expenses are paid by the two Governments, which gives them significant influence on, but not control over, the determination of expenses, to the extent that this verges on financial control, the two sides have equal power based on the requirement of equal contributions.

(b) United Nations Compensation Commission (UNCC)—claims relating to the 1990–1991 Gulf War

The UNCC has been funded with a percentage of proceeds from the export of Iraqi petroleum, which has been a source of constant fiscal tension throughout the life of this Claims Process and the mechanics of which represented one of the main challenges in the early stages of the Commission's work.

The UNCC Compensation Fund is a special United Nations account created to make payments to satisfy the Commission's awards and to finance the operations of the Claims Process. United Nations Security Council Resolution

---

[11] Claims Settlement Declaration, Article VI, paragraph 3.
[12] Iran–US CT Tribunal Rules, Article 38, paragraph 2.   [13] Ibid., Article 41, paragraph 1.

687 (1991) provided that the Fund was to be financed by Iraqi contributions based on a percentage of its oil exports.[14] Subsequently, Security Council Resolution 705 (1991) determined that Iraq's contributions ought not to exceed thirty percent of the annual value of its oil exports,[15] and Resolution 706 (1991) authorized United Nations Member States to import Iraqi oil for six months, up to a value of US$1.6 billion, establishing mechanisms for using the funds thus generated.[16] When Iraq failed to implement Resolution 706, the UNCC was forced to make other arrangements to fund its operations, including from frozen proceeds of Iraqi oil transactions held by some States that became available as a result of Security Council action.

Although not intended to be used to finance the Fund, previously frozen Iraqi assets were used for the Commission's start-up costs and initial compensation payments. Security Council Resolution 778 (1992) required Member States to transfer to the United Nations escrow account, established by Resolution 706, frozen assets and proceeds of Iraqi oil products outside Iraq.[17]

Finally, Security Council Resolution 986 (1995) established the so-called "oil-for-food" program, the revenues of which eventually became the main mechanism for ensuring payments into the Compensation Fund, channeling thirty percent of the revenues generated by Iraq's oil exports into the Fund annually.[18] (The percentage rate was modified from time to time by subsequent Resolutions.[19])

(c) Commission for Real Property Claims of Displaced Persons and Refugees (CRPC)—claims relating to the 1992–1995 war in Bosnia and Herzegovina

The constituting instrument, the Dayton Peace Agreement, provided that the parties to it (i.e., the Republic of Bosnia and Herzegovina, the Republic of Croatia, and the Republic of Yugoslavia) should bear the expenses of the CRPC and its staff equally.[20] In actual practice, however, this was provided

---

[14] UN Security Council Resolution 687 (1991) of 3 April 1991, U.N. Doc. S/RES/687 (1991) (8 April 1991), paragraphs 18 and 19.

[15] UN Security Council Resolution 705 (1991) of 15 August 1991, U.N. Doc. S/RES/705 (1991), paragraph 2.

[16] UN Security Council Resolution 706 (1991) of 15 August 1991, U.N. Doc. S/RES/706 (1991), paragraphs 1–4.

[17] UN Security Council Resolution 778 (1992) of 2 October 1992, U.N. Doc. S/RES/778 (1992), paragraph 1.

[18] UN Security Council Resolution 986 (1995) of 14 April 1995, U.N. Doc. S/RES/986 (1995) (14 April 1995).

[19] See, e.g., UN Security Council Resolution 1360 (2001) of 3 July 2001, U.N. Doc. S/RES/1360 (2001) (3 July 2001), paragraph 9, changing the level of deduction to 25% in 2001; and Resolution 1483 (2003) of 22 May 2003, U.N. Doc. S/RES/1483 (2003) (22 May 2003), paragraph 21, changing the level to 5% in 2003.   [20] Dayton Peace Agreement, Annex 7, Article X, paragraph 2.

only by the European Union, the United States, and, among others, Austria, Belgium, Canada, Germany, Ireland, Italy, Luxembourg, the Netherlands, Norway, Sweden, and Switzerland. The CRPC also received a small payment from the Republic of Bosnia and Herzegovina and contributions from non-governmental organizations for specific projects and tasks.[21]

According to Annex 7 of the Dayton Peace Agreement, compensation was to be made available to claimants whose pre-war property could not be restored to them.[22] A compensation fund was to be established for this purpose in the Central Bank of Bosnia and Herzegovina, and to be administered by CRPC. It was contemplated that compensation could be in the form of a monetary award or a compensation bond for the future purchase of the property in question, and the funds were to be financed either by grants from the international community, by the parties to Annex 7, or by proceeds from the CRPC's selling or leasing of properties it received in exchange for compensation awards.[23] However, after protracted negotiations between the CRPC and the Central Bank, the United States Departments of State and Treasury, the United States Securities and Exchange Commission, and the Federal Reserve Bank of New York, the compensation fund failed to materialize, as neither the Government of Bosnia and Herzegovina nor the international community provided the necessary funds to put it into operation. It was the view of many interested parties that the compensation plan, and the option to choose between return of property and money in lieu thereof, would undermine the fundamental goal of the Dayton Peace Agreement, namely, to restore a multi-ethnic Bosnia and Herzegovina by encouraging the return of as many refugees and displaced persons as possible to their pre-war homes.[24]

At the end of 2003, the responsibility for the financing and the operation of the CRPC was transferred to the Government of Bosnia and Herzegovina.[25]

(d) Claims Resolution Tribunal for Dormant Accounts in Switzerland (CRT-I)—first claims tribunal for assets deposited in Swiss banks

All expenses of operating CRT-I were borne by the Swiss banks who were the respondents in all the claims before the Tribunal. The potential ethical issues

---

[21] See Dayton Peace Agreement, Annex 7, Article X, paragraph 4.

[22] See ibid., Article XII, paragraph 2, affording to all refugees and displaced persons the choice between return and compensation, provided the owner has a right to compensation in lieu of return.

[23] Ibid., Article XII, paragraph 5.

[24] See CRPC End of Mandate Report, Annex B—*Annex 7 Compensation Fund Unrealised.*

[25] See Dayton Peace Agreement, Annex 7, Article XVI. The mandate of CRPC was extended beyond what Annex 7 provided.

arising from that arrangement are discussed above in the Editors' Commentary to this section 7.03.

(e) Claims Resolution Tribunal (CRT-II)—second claims tribunal for assets deposited in Swiss banks

The expenses of CRT-II are paid from the Settlement Fund in the Holocaust Victim Assets Litigation created by contributions from the defendant Swiss banks. These contributions were made pursuant to the Settlement Agreement. The banks have no obligation to make any further payment into the Settlement Fund and, as a result, they have no interest in the amount of expenses paid from it. In contrast to CRT-I, this ought to ameliorate the tension caused by the potential of purse-string control in CRT-II.[26]

(f) Housing and Property Claims Commission (HPCC)—claims relating to the 1999 conflict in Kosovo

The HPCC and the Housing and Property Directorate (HPD) are funded in part from the Kosovo Consolidated Budget of the United Nations Interim Administration Mission in Kosovo (UNMIK). However, the bulk of funding comes from donors, including various governments and the European Union. Approximately sixty percent of the annual budget is contributed by the donor community; twenty-eight percent from the Kosovo Consolidated Budget; and twelve percent from the United Nations.[27]

Funding has been one of the main challenges of this Claims Process and has severely affected the planning and productivity of its work. For example, this has resulted in difficulties of funding infrastructure development, and the inability to offer more than short-term employment contracts to staff, leading to high personnel turnover and staffing uncertainties. The root cause of the funding difficulties is said to be that the bulk of funding—seventy percent—comes from donors. Only seven percent of the budget is covered from the United Nations budget for its Development Program in Kosovo; twenty-three percent is covered by the local Kosovo Government budget, known as the "Kosovo Consolidated Budget," for UNMIK operations in Kosovo.

---

[26] See section 1.05(e) above, on the possible allocation of unclaimed residual funds from the CRT-II Claims Process.

[27] HPD/HPCC Annual Report 2004, p. 21, available at www.hpdkosovo.org.

(g) Mass Claims Processes administered by the International Organization for Migration (IOM)

German Forced Labour Compensation Programme (GFLCP)—claims against Germany and German industry for Nazi injustice

The expenses of the GFLCP Claims Process, including the Property Claims Commission and the Appeals Body for Forced Labour Claims, have to be paid from the total funds allocated to IOM by the German Foundation, pursuant to the German Foundation Act, based on an amount determined in the preceding international negotiations.[28] Like all the moneys paid into the Compensation Fund, these funds have been contributed in equal shares by the German Government and German industry.

Since expenses must be paid from a total pre-determined compensation fund, there is significant pressure, both external and internal, for efficiency and cost-effectiveness, including through continuous internal and external audits and oversight, and significant media attention.

Holocaust Victim Assets Programme (HVAP)—claims pursuant to 1999 class action Settlement

The expenses of the HVAP Claims Process are paid from the Settlement Fund established pursuant to the Settlement Agreement approved by the United States District Court for the Eastern District of New York in the class action known as the Holocaust Victim Assets Litigation. The funds have been provided by the defendant Swiss banks that participated in the Settlement.

Since expenses must be paid from a total pre-determined Settlement Fund, there is significant pressure, both external and internal, for efficiency and cost-effectiveness, including through continuous internal and external audits and oversight, and significant media attention.

(h) Eritrea–Ethiopia Claims Commission (EECC)—claims relating to the 1998–2000 war between Eritrea and Ethiopia

The 12 December 2000 Agreement provides that the two Government parties are to fund the EECC Claims Process.[29] To date, the Commission has periodically requested from the parties funds sufficient to cover approximately six months of operations at a time. These requests have been honored by the

---

[28] See section 1.01(g) above, for background of the GFLCP Claims Process.
[29] Eritrea–Ethiopia Agreement of 12 December 2000, Article 5, paragraph 15.

parties in accordance with their obligations under the 12 December 2000 Agreement, each Government party paying one half of the requested amount.

(i) Humanitarian insurance Claims Process administered by the Jewish Claims Conference (JCC) for the International Commission on Holocaust Era Insurance Claims (ICHEIC)

The ICHEIC Claims Process is funded pursuant to agreements between it and participating insurance companies (MOU Companies) and representative organizations. Funding for operations of the 8A1 humanitarian Claims Process was provided on a quarterly basis by ICHEIC to the JCC.

Funding for paying awards was supplied by ICHEIC before such payments were made. The JCC would notify ICHEIC of the number of pending claims to be paid, whereupon ICHEIC transferred the amount to a bank account from which the JCC Payment Operations Team drew checks to pay claimants. Checks ready to be paid by the Payment Operations Team were electronically forwarded to ICHEIC for an added layer of verification and authorization. The choice of using checks rather than wire transfers was made because the 8A1 humanitarian award is a one-time payment. Some regional exceptions were made, however, to allow for wire transfers or other forms of payment (e.g., private delivery of proceeds) to ensure safe receipt of payments in areas where there was uncertainty in the banking system, and local agents and local affiliate offices in such cases assisted with delivering the funds to claimants.

(j) American Arbitration Association (AAA)—an illustrative case

As part of the class action settlement in the illustrative case, the defendant insurance company paid all costs of the Claims Process, including awards to claimants and all costs and fees.

7.04 Outside Audit

Whether an outside auditor is employed to audit the Claims Process.

Editors' Commentary

All Mass Claims Processes receive and pay out money in connection with conducting their operations. In addition, some of the Claims Processes described in this book are entrusted with settlement funds, handle payments to claimants, maintain bank accounts, and perform other financial activities. It is important that they maintain public trust in their fiscal integrity. Therefore, as described below, some Claims Processes employ a firm of independent certified accountants to audit their fiscal statements periodically. Others, particularly those related to the United Nations or other public organizations, have their financial books audited, or inspected, under the procedures of those organizations.

(a) Iran–United States Claims Tribunal (Iran–US CT)—claims relating to the 1979 Islamic Revolution

The Tribunal Rules provide that:

"The Secretary-General shall transmit monthly, quarterly and annual financial statements to the Full Tribunal and to the Agents [of the two Governments]. The accounts of the Tribunal shall be audited annually by an independent qualified accountant approved by the Full Tribunal. The Secretary-General shall transmit copies of the audit report to the Full Tribunal and to the Agents. At the request of either Agent, the annual audit shall be reviewed by an Audit Committee composed of three professionally qualified persons, one appointed by each Agent and one by the President [of the Tribunal]. The Audit Committee shall submit its report to the Full Tribunal, to the Agents, and to the Secretary-General."[30]

In conformity with its Rules, the Tribunal has annually submitted its financial accounts to an independent auditor. The availability of an Audit Committee is perhaps best seen as a manifestation of the political dynamics operating at the time of the Tribunal's establishment. In practice, neither Government's Agent has ever convoked the Audit Committee.

(b) United Nations Compensation Commission (UNCC)—claims relating to the 1990–1991 Gulf War

The activities of the UNCC, including claims processing, are subject to both internal and external audit. Internal audit is conducted by the United Nations Office of Internal Oversight Services (OIOS), pursuant to memoranda of understanding entered into between the UNCC and OIOS. External audit is conducted by the United Nations Board of Auditors.

---

[30] Iran–US CT Tribunal Rules, Article 41, paragraph 4.

(c) **Commission for Real Property Claims of Displaced Persons and Refugees (CRPC)—claims relating to the 1992–1995 war in Bosnia and Herzegovina**

The CRPC Book of Regulations on Procedure does not provide for an audit mechanism. In the first two years of operations, when this Claims Process was relying on the International Organization for Migration (IOM) to administer its finances, audits were conducted by the independent auditors that audited IOM activities, i.e., the Austrian State Auditor, the *Rechnungshof.* In the later years of CRPC, annual audits were performed by an international audit firm at the request of the Commission.

(d) **Claims Resolution Tribunal for Dormant Accounts in Switzerland (CRT-I)—first claims tribunal for assets deposited in Swiss banks**

The CRT-I Claims Process was subject to two types of financial audits: regularly scheduled audits on behalf of the Board of Trustees of the Independent Claims Resolution Foundation (ICRF), and other audits conducted from time to time on behalf of the Swiss Bankers Association (SBA).

(e) **Claims Resolution Tribunal (CRT-II)—second claims tribunal for assets deposited in Swiss banks**

The ICEP (Independent Committee of Eminent Persons) audit firms[31] carried out the forensic audit of Swiss banks which became the basis for publishing names of owners of accounts who were possibly or probably the victims or targets of Nazi persecution for purposes of the CRT-II Claims Process. Provisions concerning audit appear in the CRT-II Governing Rules, which provide for the continued involvement of one or more of the ICEP audit firms. For example, ICEP audit firms may be retained by the Court-appointed Special Masters in the class action known as the Holocaust Victim Assets Litigation to conduct training of CRT-II staff in matching and research of claims data, or to perform such matching and research on behalf of CRT-II.[32]

---

[31] Arthur Andersen, Coopers & Lybrand, Deloitte & Touche, KPMG, and Price Waterhouse, see CRT-II Governing Rules, Article 46, paragraph 12.

[32] See, e.g., ibid., Article 19, paragraph 2, and Article 21, paragraph 3.

(f) Housing and Property Claims Commission (HPCC)—claims relating to the 1999 conflict in Kosovo

The HPCC Claims Process, being part of the United Nations Interim Administration Mission in Kosovo (UNMIK), is subject to regular United Nations audits. Audits have also routinely been conducted by donors of the Claims Process.

(g) Mass Claims Processes administered by the International Organization for Migration (IOM): *German Forced Labour Compensation Programme (GFLCP) for claims against Germany and German industry for Nazi injustice, and Holocaust Victim Assets Programme (HVAP) for claims pursuant to 1999 class action Settlement*

The GFLCP and HVAP Claims Processes are subject to considerable audit and oversight, both internal and external. GFLCP is audited regularly by IOM's Inspector General and by IOM's external auditors, as well as by the German Foundation and external auditors appointed by the Foundation. HVAP is audited regularly by IOM's Inspector General and by IOM's external auditors.

(h) Eritrea–Ethiopia Claims Commission (EECC)—claims relating to the 1998–2000 war between Eritrea and Ethiopia

The EECC Claims Process had not as of 31 January 2006 entered the phase of damages. The issue of outside audits had not been addressed by the parties and the Commission, and no outside audits had been carried out.

(i) Humanitarian insurance Claims Process administered by the Jewish Claims Conference (JCC) for the International Commission on Holocaust Era Insurance Claims (ICHEIC)

ICHEIC had the right to audit the JCC procedures and financial records at any time, as specified in the JCC–ICHEIC Agreement. Careful documentation of all procedures and their execution were maintained, and all work was available and subject to review by the Senior Counselor appointed by the Chairman of ICHEIC to approve evaluation criteria and supervise the payment process.

The JCC is audited regularly by an outside independent accounting firm and such audits included the 8A1 humanitarian Claims Process which the

JCC handled on behalf of ICHEIC. For example, the JCC drew checks for payments of the humanitarian awards on bank accounts of ICHEIC. The JCC's administration of the ICHEIC's bank accounts was reviewed by the outside auditor.

(j) American Arbitration Association (AAA)—an illustrative case

Independent certified public accountants conducted an audit of AAA's work in the illustrative case as part of the annual audit of the AAA. The annual audit of the defendant insurance company also included an audit of the Claims Process.

Chapter 8

Transparency

8.01 Informing the Public

Means for informing the public about the Claims Process, for example by publishing statistics on the caseload and/or texts of the awards.

Editors' Commentary

All of the Mass Claims Processes described in this book, with the exception of the illustrative case administered by the American Arbitration Association (AAA) where the parties insisted upon confidentiality, have adopted rules and procedures designed to make public their awards, decisions, or statistical information such as the number of claims, and the total amounts awarded to claimants. Typically, the Claims Processes have websites that facilitate access to such information.

Many Mass Claims Processes are conducted in the aftermath of tragic historic events, amidst much pain and public outrage. Their decisions directly affect a very large number of individuals and often generate much interest by the public at large. Thus, there is a wide belief that the more information made public about a Claims Process—the scope of its decision-making powers and the limitations imposed upon it, the pace of its progress, and the personal efforts of its staff—the greater the claimants' understanding and likely acceptance of the outcome.

The various rules typically provide that a party may request deletion of identity of parties from materials made public. The Iran–United States Claims Tribunal (Iran–US CT) and the Eritrea–Ethiopia Claims Commission (EECC) add provisions to permit a party to request, subject to the Tribunal's or Commission's approval, that trade and military secrets be kept confidential.

Annotations

(a) Iran–United States Claims Tribunal (Iran–US CT)—claims relating to the 1979 Islamic Revolution

The Tribunal Rules state that:

"All awards and other decisions shall be made available to the public, except that upon the request of one or more arbitrating parties, the arbitral tribunal may determine that it will not make the entire award or other decision public, but will make public only portions thereof from which the identity of the parties, other identifying facts and trade or military secrets have been deleted."[1]

This provision is a sharp reversal from the UNCITRAL Arbitration Rules, which the Iran–US CT is generally required to follow, which state that "[t]he award may be made public only with the consent of both parties."[2] The Tribunal made this change pursuant to its authority to modify the UNCITRAL Arbitration Rules "to ensure that [the Claims Settlement Declaration] can be carried out."[3] In doing so, the Tribunal decided that making public all awards, decisions, and separate opinions was necessary in order to ensure that all parties in future cases had equal access to the developing jurisprudence of the Tribunal, and so that Members and parties could refer to past cases in the interest of fostering uniformity.

As of 31 January 2006, the Tribunal's awards and decisions have been published in thirty-four volumes of the Iran–United States Claims Tribunal Reports, published by Cambridge University Press,[4] and are also available electronically through legal databases such as Westlaw. Recent awards and decisions are available on the Tribunal's official website.[5] The Tribunal also

---

[1] Iran–US CT Tribunal Rules, Article 32, paragraph 5.

[2] UNCITRAL Arbitration Rules, Article 32, paragraph 5.

[3] Claims Settlement Declaration, Article III, paragraph 2.

[4] IRAN–UNITED STATES CLAIMS TRIBUNAL REPORTS, A Publication of the Lauterpacht Research Centre for International Law, University of Cambridge (Grotius Publications, Cambridge University Press). An editorial note to each of the volumes of the Reports explains that:

"This series of Reports contains the texts of Decisions, Awards, Awards on Agreed Terms, Interim Awards, Interlocutory Awards, Interim and Interlocutory Awards, Selected Orders and Refusal Cases emanating from the Iran–U.S. Claims Tribunal. . . . All Decisions, Awards, Interim Awards, Interlocutory Awards and Refusal Cases are printed in these Reports. Procedural Orders are printed on a selective basis from the many thousands that have been issued by the Tribunal since its inception. Also, from time to time a section of a volume may be devoted to additional documents of a procedural nature.

Awards on Agreed Terms now largely follow a standard form and are individually of little legal significance. These therefore are also printed on a selective basis, together with some relevant supporting documents."

[5] See www.iusct.org.

releases a statistical communiqué on a quarterly basis, which lists the number of awards and other decisions, the number of cases finalized, the number of oral proceedings of various types, and the totals of the amounts awarded to United States and Iranian parties.

Although awards are made public, hearings are private at the Tribunal in accordance with the Tribunal Rules.[6]

(b) United Nations Compensation Commission (UNCC)—claims relating to the 1990–1991 Gulf War

The UNCC Provisional Rules state that:

"Decisions of the Governing Council and, after the relevant decision is made, the associated report of the panel of Commissioners, will be made public, except the Executive Secretary will delete from the reports of panels of Commissioners the identities of individual claimants and other information determined by the panels to be confidential or privileged."[7]

The panels of Commissioners conducted their work in private and all records received or produced by the Commission are confidential, except reports and recommendations that have been approved by the Governing Council. The UNCC has an extensive website which contains, among other things, Governing Council decisions, Executive Secretary reports, texts of reports by the panels of Commissioners, and statistics on the number of decisions issued and total amounts awarded in each category of claims.[8]

(c) Commission for Real Property Claims of Displaced Persons and Refugees (CRPC)—claims relating to the 1992–1995 war in Bosnia and Herzegovina

While transparency was not addressed in Annex 7 of the Dayton Peace Agreement, the CRPC did publish a newsletter, issue press releases, and air television announcements. The CRPC maintained a website containing its Books of Regulations, general information, and a database of all CRPC decisions, searchable by claimant name, municipality, or address of the claimed property.[9]

---

[6] See Iran–US CT Tribunal Rules, Article 25, paragraph 4.

[7] UNCC Provisional Rules, Article 40, paragraph 5.   [8] See www.uncc.ch.

[9] The website, www.crpc.org.ba, was taken offline at the end of the CRPC's mandate, when operations were transferred to the Government of Bosnia and Herzegovina. The contents of the site have since been made available at www.law.kuleuven.ac.be/ipr/eng/CRPC_Bosnia/CRPC%20bosnia.html, and via the website of the Permanent Court of Arbitration, at www.pca-cpa.org/MCP/index_MCP.htm "Links to Completed Mass Claims Processes."

(d) Claims Resolution Tribunal for Dormant Accounts in Switzerland (CRT-I)—first claims tribunal for assets deposited in Swiss banks

The CRT-I Rules of Procedure state:

"The decisions of the Claims Resolution Tribunal shall be made public in an appropriate manner to be determined by the Board of Trustees. If the claimant requests confidentiality, the members of the Claims Resolution Tribunal shall keep confidential all information relating to the identity of the account holder and the claimant, unless otherwise required by applicable law."[10]

In August 2000, the Tribunal, with the approval of the Board of Trustees of the Independent Claims Resolution Foundation (ICRF), published on its website forty-three decisions as examples (twenty-four in English, ten in French, and nine in German).[11] The names of claimants and banks were redacted for reasons of confidentiality. The website also contained a statistical progress report, including the number of awards issued and total amounts awarded.

(e) Claims Resolution Tribunal (CRT-II)—second claims tribunal for assets deposited in Swiss banks

The CRT-II Governing Rules state that "[t]he decisions of the CRT shall be made public in an appropriate manner as determined by the Special Masters."[12] The CRT-II's decisions and the amounts of payments to claimants are reported on its website.[13]

(f) Housing and Property Claims Commission (HPCC)—claims relating to the 1999 conflict in Kosovo

According to the procedural rules of this Claims Process, contained in UNMIK Regulation 2000/60, the Registrar of HPCC is to publish the decisions of the Commission, or summaries of the decisions.[14] The Commission and the Housing and Property Directorate (HPD) have a website which contains statistical information about claims, claims intake, and the status of claims processing.[15] The Commission's decisions may also be published on the website, subject to redaction of information for which claimants have requested confidential treatment.

---

[10] CRT-I Rules of Procedure, Article 36.
[11] After the end of its mandate, information on CRT-I has been made available at www.crt-ii. org/_crt-i. [12] CRT-II Governing Rules, Article 41.
[13] www.crt-ii.org. [14] UNMIK Regulation 2000/60, section 22.10.
[15] www.hpdkosovo.org.

(g) Mass Claims Processes administered by the International Organization for Migration (IOM): *German Forced Labour Compensation Programme (GFLCP) for claims against Germany and German industry for Nazi injustice, and Holocaust Victim Assets Programme (HVAP) for claims pursuant to 1999 class action Settlement*

Transparency and publication of decisions are not addressed in the constituting documents or rules of either GFLCP or HVAP. Decisions on individual claims and awards of the Property Claims Commission and the Appeals Body for Forced Labour Claims are not made public. IOM has, however, regularly made publicly available information on the Claims Processes it conducts, such as the issues they address, and their progress and results. This has been done through periodic activity reports (both for the German Foundation and the United States federal district court overseeing the Holocaust Victim Assets Litigation, as well as for the public), frequent press releases, fact sheets, a newsletter, distribution of information to numerous victims associations, and updates of the two Process-specific websites.[16] For HVAP, IOM's reports to the Court containing its recommendations for the resolution of batches of claims become part of the public record once they are approved by order of the Court.

(h) Eritrea–Ethiopia Claims Commission (EECC)—claims relating to the 1998–2000 war between Eritrea and Ethiopia

Publication of awards and statistics is not addressed in the 12 December 2000 Agreement. However, the Commission's Rules of Procedure provide that:

> "[a]ll awards shall be made available to the public, including by posting on an appropriate Internet website. The Commission may, at the request of a party or on its own initiative, determine that it will not make an entire award public, but will make public only portions from which the identity of individuals, other identifying facts or trade or military secrets have been deleted."[17]

This reflects the view expressed both by the Commissioners and the parties that the Commission's decisions and awards should be in the public domain. However, the Commission has taken the view that the exchanges of pleadings between the parties generally should not be public; hearings are to be held *in camera* unless the parties agree otherwise.[18] In this regard, the Commission has

---

[16] See www.compensation-for-forced-labour.org for GFLCP, and www.swissbankclaims.iom.int for HVAP.   [17] EECC Rules of Procedure, Article 18, paragraph 7.

[18] Ibid., Article 13, paragraph 5.

welcomed the parties' undertakings not to exploit publicly the proceedings and positions taken in them for publicity or political advantage. The Rules of Procedure also recognize that, in some circumstances, special measures may be required to protect the security and privacy of witnesses.[19]

(i) Humanitarian insurance Claims Process administered by the Jewish Claims Conference (JCC) for the International Commission on Holocaust Era Insurance Claims (ICHEIC)

Statistics regarding processing of ICHEIC claims were published on the ICHEIC website. ICHEIC also published press releases announcing the 8A1 humanitarian payments of March 2004 and August 2005.

(j) American Arbitration Association (AAA)—an illustrative case

In the illustrative case, pursuant to the parties' wishes implemented in the Settlement Agreement, the Claims Process was confidential and no statistics or awards were published.

---

[19] EECC Rules of Procedure, Article 13, paragraph 5.

Experience in Mass Claims Processes of Members of the Mass Claims Steering Committee of the Permanent Court of Arbitration

Each of the Members of the Steering Committee appointed by the Secretary-General of the Permanent Court of Arbitration during the preparation of this book has participated in two or more Mass Claims Processes as a decision-maker, a staff member, a government official, or a lawyer representing a party. (Those who provided key information about a particular Claims Process for this book are indicated by an asterisk.)

Howard M. Holtzmann, *Chairman of the Steering Committee and Co-Editor*

* *Judge*, Iran–United States Claims Tribunal, 1981–1994; *Substitute Judge*, 1994–present;

* *Arbitrator (CRT-I) and Senior Claims Judge (CRT-II)*, Claims Resolution Tribunals for Dormant Accounts in Switzerland, 1998–2002.

George Aldrich

Judge, Iran–United States Claims Tribunal, 1981–present;
Commissioner, Eritrea–Ethiopia Claims Commission, 2000–present.

Ronald J. Bettauer

United States Representative, Governing Council, United Nations Compensation Commission, 1991–present;

Counsel for the United States Department of State, in matters relating to:
• Iran–United States Claims Tribunal,
• United Nations Compensation Commission,
• German Foundation "Remembrance, Responsibility and Future,"
• Holocaust Victim Assets Litigation (Swiss banks), and
• Eritrea–Ethiopia Claims Commission.

Karl-Heinz Böckstiegel

Judge and President, Iran–United States Claims Tribunal, 1984–1988;
Panel Chairman, United Nations Compensation Commission, 1994–1996.

Robert Briner

Judge and President, Iran–United States Claims Tribunal, 1985–1991;
Commissioner, United Nations Compensation Commission, 1997–2004;
Arbitrator (CRT-I) and Senior Claims Judge (CRT-II), Claims Resolution Tribunals for Dormant Accounts in Switzerland, 1998–2002.

Charles N. Brower

* *Judge*, Iran–United States Claims Tribunal, 1984–1988; 2001–present; *Substitute Judge*, 1983–1984; 1988–2000;

Member, Register of Experts, United Nations Compensation Commission, 1991–present;
Counsel to parties, United Nations Compensation Commission, 1991–2004.

Thomas Buergenthal

Judge and Vice-President, Inter-American Court of Human Rights, 1979–1991;
Vice Chairman (CRT-I) and Senior Claims Judge (CRT-II), Claims Resolution Tribunals for Dormant Accounts in Switzerland, 1998–2002;
Judge, International Court of Justice, 2000–present.

David D. Caron

Legal Assistant, Iran–United States Claims Tribunal, 1983–1986;
Counsel to the Defender of the Fund, Marshall Islands Nuclear Tests Tribunal, 1994–1996;
* *Commissioner*, United Nations Compensation Commission, 1996–2003;

Commissioner, German Forced Labour Compensation Programme at the International Organization for Migration, 2000–2001;
Counsel to party, Eritrea–Ethiopia Claims Commission, 2004–2005.

John R. Crook

Agent for the United States, Iran–United States Claims Tribunal, 1983–1987;
United States Representative to United Nations Compensation Commission, 1991–1995;
* *Commissioner*, Eritrea–Ethiopia Claims Commission, 2000–present.

Jacomijn J. van Haersolte-van Hof

Author of treatise on the Iran–United States Claims Tribunal, 1991;
Consultant to Secretariat, Claims Resolution Tribunal for Dormant Accounts in Switzerland (CRT-I), 1998.

Veijo Heiskanen

Legal Assistant, Iran–United States Claims Tribunal, 1990, 1992–1994;

* *Deputy Chief*, Legal Services Branch, United Nations Compensation Commission, 1994–1998;

* *Secretary-General and Senior Claims Judge*, Claims Resolution Tribunal (CRT-II), 2001–2002;

* *Commissioner*, Housing and Property Claims Commission in Kosovo, 2000–present;

* *Deputy Director*, Claims Processing, German Forced Labour Compensation Programme and Holocaust Victim Assets Programme, International Organization for Migration, 2000–2001;

Legal Advisor on compensation claims, Government of Ethiopia, 2000.

Hans van Houtte

Commissioner, United Nations Compensation Commission, 1998–2001;
Arbitrator (CRT-I) and Senior Claims Judge (CRT-II), Claims Resolution Tribunals for Dormant Accounts in Switzerland, 1998–2002;
* *International Commissioner and Legal Chair*, Commission for Real Property Claims of Displaced Persons and Refugees in Bosnia and Herzegovina, 1996–2003;
* *President*, Eritrea–Ethiopia Claims Commission, 2000–present;

Andreas J. Jacovides

Commissioner, United Nations Compensation Commission, 1998–2002;
Arbitrator (CRT-I) and Senior Claims Judge (CRT-II), Claims Resolution Tribunals for Dormant Accounts in Switzerland, 1998–2002.

Clifton M. Johnson (alternate Member to Ronald J. Bettauer)

Deputy Assistant Legal Advisor for International Claims and Investment Disputes, United States Department of State Legal Adviser's Office, 2000–2001;
Agent for the United States, Iran–United States Claims Tribunal, 2001–present;
Counsel for the United States Department of State, in matters relating to Iran–United States Claims Tribunal.

Gabrielle Kirk-McDonald

Judge, International Criminal Tribunal for Former Yugoslavia, 1993–1999;
Judge, Iran–United States Claims Tribunal, 1991–present.

Jeffrey D. Kovar (alternate Member to Ronald J. Bettauer)

Counsel for the United States Department of State, in matters relating to:
• Iran–United States Claims Tribunal,
• United Nations Compensation Commission, and

- Commission for Real Property Claims of Displaced Persons and Refugees in Bosnia and Herzegovina.

Richard M. Mosk

* *Judge*, Iran–United States Claims Tribunal, 1981–1984, 1997–2001; *Substitute Judge*, 1984–1997;

Consultant to party, United Nations Compensation Commission, 1994–1995.

Roberts B. Owen

Legal Adviser, United States Department of State, worked on establishing the Iran–United States Claims Tribunal, 1979–1980;

Arbitrator and Vice Chairman (CRT-I) and Senior Claims Judge (CRT-II), Claims Resolution Tribunals for Dormant Accounts in Switzerland, 1998–2002.

Florence M. Peterson

* *Senior Vice President and General Counsel*, American Arbitration Association Programs, 1995–1999/1999–2004.

Michael F. Raboin

Deputy Agent of the United States, Iran–United States Claims Tribunal, 1986–1991;

Director and Deputy Executive Secretary, United Nations Compensation Commission, 1991–2005.

Lucy F. Reed

* *Deputy Agent and Agent* for the United States, Iran–United States Claims Tribunal, 1989–1992;

Deputy Assistant Legal Advisor for International Claims and Investment Disputes, United States Department of State Legal Adviser's Office, 1992–1993;

* *Co-Director*, Claims Resolution Tribunal for Dormant Accounts in Switzerland (CRT-I), 1998–1999;

* *Commissioner*, Eritrea–Ethiopia Claims Commission, 2000–present.

Arthur W. Rovine

Agent for the United States, Iran–United States Claims Tribunal, 1981–1983;

Counsel to parties, Iran–United States Claims Tribunal, 1983–2000;

Counsel to parties, United Nations Compensation Commission, 1993–2002.

Norbert Wühler

Legal Assistant to the President and Deputy Secretary-General, Iran–United States Claims Tribunal, 1983–1991;

* *Chief, Legal Services Branch*, United Nations Compensation Commission, 1992–2000;

Senior Adviser, Commission for Real Property Claims of Displaced Persons and Refugees in Bosnia and Herzegovina, 1996;
* *Director, Claims Programs* (German Forced Labour Compensation Programme, Holocaust Victim Assets Programme, and technical assistance to the Iraq Property Claims Commission), International Organization for Migration, 2000–present.

Edda Kristjánsdóttir, *Secretary to the Steering Committee and Co-Editor*

Member of Secretariat, Eritrea–Ethiopia Claims Commission, 2001–2002;
Associate Legal Officer, German Forced Labour Compensation Programme, International Organization for Migration, 2002.

Observers:

Mark Appel

* *Regional Director, Regional Vice-President and Senior Vice-President* (since 1995), American Arbitration Association, 1976–2001;

Senior Vice-President, International Centre for Dispute Resolution of the American Arbitration Association, 2001–present.

Shavit Matias

Deputy Attorney-General, Israel, 2004–present;
Commissioner, International Commission on Holocaust Era Insurance Claims, 2003–present.

Notes:

— An asterisk indicates that the Committee Member was a principal source of information concerning the Mass Claims Process marked with*.
— The term "present" means that this function was performed at least until 31 January 2006.
— The mandates of all of the Senior Claims Judges of CRT-II terminated in late May 2002, before they had any part in the reorganization of CRT-II or had decided any claims.
— The Members of the Steering Committee participated in their personal capacities, and the views they expressed were not necessarily those of the governments or organizations with which they are, or have been, affiliated.

List of Basic Documents

Iran–US CT

Algiers Accords	See General Declaration; Claims Settlement Declaration
Claims Settlement Declaration	Declaration of the Democratic and Popular Republic of Algeria concerning the Settlement of Claims by the Government of the United States of America and the Government of the Islamic Republic of Iran (19 January 1981), 1 Iran–U.S. C.T.R. p. 9, also available at www.iusct.org
General Declaration	Declaration of the Government of the Democratic and Popular Republic of Algeria (19 January 1981), 1 Iran–U.S. C.T.R. p. 3, also available at www.iusct.org
Iran–US CT Tribunal Rules	Iran–United States Claims Tribunal, Final Tribunal Rules of Procedure, adopted 3 May 1983, 2 Iran–U.S. C.T.R. 405, also available at www.iusct.org
Iran–US CT Internal Guidelines	Iran–US CT Internal Guidelines of the Tribunal, 1 Iran–U.S. C.T.R. p. 98
UNCITRAL Rules	United Nations Commission on International Trade Law (UNCITRAL) Arbitration Rules, 1976, United Nations Publication Sales No. E.93.V.6, also available at www.uncitral.org

UNCC

UNSC Resolution 674 (1990)	United Nations Security Council Resolution 674 (1990) of 29 October 1990, U.N. Doc. S/RES/674 (1990) (29 October 1990)
UNSC Resolution 687 (1991)	United Nations Security Council Resolution 687 (1991) of 3 April 1991, establishing the UNCC, U.N. Doc. S/RES/687 (1991) (8 April 1991)
UNSC Resolution 692 (1991)	United Nations Security Council Resolution 692 (1991) of 20 May 1991, U.N. Doc. S/RES/692 (1991) (20 May 1991) adopting Report of the Secretary-General of 2 May 1991

Report of the Secretary-General	Report of the United Nations Secretary-General of 2 May 1991 pursuant to paragraph 19 of Security Council Resolution 687 (1991), U.N. Doc. S/22559 (2 May 1991)
UNCC Provisional Rules	UNCC Governing Council Decision 10 of 26 June 1992, *Provisional Rules for Claims Procedure*, U.N. Doc. S/AC.26/1992/10 (26 June 1992), available at www.uncc.ch
UNCC Work Programme	UNCC Work Programme, U.N. Doc. S/AC.26/1997/WP.1 (1998), text not officially available

CRPC

Dayton Peace Agreement	See General Framework Agreement
General Framework Agreement	General Framework Agreement for Peace in Bosnia and Herzegovina, initialed in Dayton, 21 November 1995, signed in Paris, 14 December 1995, "Dayton Peace Agreement", 35 I.L.M. 75, at 138, available at www.pca-cpa.org/MCP/index_MCP.htm "Links to Completed Mass Claims Processes"
Books of Regulations	Book of Regulations on Confirmation of Occupancy Rights of Displaced Persons and Refugees (Consolidated version, 8 October 2002); and Book of Regulations on the Conditions and Decision Making Procedure for Claims for Return of Real Property of Displaced Persons and Refugees (Consolidated version, 8 October 2002), available at www.pca-cpa.org/MCP/index_MCP.htm "Links to Completed Mass Claims Processes"
Headquarters Agreement	Headquarters Agreement between CRPC and Bosnia and Herzegovina (text not officially available)
End of Mandate Report	*Commission for Real Property Claims of Displaced Persons and Refugees (CRPC) End of Mandate Report (1996–2003)*, available at www.pca-cpa.org/MCP/index_MCP.htm "Links to Completed Mass Claims Processes"

CRT-I

Memorandum of Understanding	ICEP Memorandum of Understanding, reproduced in the Independent Committee of Eminent Persons Report on Dormant Accounts of Victims of Nazi

Persecution in Swiss Banks (Volcker Report),
Appendix A, p.1 (Berne, Staempfli Publishers Ltd.
1999), available at www.crt-ii.org/icep-report.phtm

CRT-I Rules of Procedure Rules of Procedure for the Claims Resolution Process,
adopted on 15 October 1997 by the Board of
Trustees of the Independent Claims Resolution
Foundation, available at www.crt-ii.org/_crt-i

CRT-I Interest Guidelines Board of Trustees, Independent Claims Resolution
Foundation, Rules on Interest, Charges, and Fees for
Arbitral Decisions of the Claims Resolution Tribunal,
available at www.crt-ii.org/_crt-i

CRT-II

Settlement Agreement Class Action Settlement Agreement, approved, *In re
Holocaust Victim Assets Litig.*, 105 F.Supp.2d 139
(E.D.N.Y. 2000), text available at www.crt-ii.org

Plan of Allocation and Special Master's Proposed Plan of Allocation and
Distribution Distribution of Settlement Proceeds, approved, *In re
Holocaust Victim Assets Litig.*, Case No. CV 96–4849
(ERK)(MDG) 2000, WL 33241660 (E.D.N.Y. Nov.
22, 2000), aff'd., *In re Holocaust Victim Assets Litig.*,
413 F.3d 183 (2d Cir. (N.Y.) 1 July 2005), text
available at www.crt-ii.org

Governing Rules Rules Governing the Claims Resolution Process
(As Amended), available at www.crt-ii.org

Volcker Report Independent Committee of Eminent Persons, Report
on Dormant Accounts of Victims of Nazi Persecution
in Swiss Banks (Berne, Staempfli Publishers Ltd.
1999), text available at www.crt-ii.org

HPCC*

UNSC Resolution 1244 United Nations Security Council Resolution 1244
(1999) (1999) of 10 June 1999, U.N. Doc. S/RES/1244
(1999) (10 June 1999)

UNMIK Regulation UNMIK Regulation No. 1999/1 of 25 July 1999,
1999/1 *On the Authority of the Interim Administration in
Kosovo*, U.N. Doc. UNMIK/RES/1999/1

---

* See also HPD/HPCC *Housing and Property Rights in Kosovo, Collection of Basic Texts*, 2d ed.
March 2000, available at www.hpdkosovo.org.

	(25 July 1999), available at www.hpdkosovo.org and www.unmikonline.org
UNMIK Regulation 1999/23	UNMIK Regulation No. 1999/23 of 15 November 1999, *On the Establishment of the Housing and Property Directorate and the Housing and Property Claims Commission*, U.N. Doc. UNMIK/REG/ 1999/23 (15 November 1999), available at www.hpdkosovo.org and www.unmikonline.org
UNMIK Regulation 1999/24	UNMIK Regulation No. 1999/24 of 12 December 1999, *On the Law Applicable in Kosovo*, U.N. Doc. UNMIK/REG/1999/24 (12 December 1999), available at www.hpdkosovo.org and www.unmikonline.org
UNMIK Regulation 2000/60	UNMIK Regulation No. 2000/60 of 31 October 2000, *On Residential Property Claims and the Rules of Procedure and Evidence of the Housing and Property Directorate and the Housing and Property Claims Commission*, U.N. Doc. UNMIK/REG/2000/60 (31 October 2000), available at www.hpdkosovo.org and www.unmikonline.org

GFLCP

U.S.–German Agreement	Agreement between the Government of the United States of America and the Government of the Federal Republic of Germany concerning the Foundation "Remembrance, Responsibility and the Future", The Government of the United States of America and the Government of the Federal Republic of Germany, done at Berlin, 17 July 2000, available at www.compensation-for-forced-labour.org
Joint Statement	Joint Statement on occasion of the final plenary meeting concluding international talks on the preparation of the Foundation "Remembrance, Responsibility and the Future", available at www.compensation-for-forced-labour.org
German Foundation Act	Law on the Creation of a Foundation "Remembrance, Responsibility and Future" of 2 August 2000, entered into force 12 August 2000 (German Federal Law Gazette BGBl. 2000 I 1263), as amended 4 August 2001, entered into force 11 August 2001 (BGBl. 2001 I 2036), and as amended 21 August 2002, entered into force 28 August 2002 (BGBl. 2002 I 3347), available at www.compensation-for-forced-labour.org

Property Commission Rules	IOM Property Claims Commission, Supplemental Principles and Rules of Procedure, available at www.compensation-for-forced-labour.org
Rules of IOM Appeals Body	IOM Appeals Body for Forced Labour Claims, Principles and Rules of Appeals Procedure, available at www.compensation-for-forced-labour.org

HVAP

Plan of Allocation and Distribution	Special Master's Proposed Plan of Allocation and Distribution of Settlement Proceeds, approved, *In re Holocaust Victim Assets Litig.*, Case No. CV 96–4849 (ERK)(MDG), 2000 WL 33241660 (E.D.N.Y. Nov. 22, 2000), aff'd., *In re Holocaust Victim Assets Litig.*, 413 F.3d 183 (2d Cir. (N.Y.) 1 July 2005), text available at www.swissbankclaims.iom.int
Settlement Agreement	Class Action Settlement Agreement, as approved, *In re Holocaust Victim Assets Litig.*, 105 F.Supp.2d 139 (E.D.N.Y. 2000), Exhibit 1 to Plan of Allocation and Distribution. Text available at www.swissbanklaims.iom.int

EECC

12 December 2000 Agreement	Agreement between the Government of the Federal Democratic Republic of Ethiopia and the Government of the State of Eritrea, done at Algiers, Algeria, on 12 December 2000, available at www.pca-cpa.org
OAU Framework Agreement	Organisation of African Unity Framework Agreement and the Modalities for its Implementation, endorsed by the 35th ordinary session of the Assembly of Heads of State and Government, held in Algiers, Algeria, 12–14 July 1999, available at www.pca-cpa.org
Cessation of Hostilities Agreement	Agreement on Cessation of Hostilities of 18 June 2000 between Eritrea and Ethiopia, U.N. Doc. S/2000/601 (18 June 2000)
EECC Rules of Procedure	Eritrea–Ethiopia Claims Commission Rules of Procedure, available at www.pca-cpa.org
EECC Decisions	Eritrea–Ethiopia Claims Commission Decisions Number 1 to 6, available at www.pca-cpa.org

PCA Rules   Permanent Court of Arbitration Optional Rules
                                   for Arbitrating Disputes between Two States,
                                   PERMANENT COURT OF ARBITRATION BASIC
                                   DOCUMENTS, p. 41 (1998), also available at
                                   www.pca-cpa.org

ICHEIC

Memorandum of   ICHEIC Memorandum of Understanding signed
   Understanding   on 25 August 1998, by several European insurance
                                   companies, available at www.icheic.org

JCC–ICHEIC   Humanitarian Claims Processing Agreement between
   Agreement   ICHEIC and the Conference on Jewish Material
                                   Claims Against Germany (JCC), text not officially
                                   available

Point Scoring System   ICHEIC 8A1 Point Scoring System, text not
                                   officially available

Point Scoring Guidelines   ICHEIC 8A1 Point Scoring System Guidelines, text
                                   not officially available

ICHEIC policy   ICHEIC policy memoranda concerning the 8A1
   memoranda   humanitarian Claims Process, text not officially
                                   available

AAA (an illustrative case)

Settlement Agreement   Class action Settlement Agreement, approved by the
                                   United States federal district court seized of the class
                                   action, text not officially available

ANNEX C

Bibliographical Guide to Selected Sources of Information

Editors' Note:

The material that follows is not intended to be a formal bibliography, but rather a guide to finding information concerning the Mass Claims Processes described in this book. Accordingly, where a bibliography as to a particular Claims Process is available on a website or in a treatise, we refer to that bibliography, and do not repeat herein citations to all of the publications listed in it. Where no published bibliography as to a particular Mass Claims Process is available, we have cited publications related to the Process. In addition, there is a separate section citing publications that relate generally to Mass Claims Processes.

Iran–US Claims Tribunal

See "List of Publications on the Tribunal," maintained by the Secretariat of the Iran–United States Claims Tribunal, at http://www.iusct.org/publications.pdf.

See additionally:

Biography and "Guide to Sources" in David D. Caron and John R. Crook, THE IRAN–UNITED STATES CLAIMS TRIBUNAL AND THE PROCESS OF INTERNATIONAL CLAIMS RESOLUTION, Published under the auspices of the American Society of International Law (Transnational Publishers 2000).

George H. Aldrich, THE JURISPRUDENCE OF THE IRAN-UNITED STATES CLAIMS TRIBUNAL: AN ANALYSIS OF THE DECISIONS OF THE TRIBUNAL (Clarendon Press 1996).

Charles N. Brower and Jason D. Brueschke, THE IRAN-UNITED STATES CLAIMS TRIBUNAL (Martinus Nijhoff Publishers).

UNCC

See "Selected Publications" maintained by the Secretariat of the United Nations Compensation Commission, at http://www.uncc.ch.

See additionally:

Markus Eichhorst, RECHTSPROBLEME DER UNITED NATIONS COMPENSATION COMMISSION (Duncker & Humblot 2002).

Veijo Heiskanen, *The United Nations Compensation Commission*, in 296 RECUEIL DES COURS p. 255 (Martinus Nijhoff Publishers 2003).

THE UNITED NATIONS COMPENSATION COMMISSION: THIRTEENTH SOKOL COLLOQUIUM (Richard B. Lillich ed., Transnational Publishers 1995). Includes:

Carlos Alzamora, *The UN Compensation Commission: an overview*, at p. 3.

Adel Omar Asem, *Establishment of the UN Compensation Commission: the Kuwaiti government perspective*, at p. 45.

David J. Bederman, *Historic analogues of the UN Compensation Commission*, at p. 257.

Ronald J. Bettauer, *Establishment of the UN Compensation Commission: the U.S. government perspective*, at p. 29.

Charles N. Brower. *The lessons of the Iran-U.S. Claims Tribunal applied to claims against Iraq*, at p. 15.

David D. Caron, *The UNCC and the search for practical justice*, at p. 367.

Jeremy P. Carver, *Dispute resolution or administrative tribunal: a question of due process*, at p. 69.

Gordon A. Christenson, *State responsibility and the UN Compensation Commission: compensating victims of crimes of state*, at p. 311.

John R. Crook, *The UNCC and its critics: is Iraq entitled to judicial due process?*, at p. 77.

Christopher S. Gibson, *Mass claims processing: techniques for processing over 400,000 claims for individual loss at the United Nations Compensation Commission*, at p. 155.

Frederick L. Kirgis, Jr., *Claims settlement and the United Nations legal structure*, at p. 103.

Francis E. McGovern, *The intellectual heritage of claims processing at the United Nations Compensation Commission*, at p. 187.

Michael F. Raboin, *The provisional rules for claims procedure of the United Nations Compensation Commission: a practical approach to mass claims processing*, at p. 119.

Arthur W. Rovine and Grant Hanessian, *Toward a foreseeablity approach to causation questions at the United Nations Compensation Commission*, at p. 235.

Norbert Wühler, *Causation and directness of loss as element of compensability before the United Nations Compensation Commission*, at p. 207.

Roger P. Alford, *Well Blowout Control Claim, UN Doc.S/AC.2/Dec.40, 36 ILM 1343 (1997): United Nations Compensation Commission, Governing Council, December 17, 1996*, 92(2) AM. J. INT'L L. p. 287 (1998).

Mariano J. Aznar-Gómez, *Environmental damages and the 1991 Gulf War: some yardsticks before the UNCC*, 14(2) LEIDEN J. INT'L L. p. 301 (2001).

David Bederman, *The United Nations Compensation Commission and the Tradition of International Claims Settlement*, 27 N. Y. U. J. INT'L L. & POL. p. 1 (1994).

Karl-Heinz Böckstiegel, *Ein Agressor wird haftbar gemacht: die Entschädigungskommission der Vereinten Nationen (UNCC) für Ansprüche gegen Irak*, 45(3) VEREINTE NATIONEN p. 89 (1997).

Danio Campanelli, *The United Nations Compensation Commission (UNCC): Reflections on its Judicial Character*, 4(1) THE LAW AND PRACTICE OF INTERNATIONAL TRIBUNALS p. 107 (2005).

David D. Caron, *Finding Out what the Oceans claim: the 1991 Gulf War, the Marine Environment and the United Nations Compensation Commission*, in BRINGING NEW

LAW TO OCEAN WATERS p. 393 (David D. Caron and Harry N. Scheiber eds., Martinus Nijhoff Publishers 2004).

David D. Caron, *The United Nations Compensation Commission for Claims Arising out of the 1991 Gulf War: the "Arising prior to" Decision*, 14(2) J. TRANSNATIONAL L. & POL. p. 309 (2005).

John R. Crook, *The United Nations Compensation Commission: A New Structure to Enforce State Responsibility*, 87 AM. J. INT'L L. p. 144 (1993).

John R. Crook, *The UN Compensation Commission: What Now?*, 5(4) INT'L L. FORUM DU DROIT INT'L p. 276 (2003).

Veijo Heiskanen and Robert C. O'Brien, *UN Compensation Commission Panel Sets Precedents on Government Claims*, 92 AM. J. INT'L L. p. 339 (1998).

Ruth Mackenzie and Ruth Khalastchi, *Liability and compensation for environmental damage in the context of the work of the United Nations Compensation Commission*, 5(4) REV. EUR. COMMUNITY & INT'L ENV. L. p. 281 (1996).

Peter Malanczuk, *International Business and New Rules of State Responsibility?: the Law Applied by the United Nations (Security Council) Compensation Commission for Claims against Iraq*, in PERSPECTIVES OF AIR LAW, SPACE LAW, AND INTERNATIONAL BUSINESS LAW FOR THE NEXT CENTURY p. 117 (Karl-Heinz Böckstiegel ed., 1996).

Rajesh Singh, *Raising the Stakes: Evidentiary Issues in Individual Claims Before the United Nations Compensation Commission*, in REDRESSING INJUSTICES THROUGH MASS CLAIMS PROCESSES: INNOVATIVE RESPONSES TO UNIQUE CHALLENGES p. 61 (Permanent Court of Arbitration ed., Oxford University Press 2006).

Fred Wooldridge and Elias Olufemi, *Humanitarian considerations in the Work of the United Nations Compensation Commission*, 85(1) INT'L REV. RED CROSS p. 555 (2003).

Norbert Wühler, *The United Nations Compensation Commission*, in THE CLAIMS RESOLUTION PROCESS ON DORMANT ACCOUNTS IN SWITZERLAND p. 131 (Pierre A. Karrer ed., ASA 1999).

Norbert Wühler, *Institutional and procedural aspects of mass claims settlement systems: the United Nations Compensation Commission*, in INSTITUTIONAL AND PROCEDURAL ASPECTS OF MASS CLAIMS SETTLEMENT SYSTEMS p. 17 (International Bureau of the Permanent Court of Arbitration ed., Kluwer Law International 2000).

CRT-I and CRT-II

THE CLAIMS RESOLUTION PROCESS ON DORMANT ACCOUNTS IN SWITZERLAND: ASA SWISS ARBITRATION ASSOCIATION CONFERENCE IN ZURICH OF JANUARY 22, 1999: Reports and Materials (Pierre A. Karrer, ed., ASA 1999). Includes, *inter alia*:

Howard M. Holtzmann, *The Relevance of the Experience of the Iran–United States Claims Tribunal for Other Mass Claims Tribunals*, at p. 125.

Franz Kellerhans, *Review in International and Domestic Arbitration Cases*, at p. 110.

Georg Krayer, *The claims resolution process from the point of view of the Swiss banks*, at p. 15.

Owen C. Pell, *The potential for a mediation/arbitration commission to resolve disputes relating to artworks stolen or looted during World War II*, at p. 175.

Flavio Romerio, *The relationship between the Class Action Settlement of in re Holocaust victim assets and the claims resolution procedure*, at p. 18.

Urs Zulauf, *Banking secrecy and the publication of dormant accounts: did the publication of the names of holders of accounts, which had been dormant since 1945, infringe Swiss banking secrecy laws?*, at p. 94.

HOLOCAUST RESTITUTION: PERSPECTIVES ON THE LITIGATION AND ITS LEGACY (Michael Bazyler and Roger P. Alford eds., New York University 2006). Includes, *inter alia*:

Edward R. Korman, *Rewritting the Holocaust History of the Swiss Banks: A Growing Scandal*, at p. 115.

Burt Neuborne, *A Tale of Two Cities: Administering the Holocaust Settlements in Brooklyn and Berlin*, at p. 60.

Melvyn I. Weiss, *A Litigator's Postscript to the Swiss Banks and Holocaust Litigation Settlements: How Justice Was Served*, at p. 103.

Roger M. Witten, *How Swiss Banks and German Companies Came to Terms with the Wrenching Legacies of the Holocaust and World War II: A Defence Perspective*, at p. 80.

Thomas Buergenthal, INTERNATIONAL LAW AND THE HOLOCAUST (Center for Advanced Holocaust Studies, 2004).

Roger P. Alford, *The Claims Resolution Tribunal and Holocaust Claims Against Swiss Banks*, Stefan A. Riesenfeld Symposium 2001, 20(1) BERKELEY J. INT'L L. p. 250 (2002).

Michael Bazyler, *The Holocaust Restitution Movement in Comparative Perspective*, Stefan A. Riesenfeld Symposium 2001, 20(1) BERKELEY J. INT'L L. p. 11 (2002).

Sylvain Beauchamp, *The New Claims Resolution Tribunal for Dormant Accounts in Switzerland: Distribution Organ, Mass Claims Adjudicative Body or Sui Generis Entity?*, 3(6) J. WORLD INV. p. 999 (2002).

Thomas Buergenthal, *Arbitrating Entitlement to Dormant Bank Accounts*, 15 ICSID REV. p. 301 (2000).

Thomas Buergenthal, *Arbitrating Entitlement to Dormant Bank Accounts*, in LIBER AMICORUM IBRAHIM F.I. SHIHATA: INTERNATIONAL FINANCE AND DEVELOPMENT LAW p. 79 (2001).

Jacomijn J. van Haersolte-van Hof, *Issues of Evidence in the Practice of the Claims Resolution Tribunal for Dormant Accounts*, 1(4) INT'L L. FORUM DU DROIT INT'L p. 215 (1999).

Jacomijn J. van Haersolte-van Hof, *Het Claims Resolution Tribunal for Dormant Accounts: een bijzondere vorm van arbitrage?!*, 2 TIJDSCHRIFT VOOR ARBITRAGE p. 41 (2000).

Veijo Heiskanen, *CRT-II: The Second Phase of the Swiss Banks Claims Process*, in CRIMES DE L'HISTOIRE ET RÉPARATIONS: LES RÉPONSES DU DROIT ET DE LA JUSTICE p. 147 (Laurence Boisson de Chazournes *et al.* eds., 2004)

Suzannah Linton, *Righting a wrong or prolonging the agony? The Work of the Claims Resolution Tribunal for Dormant Accounts in Switzerland*, 12(2) LEIDEN J. INT'L L. p. 373 (1999).

Lucy Reed, *Arbitration Principles Prove Effective in Resolving Holocaust Bank Claims*, in Institutional and Procedural Aspects of Mass Claims Settlement Systems p. 59 (International Bureau of the Permanent Court of Arbitration ed., Kluwer Law International 2000).

Nathalie Voser, *Arbitrability and the applicable law in the claims resolution process for dormant accounts in Switzerland*, 15(3) Arb. Int'l p. 237 (1999).

Bosnia and Herzegovina (CRPC)* and Kosovo (HPCC)

See "Selected Bibliography on Housing and Property Restitution for Refugees and Internally Displaced Persons" (organized by region) in:

Returning Home: Housing and Property Restitution Rights of Refugees and Displaced Persons (Scott Leckie ed., Transnational Publishers 2003). Includes, *inter alia*:

> Marcus Cox and Madeline Garlick, *Musical Chairs: Property Repossession and Return Strategies in Bosnia and Herzegovina*, at p. 65.
>
> Alan Dodson and Veijo Heiskanen, *Housing and Property Restitution in Kosovo*, at p. 225.

Strategies for the Future of Bosnia-Herzegovina and Croatia (Guiseppe de Vergottini *et al.* eds., 2001).

Leopold von Carlowitz, *Settling Property Issues in Complex Peace Operations: the CRPC in Bosnia and Herzegovina and the HPD/CC in Kosovo*, 17(3) Leiden J. Int'l L. p. 599 (2004).

Hans Das, *Restoring Property Rights in the Aftermath of War*, 53 Int'l & Comp. L.Q. p. 429 (2004).

Mark S. Ellis and Elizabeth Hutton, *Policy implications of World War II Reparations and Restitution as Applied to the Former Yugoslavia*, Stefan A. Riesenfeld Symposium 2001, 20(1) Berkeley J. Int'l L. p. 342 (2002).

Madeline Garlick, *Protection for Property Rights: A Partial Solution? The Commission for Real Property Claims of Displaced Persons and Refugees (CRPC) in Bosnia and Herzegovina*, 19 Refugee Surv. Q. p. 68 (2000).

Lynn Hastings, *Implementation of the Property Legislation in Bosnia and Herzegovina*, 37 Stan. J. Int'l L. p. 221 (2001).

Robert M. Hayden, *The 1995 Agreements on Bosnia and Herzegovina and the Dayton Constitution: The Utility of a Constitutional Illusion*, 4 E. Eur. Const. Rev. p. 59 (2005).

Hans van Houtte, *The Property Claims Commission in Bosnia-Herzegovina: a New Path to Restore Real Estate Rights in Post-War Societies*, in International Law: Theory and Practice: Essays in Honour of Eric Suy p. 549 (Karel Wellens ed., 1998).

* For documents and reports on CRPC, see also website of the Office of the High Representative, at www.ohr.int.

Hans van Houtte, *Evidence before the Commission for Real Property Claims in Bosnia and Herzegovina*, 1(4) INT'L L. FORUM DU DROIT INT'L p. 225 (1999).

Hans van Houtte, *Mass Property Claim Resolution in a Post-War-Society: the Commission for Real Property Claims in Bosnia and Herzegovina*, 48(3) INT'L & COMP. L. Q. p. 625 (1999).

Hans van Houtte, *Mass Property Claim Resolution in a Post-War Society: The Commission for Real Property Claims in Bosnia and Herzegovina (CRPC)*, in THE CLAIMS RESOLUTION PROCESS ON DORMANT ACCOUNTS IN SWITZERLAND p. 148 (Pierre A. Karrer ed., ASA 1999).

Hans van Houtte, *Mass Property Claim Resolution in a Post-War Society: The Commission for Real Property Claims in Bosnia and Herzegovina (CRPC)*, in INSTITUTIONAL AND PROCEDURAL ASPECTS OF MASS CLAIMS SETTLEMENT SYSTEMS p. 23 (International Bureau of the Permanent Court of Arbitration ed., Kluwer Law International 2000).

Charles Philpott, *Though the Dog is Dead, the Pig Must be Killed: Finishing with Property Restitution to Bosnia-Herzegovina's IDPs and Refugees*, 18 J. REFUGEE STUDIES p. 1 (2005).

Eric Rosand, *The Right to Compensation in Bosnia: An Unfulfilled Promise and a Challenge to International Law*, 33 CORNELL INT'L L.J. p.113 (2000).

Rita Maria Saulle, *The Commission on Real Property Claims in Bosnia and Herzegovina*, in PROTECTION DES DROITS DE L'HOMME (2000).

Timothy William Waters, *The Naked Land: The Dayton Accords, Property Disputes, and Bosnia's Real Constitution*, 40 HARV. INT'L L.J. p. 517 (1999).

Rhodri C. Williams, *Post Conflict Property Restitution and Refugee Return in Bosnia and Herzegovina: Implications for International Standard-Setting and Practice*, 37(3) N.Y. U. J. INT'L L. & POL. p. 441 (2005).

Holocaust Claims (GFLCP, HVAP, ICHEIC)

See extensive bibliography on National Socialist forced labor in:

ZWANGSARBEIT IM DRITTEN REICH: ERINNERUNG UND VERANTWORTUNG: JURISTISCHE UND ZEITHISTORISCHE BEITRAGE/NS-FORCED LABOR: REMEMBRANCE AND RESPONSIBILITY: LEGAL AND HISTORICAL OBSERVATIONS: International Conference Proceedings (contributions in German and English) (Peer Zumbansen ed., Nomos 2002). Includes, *inter alia*:

Peter Van der Auweraert, *The Practicalities of Forced Labour Compensation: The Work of the International Organisation for Migration as one of the Partner Organisations under the German Foundation Law*, at p. 301.

ENTSCHÄDIGUNG FÜR NS-ZWANGSARBEIT: RECHTLICHE, HISTORISCHE UND POLITISCHE ASPEKTE (Klaus Barwig *et al.* eds, Nomos 1998).

John Authers and Richard Wolffe: THE VICTIM'S FORTUNE: INSIDE THE EPIC BATTLE OVER THE DEBTS OF THE HOLOCAUST (Harper Collins Publishers 2002).

Michael J. Bazyler, HOLOCAUST JUSTICE: THE BATTLE FOR RESTITUTION IN AMERICA'S COURTS (New York University Press 2003).

Stuart E. Eizenstat, IMPERFECT JUSTICE: LOOTED ASSETS, SLAVE LABOR, AND THE UNFINISHED BUSINESS OF WORLD WAR II (Public Affairs 2003).

Christian Pross, PAYING FOR THE PAST: THE STRUGGLE OVER REPARATIONS FOR THE SURVIVING VICTIMS OF THE NAZI TERROR (Johns Hopkins University Press 1998).

Susanne-Sophia Spiliotis, VERANTWORTUNG UND RECHTSFRIEDEN: DIE STIFTUNGSINITIATIVE DER DEUTSCHEN WIRTSCHAFT (Fischer 2003).

Ronald Zweig, GERMAN REPARATIONS AND THE JEWISH WORLD: A HISTORY OF THE CLAIMS CONFERENCE (Frank Cass 2d ed., 2001).

HOLOCAUST RESTITUTION: PERSPECTIVES ON THE LITIGATION AND ITS LEGACY (Michael Bazyler and Roger P. Alford eds., New York University Press 2006). Includes, *inter alia*:

Roland Bank, *Processing of Claims for Slave and Forced Labor: Expediency versus Accuracy?*, at p. 190.

Stuart E. Eizenstat, *The Unfinished Business of World War II*, at p. 297.

Peter Hayes, *Corporate Profits and the Holocaust: A Dissent from the Monetary Argument*, at p. 197.

Kai Hennig, *The Road to Compensation of Life Insurance Policies: The Foundation Law and ICHEIC*, at p. 251.

Roman Kent, *It's Not about the Money: A Survivor's Perspective on the German Foundation Initiative*, at p. 205.

Lawrence Kill and Linda Gerstel, *Holocaust-Era Insurance Claims: Legislative, Judicial, and Executive Remedies*, at p. 239.

Otto Graf Lambsdorff, *The Negotiations on Compensation for Nazi Forced Laborers*, at p. 170.

David A. Lash and Mitchell A. Kamin, *Poor Justice: Holocaust Restitution and Forgotten, Indigent Survivors*, at p. 315.

Gideon Taylor, *Where Morality Meets Money*, at p. 163.

Lother Ulsamer, *German Economy and the Foundation Initiative: An Act of Solidarity for Victims of National Socialism*, at p. 181.

Sidney Zabludoff, *ICHEIC: Excellent Concept but Inept Implementation*, at p. 260.

Arie Zuckerman, *The Holocaust Restitution Enterprise: An Israeli Perspective*, at p. 322.

Stefan A. Riesenfeld Symposium 2001: Fifty Years in the Making: World War II Reparation and Restitution Claims, March 8–9 2001, 20(1) BERKELEY J. INT'L L. (2002). Includes, *inter alia:*

Ronald J. Bettauer, *Keynote Address—The Role of the United States Government In Recent Holocaust Claims Resolution*, at p. 1.

Anita Ramasastry, *Corporate Complicity: From Nuremberg to Rangoon: an Examination of Forced Labor Cases and Their Impact on MNC Liability*, at p. 91.

Stephen Whinston, *Can Lawyers and Judges Be Good Historians?: A Critical Examination of the Siemens Slave-Labor Cases*, at p. 160.

Roland Bank, *The New Programs for Payments to Victims of National Socialist Injustice*, 44 GERM. Y.B. INT'L L. p. 307 (2001).

Stuart E. Eizenstat, *Imperfect justice: looted assets, slave labor, and the unfinished business of World War II*, 37(2) VANDERBILT J. TRANSNAT'L L. p. 333 (2004).

Bardo Fassbender, *Compensation for Forced Labour in World War II: The German Compensation Law of 2 August 2000*, 3 J. INT'L CRIM. JUSTICE p. 243 (2005).

Gerald Feldman, *The Historian and Holocaust Restitution: Personal Experiences and Reflections*, 23(2) BERKELEY J. INT'L L p. 347 (2002).

Hanno Goltz, *Efforts to settle insurance claims on a world-wide basis: German perspective*, in THE CLAIMS RESOLUTION PROCESS ON DORMANT ACCOUNTS IN SWITZERLAND p. 190 (Pierre A. Karrer ed., ASA 1999).

Pierre A. Karrer, *Innovation to Speed Mass Claims: the Work of the Property Claims Commission of the German Foundation "Remembrance, Responsibility and Future"*, 5(1) J. WORLD INV. & TRADE p. 57 (2004).

Pierre A. Karrer and Mohr Siebeck, *Mass Claims to Provide Rough Justice: the Work of the Property Claims Commission of the German Foundation "Remembrance, Responsibility and the Future"* in GRENZÜBERSCHREITUNGEN: BEITRÄGE ZUM INTERNATIONALEN VERFAHRENSRECHT UND ZUR SCHIEDSGERICHTSBARKEIT: FESTSCHRIFT FÜR PETER SCHLOSSER ZUM 70. GEBURTSTAG (Birgit Bachmann *et al.* eds., 2005).

Edda Kristjánsdóttir and Barbora Simerova, *Processing Claims for "Other Personal Injury" Under the German Forced Labour Compensation Programme*, in REDRESSING INJUSTICES THROUGH MASS CLAIMS PROCESSES: INNOVATIVE RESPONSES TO UNIQUE CHALLENGES p. 109 (Permanent Court of Arbitration ed., Oxford University Press 2006).

Norbert Wühler, *German Compensation for World War II Slave and Forced Labour*, in CRIMES DE L'HISTOIRE ET RÉPARATIONS: LES RÉPONSES DU DROIT ET DE LA JUSTICE p. 163 (Laurence Boisson de Chazournes *et al.* eds., 2004).

EECC

UNFINISHED BUSINESS: ERITREA AND ETHIOPIA AT WAR (Dominique Jacquin-Berdal and Martin Plaut eds., 2004).

George H. Aldrich, *The Work of the Eritrea-Ethiopia Claims Commission*, 6 Y.B. INT'L HUMANITARIAN L. p. 435 (2006).

Natalie Klein, *State Responsibility for International Humanitarian Law Violations and the Work of the Eritrea Ethiopia Claims Commission So Far*, 47 GERM. Y.B. INT'L L. p. 214 (2005).

Judith I.A. Lichtenberg, *Eritrea Ethiopia Claims Commission*, 12(3) TILBURG FOREIGN L. REV. p. 266 (2004).

AAA Illustrative Case

Donald Francis Donovan, *Arbitrating Mass Claims: the Life Insurance Class Actions in the United States*, 16(1) ICSID REV.: FOREIGN INV. L.J. p. 25 (2001).

David W. Rivkin, *ADR and Mass Claim Resolution: Life Insurance Class Action Experiences in the United States*, in THE CLAIMS RESOLUTION PROCESS ON DORMANT ACCOUNTS IN SWITZERLAND p. 163 (Pierre A. Karrer ed., ASA 1999).

William K. Slate, *Innovation to Speed Mass Claims: the Experience of the American Arbitration Association with Class Actions*, 5(1) J. WORLD INV. & TRADE p. 47 (2004).

Mass Claims Processes Generally

See Bibliography at p. 449 in:

Redressing Injustices Through Mass Claims Processes: Innovative Responses to Unique Challenges (Permanent Court of Arbitration ed., Oxford University Press 2006). Includes, *inter alia*:

John R. Crook, *Mass Claims Processes: Lessons Learned Over Twenty-Five Years*, at p. 41.
Hans Das, *The Concept of Mass Claims and the Specificity of Mass Claims Resolution*, at p. 3.
Jacomijn van Haersolte-van Hof, *Innovations to Speed Mass Claims: New Standards of Proof*, at p. 13.
Veijo Heiskanen, *Virtue out of Necessity: International Mass Claims and New Uses of Information Technology*, at p. 25.

Elazar Barkan, The Guilt of Nations: Restitution and Negotiating Historical Injustices (Johns Hopkins University Press 2006).
Richard B. Lillich, David J. Bederman and Burns H. Weston, International Claims: Their Settlement by Lump Sum Agreements, 1975–1995 (Transnational Publishers 1999).
Holocaust Restitution: Perspectives on the Litigation and its Legacy (Michael Bazyler and Roger P. Alford eds., New York University Press 2006). Includes *inter alia*:
Thomas Buergenthal, *International Law and the Holocaust*, at p. 17.

Stefan A. Riesenfeld Symposium 2001: *Fifty Years in the Making: World War II Reparation and Restitution Claims*, March 8–9 2001, Berkeley, California, 20(1) Berkeley J. Int'l L. (2002).

Richard M. Buxbaum, *A Legal History of International Reparations*, 23(2) Berkeley J. Int'l L. p. 314 (2005).
Jacomijn J. van Haersolte-van Hof, *Innovations in Mass Claims Dispute Resolution: Using New Standards of Proof*, 58(3) Disp. Res. J. p. 70 (2003).
Veijo Heiskanen, *Innovations in Mass Claims Dispute Resolution: Speeding the Resolution of Mass Claims Using Information Technology*, 58(3) Disp. Res. J. p. 79 (2003).
Howard M. Holtzmann, *Mass Claims Settlements Systems: Potentials and Pitfalls*, in Institutional and Procedural Aspects of Mass Claims Settlement Systems p. 1 (International Bureau of the Permanent Court of Arbitration ed., Kluwer Law International 2000).
Howard M. Holtzmann, *Mass Claims Processes*, 13(1–4) Amer. Rev. Int'l Arbitration p. 69 (2002).
Pierre A. Karrer, *Mass Claims Proceedings in Practice: A Few Lessons Learned*, 23(2) Berkeley J. Int'l L. p. 463 (2005).
Norbert Wühler, *The Different Contexts in Which International Arbitration is Being Used: International Claims Tribunals and Commissions*, 4 J. World Investment p. 379 (2003).

ANNEX D

Tables of Sources Cited

(Numbers following document references are the page numbers in this book.)

Table of Claims Process Documents

CRT-I (Claims Resolution Tribunal for Dormant Accounts in Switzerland)

CRT-II (Claims Resolution Tribunal)

GFLCP (German Forced Labour Compensation Programme)

Table of Legislation

Table of Resolutions

417

Checklist of Matters that Designers of International Mass Claims Processes Might Wish to Consider

This Checklist is a consolidated compilation of key issues that may arise when designing, or revising, a Mass Claims Process. It may be a useful aid for those engaged in such tasks. Commentaries and Annotations concerning each of those matters appears in the book INTERNATIONAL MASS CLAIMS PROCESSES: LEGAL AND PRACTICAL PERSPECTIVES (Howard M. Holtzmann and Edda Kristjánsdóttir eds, Oxford University Press 2006).

1—Establishing The Claims Process

1.01 Constituting Method
The types of constituting instrument(s) or procedures by which Claims Processes are created (e.g., treaty, agreement, judicial decision, or other), having regard to the major events and circumstances giving rise to the claims.

1.02 Constituting Instrument
Whether the contents of the constituting instrument are (i) a brief statement, or (ii) a detailed description of the Claims Process, with provisions, e.g., on who may be claimants, deadlines, rules of procedure, etc. If rules of procedure are not included in the constituting instrument, who is authorized to establish rules and procedures.

1.03 Modifications and Amendments
Whether there is a body (e.g., consisting of the decision-makers) or a separate policy group that is empowered to modify or augment the procedural rules, administrative procedures, or structural aspects of the Claims Process in order to reflect emerging future needs.

1.04 Jurisdiction
The jurisdiction of the Claims Process, including the types of claims that can be made. Eligible claimants, including any issues of nationality and dual nationality. Whether heirs of victims are eligible to be claimants. (Note that the types of claims may have an impact on the mass claims methodologies used to process the claims.)

1.05 Remedies
The remedies available in the Claims Process. Whether the amounts of individual compensation for various claimants, or categories of claimants, are included in the constituting instruments or rules. Whether there is a maximum aggregate amount to be paid pursuant to the Claims Process and, if there is such a maximum amount, whether the expenses of the Claims Process are included when computing the maximum amount, and the method of distribution of any funds remaining after all individual

claims are paid. (Note that the remedies may have an impact on the mass claims methodologies used to process the claims.)

1.06 Location
Where the Claims Process is physically located. Whether the location is a neutral place. Legal and practical aspects.

1.07 Privileges and Immunities
Whether privileges and immunities are provided for decision-makers and staff in the Claims Process.

1.08 Participation of Claimants in Planning
Whether representatives of the claimants take part in planning the Claims Process.

2—The Legal Nature of the Claims Process

2.01 Type of Process
Whether claims are resolved in a procedure akin to arbitration, or in an administrative proceeding, or by mediation/conciliation, or in a combination thereof.

2.02 Exclusivity of Process
Whether the Claims Process is the sole recourse available to claimants or whether and when they may choose to sue in a national court.

2.03 Applicable Law
What substantive law, if any, is applied and whether procedural law at the place where the Claims Process is located applies.

2.04 Effect of Decisions
Whether decisions made in the Claims Process are to be final and binding. Whether the principle of *stare decisis* applies within the Claims Process itself.

2.05 Approval of Decisions
Whether decisions rendered in the Claims Process require approval of another body before becoming effective.

2.06 Mandates from Other Bodies
Whether there are any aspects of claims as to which decision-makers are mandated to follow and apply decisions by another body.

2.07 Enforcement
How decisions in the Claims Process are enforced. If they are not enforceable as arbitral awards, what legal force do they have, and what is the source of their legal authority. The mechanism for paying out awards of compensation, and whether there is a special fund to secure the payment of awards.

3—Starting the Claims Process

3.01 Outreach
How potential claimants are informed of the existence of the Claims Process, including the methods and extent of outreach.

3.02 Claim Forms

Preparation of claim forms. In that connection, whether the claim forms include a waiver by which claimants agree to have their claims resolved only by the Claims Process and to forego recourse to national courts or other means.

3.03 Deadlines for Submitting Claims

Whether there is a deadline for submitting claims and whether, and by whom, deadlines may be extended in special circumstances.

3.04 Initial Screening

Whether there is a procedure for initially screening claims in order to eliminate claims that *prima facie* do not fall within the jurisdiction of the Claims Process or clearly lack merit. Whether there is a procedure by which claimants can appeal such initial screening determinations.

3.05 Preparing Schedule

Whether there is a schedule showing the sequence of activities that need to be accomplished to resolve the claims, including a general time-frame, deadlines for particular actions, and a target date for winding up the Claims Process.

4—Appointing Those who will Make Decisions

4.01 Choice of Decision-Makers

Who makes decisions on claims and by whom such decision-makers are appointed. In that connection, whether any particular criteria, expertise, or other qualifications are specified. To what extent policy-making, executive, and adjudicative functions are differentiated and allocated to the decision-makers or to different bodies.

4.02 Impartiality

Whether procedures to assure that the decision-makers are impartial and independent are included. Procedures for challenge, and the procedures to be followed in the event a challenge is successful, or a decision-maker resigns or is unwilling to act. (Those procedures may be included in the procedural rules.)

4.03 Time Commitment

Time commitments expected of the decision-makers (e.g., full-time, part-time, taking up residence at the location of the Claims Process).

5—Procedures for Conducting the Claims Process

5.01 Procedural Rules

Whether an existing set of recognized procedural rules is incorporated by reference (for example, the appropriate Permanent Court of Arbitration Rules, which are based on the UNCITRAL Arbitration Rules), and where there is such incorporation, what changes, if any, are made to reflect the particular circumstances of the Claims Process. If an existing set of rules is not incorporated by reference, whether a set of respected rules is used as a guide.

5.02 Standards of Proof
Whether the constituting instruments or procedural rules include special provisions with respect to evidence and standards of proof.

5.03 Languages
Whether the constituting instruments or procedural rules include special provisions with respect to the language(s) of the Claims Process, and determine, if applicable, how translation and interpretation services are provided (e.g., by an in-house language services department or contracted out in whole or in part). (See also section 6.01 on linguistic support.)

5.04 Hearings
Whether the constituting instruments or procedural rules include special provisions with respect to oral hearings or decisions based on documents only.

5.05 Communications
The extent to which various procedures are conducted by means other than in-person proceedings, including communications via telephone, fax, e-mail, etc. (See further section 1.06 on the location of the Claims Process, and, section 3.02 on claim forms, section 6.06 on computer support and information technology.)

5.06 Mass Claims Techniques
The use of special mass claims processing methodologies such as grouping of claims, statistical modeling and sampling, computerized matching, and standardized valuation and verification methodologies.

5.07 Coordinating Decisions
If the Claims Process involves different decision-makers acting as, e.g., Sole Arbitrators or in a number of separate panels or chambers, whether there are internal procedures for coordinating and harmonizing the work to avoid inconsistent results. (See also section 2.04 on *stare decisis*.)

5.08 Due Process
The extent to which the Claims Process includes elements to assure due process, including the right to present claims and defenses, the right for all sides to be represented and assisted by persons of their choice, the right to confront witnesses, etc.

5.09 "Voice" for Claimants
Whether there is a means by which thousands of claimants who may lack funds and legal sophistication can be provided with assistance and have a "voice" in the Claims Process, in addition to the right to be represented by their own counsel. Whether to allow *amicus curiae* briefs or similar submissions on claimants' behalf.

5.10 Costs
By whom costs of parties in the Claims Process are paid, and, if parties do not bear their own costs, how the amounts are determined. (For matters relating to the costs of running the Claims Process itself, see section 7.03.)

5.11 Awarding Interest

Whether awards of compensation pursuant to the Claims Process include interest. If so, how the interest rate is determined, for what period it is paid, and whether simple or compound interest is awarded.

5.12 Settlement

Inclusion of provisions dealing with settlement and/or withdrawal of claims.

5.13 Appeals

Whether the rules include provisions for review or appeal of decisions within the Claims Process itself. (See section 2.04 on the final and binding nature of decisions.)

6—Administration, Facilities, and Computer Support

6.01 Management and Staffing

Legal, administrative, technical, and linguistic support required to implement the Claims Process. The organizational and management structure created to execute the identified functions. The type and level of expertise of the required personnel, and the corresponding job descriptions.

6.02 Infrastructure

Whether the Claims Process creates its own staff, facilities, and administrative organization, or uses an existing institution to provide all or part of such infrastructure.

6.03 Secretariat Functions

The relationship between the Secretariat staff and the decision-makers. Defining their respective powers and functions. What role, if any, Secretariat staff has in conducting research, drafting orders and decisions, and whether the task of deciding certain claims is delegated to staff members.

6.04 Facilities

The facilities needed to implement the Claims Process (e.g., physical premises, copying and other office equipment and supplies, computers, telephone lines, etc.). What facilities need to be in place at the outset in order to handle claims as they are received.

6.05 Satellite Offices

If relevant in view of the geographic distribution of the claimant population, the various options and facilities available, including satellite offices, for reaching potential claimants, receiving and registering claims, and other functions.

6.06 Information Technology

How computers are used to facilitate the Claims Process. Whether information technology (IT) specialists are part of the initial Claims Process design team. Computer databases, systems, applications, hardware, network, and telecommunications facilities needed to provide the required level of computer support. The design of claim forms to enable and facilitate the creation of a computerized claims database. (For procedures conducted electronically and mass claims techniques, see sections 5.05 and 5.06.)

7—Funding the Claims Process

7.01 Budgeting
The costs of running the Claims Process, other than compensation payments to claimants, such as salary structure for staff, fees and expenses of decision-makers, infrastructure, and other overhead.

7.02 Budget Process
The roles, if any, which Secretariat staff and decision-makers play in establishing periodic budgets.

7.03 Funding
The source(s) of funds to pay for the expenses of the Claims Process as a whole.

7.04 Outside Audit
Whether an outside auditor is employed to audit the Claims Process.

8—Transparency

8.01 Informing the Public
Means for informing the public about the Claims Process, for example by publishing statistics on the caseload and/or texts of the awards.

Index

Please note that references to footnotes are indicated by the letter 'n' following the page number.
American spellings are used, apart from some proper names, for instance, GFLCP (German Forced Labour Compensation Programme).
Numbers are filed as if spelled out, e.g. "8A1 Claims".

439